THE EVERYTHING®
GIANT BOOK
OF EASY
CROSSWORDS

Dear Reader,

Our brains love to play with words. They can become addicted to those satisfying "aha!" moments in word games, like when a word clicks into place on a crossword grid. I love playing with words so much that I created Funster.com, a website devoted to word games and puzzles. Fortunately for people like me, researchers have determined that being addicted to word play can be healthy. Studies show that solving crossword puzzles can improve our memory and cognitive abilities as we age.

I created this book for people who are addicted to crossword puzzles. Stuffed into these pages are a huge number of crossword puzzles that will keep you entertained for a long, long time. These puzzles are designed to be slightly challenging, but you don't need to be a crossword puzzle expert. So grab a pencil (or pen, if you dare), put your brain in gear, and jump into this giant world of crossword puzzling fun!

Charles Timmerman

Welcome to the EVERYTHING® Series!

These handy, accessible books give you all you need to tackle a difficult project, gain a new hobby, comprehend a fascinating topic, prepare for an exam, or even brush up on something you learned back in school but have since forgotten.

You can choose to read an *Everything*® book from cover to cover or just pick out the information you want from our four useful boxes: e-questions, e-facts, e-alerts, and e-ssentials. We give you everything you need to know on the subject, but throw in a lot of fun stuff along the way, too.

We now have more than 400 *Everything*® books in print, spanning such wide-ranging categories as weddings, pregnancy, cooking, music instruction, foreign language, crafts, pets, New Age, and so much more. When you're done reading them all, you can finally say you know *Everything*®!

PUBLISHER Karen Cooper

DIRECTOR OF ACQUISITIONS AND INNOVATION Paula Munier

MANAGING EDITOR, EVERYTHING SERIES Lisa Laing

COPY CHIEF Casey Ebert

ACQUISITIONS EDITOR Lisa Laing

EDITORIAL ASSISTANT Hillary Thompson

Visit the entire Everything® series at *www.everything.com*

THE EVERYTHING® GIANT BOOK OF EASY CROSSWORDS

Over 300 easy and enjoyable crosswords
for your entertainment

Charles Timmerman
Founder of Funster.com

Adams Media
New York London Toronto Sydney New Delhi

Dedicated to Suzanne and Calla.

Adams Media
An Imprint of Simon & Schuster, Inc.
100 Technology Center Drive
Stoughton, MA 02072

For information about special discounts for bulk purchases, please contact Simon & Schuster Special Sales at 1-866-506-1949 or business@simonandschuster.com.

The Simon & Schuster Speakers Bureau can bring authors to your live event. For more information or to book an event contact the Simon & Schuster Speakers Bureau at 1-866-248-3049 or visit our website at www.simonspeakers.com.

Manufactured in the United States of America

14 2022

ISBN 978-1-59869-993-7

Contents

Introduction / vii

Puzzles / 1

Answers / 319

Acknowledgments

I would like to thank each and every one of the more than half a million people who have visited my website, *www.funster.com*, to play word games and puzzles. You have shown me how much fun puzzles can be, and how addictive they can become!

For her expert help and guidance over the years, I owe a huge debt of gratitude to my agent Jacky Sach.

It is a pleasure to acknowledge the folks at Adams Media who made this book possible. I particularly want to thank my editor Lisa Laing for so skillfully managing the many projects we have worked on together.

Introduction

▶ WHAT DO ROSA PARKS, Richard Nixon, Jesse Owens and crossword puzzles have in common? They were all born in the year 1913. In that year a journalist named Arthur Wynne published a "word-cross" puzzle in the *New York World* Sunday newspaper. Though it was diamond shaped, it had all of the features of crossword puzzles that we know and love today. The name evolved into *crossword* as the paper continued to publish the popular word puzzles.

It wasn't until 1924 that the first book of crossword puzzles was published. That was when the crossword craze really began. It joined other fads of the Roaring Twenties like goldfish eating, flagpole sitting, yo-yo's, and pogo sticks. Of course, not all of these fads survived (perhaps fortunately).

Besides crossword puzzles, some really beautiful things came out of the 1920s. In music, jazz surged in popularity and George Gershwin's *Rhapsody in Blue* was performed for the first time. In literature, F. Scott Fitzgerald published some of his most enduring novels including *The Great Gatsby*. In design, it was the beginning of Art Deco. That's how the world was when crossword puzzles came of age.

Crossword puzzles became popular closer to a time when entertainment required *active* participation. In those days, people actually played sports rather than watched them, told each other stories rather than turned on the television, and even sang songs rather than listened to an MP3. Like entertainment of yesteryear, crossword puzzles require your active participation. And this is a refreshing change for those of us who still enjoy a mental workout.

Today, nearly every major newspaper runs a crossword puzzle. Entire sections of bookstores are devoted to crossword puzzle books. (Thanks for choosing this one!) Indeed, crosswords are the most common word puzzle in the world.

Why do crossword puzzles continue to be so popular? Only you can answer that question since there are as many reasons to work a crossword puzzle as there are solvers. But perhaps it has something to do with the convenient marriage of fun and learning that crossword puzzles offer.

Enjoy!

PUZZLES

Puzzle 1

Across

1. Tachometer abbr.
4. Just slightly
8. Envy, e.g.
11. Close at hand
13. "The ___ Ranger"
14. Ill will
15. Comedian Johnson
16. Do a cleaning chore
17. ___ Vegas
18. Dinner bird
20. Great reviews
22. Stupid jerk
24. Window cover
26. Sounds of contentment
27. Opposite of out
29. Playtex products
32. Acumen
33. WWII plane ___ Gay
35. Thanksgiving, e.g.: Abbr.
36. Fit of bad temper
38. 1982 Disney movie
39. Rowboat blade
40. Diet guru Jenny
42. Crowded
44. Beckon to enter
46. Committing perjury
48. Mr. Turkey
49. 10 C-notes
51. Cows' mouthfuls
54. Definite article
55. Hall of Fame manager Weaver
56. Easter preceder
57. Persona ___ grata
58. Eye affliction
59. Light time

Down

1. Cell's protein producer
2. The "p" of m.p.h.
3. 2003 Nicolas Cage film
4. Gucci or Ray
5. 1976 film about Woody Guthrie
6. Electees
7. Four: Prefix
8. Eloquent
9. Wrath, to Romulus
10. "The Untouchables" lawman
12. Paper purchase
19. Prepare for a portrait
21. NYPD call
22. Old sayings
23. Goatee site
25. Move, to a Realtor
28. Prefix meaning "against"
30. Inventors' cries
31. "Of course!"
34. "___ Love Her"
37. Prefix for cycle
41. Opening bets
43. Bottom-of-letter abbr.
44. Envelope abbreviation
45. London shopping district
47. Christmas season
50. Something to doff
52. Genetic letters
53. Muddy enclosure

Solution on page 320

Puzzle 2

Across

1. Equality
4. Pea container
7. Word of amazement
10. Method
11. Follower's suffix
12. Plant fungus
14. Mtn. stat
15. Dessert choice
16. Secure, as a contract
17. Two hours before noon
19. Short races
21. Alfred E. Neuman's magazine
23. Baltimore paper
24. Each
28. Sales agent
31. Hosp. areas
32. Debtor's promise
33. Topic: Abbr.
34. Little 'un
35. Clumsy
37. Bellows of "Ally McBeal"
38. Any ship
39. Increased
43. Country singer Haggard
47. Albanian river
48. North Pole assistant
50. Smile broadly
51. Knight's lady
52. "Long ___ and far away . . ."
53. Many eras
54. Until now
55. Glove compartment item
56. Sound of rebuke

Down

1. Either end of a magnet
2. Arabian gulf
3. Overhauls
4. "Great Expectations" hero
5. "Miss ___ Regrets"
6. Dixie
7. Singer K.T.
8. Its capital is Muscat
9. Search
10. Came upon
13. NFL 6-pointers
18. Dogpatch's Daisy ___
20. Compete in a meet
22. Precision marching group
24. Indy area
25. System startup?
26. Daily grind
27. Pine-___
28. Pirate drink
29. Subside
30. Nightwear, briefly
33. Absolute certainty
35. Help
36. Skirt bottom
37. French playwright
39. Supplement
40. Low cart
41. Piece of change
42. Gold-medal gymnast Korbut
44. Collectible cars
45. Thin
46. Printer's measures
49. Beau Brummell

Solution on page 320

Puzzle 3

Across

1. Befuddled
5. Gulf of ___, off the coast of Yemen
9. Newsman Rather
12. Fish-eating eagle
13. Country way
14. Winter driving hazard
15. Doctors' charges
16. Coll. hotshot
17. Cell substance
18. Flies over the equator?
20. Leave in, editorially
21. Poet's dusk
22. "___ Believer" (Monkees hit)
24. Color variation
27. Window treatment
31. Harry Potter's best friend
32. Twice as unlikely
34. Took control
35. Surgical probes
37. Turnpike tabs
39. Grp. with a lot of pull?
40. Turkey day: Abbr.
41. Retired fast planes: Abbr.
44. Babble
48. Farming tool
49. Suffix with soft or hard
51. German river
52. Summer, in France
53. Air Force heroes
54. Cube maker Rubik
55. Crime boss
56. Salespeople, for short
57. Danson and Turner

Down

1. Went away
2. Mined metals
3. Old knife
4. Evaluated
5. Harry's veep
6. River barriers
7. Ambient music composer Brian
8. Japanese computer giant
9. Detergent's target
10. Skin woe
11. Not sloppy
19. Lose one's cool
20. Tree juice
22. Vex
23. First First Lady
24. H.S. big shots
25. In a rage
26. Unspecified amount
27. OR workers
28. Right-angled extension
29. Bro. or sis.
30. Football gains: Abbr.
33. Words before loss or standstill
36. Vegas opener?
38. Beginning
40. Long lock of hair
41. Tool storage area
42. Explorer Hernando De ___
43. One twixt 12 and 20
44. Get ready, for short
45. Weight allowance
46. Real estate
47. Piccadilly Circus figure
49. Repetitive card game
50. Flexible blackjack card

Solution on page 320

Puzzle 4

Across

1. Some Saturns
5. Nautical dir.
8. Sexist letter start
12. Sandy hill
13. Was first
14. Vietnam's continent
15. Suffix with young
16. Hit show sign
17. Blood obstruction
18. Abbr. on a contour map
20. Use an iron
21. Used up, as money
24. Sheriff Taylor's kid
26. "Peter, Peter, Pumpkin ___"
27. Many a trade-in
31. Computer screen, for short
32. "Spring ahead" hrs.
33. Yoko ___
34. Western hat
37. Highest points
39. Mozart's "a"
40. Animal stomachs
41. Fireplace remnant
44. Not punctual
46. Bit of bank business
47. The whole shooting match
48. On ___ (like much freelance work)
52. Quaint hotels
53. Domino spot
54. "Gone with the Wind" mansion
55. Not very challenging
56. Speed Wagon maker
57. Jazz performance

Down

1. Psyche components
2. Not in vogue
3. Map dir.
4. Peaceful
5. ". . . or ___!"
6. Worrywart
7. Tokyo, to the shoguns
8. Holy
9. Emerald ___ (Ireland)
10. Grande and Bravo
11. Tests for srs.
19. Env. contents
20. Key lime ___
21. Min. parts
22. Comb's creation
23. Little: Suffix
25. Calif. setting
28. Unwakable state
29. For an additional time
30. Seamstress Betsy
32. Spanish title
35. Itty-bitty
36. "To ___ With Love"
37. Perform on stage
38. High points
41. Peace Nobelist Wiesel
42. ___ Lisa
43. Outlaws
45. Purina rival
47. Auto financing letters
49. Campaign funding grp.
50. Pitcher's stat.
51. Tabby

Solution on page 320

Puzzle 5

Across

1. Relief pitcher's goal
5. Train for a match
9. Dallas hoopster, briefly
12. China's locale
13. Scale deduction
14. "I have an idea!"
15. Repressed, with "up"
16. Iowa State's locale
17. Beatnik's exclamation
18. Keep an ___ to the ground
20. Rule out
22. Channel swimmer Gertrude
25. Suffix with meth- or eth-
26. Friars' fetes
27. Summer ermine
30. Like "to be": Abbr.
31. Part of m.p.h.
33. At ___ for words
37. Spill marks
40. Railroad stop: Abbr.
41. Take into custody
42. Autumn blooms
45. Beauregard's boss
46. New Guinea port
47. Chan comment
49. Work at a keyboard
53. Wrong: Pref.
54. One of 16 chess pieces
55. Consider officially, as a judge
56. Summer coolers, for short
57. Singer Sylvia
58. Indonesian islands

Down

1. Syrup ingredient
2. Wall St. trading group
3. Beaujolais, e.g.
4. Buffet patrons
5. Gawks
6. Tennis's Shriver
7. Sports stadiums
8. Take offense at
9. Papa's partner
10. At the drop of ___
11. Wind direction indicator
19. Height: Abbr.
21. "Earth" word form
22. Silkworm
23. Wife of David Copperfield
24. English nobleman
28. ". . baked in ___"
29. Change for a $20
32. Alphabetic run
34. Sugar: Suffix
35. Handbag handles
36. Proceed nonchalantly
37. Beauty parlors
38. Three, in Torino
39. Soul singer Franklin
42. ___mater
43. Levantine ketch
44. Miss Trueheart of "Dick Tracy"
48. Personal ad abbr.
50. "___ out!" (ump's call)
51. Kung ___ shrimp
52. Before, to a sonneteer

Solution on page 320

Puzzle 6

Across

1. Box-office letters
4. Give weapons to
7. Ohio or Iowa
12. Refusals
13. Top of the corp. ladder
14. Shield
15. Savings acct. posting
16. Richard Mulligan sitcom
18. Humanitarian Mother ___
20. Kin of equi-
21. Actor Penn
22. Basketball champion's "trophy"
24. Repose
28. NASDAQ listings: Abbr.
30. Mont Blanc, e.g.
32. Crusty one?
33. Sorority letter
35. Shopper's binge
37. Country lodging
38. Draft inits.
39. Untold centuries
40. Abe's boy
42. PIN takers
44. Newsman Donaldson
46. Chest muscles, for short
49. More than impress
51. Stellar
53. Traveling salesman
57. Soccer star Hamm
58. Bus passenger
59. Tell a whopper
60. It's kept in a pen
61. Terrify

62. "How dry ___"
63. Perceive

Down

1. Angry states
2. Blakley of "A Nightmare on Elm Street"
3. Exclusion from social events
4. Great serves
5. Staff anew
6. Do the floor
7. Speaks
8. Voice range
9. Get older
10. "___ folly to be wise"
11. Boston hrs.
17. Proof of ownership
19. Brian of Roxy music
23. ___living
25. Outer skin layer
26. Break a Commandment
27. Midmorning
29. Chicago-to-Miami dir.
31. Garfield, to Jon
33. Jefferson Davis's org.
34. "The buck stops here" monogram
36. Model at work
41. Likely
43. More clearheaded
45. Madness
47. "The ___ Mutiny"
48. Allay, as thirst
50. Had been
52. Plant support
53. Tax org.
54. Personal quirk
55. Neighbor of Wash.
56. Outspoken boxer

Solution on page 321

Puzzle 7

Across

1. Revise text
5. Spanish rivers
9. Humbug preceder
12. Tiny parasite
13. Plowing unit
14. Bacardi, e.g.
15. New driver, usually
16. Track-and-field contest
17. "Who am ___ judge?"
18. Schlemiels
20. Black-and-white cookies
22. Actress Normand
25. Genetic initials
26. Popular family card game
27. Chute opener?
30. Pinup's legs
34. Sow's pen
35. Ginger cookies
37. Corp. top dog
38. Youngsters
40. Lhasa ___ (small dog)
41. Southern ___
42. Inexact fig.
44. Coffeehouse offering
46. Area of land
49. Gait between walk and canter
51. TV Tarzan Ely
52. Rose lover
54. "'Tis a shame"
58. Symbol of sturdiness
59. Charts
60. Child's building block
61. Gun lobby org.
62. Nostalgic time
63. Stolen money

Down

1. Ambulance rider, briefly
2. Conk out
3. Native: Suffix
4. Edgy
5. Turnpike exit
6. Decorates a cake
7. Unrefined metal
8. ___ Hall (New Jersey university)
9. French cheese
10. Car
11. Managed care gps.
19. Skier's mecca
21. Disreputable paper
22. Cologne scent
23. The "A" of ABM
24. Hopalong Cassidy portrayer William
25. Chews the fat
28. Biology subj.
29. Eminem's genre
31. Dept. store shopper's privilege
32. Butcher-shop buy
33. Dover ___
36. Fly like Lindy
39. Wall St. regulator
43. An E-mail doesn't need one
45. To any extent
46. Sci-fi film of 1982
47. Crowd noise
48. Crooner Paul
49. Waiter's rewards
50. Take a break
53. Cry to Bo-Peep
55. August sign
56. Give it ___ (try)
57. Juicer

Solution on page 321

Puzzle 8

Across

1. Voting coalition
5. Emily of etiquette
9. Move quickly
12. "Aargh!"
13. Person-to-person
15. Israeli statesman Weizman
16. Succession
17. Talked wildly
19. Cloudless
20. "Seinfeld" neighbor
22. Dave's "2001" nemesis
23. Untagged?
24. Attila, for one
25. JFK's successor
28. Oil cartel
29. Harmless lie
30. Formal ceremony
31. Crosses (out)
32. Auto shaft, slangily
33. First appearance
34. However
35. Double-check
36. Feline crossbreed
39. Exclude
40. Gas choice
42. Recreation area
45. More reliable
46. Place for small scissors
47. Benzoyl peroxide target
48. "The Sopranos" award
49. Money owed

Down

1. Tournament exemption
2. Fashion designer Claiborne
3. Manages
4. Earthenware
5. Puzzling problem
6. Linear, for short
7. Et ___ (and the following): Abbr.
8. Big-billed bird
9. Certain basketball defense
10. Ancient South American
11. Nobleman
14. Dickens's "Little" girl
18. Fido's doc
20. Fort ___ (U.S. gold depository)
21. Strong cord
22. Focal point
24. "She Done ___ Wrong"
25. Set free
26. HVAC measures
27. Rock singer Joan
29. Jack Sprat no-no
30. Recorded again
32. Rector's assistant
33. Belle of a ball
34. Nectar collectors
35. Towel off again
36. Figure-skating jump
37. Calvary letters
38. Overabundance
39. Regard as
41. Not too brainy
43. Abrade
44. Model airplane package

Solution on page 321

Puzzle 9

Across

1. Police alert, for short
4. Crimson Tide, briefly
8. Similar things
12. Enemy
13. Graceland middle name
14. Molecule unit
15. Boy king of Egypt
16. Plenty, and then some
17. Panhandles
18. Not wild
20. Yonder damsel
22. High-tech appt. books
25. 1983 comedy written by John Hughes
29. Shanties
32. Composer Schifrin
34. Nestegg component, briefly
35. Late actress Mary
36. Trigonometric ratios
37. Chess pieces: Abbr.
38. Part of an hr.
39. Helps
40. Second to none
41. Aromatic compound
43. Type of lily
45. Catch red-handed
47. Lad's sweetie
50. Icelandic poetry
53. "Dancing Queen" pop group
56. Prof.'s degree
58. ___ the bill (pay)
59. Naysayers' words
60. "Fantasia" frame
61. Ocean movement
62. Swindles
63. "Unaccustomed ___ am . . ."

Down

1. Toward the rear, at sea
2. Mope
3. First Greek consonant
4. Sounded sheepish?
5. Mural or sculpture
6. Barnyard sound
7. Sothern and Jillian
8. Curved sword
9. Southwest Indian
10. Gear part
11. "___ Pinafore"
19. GI cops
21. Managed-care grps.
23. Et ___ (and others)
24. Smoothes, as wood
26. Emcee's amplifier
27. Food morsels
28. Crow's-nest spot
29. Actor Cronyn
30. Novelist Leon
31. Camper's shelter
33. ___ majesty
36. ___ Lee Corporation
40. Squeezing snake
42. Growing outward
44. Bottle material
46. Judge's seat
48. Pet protection org.
49. Females
50. Little newt
51. "___ Hear a Waltz?"
52. Cabinet dept.
54. Fan's rebuke
55. Cartwright patriarch
57. Half of MCII

Solution on page 321

Puzzle 10

Across

1. NHL legend Bobby
4. Maid's cloth
7. Ancient strongbox
11. Elvis's swivelers
13. Lance of L.A. law
14. Playwright George Bernard
15. Window frame
16. NYC subway org.
17. Devoid of moisture
18. Baseball great Buck
20. Does lacework
21. Greek philosopher
24. Narrow inlets
26. Draw a bead on
27. Electrified fish
28. Unit of elec. current
31. Cowboy's rope
32. Caruso or Domingo
34. MD's helpers
35. China's Mao ___-tung
38. Make ecstatic
39. Head, in France
40. Reacts to yeast
41. Lhasa ___: small dog
44. "Am not!" response
46. ___ Flynn Boyle
47. Compete (for)
48. Cookbook measures: Abbr.
52. Winged Greek god
53. Nighttime, to a poet
54. It's for the birds
55. Song or gab add-on
56. Hosp. workers
57. "The Raven" monogram

Down

1. Surprised exclamations
2. Coastal inlet
3. Rotation meas.
4. Relative of hoarfrost
5. Clothing
6. Soccer position
7. Admin. aides
8. Flightless bird of South America
9. Golf-course vehicle
10. Impresses greatly
12. Fired upon
19. Represent with symbols
21. Catherine ___, wife of Henry VIII
22. Mortgage, for example
23. Amo, ___, amat
25. Changes
28. Anecdotal collections
29. Dust particle
30. JFK or LBJ
33. George and T.S.
36. Warded (off)
37. More weird
39. "Here's to you!" is one
41. First Hebrew letter
42. Peel, as potatoes
43. Sellout shows, for short
45. Poetic nights
49. Seek damages from
50. Pod inhabitant
51. Engine additive letters

Solution on page 321

Puzzle 11

Across

1. Chicago terminal
6. Alley lurker
9. PGA player
12. Bag carrier
13. Noah's creation
14. Marker, so to speak
15. Musical beat
16. Sense of self
17. Partner of neither
18. Middling
20. Casino transactions
21. Keebler worker
24. Lustrous velvet
26. Feel awful
27. For each
28. Have dinner at home
32. Pipe cleaner
34. Rock layers
35. Olympic sleds
36. Satisfied sounds
37. Limbo obstacle
38. "Whole ___ Shakin' Going On"
40. Devious
41. Cough syrup amts.
44. Frolic
46. Eureka!
47. Egg source
48. Book of photos
53. Pewter metal
54. Anticipatory time
55. Salary increase
56. Prone
57. Unburden
58. Like Romantic music

Down

1. Hall of Famer Mel
2. Garden implement
3. $$$ dispenser
4. Exercise unit
5. God of love
6. Salad choice
7. A noble gas
8. Ring result
9. Conifer with needles
10. Kind of vegetable
11. Mine and yours
19. 0 on a phone: Abbr.
20. Yogi or Boo-Boo
21. Jazzman Hines
22. In ___ of (substituting for)
23. Stars and Stripes, e.g.
25. Tennis dividers
27. Cozumel cash
29. File folder features
30. Emphatic type: Abbr.
31. Not (a one)
33. Sitcom diner
34. Hoax
36. Made amends (for)
39. Fountain of Rome
41. "So long!"
42. Cutter or clipper
43. Breathe hard
45. Segment
47. Boating pronoun
49. Thai neighbor
50. Storage area
51. Dos Passos work
52. "Braveheart" star Gibson

Solution on page 321

Puzzle 12

Across

1. "___ for the poor"
5. Priestly vestments
9. TGIF day
12. Cowboy's footwear
13. Ponce de ___
14. Shake off
15. ___'acte: intermission
16. Clown of early TV
17. Writer Le Shan
18. Longs for
20. Lemon and orange drinks
21. French wine
22. A.P. rival
24. Chopped
27. Hot
31. Pollution-fighting org.
32. Step inside
34. President after FDR
35. Mosque tower
37. Bridge positions
39. "No ___" (Chinese-
    restaurant sign)
40. NBC weekend revue
41. Kill
44. Try
48. Strike
49. Eclectic magazine
51. Wedding-cake layer
52. Use an ax
53. Skywalker of "Star
    Wars"
54. ___ cost (free)
55. Makeshift dwelling
56. Israeli statesman Abba
57. Remain unsettled

Down

1. Resting
2. "The ___ Ranger"
3. Witty sayings
4. Make an effort
5. Truman veep Barkley
6. Most August babies
7. Dickens's pen name
8. ___-cone (frozen treat)
9. Mr. Flintstone
10. Hitchhiker's goal
11. Lupino et al.
19. Equestrians
20. It's all around
22. Trois less deux
23. Mom or dad
24. Garment bottom
25. Prefix with dermal
26. Unnaturally pale
27. Baseball great Mel
28. Exclamations of surprise
29. WWII troop carrier
30. Sgt.'s superiors
33. Not pos.
36. Actress Madigan
38. Pub fixture
40. 17th century painter
    Jan
41. "Quiet!"
42. In ___ of (instead of)
43. Periodic table no.
44. Pop singer Paul
45. Small amount
46. Actor Sean
47. Tramped (on)
49. Suffix with glob
50. Place for a bath

Solution on page 322

Puzzle 13

Across

1. Soup samples
5. Put two and two together?
8. Church-bell sound
12. "___ something I said?"
13. Comedian Louis
14. ___ mater
15. PlayStation maker
16. Word with whiz
17. Lost traction
18. "Skip To My ___"
20. Communion plates
22. Poplars
25. Incoming flight info
26. In need of tightening
27. ER staffers
28. Mineo of "Exodus"
31. Lend a hand to
32. "It was the ___ I could do"
34. Crusty dessert
35. "Treasure Island" monogram
36. Proper
37. Set ___ (save)
39. Folk rocker DiFranco
40. Curly-tailed dogs
41. Straw bed
44. Mal de ___
45. Disembarked
46. Short flight
48. Eve's garden
52. ___ Rooter
53. Dragon roll ingredient
54. Director Ephron
55. Takes to court
56. Three, in Napoli
57. Jacket fastener

Down

1. Bro's counterpart
2. Prefix with metric
3. Bowler's target
4. Baroque and rococo, e.g.
5. Black cattle breed
6. Cover the gray
7. Becomes more profound
8. "Ristorante" course
9. Pronoun for a Parisienne
10. Ugandan tyrant
11. Boys
19. Like some rural bridges
21. On the line
22. Former orchard spray
23. Make dirty
24. Pea holders
27. Squeal (on)
28. Rotisserie rotator
29. Operatic heroine
30. Peggy and Spike
33. Nickname
38. Warning devices
39. Choir section
40. More than sufficient
41. Average figures
42. Baseball's Moises or Felipe
43. Label word for dieters
47. "___ the ramparts . . ."
49. Mafia figure
50. Elizabethan or Victorian
51. Catch a few Z's

Solution on page 322

Puzzle 14

Across

1. "The Racer's Edge"
4. Race part
7. Use needle and thread
10. ___ -tzu
11. Measured off
13. ___ snail's pace
14. Pacino and Unser
15. ___ nous (between us)
16. Sun. speaker
17. Giggling sound
19. Restlessness
21. Electrified particles
22. Make a lap
23. Feared mosquito
25. Tapioca source
29. Skater Midori ___
30. Ripken of the Orioles
31. U.S. spy gp.
32. Computer screen
35. Educate
37. Vehicle with sliding doors
38. Born and ___
39. Hologram producers
42. Gains again, as strength
45. Happy ___ clam
46. Stop by briefly
48. Ranch call
49. Paper Mate product
50. Reporter's angle
51. Charged bit
52. Dejected
53. Flock female
54. Internet pop-ups, e.g.

Down

1. Bed board
2. Fable
3. Greek god of the sea
4. Bowling alleys
5. Do not delay
6. Scrutiny
7. Lee of baking
8. Summers on the Riviera
9. Surfer's ride
11. Rounded hammer parts
12. Patron saint of France
18. Tiller's tool
20. Sci-fi invaders
23. Eye the bull's-eye
24. Ike's WWII command
25. Sedan, e.g.
26. Dean's world
27. Singer Damone
28. Satisfied sigh
30. Television cabinet
33. "___ seen enough!"
34. Field protectors
35. Senator Lott
36. Nighttime, in poetry
38. Pickling liquid
39. Swimming units
40. On the open water
41. Beach surface
43. Lumber
44. Boy babies
47. Fido's offering

Solution on page 322

Puzzle 15

Across

1. NFL team
5. Lavish party
9. Apply, as ointment
12. "___ From Muskogee"
13. Suffix with novel
14. Letter after pi
15. "Peachy-___!"
16. Wander aimlessly
17. Put the collar on
18. Old name at the pumps
19. Explosive initials
20. "Bonanza" role
21. Word of cheer
23. "___ it or lose it"
25. Statesman Sadat
28. Proportionately
32. Dairy farm sound
33. Takes out
35. Unstrict
36. Offspring
38. Michael Caine film
40. "What's more . . ."
41. Mean Amin
42. Retail complex
45. Martini maker
47. Artist's pad?
51. Relative of an ostrich
52. Pro ___ (in proportion)
53. Magician's opening
54. Knight's title
55. "___ my way"
56. Aquatic bird
57. "___ not what your country . . ."
58. Hereditary carrier
59. Nintendo alternative

Down

1. One-liner, e.g.
2. Barely manages, with "out"
3. Comes out even
4. Spanish lady
5. Bed on board
6. Heaps and heaps
7. Prestige
8. Tailor's edge
9. James Bond foe
10. Puzzle solvers' cries
11. Short hairdos
20. "Love ___ Madly": Doors hit
22. Cosmetician Elizabeth
24. "What a pity!"
25. Rock concert equipment
26. Neither's companion
27. Romance
28. Tire reinforcement
29. Politico Landon
30. ___ chi: martial art
31. Lumberjack's tool
34. Final stage
37. Guy's companion
39. Purple flowers
41. Making no sense
42. Small plateau
43. Kingsley or Martin
44. Wait in hiding
46. Lay ___ the line
48. Orchestral instrument
49. Former tadpole
50. Londoner's farewell
52. Eighteen-wheeler

Solution on page 322

Puzzle 16

Across

1. ___ Harbor, Long Island
4. Kind of stock: Abbr.
7. Tobacco mouthful
11. Coll. in Columbus
12. Bicycle part
14. Quattro automaker
15. Dairy cow
17. Put on board, as cargo
18. Walking
19. "Friendly skies" flier: Abbr.
21. Life story, in brief
22. Cut again
25. French ecclesiastic
28. Vital: Abbr.
29. Collar, as a crook
31. One with regrets
32. No ___, ands or buts
33. Island near Venice
34. NFL three-pointers
35. Chapel Hill sch.
36. Organization: Abbr.
37. Laurel and Musial
39. Soft food for infants
41. Calendar abbreviation
42. Negatively charged atoms
46. Overpublicize
49. Baptize
51. Prizms and Metros
52. Asian weight
53. Sot's interjection
54. Taunt
55. "That's incredible!"
56. Envelope contents: Abbr.

Down

1. Manhattan or London district
2. "Notes of ___ and Brother" (Henry James autobiography)
3. ___ war syndrome
4. Holy Roman emperor, 962–73
5. Connect
6. Dernier ___ (the latest thing)
7. Uses the phone
8. Mao's successor
9. Find a sum
10. Michelle of the LPGA
13. Accustoms
16. Clearheaded
20. NRC predecessor
23. Black birds
24. Rolls of bills
25. Terrier's cry
26. Computer glitches
27. Highest-quality
28. Pro Bowl team: Abbr.
30. ___ voyage
32. Bee or beetle
33. ___ lazuli
35. Former leader of Burma
38. '50s nuclear trial
39. "Gay" French city
40. Old womanish
43. Will-___-wisp
44. Opposite of "ja"
45. '60s civil rights org.
46. Elev.
47. Wood in archery bows
48. Luau side dish
50. Hardly a beauty

Solution on page 322

THE EVERYTHING GIANT BOOK OF EASY CROSSWORDS

Puzzle 17

Across

1. Sp. miss
5. Lisa, to Bart
8. Shoemaker's tools
12. Deportment
13. Derby, for one
14. Radio knob
15. Vitality
16. Goes along with
18. Always, to Keats
19. Zagreb resident
20. Sleep research tool, briefly
21. Concluded
23. One over a birdie
25. Job to be run
27. Inclines
31. Vientiane's locale
32. Humdinger
33. Drives forward
36. Visit
38. Be in session
39. Valuable rocks
40. Unreturnable serve
43. Tailoring job
45. Public-house drink
48. Abut
50. Sundries case
51. Tradition
52. Navigator's dir.
53. Nashville's st.
54. Otherwise
55. Hardly ordinary
56. Italy's Villa d' ___

Down

1. Hook's aide
2. Churn up
3. Sign of sorrow
4. Gloucester's cape
5. Had in common
6. Desdemona's enemy
7. Sandal parts
8. Sidewalk stand drink
9. Like Solomon
10. Overdue
11. Wade through the surf
17. Kin of etc.
19. MSNBC rival
22. Caravan stops
24. Actress Esther
25. Peyton Manning's younger brother
26. Aries animal
28. Beats
29. "Strange Magic" grp.
30. Day light
34. Former Italian coins
35. Portable heat source
36. Invented, as a phrase
37. Carney of "The Honeymooners"
40. Fit for the job
41. Refrigerate
42. Guesses wrong
44. Sweet on, with "of"
46. Fontanne's stage partner
47. Mozart's "___ kleine Nachtmusik"
49. "Look at Me, I'm Sandra ___"
50. Soissons season

Solution on page 322

Puzzle 18

Across

1. Bygone Fords
5. Terror
9. "Yummy!"
12. "___ Arabian Nights"
13. Web page
14. Debt acknowledgment
15. Ore-Ida product
17. Some USN officers
18. Bygone car
19. Declare to be true
21. Despotic ruler
24. Feels regret over
25. Begs
26. Minor arguments
28. Quantity: Abbr.
29. Alliance since 1948: Abbr.
31. Settees and sofas
35. Singer Twain
38. Kirghiz range
39. Painting stands
40. Mete out
42. Question's opposite: Abbr.
43. Guadalajara "Rah!"
44. Fundamentally
49. Lion or leopard
50. Kind of lily
51. Connery of film
52. Get a look at
53. Sci-fi film of '82
54. Marquis de ___

Down

1. All fired up?
2. Ode title opening
3. Decimal point
4. ___ Nevada mountains
5. Shutterbugs' settings
6. Vowel sequence
7. Rose oils
8. Get some sleep
9. Significant event
10. Witticisms
11. Can't help but
16. Boned up on
20. 4:00 social
21. Healthful retreat
22. Money for the poor
23. Private chat
27. Go yachting
30. Carrier to Sweden
32. "Float like a butterfly, sting like a bee" boxer
33. Believer in Lao-tzu's philosophy
34. Commandment breaker
35. Spring or summer
36. Author ___ Christian Andersen
37. Impose, as a tax
40. Enormous birds of myth
41. Wings: Lat.
45. Often-inflated item
46. Educator's org.
47. Dishonorable one
48. Wind direction: Abbr.

Solution on page 323

Puzzle 19

Across

1. Product makers: Abbr.
5. "Open 9 ___ 6"
8. When Hamlet dies
12. 53, in old Rome
13. Rival sch. of The Citadel
14. Rob of "Masquerade"
15. Missing a deadline
16. Save for the future
18. Letters after zetas
19. Adjective follower
20. Your, in the Bible
23. Not at all interested
27. Creative guy
31. Yup's counterpart
32. Unilever soap brand
33. Bunch of bees
36. Typist's stat.
37. Correct a manuscript
39. Unlucky
41. Went after
43. Kid's question
44. Mount from which Moses saw Canaan
47. Messenger molecules
51. American flag
55. Hercules captive
56. Malodorous
57. Universal Studios' former parent co.
58. As the ___ flies
59. Boob ___
60. Emeril's expletive
61. Cut up

Down

1. French miss: Abbr.
2. Royal order
3. Actress Hayworth
4. Afternoon rest
5. Family-room items
6. Somalian fashion model
7. Stitch's cartoon pal
8. Support group for families of drinkers
9. Dairy animal
10. Bygone airline
11. "Oy ___!"
17. Bath site
21. ___ Pinafore
22. Deviate from a course
24. Baseball's "Schoolboy"
25. Omar of "Scream 2"
26. Reps.' counterparts
27. Martinique et Guadeloupe
28. Surfer's sobriquet
29. The way out
30. "I'd rather not"
34. Like new recruits
35. Speed limit abbr.
38. Hair knot
40. Words of a song
42. Part of ITT: Abbr.
45. Broadway flop
46. Shamu or Keiko
48. Nick and ___ Charles
49. Strike ___ blow
50. Stitched up
51. Frequently, to Frost
52. Dobbs of CNN
53. Christen
54. Thanksgiving serving

Solution on page 323

Puzzle 20

Across

1. Ireland's ___ Islands
5. Pigsty
8. Put money in the bank
12. Clinton's Veep
13. WSW's reverse
14. Germany's ___ Valley
15. Sounds of disapproval
16. Estrange
18. Are: Sp.
20. Acct. earnings
21. College entrance exams
23. Correo ___ (Spanish airmail)
28. Part of ETA: Abbr.
31. Soaks, as flax
33. Burn slightly
34. Sets free
36. "Relax, soldier!"
38. Hope and Barker
39. London museum
41. Rep.'s rival
42. Pompous ones
44. ___ off (miffed)
46. Ft. above sea level, to a pilot
48. Vincent Lopez's theme song
51. Stabilized
56. "Star Wars" heroine
58. Catches rays
59. Summer clock setting: Abbr.
60. Eyeglass part
61. Bart Simpson's sister
62. Extra periods: Abbr.
63. Former fast fliers: Abbr.

Down

1. FBI employee
2. Debaucher
3. ___ and sciences
4. Birds' homes
5. Split-___ soup
6. Join the army
7. Opposite of ja
8. IRS ID
9. Motorists' gp.
10. Large tub
11. Before, to Longfellow
17. Approximate landing hr.
19. Swiss stream
22. Exam
24. WNW's opposite
25. Do one of the three R's
26. Make simpler
27. Fast-growing city near Provo
28. Goya's "Duchess of ___"
29. Aussie jumpers
30. Steals from
32. Gratify
35. Pilot's direction: Abbr.
37. Adult-to-be
40. Swear (to)
43. Unhappy
45. Barbie and Ken
47. Resort island near Venice
49. Robert E.'s family
50. ". . . and that ___ hay!"
51. Gateway Arch city: Abbr.
52. Mai ___ (rum cocktail)
53. Ems' followers
54. Stiff ___ board
55. Sot's symptoms, for short
57. Mule's sire

Solution on page 323

Puzzle 21

Across

1. Many mins.
4. Windy City, briefly
7. Short form, for short
11. Word from Miss Piggy
12. Talk wildly
14. Knight titles
15. "___ Father, who art . . ."
16. "Lonely Boy" singer Paul
17. Crotchety oldster
18. Isaac and Howard
20. Coming
22. Horner's dessert
23. Yearly records
27. Orwell's "___ Farm"
30. Minor despot
31. Devotee
32. Mamie's man
33. Group doctrines
37. Like some new lawns
40. Attack vigorously
41. Old cable TV inits.
42. In addition
43. Old sayings
47. ___ homo: Behold the man
50. Singer Erykah
52. Biblical transport
53. Lion sound
54. Interview wear
55. "Phooey!"
56. Swindles
57. Mary ___ of cosmetics
58. "A ___ Good Men"

Down

1. Med. care choices
2. Win in a runaway
3. Address for a king
4. Braincases
5. Gretel's brother
6. Calligrapher's liquid
7. Trip up a mountain
8. Life story, for short
9. Pal, in the 'hood
10. Queue before U
13. Triumphant cries
19. Dashboard abbr.
21. Merkel of moviedom
24. In need of water
25. Fishing locale
26. Drove too fast
27. Shaving lotion brand
28. Dundee turndowns
29. Vacationers' stops
34. Restaurant patrons
35. Barcelona uncle
36. Pigs
37. Sports arenas
38. At one's post
39. Crime scene evidence
44. Iron fishhook
45. New York's ___ Canal
46. Distort unfairly
47. Fraction of a joule
48. Bashful
49. Lid
51. Bering Sea bird

Solution on page 323

Puzzle 22

Across

1. December 24th and 31st, e.g.
5. Newscaster Lindstrom
8. Hushed "Hey you!"
12. Ten-cent piece
13. That thing's
14. Western Samoa's capital
15. Brit's farewell
16. Just great
17. Drop in the mail
18. Old vinyl
20. Nintendo competitor
21. Make humble
24. Ceremonial fire
27. Was in first
28. Pulitzer-winning biography of a Civil War general
30. "___ My Children"
33. Short-lived craze
34. Courtroom activity
35. Undercover org.
36. Vienna's land: Abbr.
37. Nicholas Gage title
38. Ill. clock setting
39. Uno y dos
40. Sporty Chevy
42. Broadway "Auntie"
45. Address book no.
46. "How Sweet ___"
47. "Scots Wha ___" (Burns poem)
49. Crooned
53. Clothes-dryer fuzz
54. Poem of tribute
55. On a cruise, perhaps
56. ___ Kett of old comics
57. Abbr. in an apartment ad
58. Shaker contents

Down

1. Summer D.C. clock setting
2. Route word
3. CPR administrant
4. Aquatic mammals
5. Zadora and Lindstrom
6. Los Angeles judge
7. Pose a query
8. No longer in fashion
9. German admiral
10. Croon
11. Cry of success
19. More vivacious
21. ___ Romeo: sports car
22. Gal's sweetheart
23. Does sums
24. Ballet bends
25. Bear young, as sheep
26. Experience again
29. Writer ___ Stanley Gardner
30. S&L customer
31. Santa's reminder
32. Deceased
39. Acorn's coat
41. Actress Lanchester et al.
42. 1,760 yards
43. Have a go ___ (try)
44. Julep enhancer
45. Golf ball props
47. Not vert.
48. Nimitz or Halsey: Abbr.
50. Dream Team jersey letters
51. "___ Blu Dipinto di Blu"
52. Hood's piece

Solution on page 323

Puzzle 23

Across

1. Some skirts
7. Casino employee
13. Kitchen gadgets
14. More affected
15. Lassos
16. Nasty looks
17. Hanoi holidays
18. Old what's-___-name
19. Robert E. and Spike
22. Old lab heaters
26. Derides
30. Filet of ___
31. Horse food
32. Parseghian of football
33. Cambridge sch.
34. Spanish cheers
36. Florida city
39. Roles
41. "Freeze!"
42. One ___ time (individually)
44. Colorless
47. Click beetle
50. Indian instruments
52. Mother of Dionysus
53. Hemoglobin deficiency
54. Red ink
55. Make a new home, in a way

Down

1. Follower of Mar.
2. Cafe additive
3. "Dies ___"
4. Stinging plant
5. Classroom tool
6. Leaky radiator sound
7. Move rapidly
8. Tennessee ___ Ford
9. Nuclear experiments
10. Be deceitful
11. Relative of -arian
12. Train lines: Abbr.
20. Those, in Toledo
21. Jazz singer Vaughan
23. Pitcher Hideo ___
24. Landed (on)
25. ___good example
26. Get groceries
27. "The Lion King" lion
28. One who ogles
29. Scarlett's estate
35. Says
37. Type of skiing
38. New York's ___ Island
40. Stone monument
43. Mars's Greek counterpart
45. Flimsy, as an excuse
46. Discordant deity
47. Course for new immigrants: Abbr.
48. Virgo's predecessor
49. Mornings, briefly
50. Patriotic org.
51. Fri. follower

Solution on page 323

Puzzle 24

Across

1. USAF noncom
5. Sounds of understanding
8. Be boastful
12. "___ Jury" (Spillane novel)
13. Gumshoe, for short
14. Cereal grain
15. San ___ Obispo
16. Derisive laugh
17. ___ breve (2/2 time)
18. Quaint contraction
20. Speak unclearly
21. Vocation
24. AWOL trackers
26. Maker of Space Invaders
27. Mal de ___ (seasickness)
28. IV units
31. Quagmire
32. Aptly named author Charles
34. Olive yield
35. Baden-Baden, e.g.
36. Arid
37. River to the Seine
39. Sound of disapproval
40. Pulled suddenly
41. Part of an ear
44. Two-element electron tube
46. Actress Thurman et al.
47. Sort of: Suff.
48. Ruffian
52. Carry on wildly
53. Convent member
54. Southwest Indian
55. Work measures
56. Some drs.
57. Opposed to, in Dogpatch

Down

1. Up to, briefly
2. Actor Irwin
3. Alphabet trio
4. Consumer Reports employee
5. "None of the above"
6. Learn of
7. Connived
8. Military bigwigs
9. Small stream
10. Bill of Rights defenders: Abbr.
11. Apparatus
19. Oddball
21. Truck parts
22. On the summit of
23. Indian music
25. Future doc's major
27. Mom's month
28. Bottle stopper
29. Art film theater
30. Toboggan
33. Wearing away
38. Motown's Franklin
39. Outperforms
40. ___ Hopkins University
41. Enticement
42. Sharif of film
43. Backfire sound
45. "The rest ___ to you"
49. Take more than one's share of
50. AP rival
51. Martini ingredient

Solution on page 324

Puzzle 25

Across

1. "Stormy Weather" Horne
5. TV watchdog: Abbr.
8. Tarzan creator's monogram
11. Close-fitting
12. Exclamations of triumph
14. Ghost's greeting
15. Electric co., e.g.
16. Danny of "White Christmas"
17. Wall Street order
18. Bank fixtures
20. Mizzen and jigger, e.g.
22. Harsh light
24. Suitable
25. Dug up
26. Flunky
29. Fraction of a min.
30. Mouth bone
31. "Man's best friend"
33. Trio times two
36. Serious play
38. Suffix with human or fact
39. One pointing at a target
40. Breathing room
43. Some sharks
45. Kept under wraps
46. Take rudely
48. "Voila!"
51. News-service letters
52. Casa component
53. Jr. high preceder
54. Moon craft, for short
55. Occupation
56. Be dependent (on)

Down

1. Shreveport coll.
2. Suffix for differ
3. Pain in the neck
4. Shining brightly
5. Ersatz
6. Cartoonist Addams, for short
7. Small island
8. Recedes, as the tide
9. Overwhelming victory
10. Young men
13. Large trucks
19. FBI agent
21. Bank device: Abbr.
22. Baseball VIPs
23. Doesn't tell the truth
24. Not many
26. China's Sun ___-sen
27. Water, facetiously
28. Alaskan city
30. ___ Bartlet, president on "The West Wing"
32. Narrow-bodied river fish
34. Assn.
35. Fashion model Cheryl
36. Former U.S. terr.
37. Water cannon target
40. Synagogue
41. Meerschaum or brier
42. Take ___ view (disapprove)
43. Opposite of bueno
44. Basic rhyme scheme
47. British rule in colonial India
49. Dover's state: Abbr.
50. One of Alcott's "Little Women"

Solution on page 324

Puzzle 26

Across

1. Part of T.G.I.F.: Abbr.
4. On the sick list
7. Not imit.
11. John, in Scotland
12. Evian evening
14. Italy's capital, to natives
15. Menacing sound
16. Stow, as cargo
17. Praise
18. Fished for congers
20. Most high-school students
22. "___ a Wonderful Life"
23. Form 1040 sender
24. Delicate use of words
27. Majorca Mrs.
28. Chili ___ carne
31. Thurman of "The Avengers"
32. Quaint roads
34. Patient-care grp.
35. Inside info
36. Plumber's joint
37. "Porgy and ___"
38. Coolidge's nickname
39. Horseless carriage
41. Crosses over
43. Open-mouthed
46. The one over there
47. Ferber or Best
49. Arles assent
51. Chianti or Chablis
52. Little kids
53. Flower holder
54. Chooses, with "for"
55. Toy with a string
56. Howard or Ely

Down

1. Mediterranean fruit
2. Pink, as a steak
3. Concerning: Lat.
4. Bit of land in the sea
5. A lot
6. Pot's top
7. Heraldic bands
8. Horse's color
9. Radio man Don
10. Gallivant
13. Go to bed
19. Set on fire
21. Historical times
24. Egypt's King ___
25. French friend
26. Bottle topper
27. Weekend TV revue, briefly
28. Señor Guevara
29. Mantra syllables
30. Phone book listings: Abbr.
32. Mrs. Sprat's dietary no-no
33. Raring to go
37. Bikini top
38. Actress Phoebe
39. Poem part
40. Visibly horrified
41. Ocean vessel
42. Have dog breath?
44. Serve coffee
45. Money in France
46. Company, so they say
48. Complete an "i"
50. Country hotel

Solution on page 324

Puzzle 27

Across

1. Colonel or captain
5. Ending with hard or soft
9. Part of a play
12. Asian salt sea
13. Carrier to Israel
14. ___ tai (cocktail)
15. Hit the bottle
16. 552, in old Rome
17. Do sums
18. Villainous glare
20. Strong, as feelings
22. Followed orders
24. Lowest-ranking NCO
27. Wielded the baton
28. Bothers
32. Good for farming
34. Windbag's output
36. Brilliant star
37. Note before la
38. Patient care grp.
39. Seasoned
42. Shooting marble
45. Open-handed hits
50. Big pig
51. Scrimp partner
53. Tennis player Nastase
54. Mo. after July
55. "The ___ lama . . ."
56. Tiny speck
57. Thirsty
58. Hang in the balance
59. Cashews, e.g.

Down

1. Pied Piper followers
2. Elvis Presley's middle name
3. Scruff of the neck
4. Artist Paul
5. Join in holy matrimony
6. Joined by a common cause
7. Wet, weatherwise
8. High-society group
9. The Four Seasons' "Walk Like ___"
10. Rogues
11. Bay of Fundy phenomenon
19. Bagel relative
21. Do newspaper work
23. Spelling event
24. Is able to
25. Major leaguer
26. Washroom, briefly
29. Short cheer
30. Kipling book
31. Sign of a sellout
33. Military center
34. Weeding implement
35. Cutlass automaker
37. Director Spielberg
40. Journalist Joseph or Stewart
41. Jungle vine
42. Herring kin
43. Guided vacation
44. Like a souffle
46. Portray in words
47. Baseball's Felipe or Moises
48. Actor Brad
49. Espies
52. Days of yore, in days of yore

Solution on page 324

Puzzle 28

Across

1. Place to play darts
4. Gee preceder
7. Say "pretty please"
10. ID on a dust jacket
12. Losing tic-tac-toe row
13. Flu preventers
14. Baseball great Ty
15. Balloon-breaking sound
16. Ash Wednesday follower
17. Army offense: Abbr.
19. Army posts
20. Upper atmosphere
23. Clubs or hearts
25. Milk producer
26. Discussion groups
29. 1550, in old Rome
30. Furry foot
31. German city on the Danube
33. Drunken daze
36. Easy putt
38. ___ care in the world
39. ". . . and ___ grow on"
40. Sweater size
43. Bit of force
45. British noble
46. Hyundai competitor
47. Ukraine's Sea of ___
51. Going ___: fighting
52. Jerusalem's land: Abbr.
53. Casanova type
54. Barbie's guy
55. Signed like an illiterate
56. Neighbor of Braz.

Down

1. Snapshot, for short
2. Mil. entertainment group
3. Consumer protection org.
4. Trade show, for short
5. State of false hope
6. Dandy dresser
7. Hive dwellers
8. Seaside soarer
9. Mobsters' guns
11. Pro hoopster
13. Blackboard material
18. Dryly humorous
19. Receptacle
20. Teacher's deg.
21. Very small amounts
22. Sword handle
24. Detroit labor org.
27. Old-time actress Velez
28. Skirt opening
30. Stew vessel
32. L-P link
34. Not yet rented
35. Legislator, for short
36. Bricks measure
37. Lend___ (listen)
40. Where Mt. Rushmore is
41. Trumpet muffler
42. Similar (to)
44. Football field measure
46. General Mills cereal
48. Animals: Suffix
49. Your and my
50. Relax, with "out"

Solution on page 324

Puzzle 29

Across

1. Wise bird
4. Longtime Chinese chairman
7. Road grooves
11. "Here comes trouble!"
13. Benevolent guy
14. Oklahoma Indian
15. Angelic topper
16. "CSI" network
17. Hollywood's Bruce or Laura
18. Radio woe
20. Balance sheet plus
21. Big bangs
24. Russian workers' cooperative
27. How the weasel goes
28. Church lady
31. Whole bunch
32. Set down
33. Role for Lorre
34. Western omelet ingredient
35. Fragrant tree
36. Basted
37. Sour brew
39. Irish patron, briefly
43. Ox or fox
47. Afternoon socials
48. Move among the moguls
50. Unthreatening
51. American, to a Brit
52. Reunion attendees
53. "Saturday Night Live" piece
54. Bits of work
55. QB's gains
56. Sullivan and Bradley

Down

1. Partner of aahs
2. One of the five W's
3. She gets what she wants
4. Pilgrimage site
5. Mass vestment
6. Authorizes
7. Fishing poles
8. All-purpose trucks
9. Went like the blazes
10. Transmitted
12. Place of rapid growth
19. In need of a doctor
20. Dangerous snake
22. Trunk contents
23. Trifle (with)
24. Cigarette tip
25. Nipper's company
26. Scot's cap
28. "Immediately!"
29. Salt Lake City college athlete
30. Silent assent
32. Abner's adjective
33. Is worthy of
35. ___ Tuesday (Mardi Gras)
36. ___ Diego
38. Acquires
39. Eye irritation
40. Go like heck
41. Feeling of hunger
42. Gets inquisitive
44. Model's partner
45. At the center of
46. Cole Porter's "___ Do It"
48. "Lucy in the ___ with Diamonds"
49. Tease

Solution on page 324

Puzzle 30

Across

1. Mouths
4. "Send help!"
7. Over-50 grp.
11. ___ Jones Average
12. Ensnare
14. Elisabeth of "Leaving Las Vegas"
15. One way to see
17. Pretzel topper
18. Light switch settings
19. ___ Peanut Butter Cups
21. En ___: as a group
24. Composer Bacharach
25. Days before big events
26. Puts up a fight
29. Pointer
30. Elaborate parties
31. Horror director Craven
33. Appetizer
35. German composer
36. Psychiatrist Jung
37. Insolent
38. Taste center
41. Small speck
42. Centrally located
43. Wake-up calls
48. Not yet final, at law
49. Shredded
50. Drenched
51. Words before job or life
52. Mom's mate
53. Sitting site

Down

1. Exaltation in verse
2. Cowboy Rogers
3. Overwhelming wonder
4. British weight
5. Mine rocks
6. Declare
7. Desirable qualities
8. "Gotcha!" cries
9. Regulation
10. Cats and canaries
13. Reader
16. Prepare, as a salad
20. Discord goddess
21. Shea player
22. Rival of Hertz
23. Back-to-school mo.
24. Asian palm
26. Turn tail
27. "___ the night before . . ."
28. "Be with you in a coupla ___"
30. College club
32. Not outgoing
34. Maine's ___ National Park
35. Cubs' clubs
37. In good condition
38. Sudden pain
39. Pierre's girlfriend
40. Santa checks it twice
41. "Dumb ___" (old comic strip)
44. Serling of "The Twilight Zone"
45. Hole-punching tool
46. Open meadow
47. Indy sponsor

Solution on page 325

Puzzle 31

Across

1. Trite saying
4. Nexus
8. Builder's detail, in brief
12. Crazy eights cousin
13. In unison, musically
14. Prom night transportation
15. Calligraphy need
16. Feel sorry for
17. Bar member: Abbr.
18. One of the senses
20. Catch some rays
22. European range
25. Moonshine maker
29. Retired airplanes: Abbr.
32. Fleming and Paisley
34. Narc's agcy.
35. Fleecy females
36. Paid athlete
37. Army beds
38. Tire filler
39. Detach gradually
40. Gofer: Abbr.
41. Show pleasure
43. Gas in bright signs
45. Brain scan: Abbr.
47. Delay
51. Defeat
54. Swedish pop group
57. Shake a leg
58. Malt kiln
59. Target
60. Doctors' gp.
61. Diving birds
62. Porch for Pericles
63. High-jumper's hurdle

Down

1. Diamonds, for example
2. Singer Moffo
3. Canton cookware
4. Mike site
5. Infamous Amin
6. Pecan
7. Door openers
8. Incline
9. Indy tire-changing area
10. Hwy. mishap respondent
11. Flirtatious
19. ITAR-___ (news agency)
21. Carrier letters
23. Tobacco holder
24. Brand of wrap
26. Wedding-ceremony exchanges
27. Response to "Shall we?"
28. Keep going
29. Large bodies of water
30. Do some laps at the Y
31. Actress Garr
33. ___ of the above
37. Bevel
39. Itsy-bitsy
42. Latvians
44. City near Kyoto
46. Legs, in slang
48. Melville hero
49. Peru's largest city
50. Tragic king
51. Feathered stole
52. Agua, in Arles
53. Seek information
55. Take one's cuts
56. Sis's sib

Solution on page 325

Puzzle 32

Across

1. Small pieces
5. Last year's senior
9. DX divided by V
12. Disney's "___ and the Detectives"
13. Chauffeured vehicle
14. ___ Ronald Reagan
15. In ___ straits
16. Scissorhands portrayer Johnny
17. Novak or Basinger
18. Sports artist LeRoy
20. Own (up to)
21. Soldiers
22. Italian monk
24. Omega's opposite
27. White-collar workers?
31. Oversized
32. "The Mod ___"
34. "___ Sera, Sera"
35. Asserted
37. County in East England
39. Real heel
40. Soak
41. Pretentiously cultured
44. Least wild
47. Boxing punch
48. Letters before zees
50. Raindrop sound
52. Out-of-date: Abbr.
53. Pursuit
54. Sunscreen ingredient
55. Puppy's bark
56. Ye ___ Shoppe
57. Stunt man Knievel

Down

1. Garden plot
2. Poker player's declaration
3. Goodyear product
4. Santa's transport
5. Actors Robert and Alan
6. Lender's security
7. Diamond head
8. Item in a bucket
9. Salad veggie
10. Horus's mother
11. Distinctive doctrines
19. Noxious atmosphere
20. "So ___, so good"
22. Neighbor of Ala.
23. Cash in
24. Disney division
25. Abner adjective
26. Tour organizer, for short
27. Jersey chew
28. Figs. averaging 100
29. Billiards stick
30. Questionnaire question
33. Abbr. at the end of a proof
36. Very cold
38. Eurasian treeless plain
40. Toxic ___
41. "A thing of beauty is ___ forever"
42. 1944 Nobel physicist Isidor
43. Cookbook amt.
44. Be inclined (to)
45. Croat or Bulgar
46. Choice for Hamlet
48. One of the five W's
49. Bald Brynner
51. Good buddy

Solution on page 325

Puzzle 33

Across

1. 2002 Winter Olympics site
5. Peter out
8. Reddish-brown horse
11. "___ Lisa Smile" (2003 film)
12. Margarita fruit
14. Cereal box letters
15. Attack, as a fly
16. Cereal serving
17. Suffix with peace or neat
18. Cod and May
20. Leopard features
22. Campfire treat
24. Hairpiece
25. Greek column type
26. Henchman of Daddy Warbucks
29. Marked a ballot
30. "Citizen Kane" studio
31. ___ a plea
33. Body art
36. Boxing site
38. Ross musical, with "The"
39. "Peter Pan" girl
40. Portugal neighbor
43. Lightweight wood
45. Director's "Stop!"
46. Informal conversation
48. Clapton who sang "Layla"
51. Israeli weapon
52. "The Wizard of Oz" dog
53. Train line to NYC
54. Unruly mane
55. Candy in a dispenser
56. Mischievous Norse god

Down

1. Sounds of hesitation
2. Disabled vehicle's need
3. Jungle crusher
4. John Wayne film set in Africa
5. North Sea tributary
6. Life stories, briefly
7. Mercedes rival
8. Czech city
9. Mine opening
10. Tibetan bovines
13. Borden's cow
19. Chest muscle, for short
21. Ernie Els's org.
22. Half a dozen
23. Big name in champagne
24. "___ asked you?"
26. Boxing match ender
27. Plot outline
28. Golden or Walden
30. Peri Gilpin's "Frasier" role
32. Take care of a bill
34. Prefix with light or night
35. Touch of color
36. Shoemaker's tool
37. Market again
40. Pond gunk
41. Vito Corleone's creator
42. "Take ___ from me . . ."
43. Lessen
44. From ___ (completely)
47. Jump on one leg
49. Get on one's nerves
50. Dernier ___ (latest thing)

Solution on page 325

Puzzle 34

Across

1. Write quickly
4. Theater seating
8. Comical Laurel
12. Be in the red
13. Deep black, in poetry
14. Singer-actress Lane
15. Deli sandwich
16. Pebbles' pet
17. Cotton quantity
18. Attention getter
20. Kept out
22. Huxley's "___ in Gaza"
26. Persian Gulf port
27. Like slasher films
28. De Mille specialty
30. Astronaut Grissom
31. Understood
32. Soaking spot
35. Bovine sounds
36. Stadium level
37. Song refrain
41. Boris' partner
43. Let up
45. "What can brown do for you?" sloganeer
46. Earthenware jar
47. Help in crime
50. Switch setting
53. Page of a book
54. Letter for Gandalf
55. Miles and miles
56. Spyglass part
57. Fairy tale's first word
58. "Most wanted" org.

Down

1. Employment
2. One who gives a hoot
3. Restraining ropes
4. Try another shade
5. ___-Wan Kenobi
6. Took the trophy
7. Snooty type
8. Tel Aviv native
9. Skiers' transport
10. More qualified
11. "I ___ vacation!"
19. England's Isle of ___
21. 2 on a phone dial
22. Omelet need
23. "___ Light Up My Life"
24. Showy lily
25. Part of a place setting
29. "___ small world!"
32. Do effortlessly
33. "Gross!"
34. Actress Arthur
35. "Whew!"
36. Once around the track
37. Fish, in a way
38. U.S. Grant's counterpart
39. Edgar ___ Poe
40. Pages (through)
42. Student getting one-on-one help
44. Tropical root
48. Hair style
49. SASE, e.g.
51. "Groovy!"
52. Cal. column

Solution on page 325

Puzzle 35

Across

1. Domino dot
4. Gist
8. EMT's specialty
11. Like the Sahara
13. Huron, for one
14. "Look at that!"
15. Fashion initials
16. Worry, perhaps
17. Stage help
18. Mind reader's gift
20. Deliver an address
22. Stock unit
25. Cab
27. Finished first
28. They give people big heads
30. Choir member
34. Try to find out
35. Took to the station house
37. Luau fare
38. Oscar-winner Patricia
40. Singer Horne
41. NBC weekend comedy, briefly
42. Frozen treats
44. Spaghetti sauce brand
46. Wee
49. Shar-___ (wrinkly dog)
50. Twain portrayer Holbrook
51. Holds the deed to
54. Barbed remark
58. Hurricane hub
59. Belles of balls
60. Hoity-toity sort
61. Evening hour
62. Ballpark figure?
63. Hack's auto

Down

1. Place to crash
2. Bug
3. Lapel attachment
4. Lend a hand?
5. Joplin composition
6. Luau instrument
7. Canon competitor
8. Caesar's comedy partner
9. Be sullen
10. Former South Korean president Syngman
12. Textile worker
19. Palm reader, e.g.
21. Tease
22. Long-necked bird
23. Garden waterer
24. "Puppy Love" singer Paul
25. Shadings
26. A-apple link
29. Stiff wind
31. Cathedral recess
32. Carol
33. Farm storage
36. Neck part
39. Like Abner
43. Clumsy ones
45. Big trucks
46. "___ a Lady"
47. "___ help you?"
48. "'World Capitals' for 200, ___"
49. Furtive "Hey, you!"
52. Soggy
53. Wizards and Magic org.
55. Corp. abbr.
56. Serpentine squeezer
57. Decline

Solution on page 325

Puzzle 36

Across

1. Huron or Erie
5. Purpose
8. Atty.-to-be's exam
12. Mr. Potato Head pieces
13. Matamoros Mrs.
14. Seafood order
15. Outdoor accommodation
16. Chicago-Miami dir.
17. Hawkeye portrayer
18. Sea bird
20. Screwdriver, e.g.
21. Lower in prestige
24. ___ serif
27. Umbrella part
28. Stood up
30. Mus. version
33. The Braves, on scoreboards
34. Cultural customs
35. Chinese "path"
36. Quilting party
37. Bother continuously
38. Play a part
39. Appends
40. Mine bonanzas
42. Chimney residue
45. Blanc or Brooks
46. Nest eggs: Abbr.
47. Suffix with Canaan
49. Highland girl
53. Sampras of tennis
54. Put on TV
55. "The Thin Man" dog
56. Wrigley Field slugger
57. Stooge with a bowl cut
58. Salon cut

Down

1. Replayed tennis shot
2. Sailor's yes
3. Baseball's Griffey
4. Politician Kefauver
5. Part of AMA
6. April 15 org.
7. West of "My Little Chickadee"
8. Exams for future attys.
9. Unassisted
10. Moro of Italy
11. Pond duck
19. Cleaned, as a pipe
21. Saudi citizen
22. Angler's quest
23. Ready and willing partner
24. Puts into piles
25. En route to England, maybe
26. Cuddle up
29. Thoroughfare
30. Just slightly
31. Go quickly
32. Deteriorates
39. On a cruise
41. Earthenware pots
42. Doesn't guzzle
43. Black-and-white cookie
44. Meal for a horse
45. "A ___ formality!"
47. "___ the Walrus"
48. Juan's uncle
50. Fire residue
51. Stop on a line: Abbr.
52. Go limp

Solution on page 326

Puzzle 37

Across
1. Superabundance
5. P-T connection
8. Internet abbr.
11. Composer Edouard
12. Flying geese formation
13. Housekeeper
14. "Love the skin you're in" company
15. Cleveland cager, briefly
16. 10-percenters: Abbr.
17. "Look ___ hands!"
18. Former Spice Girl Halliwell
20. West Point letters
23. Perfume resin
27. Cathedral seat
30. Hardly ruddy
31. Male and female
32. Playwright Sean
34. Tennis star Williams
35. Emulated a siren
36. Day: Sp.
37. "Stop the cameras!"
38. Soup utensil
39. World Series mos.
41. WWII transports
43. Police officers
47. Bilko's mil. rank in "The Phil Silvers Show"
50. Fix illegally
52. "___ Wanna Do" (Sheryl Crow tune)
53. Pacific salmon
54. Joseph of ice cream fame
55. Group that votes alike
56. 111, in old Rome
57. Bread, for stew
58. Actress Thompson of "Family"

Down
1. Latch (onto)
2. In ___ land (spaced out)
3. ___ Bator (capital of Mongolia)
4. "Happy Birthday ___"
5. Shopping channel
6. Carter's successor
7. Ballesteros of golf
8. Move from side to side, as a tail
9. Mental quickness
10. Dict. entries
13. Writer Norman
19. Move to the front row, maybe
21. Stockholm natives
22. "Merry" month
24. Prez, e.g.
25. Bistro handout
26. "Peace ___ hand"
27. Gallup specialty
28. Quito's country: Abbr.
29. Beaver Cleaver's dad
33. Do business with
34. Attack command to Fido
36. Square-dance move
40. Strikebreakers
42. Very: Fr.
44. Spanish cooking pot
45. Trudge (along)
46. Director Vittorio De ___
47. 1200, to Caesar
48. Chicago White ___
49. 4, on the phone
51. Cheat

Solution on page 326

Puzzle 38

Across

1. Scores to shoot for
5. ___ standstill (motionless)
8. London subway, with "the"
12. "The Sopranos" Emmy winner Falco
13. Trouser part
14. Geological periods
15. Uncool fellow
16. Things kept under wraps?
18. Caribbean and others
20. Usher's find
21. Day's opposite in commercials
23. New ___, India
27. 16 1/2 feet
30. Hardly cooked
32. Wind-instrument insert
33. Chalk remover
35. Car lot transaction
37. Western lawman Wyatt
38. Narrative
40. Cup part
41. Hightails it
43. Hair goops
45. Jules Verne captain
47. Guesstimate
50. Builders
54. Oodles
56. Bowling alley
57. Sound of relief
58. Ancient portico
59. Tea leaves reader
60. Golf ball raiser
61. Freight hopper

Down

1. Coop
2. Fruity coolers
3. To laugh, to Lafayette
4. Four-door car
5. Matterhorn, e.g.
6. Less long-winded
7. "The African Queen" screenwriter James
8. Wobbles
9. Large coffee container
10. Cave dweller
11. Sharp curve
17. Gloomy
19. Regal address
22. Fruit-filled pastry
24. "All in the Family" producer Norman
25. Prefix with port
26. The same as before
27. Atoll protector
28. Exam sans pencils
29. Madonna's "Truth or ___"
31. Mystery writer ___ Stanley Gardner
34. Princess Diana's family name
36. Snakelike swimmers
39. Greek markets
42. Matched items
44. Hidden stockpile
46. Trench around a castle
48. Certain chorister
49. Dunce
50. Overhead rails
51. Norma ___
52. Opposite of WSW
53. Female pronoun
55. Path for Confucians

Solution on page 326

Puzzle 39

Across

1. Tiny legume
4. Bleats
8. Muffin type
12. Spot for a napkin
13. Not on tape
14. Verdi heroine
15. Seagoing letters
16. Arabia's Gulf of ___
17. Neuter
18. Do the driving
20. Bambi's mother, e.g.
22. Camera eye
25. Traffic snarler
29. Nap sacks?
32. Malt-drying kiln
34. Early Beatle Sutcliffe
35. Charles Lamb's nom de plume
36. Hoops org.
37. Secures, as a shoelace
38. Small bite
39. Maui necklaces
40. Courtroom pledge
41. In a peevish mood
43. House made of twigs
45. Striped shirt wearer
47. Winter ailments
51. Mayberry tyke
54. Palindromic pop quartet
57. Shale extract
58. Similar to
59. Dress line
60. Police blotter abbr.
61. Owner's certificate
62. Short-term worker
63. Original

Down

1. +
2. Sunrise direction
3. Church nook
4. Loud noise
5. Support
6. N.Y.C.'s Park, e.g.
7. Ship off
8. More despicable
9. Kind of cord
10. Tooth care org.
11. Negative vote
19. Adamson's lioness
21. Fall mo.
23. ___ the wiser
24. Polio vaccine developer
26. Where Siberia is
27. Don't delete
28. "Shh!"
29. Needing straightening
30. "Night" author Wiesel
31. Cocktail hour assortment
33. Manuscript encl.
37. "The Wizard of Oz" pooch
39. High-pH substance
42. Brought to bay
44. Rapscallion
46. Go on a hunger strike
48. Money to tide one over
49. Sea wall
50. Cabbage salad
51. From a prior era
52. Cutie ___
53. 34th Prez
55. Spelling contest
56. Loud noise

Solution on page 326

Puzzle 40

Across

1. Quit, with "out"
4. Farmer's place, in a song
8. Sawyer or Seaver
11. Rajah's mate
13. Sandwich-cookie name
14. Possess, to Burns
15. Deli orders, briefly
16. First miracle site
17. Where the rudder is
18. "Schindler's ___"
20. Heavy, as fog
22. More dishonorable
25. Sweet suffix
26. Rankle
27. Israeli Abba
30. D-day carriers
34. Cowboy actor Rogers
35. Wise advisors
37. 102, in old Rome
38. Prescription quantity
40. Outscore
41. Web address: Abbr.
42. ___ Constitution
44. Actor M. ___ Walsh
46. Stravinsky's "Le ___ du printemps"
49. Realtor's unit
51. A braggart has a big one
52. "Show Boat" novelist Ferber
54. "Lion King" baddie
58. Marks a ballot
59. Goes bad
60. "For heaven's ___!"
61. Although
62. The Beatles' "___ a Woman"
63. "Out of sight!"

Down

1. Round figure
2. Friend
3. Blasting stuff
4. Physicians, for short
5. Middle of QED
6. "Yesterday's Spy" author Deighton
7. Fills, as a camera
8. "More ___ You Know" (1929 song)
9. Clumsy sorts
10. Ration (out)
12. Dot in the sea
19. Enrages
21. Conger or moray
22. Feathered friend
23. Buck add-on
24. "The ___ the limit"
25. Prime draft status
28. Nickname for Barbara
29. Mature, as wine
31. Refuse
32. Start to sag
33. River sediment
36. Suffix with young or old
39. Pt. of EEC
43. Crystal-ball gazers
45. Meal at boot camp
46. Like Marilyn Monroe
47. Pulitzer writer James
48. Price paid
49. Poker entry fee
50. Elliot of the Mamas and the Papas
53. Homer Simpson's exclamation
55. Tourist's rental
56. Wanted-poster initials
57. Claret color

Solution on page 326

Puzzle 41

Across

1. 1973 French Open winner Nastase
5. "Be Prepared" org.
8. Three- ___ sloth
12. Cooing bird
13. Tach letters
14. Prefix with -syncratic
15. Sign-making aids
17. Macy's department
18. Dauphin's dad
19. Take in again
20. Rio de la ___
24. Hair No More alternative
26. "The Planets" composer Gustav
27. Wrecks completely
30. Not doing anything
31. Sandra or Ruby
32. 1930's boxing champ Max
34. Book after Nehemiah
36. Float ___ (provide financing)
37. Ballad, for example
38. Gnats and mice
39. Skin openings
42. Urban vermin
44. Santa's landing spot
45. Clear soup
50. Part of IBM: Abbr.
51. Over's partner
52. Flying jib, e.g.
53. Simple
54. Photo ___ (media events)
55. Like Playboy models

Down

1. Passports, for example: Abbr.
2. His wife took a turn for the worse
3. "___ Got a Secret"
4. Bard's twilight
5. Gusto
6. Organizational offshoot
7. Pre-noon hrs.
8. Schedule
9. Some Keats poems
10. One, in Weimar
11. Prescription amount
16. Auto or pluto follower
19. Gen. Powell's status
20. Sorority letter
21. Miner's strike
22. "___ Well That Ends Well"
23. African insect
25. Fair-hiring letters
28. Neighbor of Vietnam
29. Bench or chair
31. Couch potato's hangout
33. T.L.C. givers
35. Sounds from Santa
36. Places for rent: Abbr.
39. ___-dieu (kneeling bench)
40. The last Mrs. Charlie Chaplin
41. Decomposes
43. Colonizing insects
45. Speak lovingly
46. CIA forerunner
47. West of old films
48. Blend
49. TV Tarzan Ron

Solution on page 326

Puzzle 42

Across

1. Geese formation
4. 60's hairdo
8. Release, as lava
12. Toronto's prov.
13. Sitcom star Carey
14. Yesterday: Fr.
15. Took the prize
16. Cote dweller
17. Like quiche
18. Corduroy ridge
20. Weep audibly
22. Celestial spheres
25. Trousers
29. Guys-only party
32. Santa Anita event
34. "All systems go"
35. Marciano stats
36. Course with lettuce
37. Next-to-last Greek letter
38. Covenant holder
39. Shed tears
40. Acting group
41. Puccini heroine
43. Laundry need
45. "That's yucky!"
47. Richie's mom, to the
    Fonz
50. Tex. or Mex., e.g.
53. "___ Karenina"
56. Raincoat
58. Nominate
59. Soldiers in gray
60. ET carrier
61. Sails temporarily off
    course

62. "___ the night before
    Christmas . . ."
63. Hair fixative

Down

1. "I'll never do it again," e.g.
2. Plenty, to a poet
3. Volcano in Sicily
4. Calculating snake?
5. To's companion
6. Gun the engine
7. Is in arrears
8. Biblical land with a queen
9. Corkscrew-tailed animal
10. Brain-wave test, briefly
11. Like some smiles
19. Captain's record

21. Essay page, for short
23. Highlands hillside
24. Business department
26. West Coast wine valley
27. Easy throw
28. Comical playlet
29. Three-person card
    game
30. Corrida foe
31. Says "When?"
33. Mafia boss
36. Ill-gotten gains
40. EMT specialty
42. Remedies
44. Collect in abundance
46. Male deer
48. Pleased with oneself

49. Sidewalk eatery
50. "Pick a card, ___ card"
51. Farmyard sound
52. Big name in luxury autos
54. Modern
55. Hoops grp.
57. Maj.'s superior

Solution on page 327

Puzzle 43

Across

1. "No ___, ands or buts"
4. Cry a river
8. Auction offers
12. Calendar square
13. Job conditions agcy.
14. Old Testament twin
15. Mensa members have high ones
16. Variety of chalcedony
17. Weakling
18. Subject of a will
20. Stinging insects
21. Airedale, for one
24. Hand covering
27. Reception aid
31. Managed care gp.
32. Get a blue ribbon
33. Chicken ___
34. Belongs
37. Comic pianist Victor
39. Defamed in writing
41. 1983 Mr. T flick
44. Ultimate purpose
48. Easy win
49. Mississippi Senator Cochran
51. Miss Piggy, to Miss Piggy
52. Kathryn of "Law & Order: CI"
53. Bestow
54. Grain beard
55. Below-average grades
56. Cake decorator
57. Pa Clampett

Down

1. "Each Dawn ___" (Cagney film)
2. Internet info sources
3. Method: Abbr.
4. Tot's tootsy cover
5. "Lou Grant" actor
6. For what reason
7. Calif. airport
8. "___ the Ides of March"
9. Sister of Osiris
10. Somewhat moist
11. Has a late meal
19. Off-road transport: Abbr.
20. Moist
22. Increase
23. Rural hotel
24. Touch-tone 4
25. K-O connection
26. ___ and aah
28. "All Things Considered" airer
29. Egg drink
30. Tool that's swung
32. Spider's creation
35. Makes ecstatic
36. Make fun of
37. Drinking spree
38. Strange
40. Exit the premises
41. ___ Scott Decision, 1857
42. Apple discard
43. Six-sided solid
45. Key related to F# minor: Abbr.
46. Rob or Chad
47. Swedish soprano
49. ___F: end-of-the-week sigh
50. Here: Lat.

Solution on page 327

Puzzle 44

Across

1. Ladies of Spain: Abbr.
5. NFL six-pointers
8. African lake
12. "I could ___ horse!"
13. New Deal org.
14. Queen of Olympus
15. Refines, as wine
16. Letter after kay
17. B & B's
18. Hearing and sight
20. Sculpted figure
22. Mag. executives
23. Kennel sound
24. Ropes, as a dogie
28. Pre-1917 Russian rulers
32. Modern composer Brian
33. Mineo of film
35. One of the Stooges
36. Adds seasoning to
39. More dweeblike
42. Elongated fish
44. Average grade
45. Sudden outpouring
47. Petting zoo animal
51. "Who ___ there?"
52. Tax filing mo.
54. Comedian King
55. Suffix for million
56. Hide ___ hair
57. Slashes
58. Sandwiches, for short
59. Uno y due
60. Spanish snack

Down

1. Caribbean and Bering
2. Fury
3. ___ o'clock scholar
4. Gives some lip
5. Long locks
6. Neighbor of Penna.
7. Like most pretzels
8. Bird sounds
9. Egg layers
10. The New Yorker cartoonist Peter
11. "___ Rheingold"
19. Tokyo, long ago
21. Cheerios grain
24. Guitarist ___ Paul
25. Santa ___, Calif.
26. Note between fa and la
27. ___ Fernando Valley
29. "What a good boy ___!"
30. Beluga eggs
31. Sun. homily
34. "Tinker, Tailor, Soldier, Spy" author
37. Acts the coquette
38. Prepare, as a table
40. Kin: Abbr.
41. Leave the premises
43. Listed
45. Flower pot filler
46. Sprightly
48. Inter ___: among others
49. Li'l Abner creator
50. Looped handle
51. Gossip
53. ___ favor (please, in Spanish)

Solution on page 327

Puzzle 45

Across

1. Comic Rock
6. Attack word
9. Ship pronoun
12. Microwave brand
13. Señora Peron
14. Proof finale
15. First-rate
17. Cycle starter
18. Acorn dropper
19. Hiking path
21. Old gas name
24. African snake
27. Oak or apple
28. Oyster product
30. Actress Anouk
32. Whatever amount
33. Plant sheath
35. Antediluvian
38. Newswoman Connie
40. Start a closeup shot
42. Workplace safety group: Abbr.
44. American composer Rorem
46. Mother of Helen of Troy
47. Wind-borne soil
49. Red-white-and-blue inits.
51. Ike's monogram
52. In a precarious situation
58. Freudian topics
59. Response to a bad call
60. Eats in style
61. Gaze at
62. Home on the farm
63. Prevent, in legalese

Down

1. Garfield, e.g.
2. Med. ins. plan
3. Coolio's genre
4. Not outside
5. Mystery writer Paretsky
6. Do tailoring
7. "___ been had!"
8. Golfer's vehicle
9. Place to go back to
10. Three-time skating gold medalist
11. Roman magistrate
16. Police blotter letters
20. Hwy.
21. Antipollution org.
22. One of a D.C. 100
23. Photographer's request
25. "Beetle Bailey" character
26. Dessert with a crust
29. R and B singer Rawls
31. Rand McNally product
34. Atlanta's ___ Center
36. Pot top
37. Genetic initials
39. Contains
41. "Ironic" singer Morissette
42. Any '50s tune
43. Like a new lawn, maybe
45. "I am such a dope!"
48. Blubbers
50. Hypotenuse, e.g.
53. "Wayne's World" denial
54. Play (with)
55. Acct. amount
56. Boardroom VIP
57. Second sight, for short

Solution on page 327

Puzzle 46

Across

1. Soak up the sun
5. Eye
8. Gang's territory
12. Reason for a backrub
13. Speed along
14. Where Korea is
15. "___ here long?"
16. Well-worn
17. Hit the horn
18. Little whirlpool
19. "___ we forget . . ."
21. Abet
24. Gondola guider
28. Fireplace shelf
31. Beautiful woman of paradise
32. Charlie Parker's instrument
33. Derogatory in manner
35. One of the Smothers Brothers
36. Spoken language
38. Rich pastries
40. 1983 Streisand film
41. Golf ball prop
42. Newts in transition
45. Degrees for CEOs
49. Having sufficient skill
52. The guy's
54. El ___, Tex.
55. Map line
56. Batting stat
57. Common newspaper nickname
58. Vaudevillian family of note
59. Naval initials
60. Backtalk

Down

1. Legendary ox
2. Got 100 on, as a test
3. Storage building
4. Nairobi native
5. "Caught you!"
6. Tiny stream
7. "Venerable" English writer
8. Arm art
9. G.I. morale booster
10. Brazilian city, familiarly
11. "Spare tire," essentially
20. Field of knowledge
22. Reflexive pronoun
23. Room to relax in
25. Mandolin cousin
26. Piccadilly figure
27. Net holder
28. Equine mom
29. Part of a neuron
30. Burning
32. Double agent, e.g.
34. "i" piece
37. Fine horses
39. Entices
43. Not exiting, as traffic
44. Brothers and sisters
46. Theda of the silents
47. Garage sale tag
48. Doesn't just tear up
49. Canine line
50. Ride the ump
51. Put down
53. Female sib

Solution on page 327

Puzzle 47

Across

1. Ill-humored
5. Corporate symbol
9. Brother's address
12. Flow like molasses
13. Kind of sch.
14. Bagel go-with
15. Cleft locale
16. Humdrum
18. Muscat is its capital
20. Was slack-jawed
21. Short race
24. Jurisprudence
25. Oldsmobile model
26. Be accepted as
30. Thanksgiving vegetable
31. Simonize
32. "Ick!"
33. Impassive
36. Mrs. Phil Donahue
38. Twice-chewed food
39. Has a feeling
40. More suitable
43. Featherbrain
44. In the wrong
46. ___-bitsy
50. Concert equipment
51. Triangle tone
52. Quote as an example
53. Owns
54. Breyers competitor
55. Bunny's tail

Down

1. Scrubs wearer
2. Surprised cry
3. Israeli submachine gun
4. "The Bathers" painter
5. Sic on
6. Hollywood's Ken or Lena
7. Neighbor of Lux.
8. Alphas' opposites
9. Complete failure
10. Vatican City's
    surroundings
11. Took a bough?
17. Toothed tools
19. L-P filler
21. Recites
22. Survey chart
23. San ___, Italy
24. Careless
26. Amigo
27. Expensive coats
28. Girl-watch or boy-watch
29. Greek R's
31. Gum amount
34. "Original Gangster"
    rapper
35. Parish priest, e.g.
36. Actor Gibson
37. Pranks
39. Musical numbers
40. Eastern nursemaid
41. Strong cotton
42. Recipe measurements:
    Abbr.
43. When said three times, a
    liar's policy
45. Young goat
47. Idiosyncrasy
48. Onetime Beatle Sutcliffe
49. Up to now

Solution on page 327

Puzzle 48

Across

1. Homer Simpson's father
4. Sword fight
8. Auction caution
12. Tax dept.
13. Words to an old chap
14. Down with the flu
15. Set afire
16. Marquis's inferior
17. Deuce topper
18. Begin
20. Hawaiian bird
22. Put into action
24. "___ we devils?"
28. Job for a lawyer
31. Not at home
34. Hawaiian neckwear
35. Dull routine
36. Three English rivers
37. Anatomical container
38. Western tribesman
39. Bumper mishap
40. Shea Stadium team
41. Look for water
43. "Hallelujah, ___ Bum"
45. Plenty, old-style
48. Imogene et al.
52. Villa d'___ (Italian landmark)
55. Comic Bert
57. "___ Miz"
58. Byway
59. Enjoying a cruise
60. Hockey legend Bobby
61. Floor coverings
62. Tarzan's transportation
63. Windows forerunner

Down

1. Is under the weather
2. Londoner, e.g.
3. This, in Havana
4. Tries to lose weight
5. It's between Can. and Mex.
6. Make, as a living
7. Country singer Lovett
8. Late-blooming flower
9. Term of respect
10. Zamboni's surface
11. Cloud backdrop
19. Feel sorrow about
21. No votes
23. Roof overhang
25. Option word
26. Like a pin?
27. Muscle twitches
28. Gunk
29. Sedan or coupe
30. Irish ___
32. Got the gold
33. Prefix meaning "opposed to"
36. The Mideast's Gulf of ___
40. '60s Chinese chairman
42. Watermelon features
44. Jazz singer Carmen
46. Norway's patron saint
47. "Now, where ___?"
49. Clumsy one
50. Dynamic lead-in
51. C.I.S. members, once
52. Make a goof
53. Not worth a ___
54. Schoolyard game
56. Egg layer

Solution on page 328

Puzzle 49

Across

1. Follow, as orders
5. Sandwich order
8. Elevator maker
12. "___ fair in love and war"
13. Karel Capek play
14. Former "Entertainment Tonight" host John
15. Fanciful yarn
17. "Stand By Me" singer ___ King
18. "The Sopranos" network
19. Cold-shoulders
21. Doze (off)
22. Toast topping
23. Lowers, as a light
25. Soft felt hat
28. Ruined
31. Used a credit card
32. "Hud" Oscar-winner
33. Fixes Junior's laces
36. Like grams and liters
38. Start of a counting-out rhyme
39. "___ Got Sixpence"
40. New Deal pres.
42. Oreo filling
44. Foldaway bed
47. Seniors' org.
49. Pots and pans, e.g.
51. "___ a man who wasn't there . . ."
52. Iron pumper's pride
53. Declare with confidence
54. Commies
55. Cultural underwriting org.
56. Prefix for sphere

Down

1. Swearing-in words
2. Divulge a secret
3. Cockney greeting
4. Couture monogram
5. Rodeo bull
6. Ripsnorter
7. Current fashions
8. Gambling site, briefly
9. Comparatively small
10. "That ___ excuse"
11. Tool building
16. Russian autocrat
20. Nurse a drink
22. Oscar winner Foster
24. ___ Carlo, Monaco
25. Part of F.Y.I.
26. Female in a flock
27. Discouraged
29. Chou En-___
30. Pampering, initially
34. SASE, perhaps
35. Native of Damascus
36. Brunch drink
37. Odd's opposite
40. So-so
41. Titled British woman
43. Kathryn of "Law & Order: Criminal Intent"
44. Underground chamber
45. City NNW of Provo
46. Hatcher or Garr
48. Barnum and 109, e.g.
50. Baby's cry

Solution on page 328

Puzzle 50

Across

1. Slithery swimmers
5. Get done with
8. Canned meat product
12. Keep ___ (persevere)
13. Prefix with classical
14. Frat-party wear
15. Caracas lass: Abbr.
16. Uncle ___
17. Fencing sword
18. One 'twixt 12 and 20
19. MTV segment?
21. Union toe: Abbr.
24. Choir group
28. Flier Earhart
31. One of Franklin's two certainties
32. Stage signal
33. Ban rival
35. Cheering word
36. Sharp as ___
38. Versailles document
40. ___ Dame de Paris
41. Compass doodle
42. Egyptian vipers
45. History Muse
49. Stock exchange position
52. Always, poetically
54. Banjo-plucking Scruggs
55. Derby, e.g.
56. Ostrich-like bird
57. Move laboriously
58. Double-play duo
59. Margin
60. Turns bronze

Down

1. Vane direction
2. To be, to Gigi
3. Lo-cal
4. Golfer's position
5. Printer's spaces
6. In apple-pie order
7. Rotunda feature
8. Addison's literary partner
9. Old man
10. Ripen, as cheese
11. Author Rita ___ Brown
20. Eloper's need, maybe
22. Satisfies
23. Ventilate
25. Bakery bite
26. Our Gang assent
27. Librarian's admonition
28. Detroit product
29. Vegetarian's no-no
30. "Wherefore ___ thou . . ."
32. Give a pink slip to
34. 401(k) alternative: Abbr.
37. Jalopies
39. Agree to
43. Duke or earl
44. 18-wheeler
46. Tra-___
47. Laundry appliance
48. General Motors line, for short
49. Sellout letters
50. Perfumery word
51. Group of scenes
53. Metal ingredient

Solution on page 328

Puzzle 51

Across

1. Spherical opening?
5. Shea Stadium nine
9. Still and all
12. De ___ (too much)
13. "Dies ___"
14. Bullring cheer
15. Grabber's cry
16. Neighbor of Wis.
17. "Kidnapped" author's monogram
18. Napoleon's force
20. Frozen rain
22. French city on the Strait of Dover
24. Catch sight of
25. Pension-legislation acronym
26. Stairway parts
29. Many "Star Wars" characters
30. Barfly
31. Suffix with chariot
33. Cowboy's seat
36. Try to locate
38. "Hollywood Squares" win
39. Mountaintops
40. Of interest to John Paul
43. Lean-tos
44. Cotton State: Abbr.
45. Low-fat designation
47. Baby-faced
50. Home of the NFL's Rams
51. Mayberry man
52. Asia's shrinking ___ Sea
53. "Erie Canal" mule
54. Starboard's opposite
55. Coatrack parts

Down

1. Banking convenience: Abbr.
2. Three: Prefix
3. Louvre highlight
4. La Scala offerings
5. Street performers
6. ___-Lackawanna Railroad
7. Ecru
8. Sight and hearing
9. Time long past
10. Woman's magazine
11. Trial run
19. She played Hannah in "Hannah and Her Sisters"
21. Actress Remick
22. Fair grade
23. Partner of crafts
24. Command for Fido
26. ___ v. Wade
27. Restore confidence to
28. The Amish, e.g.
30. ___-mo replay
32. High-___ monitor
34. ___ double-take
35. Blob
36. Quattro minus uno
37. Pullman porter
39. Treasure container
40. Quarterback's throw
41. Calgary's prov.
42. Lose interest
43. Mix the batter
46. Lance of the bench
48. Luggage attachment
49. South African golfer Ernie

Solution on page 328

Puzzle 52

Across
1. Online periodical
5. Rock's Fleetwood ___
8. Topers
12. Nuts or crackers
13. Stowe's little girl
14. Fishing device
15. Deposited
16. It's another day
18. Come to a conclusion
19. Penalized, as a speeder
20. Opposite of ant.
21. Syngman of South Korea
23. Sales agent, briefly
25. Kitchen gadget
27. Like our numerals
31. Merle Haggard's "___ From Muskogee"
32. University mil. group
33. Detecting device
36. Puts forth, as effort
38. Fill in ___ blank
39. Elevated flat land
40. WWII lady in uniform
43. Leaf stalks
45. Air gun pellets
48. Not fully developed
50. Robert Frost work
51. Kitchen-flooring piece
52. Tiresome grind
53. Sea flyer
54. Lose one's footing
55. Morse code sound
56. Stare, as at a crystal ball

Down
1. She: Fr.
2. Sound of distress
3. Environmental problem
4. Deity
5. Profession
6. Company that might ring a bell?
7. Photographer's need
8. Certain camera, for short
9. Possessive pronoun
10. Where Helen was taken
11. Stitched
17. River to the Baltic Sea
19. Lawyer's payment
22. Bikini Atoll event, briefly
24. Peels
25. Fenway Park team, on scoreboards
26. ___ out (supplement)
28. Island near Tahiti
29. "The Addams Family" cousin
30. Syringe amts.
34. Extremely
35. Impede
36. Circus clown Kelly
37. Obliterates
40. Ingenuity
41. Indigo dye source
42. 251, in old Rome
44. Pins and needles holder
46. Mercedes-___
47. Hook's underling
49. Not square
50. Cribbage board insert

Solution on page 328

Puzzle 53

Across

1. "This ___ better be good!"
4. Copenhagen citizen
8. Remove the peel
12. Cellular letters
13. Widemouthed jug
14. "First Wives Club" members
15. Steamy
16. Run across
17. High five, essentially
18. Yegg
21. Greyhound vehicle
22. Direction
23. Literary collections
25. Car for hire
26. Also
29. Ira Levin novel
33. Suffix with brom-
34. Khan married to Rita Hayworth
35. Without change
36. ___ Amin
37. RNs' coworkers
38. Children's game
43. Cotton bundle
44. Port ___, Egypt
45. Mustache site
47. Luau instruments, for short
48. Conoco competitor
49. "Evil Woman" group
50. Bird's dwelling
51. Fifth Avenue name
52. i topper

Down

1. Royal initials
2. Calendario units
3. Information bank
4. Rounded roofs
5. Actor Baldwin
6. N.Y. Met or L.A. Dodger, e.g.
7. Erode
8. Like Dennis the Menace
9. Rod for a hot rod
10. Back section
11. Sixth sense: Abbr.
19. Electrical safeguard
20. Urban vehicles
23. Jackie's second husband
24. Unspoken assent
25. Boo-hoo
26. Like a mortarboard
27. Japanese sash
28. Yiddish plaints
30. Manufactured
31. Assumed names
32. Expressed, as a welcome
36. That is: Lat.
37. Early PC environment
38. Cod relative
39. French islands
40. Astronauts' org.
41. Tiddlywink, e.g.
42. Narc's unit
43. Hamburger holder
46. Flower holder

Solution on page 328

Puzzle 54

Across

1. Recipe abbr.
4. Dr.'s group
7. Movie canine
11. Its members often get motel discounts: Abbr.
12. Male offspring
14. Knee-ankle connector
15. "I'm freezing!"
16. Journey
17. Mail away
18. Word before Nevada or Leone
20. Had a snack
22. Yahoo! competitor
23. Puts back to zero
27. Bed supports
30. Scarlet
31. Grief
32. Green shade
33. LP successors
34. Trillion: Pref.
35. Dada founder
36. Pas' mates
37. Sells for
38. Beaux ___: noble deeds
40. Rapping Dr.
41. Lab runner
42. It parted in Exodus
46. Use a dishtowel
49. "Garfield" canine
51. Deli meat
52. On an ocean liner
53. Dice toss
54. "Just ___ thought!"
55. "Stop that!"
56. Gore and Roker
57. Hibernation location

Down

1. Bar bills
2. Calcutta garb
3. Whittle down
4. Houston baseballers
5. Upstanding
6. Folk singer DiFranco
7. Surefooted animals
8. That lady
9. ___ Pan Alley
10. Also
13. Bowling scores
19. Tempo
21. Kennedy in Congress
24. Rams' dams
25. Reason to sue
26. Black and Baltic
27. Smelting residue
28. Money in Milano
29. Sound boosters
30. Byways: Abbr.
33. Pollux's twin
34. ___ the line (obeyed)
36. "Are you calling ___ liar?"
37. Angler's baskets
39. Pleasant surprise
40. Dentist's tool
43. Kind of herring
44. Comfortable state
45. Ugandan dictator
46. Gum unit
47. Prefix meaning "equal"
48. Ballpoint
50. Film noir classic

Solution on page 329

Puzzle 55

Across

1. Morse code bits
5. Greedy sort
8. "The ___ Baltimore" (Lanford Wilson play)
12. Barbell metal
13. Average guy?
14. Gone
15. Ultimatum conclusion
16. Total
17. Pivot around
18. Be too fond
19. Georgia and Ukraine, once: Abbr.
21. LBJ successor
24. Writer Horatio
28. Et cetera
32. Defense gp. dissolved in 1977
33. 7, on a sundial
34. Like some wits or cheeses
36. Palindromic cheer
37. "___ a monkey's uncle!"
39. Noblewoman
41. Postpone
42. Govt. Rx watchdog
43. Quickly: Abbr.
46. On the ___ (separately)
50. Very little
53. Carry-on item
55. Tortilla sandwich
56. Court org.
57. ___ Dhabi (Gulf emirate)
58. Unattributed: Abbr.
59. Caffeine source
60. Prohibit
61. Payroll dept. IDs

Down

1. Fizzled out
2. Guthrie the younger
3. Throw a party
4. Villainous looks
5. Sleepwear, for short
6. Cash substitutes
7. Tiara inlays
8. Give a hard time
9. "Wise" bird
10. Sigma's follower
11. Basic cleaner
20. Spoke scratchily
22. Ambles
23. Drama in Kyoto
25. Marvin of Motown
26. Zeta followers
27. Rogers and Bean
28. Fanatical
29. Blue or green shade
30. Gherkin kin
31. 40 winks
35. Football official
38. Nursery rhyme opening
40. Dreadlocks wearers
44. Quatrain rhyme scheme
45. Sunblock ingredient
47. Actors Holm and McKellen
48. Raid rival
49. Forever, figuratively
50. Diving seabird
51. Brit. medal
52. The "A" in NATO: Abbr.
54. Revolver

Solution on page 329

Puzzle 56

Across

1. Augments
7. Nissan, once
13. Sailed
14. Actress May
15. Octad plus one
16. From Scandinavia
17. ___ out a living (gets by)
18. However, for short
19. Pull apart
22. In any respect
26. Medic's treatment
30. "Go away!"
31. Friend of Pooh
32. Major-leaguer
33. Actress Gabor
34. Unfooled by
36. Flowed copiously
39. "Miracle on 34th Street" store
41. Down-home pronoun
42. "Keep it down!"
44. Chess finale
47. Words of agreement
50. Disney duck
52. Gift recipients
53. Stimulate
54. Oscar and Edgar
55. ___ floss

Down

1. Lincoln's nickname
2. "Been there, ___ that"
3. Like a dungeon
4. Beef on the hoof
5. China grouping
6. Like 7 or 11
7. Bumper bump
8. Hawaiian greeting
9. Mystical cards
10. Half brother of Tom Sawyer
11. Mono- relative
12. Toshiba competitor
20. Brief sleeps
21. Unwashed
23. Pause filler
24. Affection
25. Laundry measure
26. "___ Here to Eternity"
27. Inner Hebrides island
28. Campus recruiting org.
29. Dumb ___
35. Seafood in a shell
37. Author ___ Leonard
38. Support group for drinkers' families
40. Did a blacksmith's job
43. Dan Blocker role
45. Drawn tight
46. "Born Free" character
47. Boise's state: Abbr.
48. Wall Street index, with "the"
49. ___ roll (winning)
50. "Dear old" guy
51. Neighbor of Md.

Solution on page 329

Puzzle 57

Across

1. Tango requirement
4. Atlantic food fish
8. Buy on ___
12. Cranberry-growing site
13. Mata ___ (infamous spy)
14. City in Arizona
15. Part of GPA: Abbr.
16. McGregor of "Moulin Rouge"
17. Surprise greatly
18. Royal rule
20. "___ we forget"
22. British fliers: Abbr.
24. Sugary
27. Bedecked
31. Arab prince
33. Large coffee brewer
34. Mirror reflection
36. Eloise creator Thompson
37. Labor camp
39. French artist Henri
41. Pianist Hess and others
43. Performed
44. "___ pronounce you . . ."
46. Windblown
50. Banned pollutants
53. Item on an end table
55. Letterhead abbr.
56. "The Andy Griffith Show" role
57. Italian wine district
58. 49ers' org.
59. Beer steins
60. Speak wildly
61. Keystone comic

Down

1. Lift in Aspen
2. Created a basket
3. Today, in Turin
4. Prank
5. Crow's call
6. ___ Mountains (Eurasia divider)
7. Evergreen trees
8. Gambler's method
9. Deposited
10. Flightless Aussie bird
11. Soda container
19. Dog's warning
21. Term of endearment
23. Not masc.
25. Squeals of fright
26. 4:00 socials
27. 31-day mo.
28. Percussion instrument
29. "If ___ I had known"
30. River blocker
32. Loaf with seeds
35. Zooks lead-in?
38. Wakes up
40. Wedding phrase
42. Of the sun
45. "It ___ Very Good Year"
47. Chain unit
48. Data, for short
49. Initials on Sputnik
50. Small dog, for short
51. PC's "brain"
52. Large
54. VH1 rival

Solution on page 329

Puzzle 58

Across

1. The "p" in r.p.m.
4. Groceries holder
7. ___ and Coke
10. Campbell of "Wild Things"
11. Dept. head
12. Pinza of "South Pacific"
14. Type of type: Abbr.
15. Miniscule
16. Check mark
17. Toyota model of the 1990s
19. Contrives
21. The Big Apple, initially
23. Short snooze
24. Alcott sequel
28. Attila, e.g.
31. Budget competitor
32. Actress Myrna
33. Spiritual leader
34. Workout site
35. Bug spray
37. Delivery co. with brown trucks
38. Batman and Robin
39. Rock for a monument
43. Yucky
47. Soaks flax
48. "May ___ now?"
50. Everyone, in the South
51. Ancient alphabetic character
52. CIA operative
53. Donkey's sound
54. Poker winnings
55. Toss
56. Sixth sense, initially

Down

1. Anti-fur grp.
2. Gabor and Peron
3. Caves in
4. Mercedes competitor
5. Sat in a cask
6. Jealous
7. Fix, as a pool cue
8. Israeli guns
9. Rat relatives
10. Autumn chill
13. Says "yes" to
18. Olive of "Thimble Theatre"
20. Mover's vehicle
22. Heavenly
24. Bring up the rear
25. Clinging vine
26. Comic Conway
27. Cleaning tool
28. Shade of color
29. Large coffee maker
30. Enthusiast, slangily
33. "Good gracious!"
35. Sch. in Troy, NY
36. Big ape
37. Not yet decided
39. Canine warning
40. Do another hitch
41. 1 for H, or 2 for He
42. Frozen waffle brand
44. Rowing equipment
45. Strike with open hand
46. Clever
49. Wagering locale, for short

Solution on page 329

Puzzle 59

Across

1. Cat's feet
5. Canine sounds
9. Celestial body
12. A Great Lake
13. Bottom of a shoe
14. "The Raven" author
15. Lean slightly
16. Ice pellets
17. Joad and Kettle
18. Beelzebub
20. Rd. or hwy.
21. Scrap for Rover
22. Poetic "before"
24. Mama's boy?
26. Co. that merged into Verizon
29. Danson and Koppel
31. ___ vu
34. "Say it ___, Joe!"
36. Porter's pen name
38. Rose of baseball
39. "Will Be," in a Doris Day song
41. Taoism founder Lao-___
42. Suffix with exist
44. Tennis divider
45. Metal container
47. Big inits. in long distance
49. Pierces
54. Elev.
55. Dietary component, for short
57. Oodles and oodles
58. ___ Jeanne d'Arc
59. Scone spread
60. Trig ratio
61. ___-been
62. Noticed
63. Don't move

Down

1. Beloved animals
2. Prima donna's song
3. Sag in the sun
4. ___bad example
5. Cigar remnant
6. Sounded like a lion
7. Fly like a butterfly
8. Tennis's Monica
9. Adversary
10. Lion's warning
11. Most outstanding
19. Fishing aids
23. Vintage cars
25. "___ on a Grecian Urn"
26. Interruption
27. Father's Day gift
28. International pacts
30. Touchy
32. PSAT takers
33. Reply to a captain
35. Perfect score in gymnastics
37. Derbies and berets
40. Appetizer follower
43. Mexican meals
45. Moolah
46. Neighbor of Sask.
48. Chronicle
50. Soviet news agency
51. Reached terra firma
52. Sonny of Sonny and Cher
53. Stair part
56. ___ vivant

Solution on page 329

Puzzle 60

Across

1. Deuces
5. Cooking additive
9. Not sweet, as wine
12. Boxer Oscar De La ___
13. Thomas Edison's middle name
14. Engage in rivalry
15. The Runnin' Rebels of NCAA basketball
16. In need of directions
17. Pixie
18. Sign of the future
20. Wrongly
22. More cheerful
25. Crone
26. Deprive of weapons
27. Scam artist
30. Listening device
31. ___ Jones Industrial Average
32. "That's show ___"
34. Biblical strongman
37. "Alfie" star Michael
39. Carpet cleaner, for short
40. Serving bowl
41. Basketball star Baylor
44. English noble
45. Mink or ermine
46. Omelet needs
48. ___ out: makes do
52. Winter malady
53. Brings to court
54. Expected soon
55. Sizable sandwich
56. Beginner
57. Nervously irritable

Down

1. Day before Fri.
2. Came in first
3. Animated Olive
4. ___-faire
5. More healthy
6. North Carolina's ___ University
7. Homes on wheels, for short
8. Philippine peninsula
9. 507, to Caesar
10. Drum parts
11. Slangy assents
19. Dues payer: Abbr.
21. RKO competitor
22. Cause friction
23. Tough task
24. Heroic tale
25. "In what way?"
27. Pro and ___
28. Irish Rose's beau
29. Highest digit
31. "What's up, ___?"
33. Method of meditation
35. 11th-century date
36. Most sensible
37. Common canine
38. Actress Dahl
40. Renaissance Italian poet
41. Failing grades
42. Little comics girl
43. Cowhand's chow
44. Hungarian spa town
47. Gal's date
49. Joke around with
50. Future chick
51. Bashful

Solution on page 330

Puzzle 61

Across

1. Devils' org.
4. German auto
8. Brilliantly colored fish
12. When it's light
13. 1973 Supreme Court decision name
14. Seized vehicle
15. Legendary sunken island
17. "Pirates of the Caribbean" star Johnny
18. Most perceptive
19. Toy dog, for short
20. Like Chianti
21. Captain Kidd, for one
23. Learns
26. Kind of code
27. Hanks film
28. Spot of land in the sea
29. American Legion member
30. Composer Nino
31. Keystone figure
32. Fleeting fashion
33. Made dove sounds
34. "Sleepless in Seattle" director Nora
36. Tea holder
37. Barber's concern
38. Round Table locale
42. Taxis
43. Fall behind
44. Author of "A Death in the Family"
45. "___ a man with . . ."
46. Atlanta-based network
47. Mental acuity
48. Actor Mostel
49. Joke (around)

Down

1. Bismarck's home: Abbr.
2. Detest
3. Singer Lovett
4. Title holders
5. Singer Cline
6. Revise a mistake
7. Guitar master Paul
8. "___ in the court!"
9. Tot's game
10. Desire for food
11. Bounce
16. Agassi of tennis
19. Lulu
21. Band's place on Broadway
22. Old-style exclamation
23. Go backpacking
24. Gullets
25. Kindergarten lesson
26. End of the English alphabet
29. Moving truck
30. Thesaurus compiler
32. In favor of
33. Awoke
35. Greets the day
36. More vile
38. Arrive
39. Beat soundly
40. All: Prefix
41. Baby-sit
42. Crow's sound
43. Gossip columnist Smith

Solution on page 330

Puzzle 62

Across

1. Band's booking
4. Cain's dad
8. Dog sounds
12. Nutritional std.
13. Rhapsodize
14. "Star Trek" character
15. Director Reiner
16. Fireballer Nolan
17. Spring formal
18. Swan's mate, in myth
20. Comeuppance
22. Workplace safety agcy.
25. Prefix with -plasm
29. '60s protest singer Phil
32. Priests' robes
34. Tom Collins liquor
35. Philandering fellow
36. Victory sign
37. Hudson Bay Indian
38. Capture
39. Actress Miles
40. A smaller amount
41. Plagiarized
43. Forest component
45. Tout's hangout, for short
47. At a ___ for words
50. TV attachments
53. Prefix with dextrous
56. ___ goes it?
58. Tyke of '60s TV
59. Neck wraps
60. Cry of discovery
61. Tail movements
62. Eye annoyance
63. Sound of a sock

Down

1. Fido's warning
2. Fan-club favorite
3. Comic Kaplan
4. Hung tapestry
5. "The ___ of the Jackal"
6. An ex of Frank
7. Repair
8. In accordance with
9. Robot drama
10. Waitress at Mel's
11. Add
19. Two tablets, often
21. FedEx rival
23. "___ a nice day!"
24. Fully awake
26. Folklore meanie
27. Ascots
28. Change from a five
29. Planets
30. Parka, for one
31. Justice Black
33. Stand
37. Nile queen, for short
39. One who looks Rover over
42. Comes in last
44. Beethoven honoree
46. Streisand, in fanzines
48. Patronize a mall
49. Part of London or Manhattan
50. Oath
51. Tax pro, for short
52. Fix, as a fight
54. Witty remark
55. Cargo compartment
57. "Unbelievable!"

Solution on page 330

Puzzle 63

Across
1. Math branch: Abbr.
4. Irate
7. Thin cut
11. Tool and ___
12. Calla-lily family
14. "___ Can" (Sammy Davis Jr. book)
15. Tuscaloosa's state: Abbr.
16. Frost
17. Prefix with "second"
18. Cop's postarrest recitation
21. Nectar gatherer
22. Like Bach's Violin Sonata No. 3
23. Folk story
26. Altitudes: Abbr.
27. Triumphant shout
30. "The Breakfast Club" actor
34. 2,000 pounds
35. Pig's place
36. Lab-maze runners
37. Western Indian
38. Blood grouping syst.
40. "Running on Empty" singer
47. Mine, in Paris
48. "The Sweater Girl" Turner
49. ___ Lingus
50. Outfielder's call
51. Summers, in France
52. ___ la-la
53. Four-posters
54. Surgery sites, for short
55. Small child

Down
1. Abel's dad
2. Role for Leslie Caron
3. PRNDL pick
4. WWI battle site
5. Hitch ___ with
6. Old Russian assembly
7. "The Playboy of the Western World" author
8. First wife of Jacob
9. Common contraction
10. Spanish uncles
13. Earns
19. Eve's second son
20. Technical sch.
23. Holiday in Vietnam
24. "I love," in Latin
25. Author ___ Yutang
26. "Watch it, buster!"
27. Lab eggs
28. Steamed (up)
29. Parts of lbs.
31. Followers
32. Peter of "My Favorite Year"
33. Suffix with switch
37. The Joads, e.g.
38. "Li'l" Capp creation
39. Button material
40. Door frame
41. Parisian lady friend
42. RR employee
43. Pact since 1949
44. Light bulb unit
45. Infamous Roman emperor
46. The "E" in Q.E.D.

Solution on page 330

Puzzle 64

Across

1. Cash dispenser
4. Farm animal
7. Sales pitch
12. Coffee alternative
13. "Evil Woman" band
14. Like Bigfoot
15. Bruin Bobby
16. QB gains
17. Get out of bed
18. D-Day craft
19. Hair-raising
21. Guide
23. Antonym's antonym: Abbr.
24. Change the color of
27. Astern
29. Chased away
32. Russian coin
35. Dalmatian markings
36. The East
38. One ___ time (singly)
39. Tie the knot
40. Haifa's country: Abbr.
42. Night-table light
46. Fill to the brim
47. Prefix with colonial
48. Cash, casually
52. Thieve
54. Realm of Ares
55. Had title to
56. Cray or pay ending
57. Slow-pitch pitch
58. Seed covering
59. Cooking spray brand
60. Pep rally word

Down

1. Coral ensemble?
2. Brief and to the point
3. "I Remember Mama" mama
4. Attention-getting call
5. Born first
6. Meddlesome
7. Open carriage
8. 72, at Augusta
9. Midafternoon, on a sundial
10. Triage ctrs.
11. Soap ingredient
20. Hosp. workers
22. Over hill and ___
24. ___-wop
25. However
26. Sullivan and Wynn
28. Marshy area
30. FDR follower
31. Silica gem
32. Column's counterpart
33. Suffix with fail
34. Signal at Sotheby's
37. ___ Maria (coffee liqueur)
38. Colorful ring
41. Razor sharpener
43. Sadat of Egypt
44. Stiller and ___
45. Veranda
46. Thompson of "Family"
48. Pithy saying
49. Be in debt
50. Switch statuses
51. Court do-over
53. Crashing sound

Solution on page 330

Puzzle 65

Across

1. Future atty.'s exam
5. Successful accomplishment
9. Switz. neighbor
12. From Bangkok
13. Radiant glow
14. World Baseball Classic team
15. Academic honor
17. Cole who was "King"
18. Letters on a Cardinal's cap
19. An outer planet
21. San ___, TX
24. High return
25. Deodorant type
26. Baldwin and Guinness
29. Dove sound
30. Combat pilot pro
32. Sears rival
36. Acela Express runner
39. ___ Majesty
40. Move in a circle
41. Gilbert and Sullivan operetta, with "The"
44. Pierre's friend
45. Suffix with Manhattan
46. Unsportsmanlike conduct
51. Lunar New Year
52. Muskogee native
53. Find attractive
54. CPR specialist
55. Practical jokes
56. Noted lioness

Down

1. India "Inc."
2. "___ Drives Me Crazy" (Fine Young Cannibals hit)
3. Hwy. helper
4. Christmas tree decoration
5. Pay a visit to
6. Opposite of non
7. Andress of film
8. Walk a beat
9. Old TV detective Peter
10. Brother of Jacob
11. Squealers
16. WW II battle site
20. Figure on a fiver
21. Circuitous path
22. Niche
23. ___ onto (grab)
27. "Fame" singer
28. "Get away!"
31. Just manage, with "out"
33. Melodramatic cry
34. Football blitz
35. Ruling threesome
36. Glass marbles
37. "Goodness gracious!"
38. Not quite a homer
41. Tiny pest
42. Agenda element
43. Etta of the funnies
47. Tractor-trailer
48. Lubricate
49. Sanctions
50. Shepherd's domain

Solution on page 330

Puzzle 66

Across

1. Dawn drops
4. Ye ___ Tea Shoppe
8. Tiptop
12. Hollywood's Thurman
13. Actor Neeson
14. Hockey's Gordie
15. Overeat, with "out"
16. "Medea" playwright
18. "Maria ___" (1941 hit song)
20. Hard journey
21. Bank acct. earnings
23. Chart again
27. Potato holder
30. "Where the heart is"
33. TV hosts
34. Civil War org.
35. Walks back and forth
36. Third-to-last Greek letter
37. Nocturnal bird
38. Hayworth or Moreno
39. Dessert options
40. T, in physics
42. Stanley Cup org.
44. "Blame ___ the Bossa Nova"
47. Sing in the Alps
51. "Fame" singer
55. Seeded bread
56. Zero, to Sampras
57. Waste allowance
58. Ornamental vase
59. Skating champ Michelle
60. Part of CPA: Abbr.
61. Prefix with political or logical

Down

1. Patsy
2. Jannings of old movies
3. Worker's compensation
4. Upstate New York city
5. Lucy of "Lucky Number Slevin"
6. Move abruptly
7. Ruler of Qatar
8. "Take ___!" ("Get lost!")
9. Pea place
10. Full-grown sheep
11. Marks, as a ballot
17. Former Israeli prime minister
19. Ending for beat or neat
22. Laotian's neighbor
24. Start of the next century
25. Throbbing pain
26. Pitchfork-shaped Greek letters
27. Dundee native
28. ". . . ___ forgive our debtors"
29. Ripken et al.
31. Halloween mo.
32. Cruel
35. Ramble on
39. Mahmoud Abbas's org.
41. Bedding material
43. Big name in hotels
45. Penta- plus three
46. Drug-fighting cop
48. Pharmaceutical
49. Bronte's fictional governess
50. Late-night comic
51. Family
52. Line of seats
53. Ms. Peron
54. Camcorder abbr.

Solution on page 331

Puzzle 67

Across

1. Unit of electrical resistance
4. ___ for oneself
8. Island near Java
12. Seek the affection of
13. Hollow-stemmed plant
14. Ovid's love
15. Baloney
17. "___ fan tutte" (Mozart opera)
18. Piano-playing Dame
19. Traffic diverters
20. Rum-soaked cakes
23. Land on the Caspian Sea
25. Writer Hunter
26. Pop music's Bee ___
27. Ballpoint brand
30. Fill with fizz
32. Mexican cowboy
34. Major TV maker
35. Rat-___
37. Crumbly soil
38. Swimsuit tops
39. Deep-voiced singer
40. Aspirations
43. Mortgage, for example
45. Lake that Canada's Point Pelee National Park is on
46. Have second thoughts about
50. Pre-Easter time
51. Where Samson slew the Philistines
52. "That's a laugh!"
53. Sorts
54. Made, as a web
55. Univ., e.g.

Down

1. Confess, with "up"
2. Boo follower
3. Sun. follower
4. Turns loose
5. Poetic dusks
6. Scottish monster's nickname
7. President before JFK
8. Part of BLT
9. Egyptian deity
10. Be defeated
11. Spring flower
16. Author Alexander
19. Money in a wallet
20. Yellowstone beast
21. With: Fr.
22. Silents star Theda
24. Four-sided fig.
26. "___ move on!"
27. Male sibs
28. Some nest eggs: Abbr.
29. Crooner Perry
31. Old salts
33. Astronauts Bean and Shepard
36. Out for the night
38. Borscht vegetables
39. Place to wash up
40. Prefix with port or pad
41. Russian city on the Oka
42. Nursery color
44. Waikiki's isle
46. "Treasure Island" author's inits.
47. Querying sounds
48. Anatomical pouch
49. "No talking!"

Solution on page 331

Puzzle 68

Across

1. Patty Hearst's kidnap grp.
4. Future blossom
7. Writer John Dickson ___
11. One, in Germany
12. Son in Genesis
14. "When I was ___"
15. Bert Bobbsey's twin
16. "Thanks___!"
17. Untidiness
18. Deepen, as a canal
20. Ended a fast
22. Blanc and Brooks
23. Hit the hay
27. Glacial ridges
29. Swiped
30. Mauna ___ (Hawaiian volcano)
31. Football great Dawson
32. Some noblemen
36. Sergeant's command
39. Ark's landing spot
40. ___ we forget
41. Remark from Chan
42. Walks in
45. Office helper: Abbr.
48. Some French paintings
50. Ooh and ___
51. Brief letter
52. Building manager, briefly
53. Tiny, in Troon
54. Hydrocarbon suffixes
55. Silent acknowledgment
56. Abbr. after an attorney's name

Down

1. Cell-phone button
2. Fibber
3. Jerry Stiller's partner
4. Snoopy, for one
5. Except
6. Scooby-___ (cartoon dog)
7. Recovered consciousness
8. British brew
9. ___ Tafari (Haile Selassie)
10. Highways: Abbr.
13. Constellation components
19. NYPD figure
21. Vietnamese festival
24. Uncomfortable
25. "Cheers" actor Roger
26. Feminine suffix
27. Jessica of TV's "Dark Angel"
28. Leonine sound
33. Speaks pompously
34. "Illmatic" rapper
35. Greek promenades
36. Syrian city
37. Became strained
38. Letters on a cornerstone
43. Crashes into
44. NBAer O'Neal
45. Anecdote collection
46. Dad, to Grandpa
47. French holy woman: Abbr.
49. Do a marathon

Solution on page 331

Puzzle 69

Across

1. Protest gone bad
5. Waiter's burden
9. "CSI" evidence
12. School for a future ens.
13. Come in last
14. NASA thumbs-up
15. Luge, e.g.
16. Water-to-wine site
17. ___ one-eighty
18. Taunt
20. Gymnast Mary Lou
22. Not plentiful
24. Hack (off)
27. Poker prize
28. "Livin' la Vida ___"
32. Director May
34. High schooler
36. Former Speaker Gingrich
37. Little shaver
38. Private eye
39. Cuba, e.g.
42. Surgical instrument
44. Tin Pan Alley grp.
49. School transportation
50. Elevator pioneer
52. Golfer's goal
53. Acorn maker
54. Voice quality
55. Periods in history
56. Gloomy guy?
57. Skiing surface
58. Hand, to Hernando

Down

1. Metal corrosion
2. Maui or Tahiti
3. Fit for duty
4. Tiny bits
5. Pampering, briefly
6. Greet with loud laughter
7. Ed who played Lou Grant
8. 1923 Literature Nobelist
9. Carpenter's groove
10. Lunch time, often
11. Letters before an alias
19. Fox Sports alternative
21. Prefix with vision
23. Mystery story pioneer
24. NFL Hall of Famer Dawson
25. Bullfight bravo
26. Terrier tootsy
29. Canadian prov.
30. Mediocre mark
31. Rainbow path
33. Put ___ writing
34. Beachgoer's shade
35. Icelandic poetry collection
37. Mexican-American, e.g.
40. Glasgow residents
41. Give away
42. Waikiki feast
43. Requests
45. One of Noah's sons
46. Julius Dithers's wife, in "Blondie"
47. A.A. Milne's first name
48. Mexican coin
49. Swampy area
51. Embroider

Solution on page 331

Puzzle 70

Across

1. Jack's partner
5. Envelope part
9. J.F.K.'s successor
12. Tennis champ Nastase
13. Introduction to marketing?
14. "___ Are My Sunshine"
15. Fetches
16. Auto racer Yarborough
17. Yuletide beverage
18. Dutch master Jan
20. Matures
22. Writer Hemingway
24. Jan. 15th monogram
27. Anti-Prohibition
28. Campus building
32. "Little Red Book" ideology
34. Bacon strip
36. Modern movie buff's purchases
37. Classic drama of Japan
38. 1006, to Caesar
39. ___-Lorraine
42. Lease signer
44. Dillon and Damon
49. Binge
50. Seriously injure
52. University official
53. Heart chart, for short
54. Awed
55. Mini's opposite
56. Actor Turhan
57. Some paycheck IDs
58. Lingerie item

Down

1. Irish dances
2. "___ a Song Go . . ."
3. Dieter's label word
4. ___ majesty (high treason)
5. Anti-fraud agcy.
6. Memorized
7. Kate's TV friend
8. Chick's chirps
9. Actress Redgrave
10. Greets the villain
11. Wine container
19. Six o'clock broadcast
21. LAX announcements
23. Sleep phenom.
24. CCL x X
25. Restroom, informally
26. Down for the count
29. Measure of resistance
30. Minister: Abbr.
31. CAT scan alternative
33. "No man ___ island . . ."
34. Fabled bird
35. "Um, excuse me"
37. ". . . one ___ under God"
40. Tibetan monks
41. Hosiery problems
42. ___ five (rest)
43. Like an omelet
45. USN bigwigs
46. Mallard cousin
47. Car for hire
48. Scissors cut
49. Confederate general Stuart
51. Brit. sports cars

Solution on page 331

Puzzle 71

Across

1. NY time
4. Ladder part
8. Pharmacist's weight
12. Watering hole
13. Actress ___ Flynn Boyle
14. Scottish isle
15. Maple fluid
16. Primates
17. Cartoonist Groening
18. Like some computer maintenance
20. Have a premonition
21. Gobi or Mojave
24. Soho so longs
27. Beam of sunshine
28. Disconsolate
31. WSW opposite
32. "You ___ There"
33. Plus
34. Grow old
35. "___ Te Ching"
36. Dull finish
38. Cold-weather cap attachment
40. March 17 honoree, for short
44. Sports sites
48. Darjeeling and oolong
49. "Q ___ queen"
51. Latin 101 verb
52. Sculling poles
53. Wrapped up
54. Caribbean, e.g.
55. Brown songbird
56. Unique person
57. African slitherer

Down

1. Bygone pump name
2. Wing measurement
3. Bugler's signal
4. Candidate lists
5. Presses the "Record" button
6. Before, in poems
7. Daddies
8. "Thin" coin
9. Speckled steed
10. Tiny tunnelers
11. Spouse
19. Cretan Mount
20. Slovenly place
22. Proofreader's find
23. "Norma ___" (Field film)
24. Hot drink
25. Filmmaker Lee
26. Driver's peg
28. Posed for a portrait
29. Colony insect
30. He followed HST
32. Auto club letters
35. Asian New Year
36. Fictional weaver
37. Gorilla, for one
39. Cleo or Frankie
40. Stash away
41. Get misty-eyed
42. Scale down
43. Trade org.
45. Cape Canaveral agency
46. Iowa State's town
47. Source of suds
49. Bustling commotion
50. Michael Douglas, to Kirk

Solution on page 331

Puzzle 72

Across

1. Dulles Intl. posting
4. Stocking's end
7. Vulgar
12. Down Under hopper
13. Shirt-sleeve filler
14. Convent attire
15. Unruly group
16. ___ ipsa loquitur
17. Field of play
18. Surgeon's tube
20. Stopwatch button
21. Snake shape
23. Long-eared beast
24. Enc. with a manuscript
27. Sunset time, in verse
29. Koppel and Turner
33. Suffix with Israel
34. Auction grouping
35. Thumbs-up response
36. Butter squares
38. Brian of rock music
39. Pollen spreaders
40. Middle muscles
42. Eavesdropping org.
44. Traffic tangle
47. Locker room powders
51. Rich pastry
52. ___ matter of fact
54. Sigh of relief
55. Greek marketplace
56. Came down with
57. West of "I'm No Angel"
58. Group of nine
59. TV show interrupters
60. Reply: Abbr.

Down

1. Sofa parts
2. Cheer (for)
3. Judge's gown
4. Fruity desserts
5. Mine rock
6. Printer's widths
7. Burns the surface of
8. Least cooked
9. Fortas and Burrows
10. Trig function
11. Numerical fact, for short
19. Abigail Adams, ___ Smith
22. Tennis champ Monica
23. Dramatist Chekhov
24. Drink gingerly
25. Words before glance or loss
26. Band performance
28. Looooong time
30. Needle hole
31. Actor Billy ___ Williams
32. Puncture sound
37. French existentialist
39. Ovine entreaty
41. Sound sheepish?
43. RBI and ERA
44. Comic Laurel
45. Canceled, as a launch
46. "Moses und ___"
48. Tibetan monk
49. James of TV's "Las Vegas"
50. Ladies
52. Turkish bigwig
53. Instant lawn

Solution on page 332

Puzzle 73

Across

1. Keystone characters
5. Hebrew letter
8. Scenes of action
12. Give off
13. Start of a Latin 101 trio
14. "Love ___ leave it"
15. Japanese aboriginal
16. Convent dweller
17. Peter of the Monkees
18. Walking sticks
20. Perfumer Lauder
22. It's south of Ga.
23. "The King and I" name
24. Shooting stars
28. Rays
32. Dry, as a desert
33. Dah's partner
35. Harbor marker
36. Irregularly edged
38. Speaks highly of
40. Skirt border
42. Student's stat.
43. "All My Children" regular
45. North African desert
49. Marlin or Met, for short
50. President after U.S.G.
52. Oil cartel acronym
53. Denominational offshoot
54. Feed lines to
55. Ready to be harvested
56. Government agents, for short
57. Delivery room doctors, for short
58. Ancient temple

Down

1. New Zealand parrots
2. Forget to mention
3. ___ colada
4. Pompous types
5. Roof style
6. Cousin of an ostrich
7. Dough
8. Site of Custer's last stand
9. Sioux Indian
10. Apple center
11. Irritate
19. Mel's Diner waitress
21. Long sandwich
24. Fannie ___ (federal mortgage agency)
25. "To ___ is human"
26. Uncle: Sp.
27. Imbibe slowly
29. Vienna is its cap.
30. Brother of Curly and Shemp
31. The "S" of CBS: Abbr.
34. Speaks disparagingly of
37. Common Market inits.
39. Gardner of Hollywood
41. Voyager Polo
43. Gen. Robert ___
44. Shipping dept. stamp
46. Samoan seaport
47. "___ Man" (1984 cult film)
48. Poker pair
49. Stamp on a bad check
51. Fella

Solution on page 332

Puzzle 74

Across

1. Titled lady
5. Ice cream order
9. Couples: Abbr.
12. Lamb pseudonym
13. "The Clan of the Cave Bear" author
14. Interjection of disgust
15. Chamberlain of the NBA
16. Elm or oak
17. Govt. media watchdog
18. Lead head?
20. Pigeon shelters
22. Window parts
25. Bering Sea isle
27. Letter before sigma
28. Early 12th-century date
30. Messy type
34. Ambulance personnel, for short
36. 1550
37. Polynesian tuber
38. Sir ___ Connery
39. Wooded valley
41. Actor Kilmer
42. Portions of corn
44. Commandment verb
46. Points on a diamond?
49. Pool stick
50. Britney Spears's "___ Slave 4 U"
51. "___ la Douce," 1963 film
54. Raggedy Ann's friend
58. Account amt.
59. Christens
60. Pope from 440 to 461
61. Octopus's defense
62. Chunks of history
63. Any day now

Down

1. Morning droplets
2. Boxer Muhammad
3. 1,000 gees
4. Wonderland cake words
5. Tabbies
6. Wilder's "___ Town"
7. Mary Lincoln ___ Todd
8. Vote into office
9. Kaput sound
10. Jambalaya ingredient
11. Parts of a min.
19. Credo
21. Boot from office
22. Air Force One passenger: Abbr.
23. Sighed words
24. "___ creature was stirring . . ."
25. Assistants
26. Money drawer
29. USN rank
31. Liquid rock
32. Nonwritten exam
33. Length of fabric
35. Dagger
40. Baton Rouge coll.
43. All kidding ___
45. Gets well
46. Actress Osterwald
47. "___ Called Horse"
48. Polio-vaccine discoverer
49. Mama of pop music
52. Karel Capek robot play
53. Executive's deg.
55. Prefix meaning "recent"
56. "Inka Dinka ___"
57. Yang's counterpart

Solution on page 332

Puzzle 75

Across

1. Some PCs
5. Kiss and cuddle, in British slang
9. Negative prefix
12. Skipper: Abbr.
13. Part of Batman's costume
14. Squid's defense
15. Jewish youth org.
16. ___ time (never)
17. Bush Sr. once headed it
18. Distribute, with "out"
20. Comic Butler
22. Adjust to something new
25. Prefix with political
26. Ring victories, for short
27. Farmer's measurement
30. Low in pitch
34. Nationality suffix
35. Was brilliant
37. Right away
38. Prerequisite
40. On vacation
41. Cagers' grp.
42. Away from the bow
44. Bake in an oven
46. "The Devil Wears ___"
49. Catches a glimpse of
51. Brunch fish
52. Hot Springs and others
54. Astrological border
58. Western tribe
59. Change for a fifty
60. Imitative sort
61. Hairstyling goo
62. Slaw or fries
63. "Little Caesar" role

Down

1. Real cold
2. Emeril's exclamation
3. Radar gun meas.
4. Imprint
5. "Scram!"
6. Middle C, e.g.
7. Hold the deed on
8. Shakespeare's theater
9. Backgammon equipment
10. "What's ___ for me?"
11. Three-handed card game
19. Hellenic H's
21. Shoplift from
22. Comparable (to)
23. Medicinal amount
24. Court great Arthur
25. Filmdom's Rowlands
28. Make small talk
29. Set-to
31. "The King and I" teacher
32. Cries convulsively
33. Hit, as a fly
36. Bronte's "Jane ___"
39. Scoutmaster, often
43. Eschews food
45. Movie award
46. Blatant promotion
47. Memorization method
48. Rink leap
49. Hourglass fill
50. Being, in Latin
53. Architect I.M.
55. Wire service
56. "Hold on a ___!"
57. Former amateur

Solution on page 332

Puzzle 76

Across

1. TV channels 14 and up
4. Hall of Famer Speaker
8. Super, to a Beatles fan
11. Scottish refusals
13. Help for the puzzled
14. Three, on a sundial
15. Moslem cleric
16. Italian peak
17. Hall-of-Famer Roush
18. Paris bisector
20. Makes angry
22. Church song
24. Hill nymph
26. Tokyo of old
27. ___ Romeo (Italian car)
29. Have a bite
32. Sea: Fr.
33. Full of flavor
35. Agcy. for homeowners
36. Buffoons
38. Western novelist Grey
39. "That's obvious!" in teen talk
40. Buenos ___, Argentina
42. Ranchland measures
44. Brazilian ballroom dance
46. Room, in Rouen
48. Sash in Sapporo
49. Entice
51. Roof's edge
54. King ___ Saud
55. Barely beat, with "out"
56. "Rubaiyat" poet
57. Bread with seeds
58. '50s sitcom mom Donna
59. Foxlike

Down

1. Prefix meaning "one"
2. Lunch meat
3. Availability extremes
4. Every now and ___
5. Bar mitzvah, e.g.
6. Place for the night
7. Fixed gaze
8. 1989 Kevin Costner film
9. Intern
10. Bridge calls
12. Captain Hook's assistant
19. "Play ___ it lays"
21. Fleming who created 007
22. Office missive
23. Ancient concert halls
25. Ballgame spoiler
28. Emulate a couch potato
30. Actress Elisabeth
31. Cries of triumph
34. Card game start
37. Bro or sis
41. Indy competitor
43. Nile queen, informally
44. Evening: Fr.
45. "Dear" advice-giver
47. Chopped down
50. Pindar poem
52. Kilmer of "At First Sight"
53. Suffix with station

Solution on page 332

Puzzle 77

Across

1. Islands off Ireland
5. Watch the kids
8. Being: Lat.
12. Warsaw resident
13. Collection of anecdotes
14. Walrus relative
15. Football officials
16. Turner or Danson
17. Makes leather
18. Fearsome dinosaur, for short
20. Rationality
21. Post office device
24. Like the driven snow
26. "Our Gang" dog
27. Tooth coverings
31. Big fuss
32. Former White House spokesman Fleischer
33. Bunion's place
34. End points
37. Italian cheese city
39. In ___ (even)
40. Heat source
41. Hardly enough
44. Wall Street inits.
46. Is sick
47. Writer Umberto
48. "___ fair in love . . ."
52. Weak, as an excuse
53. In mint condition
54. Sauce bean
55. Soft throw
56. '60s radical org.
57. Hot times in Paris

Down

1. Mar. follower
2. Caviar source
3. 1936 candidate Landon
4. Curl up
5. Satisfy a hankering
6. Green
7. "Just a ___"
8. Hold in high regard
9. Actor Connery
10. Avec's opposite
11. "What ___ can I do?"
19. Actor Alejandro
20. Spanish Mrs.
21. Little argument
22. Yield, as property
23. Fabric finish?
25. Prefix with cycle
28. Being, in Bordeaux
29. ___ Linda: San Bernardino suburb
30. Coal bed
32. Cuckoo
35. Parsons' places
36. Corp. giant
37. Ltr. addenda
38. "Relax, soldiers!"
41. Pepper's partner
42. Toodle-oo, in Turin
43. Gifts to the poor
45. Cries of pain
47. Lt.'s inferior, in the Navy
49. Parcel of land
50. Soapmaking need
51. Flier to Stockholm

Solution on page 332

Puzzle 78

Across

1. Product to flick
4. Stare stupidly
8. Tony Blair, for one
12. Pass receiver
13. The Bard of ___
14. Newspaper section
15. Hodges of the Dodgers
16. Emcee's aid
17. Gulf near Yemen
18. Mark of infamy
20. Church officials
22. Ashen
23. Settle a debt
24. Be in harmony
27. Take into custody
28. Joke or choke
31. Model married to David Bowie
32. Massachusetts' Cape ___
33. "I ___ Song Go Out of My Heart"
34. Speed meas.
35. Reporter's query
36. Jealousy
37. Mangy mutt
38. LAPD rank
40. Op-Ed piece
43. Monopoly buys
47. Vietnam neighbor
48. Spreadsheet pros
50. Industrial tub
51. Breakfast chain
52. Shield border
53. Yale, for one
54. Plays on words
55. Computer data unit
56. Hardly strict

Down

1. Entreats
2. Monogram part: Abbr.
3. 451, in old Rome
4. Beta's follower
5. Relating to birds
6. Stir-fry pan
7. Patella protector
8. Diamond Jim
9. Took the bus
10. Road for Caesar
11. Heavy weights
19. Dancer Verdon
21. Chem class
24. Muppeteer Henson
25. Little devil
26. Exclamation of contempt
27. Here's partner
28. Col.'s superior
29. Off-road transport, for short
30. Happy
32. Pipe type
33. Latvian
35. Engine sound
37. Pointed ends
38. Commandment word
39. "Take a look!"
40. Football foul
41. Third-largest Hawaiian island
42. Crazy bird?
44. Like Hannibal Lecter
45. Volcano outflow
46. Underworld river
49. Act the snoop

Solution on page 333

Puzzle 79

Across

1. Ltr. holders
5. Nixon pal Rebozo
9. TV sked abbr.
12. Drudgery
13. Rivers, in Spain
14. Drill sergeant's syllable
15. To the degree that
17. Grammar school basics, briefly
18. Cornmeal bread
19. Imitative types
21. State positively
24. Old Greek stringed instrument
25. Dracula, at times
26. Most sage
28. Unlocks, poetically
30. River bottom
31. Food preparer
33. Spicy dips
35. "Oh, give ___ home . . ."
36. Racing circuits
37. Most skilled
40. Diminish in intensity
42. Italian money
43. Dogpatch denial
44. Himalayan danger
49. Double-helix molecule
50. Movie "Citizen"
51. Impact sound
52. Frigid
53. Multitude
54. "Elephant Boy" star

Down

1. UK record label
2. French negative
3. Word on either side of "-a-"
4. Mountain incline
5. Type of goose
6. Cork's land
7. Snake that squeezes its prey
8. School papers
9. The Stooges, e.g.
10. TV's Perry Mason
11. Spring mos.
16. Part of FYI
20. Before: Abbr.
21. Blood-type group
22. Maple fluids
23. Leave on the sly
24. Coffee-to-go topper
26. Filmmaker Craven
27. Tot's "little piggies"
29. Blinds crosspiece
30. ___-relief
32. Krazy ___ of the comics
34. Pipes up
37. Troubled
38. Uplifting undergarment
39. Fasting times
40. "Me, myself ___"
41. Judge's bench
42. Turner of movies
45. Rug cleaner, for short
46. When repeated, a Latin dance
47. Airline's home base
48. College website letters

Solution on page 333

Puzzle 80

Across

1. Poor mark
4. Jacuzzi
7. Lawyer: Abbr.
10. Lyrical poems
12. Egyptian king
13. Gin flavor
14. Donkey, in Dusseldorf
15. Quick-wink link
16. Big-eared hopper
17. Solemn word
19. Musical sounds
20. Better qualified
23. Peter Fonda role
25. Pigeon perch
26. Bearlike beasts
29. Aves.
30. Buffalo's summer hrs.
31. All the rage
33. "___ by Starlight"
36. Make a beginning
38. Neighbor of Senegal
39. Takes it easy
40. After, in Arles
43. Slugging Sammy
45. One billion years
46. Spanish aunt
47. Scottish girl
51. Relax with a good book
52. No longer working: Abbr.
53. Dagger of old
54. White-tailed eagle
55. Pluralizing letter
56. Animal pouch

Down

1. Female deer
2. Mag. officials
3. Wide shoe spec
4. Number on a baseball card
5. Be dead and buried
6. One ___ time
7. Actor Alda
8. Drove like mad
9. Golf pegs
11. Blackthorn shrubs
13. Did a smith's job
18. Paintings and sculpture
19. Commandments count
20. Incoming flight: Abbr.
21. Physiques, informally
22. "___ in Space"
24. Counterpart of long.
27. Part of a Latin trio
28. Do postal work
30. Kay follower
32. Sot's affliction
34. Change text
35. "Deck the Halls" words
36. June grads: Abbr.
37. Marsh ducks
40. River of Bern
41. Social equal
42. Reddish horse
44. Horse's meal
46. Uno, due, ___
48. Reply to a ques.
49. Caspian or Caribbean
50. NYSE watchdog

Solution on page 333

Puzzle 81

Across

1. Fictional Uriah
5. Tit for ___
8. Beavers' constructions
12. "Dies ___" (hymn)
13. Astronomical altar
14. Buck follower
15. Sunrise direction, in Sonora
16. Stimpy's partner
17. Circus safety equipment
18. Jeanne d'Arc, for one
19. Griffey of baseball
20. Gaucho gear
21. Sally Field's "Norma ___"
23. Iowa State University site
25. Canonized one
27. Plopped (down)
28. Family M.D.'s
31. Not rejecting out of hand
33. Close again, as an envelope
35. Negative votes
36. Before Vegas
38. ___ Domingo (Caribbean capital)
39. Very dry
40. When doubled, an African fly
41. Fountain orders
44. Four Monopoly properties: Abbr.
46. Mas' partners
49. Maverick of TV
50. Use a chair
51. Shed one's skin
52. Sicilian commune
53. Golf platform
54. Shoe bottom
55. Take a catnap
56. Old draft letters
57. Blinds strip

Down

1. Scurries
2. Formerly
3. Diners
4. ___ Dee river
5. Shipping weight deduction
6. Sports centers
7. Earth tone
8. Citizens of Copenhagen
9. Length x width, for a rectangle
10. Feminist Lucretia
11. Sammy of baseball
19. Soup pots
20. Tries again
22. Advice giver Landers
24. Month after Feb.
25. Junior, to Senior
26. PFC's address
28. Hereditary collection
29. Margarine serving
30. School-zone sign
32. Rowboat implement
34. Flier out of Stockholm
37. Sequence
39. Assail
41. Trucker who broadcasts
42. Writer Sarah ___ Jewett
43. Ranges of knowledge
45. Highways: Abbr.
47. "It's ___ big mistake!"
48. Editor's "leave it"
50. Ave. intersectors
51. Ed.'s concerns

Solution on page 333

Puzzle 82

Across

1. Tried to avoid the tag
5. Great merriment
9. Increases
12. Prefix with legal
13. Eugene O'Neill's daughter
14. Atlas feature
15. Printer's primary color
16. Harbor sights
17. Harper Valley grp.
18. Portfolio holding
20. Made simpler
22. One who makes a scene?
26. Took cover
29. Brought into the world
30. Retailer's gds.
34. Whitney et al.
36. Take the title
37. Coal streak
38. Hide-and-go-___
39. The "A" in DNA
41. Roast hosts, briefly
42. Bronx Bomber
44. Church nooks
47. Student group
52. Frisk, with "down"
53. Farce
57. Spoken exam
58. Night before a holiday
59. Prefix with pilot
60. Medley
61. Morning moisture
62. Alice doesn't work here anymore
63. Prevailing style

Down

1. Shelter org.
2. Sets (down)
3. Keogh alternatives
4. Copenhagen native
5. Acquired
6. Gehrig of baseball
7. Part of ESL: Abbr.
8. Makes simpler
9. Baseball officials
10. Hors d'oeuvre spread
11. WWI plane
19. Bar bill
21. S&L devices
23. Atkinson of "Mr. Bean"
24. Halloween choice
25. Navel type
26. Cocks and bulls
27. Spot of land in the Seine
28. Backgammon cube
31. FDR or JFK
32. Kangaroo pouch
33. Typesetter's units
35. ___ terrier
40. Xmas time
43. State of NE India
44. Parroted
45. Finish a drive?
46. Slow-cooking dish
48. Weaver's machine
49. Guthrie of folk
50. Stated
51. Tart plum
54. ___ and cry
55. U.S./Eur. divider
56. Yr. parts

Solution on page 333

Puzzle 83

Across

1. Some college tests, for short
5. 26th of 26
8. Places for experiments
12. Former Italian coin
13. ER hookups
14. "For the life ___ . . ."
15. Hertz competitor
16. Precious stone
17. Grand Canyon St.
18. Hockey feint
19. Hair removal brand
21. Wood-cutting tools
24. Polo or tee
28. Speak hesitantly
31. ___ Schwarz (toy store)
32. Chest-maker's wood
33. Waiting to talk
35. Betting setting
36. Bridge bid, informally
37. Part of a litter
38. Scram, oater-style
39. One of Columbus's ships
40. Town near Provo
42. Pertaining to the ear
44. LAPD alerts
48. Tulsa's state: Abbr.
51. Soft mass
53. Absconded with
54. Mediterranean fruits
55. Wildebeest
56. Become tiresome
57. Ridge on a guitar neck
58. Day in Jerusalem
59. Aspiration

Down

1. Thrilled
2. Tear apart
3. "The Devil in the White City" author Larson
4. Ms. enclosures
5. Sharp turn
6. All the same
7. Salinger heroine
8. Abhors
9. Continent south of Eur.
10. ASCAP counterpart
11. Utters, informally
20. Fly the coop
22. Not sinking
23. Money roll
25. "Understood," hippie-style
26. Rajah's wife
27. Gait faster than a walk
28. Basketball target
29. Years, in old Rome
30. "Stop pouring!"
34. How tuna may be ordered
35. Snarling dog
37. Pennsylvania's ___ Mountains
41. "Concentration" objective
43. Pop of punk
45. Palm Beach sport
46. Cartoon character Betty
47. Hebrides island
48. Not at work
49. White wine cocktail
50. Size above med.
52. Bleacher creature?

Solution on page 333

Puzzle 84

Across

1. Exec's "Right now!"
5. Hot springs
8. Spherical hairdo
12. Constructed
13. It's often pierced
14. "Go, ___!"
15. Med school subj.
16. ___ Baba
17. Turner of Hollywood
18. Concerning, in legalese
20. Fax cover sheet abbr.
21. Outpourings
24. Some coll. students
26. Singers Hall and ___
27. Battery size
28. Old cloth
31. Blubber
32. Examinations
34. Mrs. Lennon
35. Make an effort
36. Chicago transports
37. Was wearing
39. Highlands hat
40. Calm
41. Monotonous learning
44. Go down to defeat
45. Two-dimensional measure
46. Have a fever
47. Cape Canaveral org.
51. Come clean, with "up"
52. "Get the picture?"
53. Port of Yemen
54. Carry
55. Program interrupters
56. Religious subdivision

Down

1. Drs.' org.
2. ___ Quentin
3. Oklahoma city
4. Small size
5. Roebuck's partner
6. Drained of color
7. Shipping magnate's nickname
8. Rand McNally book
9. Heroic deed
10. Make a scene
11. Muscat and ___
19. Lipton rival
21. Cushy
22. Host before Carson
23. Trial fig.
24. Formed a lap
25. Spates
27. Pompous one
28. Took a cab
29. Prolific author?: Abbr.
30. Disappeared
33. House shader
38. Pugs' venues
39. Backcomb hair
40. Cobbler's supply
41. Huck Finn's transport
42. Creme treat
43. Midterm, say
44. Emulated Pinocchio
46. Proud ___ peacock
48. Fruity quencher
49. Two shakes
50. Little scurrier

Solution on page 334

Puzzle 85

Across

1. U.S. Army medal
4. "The ___ Love" (Gershwin tune)
8. Prom-night safety gp.
12. Keystone lawman
13. Etc., for one
14. Key with four sharps: Abbr.
15. Big Apple sch.
16. Landing pier
17. Yanks' adversaries
18. Arafat of the P.L.O.
20. Ugly Duckling, ultimately
22. Set of tools
23. Movie awards
26. Flat sign?
29. Autobahn auto
30. Network on the telly
31. Dog in "Garfield"
32. "Average" guy
33. Roman 152
34. "I ___ You Babe"
35. Irk
36. Rich soil deposit
37. Retort to "Am too!"
39. Yeshiva student
40. Lines of theater seats
41. Having a handle
45. "Say ___?"
47. Lena or Ken of film
49. Kernel
50. "___ sight!"
51. "20,000 Leagues . . ." captain
52. Corporate-alias abbr.
53. Sharpen, as an appetite
54. Swedish cinematographer Nykvist
55. "Yippee!"

Down

1. Designer label letters
2. Type of bean
3. PC "brains"
4. Achieved success
5. Cancel, NASA-style
6. Peacock network
7. Annoying
8. Glacial pinnacle
9. Open to advice
10. Perfume amount
11. Radio staff, for short
19. ___-Ball: arcade game
21. Opposite ENE
24. Slugger's stats
25. Chem. and bio.
26. Ancient Roman garb
27. Annoying smell
28. Well-read
29. Be a pugilist
32. Futuristic toon family
33. Dairy animals
35. Solemn promise
36. "Instant Karma" singer
38. ___ home: out
39. "The Bionic Woman" role
42. Mayberry sheriff
43. "Oompah" instrument
44. Auctioneerless auction site
45. Really impress
46. "What'd you say?"
48. "My Name Is Asher ___"

Solution on page 334

Puzzle 86

Across
1. Cookbook abbr.
4. Naughty
7. Fabric measures
12. Yours and mine
13. Storekeeper in "The Simpsons"
14. Guiding philosophy
15. Day-___ paints
16. "The San Francisco Treat"
18. Rite places
20. 23rd Greek letter
21. Gawker
22. Fellows
24. Photos
28. Race in a slalom
30. Soft toss
32. Six-pack component
33. Tiny bit
35. Chiropractor's concern
37. Plumbing connection
38. "___ Gotta Crow"
39. Crimson
40. Playful bite
42. Klinger player
44. Iron-pumper's unit
46. Of churchgoers
49. Sky light?
51. "That's good enough"
53. Like-minded
57. Money machine
58. Warning signal
59. Bout stopper, for short
60. Truck feature
61. Vetoes
62. Dict. entry
63. Self-image

Down
1. Forum robes
2. Besmirch
3. Sit-in participant
4. "Roseanne" star
5. Prone to imitation
6. Vietnam's Le ___ Tho
7. Thumbs-up votes
8. Just free of the bottom, as an anchor
9. 17th Greek letter
10. Clamor
11. Poly-___ (college major)
17. Big name in printers
19. Noah's craft
23. Leave out in pronunciation
25. 1960 Richard Burton film
26. Ripken of the diamond
27. NBC show with skits
29. Medit. country
31. Golfer Hogan
33. Skippy competitor
34. Fertilization targets
36. H. Ross ___
41. "___ be a monkey's uncle!"
43. Coin of India
45. Hard to please
47. Pet pendant
48. Jazz group
50. Aficionados
52. Bugs Bunny, e.g.
53. Nine-digit ID
54. Sundial number
55. Mystery man
56. "___ Howdy Doody time!"

Solution on page 334

Puzzle 87

Across

1. Grain bristle
4. Dress style
8. "An Iceland Fisherman" author Pierre
12. "Now I ___ me down . . ."
13. Getting ___ years
14. Has ___: has connections
15. Railroad spans
17. Proverbial inheritors
18. As a substitute
19. Gooey hairdo holders
20. Prince ___ Khan
21. A B C's
23. ___-fatty acid
26. Porky or Petunia
27. Lon of Cambodia
28. Ranch worker
29. Excavated
30. "Tootsie" star Garr
31. Big coffee holder
32. Warm welcome
33. Was father to
34. Leaked
36. Spying device
37. ___ accompli
38. Welsh ___
42. Coated with gold
43. Grand Prix racer
44. "___ pin and pick it up . . ."
45. Currier's partner in lithography
46. Possum's pouch
47. Does simple arithmetic
48. Dinero
49. Animal with antlers

Down

1. Some choir voices
2. Alert
3. Louis and Carrie
4. Roadside stops
5. Dental filling
6. Went out, as a fire
7. ___ and outs
8. Fabrics with metallic threads
9. Short joke
10. Reason for overtime
11. Sign, as a contract
16. Easel, for one
19. Comedian's bit
21. Immense
22. Avoided the tag
23. Ergo
24. Lofty
25. Toughened, as glass
26. Dog with a wrinkly face
29. Defective firecracker
30. Fierce feline
32. All ___ up (irate)
33. Most confident
35. Breads with pockets
36. Swiss city on the Rhine
38. Rant and ___
39. Military installation
40. Slanted type: Abbr.
41. Clock sound
42. Fed. purchasing org.
43. Russian-built fighter

Solution on page 334

Puzzle 88

Across

1. Shoe part
5. Down times
9. TVA project
12. "___ does it!"
13. Author ___ Easton Ellis
14. Half of deux
15. Quickly
17. Tackle a slope
18. Pertaining to planes
19. Pave again
21. Lads' partners
24. No longer working. Abbr.
25. NYC hrs.
26. Owl
28. Planet between Earth and Jupiter
30. Cyclotron bit
31. Rara ___
33. Roof of the mouth
35. Neighbor of Mont.
36. Buddies
37. Jewish campus group
40. Conductor Sir Georg
42. July 4, 1776, e.g.
43. Miner's load
44. Redhead, slangily
49. "___ Liaisons Dangereuses"
50. "Since ___ You Baby" (1956 hit)
51. Grab
52. MS-___
53. Office staffer
54. Slammin' Sammy

Down

1. Gas additive
2. "NOW I get it!"
3. ___ Cruces, New Mexico
4. James and Jones
5. Angle irons
6. Words of approximation
7. Dampen
8. Not mono
9. Desert whirlwind
10. "My Way" singer
11. Dayan colleague
16. Half a bray
20. Jazz singer ___ James
21. NASA moon craft
22. Letters of haste
23. Like some gowns
24. Howard of "American Graffiti"
26. Gardener's tool
27. Theme park attraction
29. Jalousie part
30. "___ not my problem"
32. Mr. Mineo
34. Silverstone of "Clueless"
37. Western writer Bret
38. Judge Lance ___
39. Baltic natives
40. Auctioneer's final word
41. Cookie with a creme center
42. Great Scott of 1857
45. Pal for Pierre
46. Universal ideal
47. Gives a thumbs-up to
48. Veggie in a pod

Solution on page 334

Puzzle 89

Across

1. ER equipment
4. Presidents' Day mo.
7. Ping-___
11. Grazing place
12. Part of U.S.A.
14. Funny Martha
15. Mystery writer Deighton
16. Racing sled
17. Rt.-hand person
18. Kinski role
20. Treats with malice
22. Ear pollution
24. IRS-form experts
25. Asian salt lake
26. Caboose, e.g.
29. One-liner
30. Romantic adventure
31. Cannes water
33. "Forget about it!"
35. Ill-fated Supreme Court nominee
36. Said "not guilty," perhaps
37. From that time
38. Balance-sheet pluses
41. Without: Fr.
42. "Fargo" director Joel
43. Siesta times: Abbr.
45. "___ bin ein Berliner"
48. Was sorry about
49. Mineo and Maglie
50. Sludgy substance
51. Shore birds
52. Artist Lichtenstein
53. TV's "Science Guy" Bill

Down

1. Chicago's state: Abbr.
2. Sign from Churchill
3. South American capital
4. Not true
5. Ostrichlike birds
6. Canine command
7. Tout
8. Tobacco-curing kiln
9. NASDAQ rival
10. Catches on to
13. Time off
19. Subj. for immigrants
21. Hardly tanned
22. Racehorse, slangily
23. Algerian seaport
24. Checked out before the heist
26. Brewer and Wright
27. Advertising lure
28. Ste. Jeanne ___
30. Expensively finished
32. Hawaiian instrument
34. Disburses
35. Storage box
37. Smart-mouthed
38. Land measurement
39. Kind of grapes
40. Laid eyes on
41. Normandy campaign town
44. Not near
46. Artfully shy
47. Groundbreaking tool

Solution on page 334

Puzzle 90

Across

1. Bic products
5. Poet Sandburg
9. Overhead railroads
12. Philosopher Zeno of ___
13. Logical beginning?
14. ___-Tzu (Chinese philosopher)
15. Emulate Pisa's tower
16. Bell hit with a padded hammer
17. That, in Tijuana
18. Noggin, in Nantes
19. Arthur of "Maude"
20. One whose name is followed by "esq."
21. Not easily found
24. Indian bread
26. Floor covering
29. Arnaz of "I Love Lucy"
31. Telephone wire
34. Planned schedule
36. Home audio system
38. Unit of loudness
39. Narrow path
41. Parliamentary response
42. Tooth-care org.
44. Howard and Silver
46. Give no stars to
48. General Grant's foe
50. Deadly sin
54. Tiny hill dweller
55. Suffix with origin
57. Range below soprano
58. Point opposite SSW
59. SWM part
60. Kind of pressure
61. Sen. Kennedy
62. Dairy-case purchase
63. Medical fluids

Down

1. Animal skin
2. Robert ___
3. Well-ordered
4. More levelheaded
5. Smoke, informally
6. Pueblo homes
7. Descartes
8. Boston's airport
9. Billie Holiday's real first name
10. Losing badly
11. Chimney grime
22. Tally (up)
23. Kind of estate
25. Poker card
26. Kettle and Barker
27. "Fourscore and seven years ___ . . ."
28. Occupied
30. "Money ___ object"
32. Actor Fernando
33. Deer female
35. Beatty or Buntline
37. Coffee-break time, often
40. Small cavity
43. Crockett's last stand, with "the"
45. High-five sounds
46. Breathe rapidly
47. Diarist ___ Frank
49. And others: Abbr.
51. "___'s Gold" (1997 Peter Fonda movie)
52. Suffix with gang
53. When tripled, a 1970 war film
56. Classic auto

Solution on page 335

Puzzle 91

Across

1. Guitar's cousin
4. Nigerian native
7. Barbecued treat
10. Certain Ford, for short
12. Reel partner
13. Mrs. Dithers of the comics
14. Non-winners
16. Barber's expertise
17. Darn, as socks
18. Firmly packed
19. Eucharist plate
22. Another name for Jupiter
24. "At once!"
25. Singing sisters
29. By the same token
30. Letters after els
31. Not of the clergy
32. Having a valid will
34. Cube inventor Rubik
35. "___ Tu": 1973 tune
36. French impressionist
37. Brit's cavalry sword
40. Pitt of "Babel"
42. Saroyan's "My Name Is ___"
43. Unresolved detail
47. Rocky ridges
48. Hill-building insect
49. Aussie hoppers
50. ". . . or ___ thought"
51. Long-term S&L investments
52. Broadway hit letters

Down

1. Thurman of "Kill Bill" films
2. Kenan's Nickelodeon pal
3. Ambulance destinations, for short
4. Tehran's country
5. 007's introduction
6. Pigs out (on), briefly
7. Speckle-coated horse
8. Part of the eye
9. Unclothed
11. Agree
13. Team booster
15. Stimpy's cartoon buddy
18. Movie format
19. H.S. jr.'s exam
20. Tamarisk tree
21. Merged Soviet news agency
23. Switch words
26. Get, as a salary
27. Burgundy or Bordeaux
28. Glasgow guy
30. High season, on the Riviera
33. "The best things in life ___ free"
36. Mothers
37. Matinee days: Abbr.
38. Ending for buck
39. Italian seaport
41. Putrefies
43. Resinous substance
44. Greek dawn goddess
45. "Neither a borrower, ___ . . ."
46. Mil. award

Solution on page 335

Puzzle 92

Across

1. Taj Mahal locale
5. Place for peas
8. Gullible sorts
12. Surveyor's work
13. Lamb's mama
14. Felipe, Matty, or Jesus of baseball
15. Not straight
16. Special attention, for short
17. Place for trash
18. Binding orders
20. Stereo parts
21. "Crying" singer Orbison
22. L.A. hours
24. ___ up (accumulated)
27. Spoil
28. By what means
31. Fight stopper, briefly
32. Window curtain
34. Area 51 craft
35. Follow a pattern?
36. Trip segment
37. Golfer Calvin
39. Society newcomer
40. Kind of artist
41. Submarine command
44. Iran-___ Affair
47. Drought relief
48. Unit of bricks
49. ___ Hashanah
51. Bronze and Iron
52. Giant slugger Mel
53. Pierre's paramour
54. Manner
55. Itty-bitty
56. Gives zero stars to

Down

1. L.A.P.D. alert
2. Tickled-pink feeling
3. Cape Town currency
4. Get-up
5. Trifling
6. Temple athletes
7. Yule mo.
8. Former Egyptian leader
9. Graduate, for short
10. Splendid display
11. Dines
19. Treat tenderly
22. Rice Krispies sound
23. Walk over
24. Scoreboard nos.
25. 1950s campaign nickname
26. Temperature extreme
27. Scott Joplin piece
28. Tint
29. Frequently
30. Heartache
33. Yank's foe
38. Lure into wrongdoing
39. Not too bright
40. Italian noble
41. Ounce part
42. Shakespeare villain
43. Contended
44. Pigeon coop
45. "Arrivederci ___"
46. N ___ Nancy
48. Drag along
50. "For ___ a jolly good . . ."

Solution on page 335

Puzzle 93

Across

1. Editorial submissions: Abbr.
4. Le Pew of cartoons
8. Rotten kid
12. Mikhail of chess
13. Irish island
14. Suffix for billion
15. Coll. seniors' test
16. Long-snouted fish
17. One of the Aleutians
18. Imagine
20. Make holy
21. Noisy sleeper
23. Casual talk
26. Surgical beams
31. Abase
34. Reveals
35. Strand like Crusoe
36. Prefix with tiller
37. Quick ballet movement
41. Spanish houses
45. La Brea attraction
48. Jordanian, for one
49. Numerical information
50. "Uno" + "uno"
52. Turkey-stuffing herb
53. Character actor Jack
54. HBO competitor
55. Fruit of the blackthorn
56. Animation units
57. Capuchin monkey

Down

1. Office conference: Abbr.
2. Dress of India
3. Luge or toboggan
4. Idolater
5. Muse who inspires poets
6. Kitchen utensil
7. Annapolis grad: Abbr.
8. Jezebel's god
9. Baptism or bar mitzvah
10. Clumsy ships
11. Oolong and pekoe
19. 1950's candidate Kefauver
20. Loch Lomond hill
22. House extension
23. B followers
24. Barnyard bird
25. "___ seeing things?"
27. Throat malady
28. "___ Beso" (1962 song)
29. Tommy follower?
30. ___-Cat (off-road vehicle)
32. Bitter brews
33. "___ blu, dipinto di . . ."
38. "___ of Two Cities"
39. Pertaining to birth
40. Stuffs
41. Mama ___ of the Mamas and the Papas
42. Landlocked Asian sea
43. Kind of tropical palm
44. ". . . sting like ___"
46. Mrs. McKinley and others
47. Tony Musante cop series
49. Santa's mo.
51. Poli ___ (college major)

Solution on page 335

Puzzle 94

Across

1. Chow mein additive
4. Santa's little helper
7. Prefix meaning "tenth"
11. Galley slave's tool
12. Opposite of alway
14. Whitney and Wallach
15. Pilot's heading: Abbr.
16. Attractive person
18. Buster or Diane
20. A long way off
21. Akron product
22. More hackneyed
26. Have a cross ___
28. Bun-seed source
29. Expose, poetically
30. Beer container
31. Hole-enlarging tool
35. Loafers
38. Make angry
39. Finch's home
40. Elephant's weight, maybe
41. Ringed planet
44. Ottoman
48. Rock's ____ Speedwagon
49. Four-star
50. One-and-only
51. '60s battleground
52. Peasant
53. Pay-___-view
54. ___-mo (replay speed)

Down

1. Monastery resident
2. Mentally sound
3. Ursa Major
4. "Bewitched" witch
5. Loewe's Broadway partner
6. Membership charge
7. Wreckage
8. "Xanadu" group
9. Spy org.
10. Believer's suffix
13. Rapids transits
17. Filly's mother
19. Item with a clip or a pin
23. Alternate
24. Part of EMT: Abbr.
25. Rules, informally
26. Ruptured
27. Word on a store sign
32. Be important
33. Items often bruised
34. Takes an apartment
35. Dr. Scholl's product
36. Casino worker
37. D-Day transport
42. Not imaginary
43. Hurler Hideo
44. Tide competitor
45. Tic-tac-toe winner
46. Lennon's Yoko
47. Alley-___

Solution on page 335

Puzzle 95

Across
1. Dan Rather's employer
4. "The ___ Divorcee"
7. Switch positions
11. Lumber source
12. Mine access
14. Roly-___
15. Commit an unabetted crime
17. Cell impulse transmitter
18. Leader of the flock
19. Bruins' org.
21. Triumphed
22. Wish for
26. Mr. Chips portrayer Robert
29. Go a few rounds
30. Strike smartly
31. Hebrew measure
32. Sisterhood member
33. Hand: Sp.
34. Slangy denial
35. Buddhism school
36. Ayn and Sally
37. Chickasaw and Choctaw
39. Atlantic City casino, with "the"
40. L-1011, e.g.
41. Theater district
45. "The Godfather" author
48. Discharge
50. The Munsters' pet bat
51. Fully cooked
52. Take wing
53. "What happened next . . ."
54. ___-Atlantic
55. Prom wear

Down
1. Sound of thunder
2. ___ Raton
3. Some NCO's
4. Awkward bloke
5. Make pretty
6. Yang's partner
7. Fiery gems
8. Sly sort
9. Showman Ziegfeld
10. Thesaurus entry: Abbr.
13. Muscle/bone connector
16. In armed conflict
20. Evil spell
23. Teheran's land
24. Author Ayn
25. Narrative poetry
26. No-no
27. WWII general Bradley
28. Royal Crown Cola brand
29. Hot dog holder
32. Fitted one within another
33. Goya subjects
35. Snore letter
36. Reared
38. Borg of tennis
39. Alvarado of "Little Women"
42. London elevator
43. Balsam
44. Intaglio stone
45. Peach center
46. "That's disgusting!"
47. Playwright Akins
49. Dad's mate

Solution on page 335

Puzzle 96

Across

1. Cleopatra's love ___ Antony
5. Title
9. Umbrella stiffener
12. ___ Khayyam
13. Verbal exam
14. Marriage vow
15. Jab playfully
16. Christmas saint
17. Church seat
18. Get really steamed
20. Mama of pop
21. Ring results
22. "___ Haw"
24. Haunted-house spirit
27. Given a conditional release
31. Flightless Australian bird
32. Porous gems
34. Like an unmatched sock
35. Went for a drive
37. Monster with 100 eyes
39. Clock setting at LAX
40. Extreme degree
41. Exam for a jr.
44. Sorting devices
47. Approves
48. Death notice
50. Absorbs, with "up"
52. Back talk
53. Had on
54. Voice of America org.
55. What DJs spin
56. Votes against
57. Crooned

Down

1. Unruly head of hair
2. "Famous" cookiemaker
3. Gather leaves
4. Small streams
5. Roman date
6. Sere
7. Scottish surname starter
8. Lodge brother
9. Philbin co-host
10. 15th of March
11. Violinists' needs
19. Chopper parts
20. Corp.'s top dog
22. Fictional supercomputer
23. Imitation
24. Thing in a ring
25. Med. insurance plan
26. Umpire's call
27. Expand unnecessarily
28. Journal
29. Univ. web address suffix
30. Orthodontist's deg.
33. Poodle or parakeet
36. Make a decision
38. Monkey used in research
40. Evenings, informally
41. Opinion taker
42. Omit
43. Venomous vipers
44. What to call a king
45. Civil rights leader Parks
46. Laundry cycle
48. Have title to
49. Ghost's cry
51. Droop

Solution on page 336

Puzzle 97

Across

1. Yeses at sea
5. Chem. pollutant
8. Parts of feet
12. Humorist Sahl
13. China's Chou En-___
14. Actor ___ Ray
15. A.D. part
16. Enero to diciembre
17. Golda of Israel
18. Stringed instrument
20. Moisten, as a roast
21. Sneaker bottoms
24. Have something the matter
25. Lacking couth
26. Makes beloved
30. Matterhorn, for one
31. Those holding office
32. Nev. neighbor
33. Sweet course
36. Angry
38. That schooner
39. Made a memo
40. Puff snake
43. Read rapidly
45. Read (over)
46. Cuban hero Guevara
47. Quarterback Flutie
51. Enthusiastic vigor
52. Play on words
53. Greek mountain
54. Words before record or trap
55. On, as a lamp
56. Escape slowly

Down

1. MD's org.
2. Hither's opposite
3. Suffix with north or south
4. Shoulder wraps
5. Real-estate map
6. Rattan
7. Life story
8. Burrito kin
9. Bullring shouts
10. Do magazine work
11. Feeling achy
19. "Enterprise" initials
20. Bridge action
21. Great number
22. Heraldic border
23. Trips around the track
24. Opposite of a ques.
26. Tolkien being
27. One-___ (ball game)
28. Hotel price
29. Santa's vehicle
31. Like some vbs.
34. Singer Easton
35. Suffix for ballad
36. Buy a pig ___ poke
37. Sonata movements
40. Gorillas and chimps
41. Mete (out)
42. "Darn!"
43. Feng ___
44. Word on a penny
46. Sgt.'s underling
48. Suffix meaning "full of"
49. Implement
50. Cumberland ___

Solution on page 336

Puzzle 98

Across

1. Brit. flying group
4. Fizzling-out sound
8. Certain herring
12. Latin eggs
13. Straight line
14. Italian lake
15. Cyrano de ___
17. "Chestnuts roasting ___ open fire"
18. Shell rival
19. British weapons
20. Enlarge
23. Owl sound
25. "___ Fire" (Springsteen hit)
26. Do some logrolling
27. Popular tattoo word
30. Look-alike
33. President after F.D.R.
34. Aardvarks' snacks
35. Dresden donkey
36. Fanny
37. Defeated at chess
38. Ore deposits
41. River through Hesse, Germany
43. Kazan who directed "On the Waterfront"
44. Ran, as machinery
48. False locks
49. Broccoli ___ (leafy vegetable)
50. Give ___ shot
51. Amount of medicine
52. "Last one ___ a rotten egg!"
53. 1900

Down

1. Hold up, as a bank
2. Street map abbr.
3. Not in the neighborhood
4. Fuss at the mirror
5. Expensive wraps
6. Short-lived success
7. Private eye, for short
8. "Patton" star
9. Sharpen, as a razor
10. To ___ (unanimously)
11. Slips into
16. Capital of East Flanders
19. Songs for one
20. Fond desire
21. Little troublemakers
22. "Just ___": Nike slogan
24. Assns.
26. Coal holders
27. Ship's pole
28. Decorative molding
29. Merge
31. Greek consonants
32. Stiller's mate
36. Annoy
37. French mothers
38. Indelicate
39. Bit of this, bit of that
40. Uses a shovel
42. Figure skater Thomas
44. "Either you do it, ___ will!"
45. "Tiny" Dickens boy
46. List ender: Abbr.
47. Beaver creation

Solution on page 336

Puzzle 99

Across

1. Talk, talk, talk
4. And so on, briefly
7. Injection
11. Has debts
13. "I didn't know that!"
14. Bop on the bean
15. Bone near the humerus
16. Guy's partner
17. Folkie Guthrie
18. "Heidi" author
20. Deposits
21. Not these
24. City near Tulsa
26. Four-star reviews
27. Sleep acronym
28. Applicant's goal
31. ___-France
32. First Lady's first name
34. For each one
35. Actor Robbins
38. "Lou Grant" star
39. Royal sari wearer
40. Not those
41. See socially
44. More clever
46. Gets older
47. Pup's bark
48. Actor Griffith
52. Deceptive plan
53. Prefix with classic or natal
54. Central American Indian
55. Home on a branch
56. Cow's chew
57. Ruby, for one

Down

1. "Hey, ___!"
2. Piercing tool
3. Author Follett
4. Like custard
5. Ripper
6. Singer Dion
7. Burn with hot water
8. Bar mitzvah dance
9. The "O" in S.R.O.
10. Ring decisions
12. Talked back to
19. Spanish coin
21. Stumble
22. Revolutionary Nathan
23. Partner of "done with"
25. White Rabbit's cry
28. Father's Day month
29. Native minerals
30. Like Hubbard's cupboard
33. Guru's residence
36. On the same wavelength
37. Surroundings
39. Bowling button
41. "Oh, heck!"
42. Fluish feeling
43. "___ of the D'Urbervilles"
45. Digital music player
49. Pick on
50. Stain
51. Thanksgiving staple

Solution on page 336

Puzzle 100

Across

1. ___ of war
4. "Let's get crackin'!"
8. One of Lawrence's men
12. "___ as directed"
13. ___kiri
14. Be overly picky
15. Erodes
17. Puerto ___
18. Party giver
19. Sight or smell
20. Multiplied by
23. Celebratory poems
25. Oscar-nominated Peter Fonda role
26. Ontario tribe
27. Prattle
30. Infant's toy
32. Punish by fine
34. "Bill ___, The Science Guy"
35. Biblical garden spot
37. Deadlocked
38. Bar mitzvah boy, barely
39. Makes smooth
40. Seed spreader
43. Knucklehead
45. Grows older
46. Goes first
50. In good order
51. Soft French cheese
52. "For shame!"
53. Cozy rooms
54. Grounded planes: Abbr.
55. Cook, as bacon

Down

1. Calendar col.
2. Cuba's neighbor
3. Fetch
4. Mass confusion
5. Gaping mouths
6. Speechmaker
7. Not yea
8. Zoning units
9. Precipitation
10. Compass doodles
11. Fraternal gp.
16. Piece of paper
19. Appear to be
20. Go right or left
21. "Now ___ me down to sleep . . ."
22. Apportion, with "out"
24. Dizzy of baseball
26. Give up, as territory
27. Look of contentment
28. Scored 100 on
29. Hotel capacity
31. Look slyly
33. French political divisions
36. Keys in
38. Finals and midterms
39. Allies (with)
40. Beach composition
41. Type of arch
42. Gradually withdraw
44. Bide one's time
46. Weight abbr.
47. Inaccurate
48. Spruce relative
49. Enchanted

Solution on page 336

Puzzle 101

Across

1. Hi-fi component
4. Ace or deuce
8. Japanese drink
12. Hamm of soccer
13. Computer operator
14. Tel ___, Israel
15. "Harper Valley ___"
16. Kojak's first name
17. Greek-salad cheese
18. Glacial ridge
20. Capital of Peru
22. Glop
24. Actress Day
27. City near Naples
31. Soars
33. A numero
34. Time being
36. Hawaiian garland
37. Roman judge
39. Most quickly
41. Traffic tie-up
43. Like zinfandel
44. Ivan or Nicholas
46. Starring roles
50. Cattle
53. "Don't stop!"
55. Pigeon sound
56. Pre-holiday times
57. Eve's grandson
58. Fox News rival
59. Without ice or mixer
60. Sun emanations
61. Price indicator

Down

1. Elec. units
2. Small contribution
3. Carson predecessor
4. Economize
5. Combustion residue
6. Fishing-rod attachment
7. C-3PO, for one
8. African outing
9. ___ Maria
10. Caboodle complement
11. Zsa Zsa's sister
19. "___ before beauty"
21. Approximately
23. Lennon's widow Yoko
25. The Emerald ___ (Ireland)
26. Envisions
27. Lyon of "Lolita"
28. "No ifs, ___, or buts"
29. Cut of pork
30. Switch positions
32. Take a chair
35. Fish-and-chips fish
38. Hottest, as news
40. Bill, the "Science Guy"
42. Less plausible, as an excuse
45. Gossip's Barrett
47. Depositor's holding: Abbr.
48. Lisbon lady
49. Ballad
50. Barbie's ex-beau
51. "___ said it before . . ."
52. Grant-giving org.
54. Siegfried's partner

Solution on page 336

Puzzle 102

Across

1. Soldiers and carpenters, e.g.
5. Bankbook abbr.
8. Opera parts
12. Horse controller
13. Prefix with classic
14. Hide's partner
15. Foal's mother
16. Website address part
17. Spelling on television
18. Man of ___ (Superman)
20. Unbeatable foe
22. Ministerial nickname
24. Impair
25. Handel masterwork
29. Related on the mother's side
33. ___ -de-France
34. Four-in-hand
36. Wall Street barometer, with "the"
37. Home products seller
40. Starting point
43. Haw's partner
45. Thrilla in Manila boxer
46. Spray can
50. Singers' refrains
54. Top-billed performer
55. Use oars
57. Desert monster
58. Yard sale labels
59. Regret
60. Household power: Abbr.
61. "NOW it's clear!"
62. "___ to a Nightingale"
63. Clock sound

Down

1. Hug givers
2. Uncluttered
3. Firestone product
4. Contemptuous looks
5. Unaffiliated: Abbr.
6. Gas used in signs
7. Indian carving
8. Toward the rudder
9. Corp. heads
10. Ms. Garr of "Mr. Mom"
11. Slaloms
19. Floral chain
21. West from Brooklyn
23. Dye container
25. Woody's ex
26. Freddy Krueger's street
27. Use a needle
28. "___ master's voice"
30. "Much ___ About Nothing"
31. Large amount
32. Lamb's mother
35. Airport info: Abbr.
38. In the saddle
39. "Indeed!"
41. Plumbing joint
42. Swiss child psychologist Jean
44. ___ Castle (Havana landmark)
46. Spumante city
47. Greek letters
48. Craze
49. Noisy
51. Disney's "___ & Stitch"
52. Author Waugh
53. Big bag
56. Lilliputian

Solution on page 337

Puzzle 103

Across

1. Record producer Brian
4. Oft-pierced body part
7. Place to get pampered
10. Horse's hair
12. Activity
13. Char
14. Mall habitue
15. Make a quilt
16. Cabbie
17. Tailless primates
19. Fills
20. Votes into office
23. Cargo weight
24. Ushers in
25. Least loony
28. Martians and such
29. Align the cross hairs
30. You ___ here
32. Goes first
35. Cherbourg shes
37. Fish eggs
38. Picks on
39. Desirable quality
42. Put into pigeonholes
43. Singer Falana
44. Do lunch
45. Jackrabbit
49. Iowa city
50. Easter egg need
51. Writer-illustrator Silverstein
52. Beatty of "Superman"
53. Draft initials
54. Everyone

Down

1. CPR performer
2. Scottish refusal
3. Lonely number
4. Backs off, with "up"
5. Citrus drinks
6. Tier
7. Install in office
8. Stride
9. Boats like Noah's
11. Make official, as a law
13. Alan Ladd role
18. NBA stats
19. "Sanford and ___"
20. Ending with Siam or Japan
21. Answer to "Shall we?"
22. Near or Far follower
23. Highland topper
25. Bro's relative
26. Actor Mineo et al.
27. Forest element
29. Had dinner
31. Shape of some hooks
33. General vicinities
34. Stuff and nonsense
35. Always, to Byron
36. Wooden slats
38. Carryalls
39. Fed chairman Greenspan
40. Not all
41. Snow coaster
42. Verbalizes
44. Sullivan and McMahon
46. "I found it!"
47. Family member: Abbr.
48. Angled annex

Solution on page 337

Puzzle 104

Across

1. Hack's customer
5. Mylanta target
8. Golf score
11. Spy Aldrich ___
12. Spy Mata ___
13. Dr. provider
14. Beef or pork
15. Make the first bid
16. Indistinct
17. Mesmerized
19. Big name in small planes
21. Canadian capital
23. Dashboard abbr.
26. "Obviously!"
27. Room meas.
31. Beekeeper played by Peter Fonda
33. Bit of luggage
35. Natural successor
36. Workout centers
37. "Awesome!"
39. Uninteresting
40. Third-generation Japanese-American
43. Former San Francisco Mayor Joseph
46. Handbag holders
51. Disencumber
52. "Damn Yankees" siren
54. Slanted: Abbr.
55. Former Chinese leader
56. Med. course
57. Dark soft drink
58. Last year's jrs.
59. Spider's handiwork
60. Was certain of

Down

1. Fortune's partner
2. Prayer's last word
3. Raise, as a child
4. Spanish 101 verb
5. Wide divergence
6. Palm
7. Muscle
8. Advanced degs.
9. Idi ___
10. Italia's capital
12. Home-spa device
18. Pea's home
20. Accessory for a Miss America contestant
22. Defrosts
23. Stein
24. Wield
25. Dress's bottom
28. Logician's abbr.
29. Coniferous tree
30. Undertake
32. Gas of the past
34. Attacks
38. Clever sort
41. Attorney-___
42. Opposite of everybody
43. Equips for war
44. Teller of tall tales
45. Nuptial vows
47. "Casablanca" cafe owner
48. Oodles
49. Wan
50. Cole ___
53. Research building

Solution on page 337

Puzzle 105

Across

1. Circumference segment
4. Poorly behaved
7. Toys for ___
11. Where Ipanema is
12. Gets one's goat
14. Baseball's Matty or Moises
15. Office seeker, for short
16. Cabinet div.
17. Roadside guide
18. Heads, in Le Havre
20. Choir voices
22. G.I. entertainers
23. Etch A Sketch, e.g.
24. Big stack
27. Half a quartet
28. Lifesaving skill, for short
31. "This ___ recording"
32. Actress Bo
34. Worthless coin
35. Thanksgiving mo.
36. Lowest bill
37. Encl. for a reply
38. Common conjunction
39. U.K. music label
41. "The Canterbury ___"
43. Give more cushioning
46. Game on horseback
47. Voice of America grp.
49. Bird's beak
51. Units of current
52. French bridge
53. ___ Bingle (Crosby)
54. Untidy condition
55. Letter add-ons: Abbr.
56. California's Big ___

Down

1. Dada cofounder Jean
2. Unruly event
3. Nat King ___
4. Tarries
5. "Am not!" rejoinder
6. Bankbook abbr.
7. Delicious
8. Mishmash
9. Clothing
10. Natural tanner
13. Rodin work
19. Mon. follower
21. Appearance
24. Wrestling finale
25. Prefix for metric
26. Restroom, for short
27. Rapper Dr. ___
28. Jefferson Davis org.
29. Not neg.
30. Wish it weren't so
32. Completed
33. Ultimately becomes
37. Taste of tea
38. Thrown for ___
39. Moran and Brockovich
40. Butchers' offerings
41. Thick textbook
42. European peaks
44. "No ifs, ___ or buts"
45. Prie-___ (prayer bench)
46. Shriver of tennis
48. Absorb, with "up"
50. "Gosh, it's cold!"

Solution on page 337

Puzzle 106

Across

1. "I Do, I Do, I Do, I Do, I Do" singers
5. Civil War side: Abbr.
8. Wrestling victory
11. Neighbor of Thailand
12. Arkin of films
13. Canterbury can
14. Seabirds
15. Frat party attire
16. Printer's widths
17. Formally surrender
18. Flowery voroo
19. Manuscript enc.
20. Prince, to a king
22. Scurried
24. Roast hosts, for short
27. Butt into
29. Belt holders
33. Same old same old
34. Silent star Bow
36. Cracker Jack bonus
37. Nasal dividers
39. Luau chow
40. Jerry's ice-cream partner
41. Egyptian cobra, e.g.
43. A, in Ardennes
45. Great quantity
48. Brief writer, briefly
50. Cement piece
54. 007 creator Fleming
55. Barre bend
56. ___ avail
57. Org. with many arms?
58. Coop denizens
59. Tuscany river
60. NYC clock setting
61. Pseudonymous surname
62. Spelling contests

Down

1. Baldwin brother
2. Unadorned
3. 007
4. Beasts of burden
5. Clump of earth
6. Lyricist Carole Bayer ___
7. California's Santa ___ winds
8. Courtroom statement
9. Charged particles
10. Bloodhound's asset
12. Lacking a key, in music
19. ___-Caps (concession stand candy)
21. Predatory whales
23. French actor Delon
24. Lady's title
25. Actor's prompt
26. Nascar sponsor
28. Atlas page
30. Wagering loc.
31. "Lenore" poet
32. Ant. ant.
35. Itineraries
38. Small amount
42. Prefix with -lithic
44. Founded: Abbr.
45. Cosecant's reciprocal
46. Cougars and Jaguars
47. Med. school course
49. Fork point
51. Folk stories
52. ___ of Cleves
53. Ghostly greetings
55. Advanced degree

Solution on page 337

Puzzle 107

Across

1. Avoid
6. Dictator Amin
9. "Be quiet!"
12. One beyond hope
13. Energy source
14. Gradation of color
15. Bone below the femur
16. Former "Grand Ole Opry Live" network
17. "The Wizard of Oz" studio
18. Tiny criticisms
20. Fragrant East Indian wood
22. Number on a bank sign
25. Highway: Abbr.
26. Architect I.M. ___
27. Ream units
30. Has outstanding bills
32. Outdoor parking area
33. Green around the gills
36. Find
38. Fetch with force
39. Sounds of doubt
40. Savoir-faire
43. Dark brown fur
46. Con ___ (vigorously)
47. Online chuckle
48. Batter's stat.
50. Cavaradossi's love, in opera
54. Crazy eights spinoff
55. Hagen of Hollywood
56. Clues
57. Kitten's sound
58. Commuter vehicle
59. Psalms word

Down

1. Lt.'s subordinate
2. Japanese carp
3. Bach's "Mass ___ Minor"
4. Spanish queen
5. Blue eyes or baldness, e.g.
6. Followers: Suffix
7. Demand payment
8. Hereditary
9. Bumbling sort
10. Massive
11. ___ and haws
19. Units of magnetic flux density
21. Enthusiastic response
22. Naval noncom: Abbr.
23. Morning condensation
24. Cambodian currency
25. Rip again
28. Like stolen goods
29. Grain-storage building
31. "Heart and ___"
34. Magna ___ laude
35. Former Soviet spy agcy.
37. Little angel
41. Cores
42. Sarge's superior
43. Run-down neighborhood
44. High rating
45. Play a trumpet
46. Diagonal
49. Air-conditioning unit: Abbr.
51. "Live from N.Y." show
52. Windy City train initials
53. Blaze remnant

Solution on page 337

Puzzle 108

Across

1. "What was ___ do?"
4. Improvise, musically
8. Prof's degree
11. Slave Turner
12. Informal refusal
13. Become frayed
14. Dove's cry
15. Business envelope abbr.
16. No ifs, ___, or buts
17. Burn a bit
19. Complete collections
21. ___ Royal Highness
23. Fork parts
26. Holy
30. ". . . a poem lovely as ___"
32. Get ___ of (eliminate)
33. Scratch and dent
35. No. on a business card
36. Preferred invitees
39. Cassandra, e.g.
42. Signs of sorrow
44. Org. with Eagles
45. Homebuilder's strip
47. Fakery
50. Small snack
53. Outward glow
55. Wrestler's pad
57. ___ out (barely gets)
58. Pottery material
59. French affirmative
60. Place for thieves
61. Puppy patter
62. Backboard attachment

Down

1. Small-business magazine
2. New Mexico art colony
3. Oklahoma tribesman
4. Entraps
5. Barracks bunk
6. Bldg. units
7. Church principle
8. Parker product
9. Owned
10. Salk and Pepper: Abbr.
13. "Rome ___ built in a day"
18. Sighing sounds
20. Padre's sister
22. Sleep phenomenon
24. Art Deco name
25. Observes
26. Bathing suit top
27. Pleasant tune
28. Chanteuse Adams
29. Court figs.
31. Aboveground trains
34. Soldier in gray
37. Corporate division
38. La-la preceder
40. Some exam answers
41. Bleachers cry
43. Keach of "The Pathfinder"
46. Oahu dance
48. Roman love god
49. Hawaiian isle
50. Sleeping spot
51. Tina Turner's ex
52. Perfect score, sometimes
54. Hip-hop
56. Lyricist Rice

Solution on page 338

Puzzle 109

Across

1. Actress Lollobrigida
5. Fuzzy member of Skywalker's army
9. Noticed
12. Aid in a crime
13. Be sulky
14. Els org.
15. Roof support
16. Soup vessels
17. Albanian currency
18. Took deliberate steps
20. Withdraw from an alliance
22. "The A-Team" muscleman
24. Hither and ___
25. Calendar divs.
28. Menagerie
29. Prefix meaning "thought"
32. Certain paintings
34. ___ Van Winkle
36. "Damn Yankees" seductress
37. Interweave
38. Bagel accompaniment
40. D.C. stadium
41. 7, on a phone
43. Topic for Dr. Ruth
44. Teaching session
47. Sums
52. Show to a seat, informally
53. Canoeing locale
55. Go gaga
56. Mail HQ
57. Rosary prayers
58. "Don't look ___ like that!"
59. Boundary
60. Rules, briefly
61. Run with an easy gait

Down

1. Talks a lot
2. Skeptic's remark
3. Not distant
4. Prefix for sphere
5. Supreme ruler
6. It's pitched by a suitor
7. Acts on a preference
8. "One Flew Over the Cuckoo's Nest" author Ken
9. Magnificence
10. Matured, as wine
11. Rouse from sleep
19. Area between N. and S. Korea
21. Form spirals
23. Works hard
25. Chinese frypan
26. Aunts, cousins, etc.
27. Careless
30. Folklore sprite
31. Acorn product
33. Violins and violas: Abbr.
35. Emily Dickinson, e.g.
39. Tic-tac-toe loser
42. Like some renewable energy
44. Winter Olympics sled
45. Channel for armchair athletes
46. Central church section
48. Nonstick cookware brand
49. Female voice
50. Not stiff
51. German battleship Graf ___
54. Frat party container

Solution on page 338

Puzzle 110

Across

1. Playground game
4. Baby syllable
7. Comic Amsterdam
12. Coronado's gold
13. Exclamation of triumph
14. "Go fly ___!"
15. "___ many cooks . . ."
16. Acknowledges applause
18. Lent ender
20. Wild blue yonder
21. ___ Scott Decision
22. End a fast
24. Numerical datum
28. Winding road shape
30. Wager
32. Put ___ good word for
33. Mo. with no holidays
35. Clean the blackboard
37. Furious
38. Having one sharp, musically
39. "To be or ___ to be"
40. Links peg
42. Sail supporter
44. "The Ipcress File" author Deighton
46. Latticework feature
49. Gorilla or orangutan
51. Garb
53. Get out of the way
57. Ott or Gibson
58. All gone, as food
59. Sun. delivery
60. Suffix with Benedict
61. Tacky
62. Provide weapons for
63. Levy

Down

1. Lugged along
2. Bellowing
3. Zeros
4. Prize fight's take
5. Chicago airport
6. Acorn producer
7. Lone Ranger attire
8. Approvals
9. Chest protector?
10. Ike's WWII command
11. Archery wood
17. ___ Park, CO
19. Super Bowl scores, for short
23. Let up, as a storm
25. "Final Jeopardy" feature
26. Actress ___ Alicia
27. Itsy bit
29. Upper House member: Abbr.
31. Saigon New Year
33. Sharpshooter's asset
34. Acapulco article
36. Parts in plays
41. Phila. clock setting
43. Cassettes
45. Common Cause founder
47. Sports complex
48. Fax predecessor
50. Gives a bad review to
52. School semester
53. "Hold on just a ___!"
54. Part of cigarette smoke
55. When a plane is due in: Abbr.
56. "Life ___ cabaret . . ."

Solution on page 338

Puzzle 111

Across

1. That guy
4. Traveler's guide
7. Wearing loafers
11. Penn. neighbor
12. College grad
14. Singer Perry
15. Gab
16. Like Tim Cratchit
17. Silver wear?
18. Catch some Zs
20. California mount
22. Rock's ___ Jovi
23. Harbor workhorse
24. "What've you been ___?"
27. Henson of Muppets fame
28. Toddler's question
31. Apply macadam to
32. Happy associate
33. "Vaya Con ___"
34. IV measurements
35. Kan. neighbor
36. Part of IHOP: Abbr.
37. Spitfire fliers, for short
38. "For shame!"
40. Assert without proof
43. Glacial period
47. Vientiane's country
48. Raleigh's state: Abbr.
50. Four qts.
51. The Beatles' "Let ___"
52. "___ the Explorer": kids' TV show
53. Mouse spotter's cry
54. Boxer's weapon
55. Looker's leg
56. "Kidnapped" author's inits.

Down

1. Major rtes.
2. Infamous czar
3. Dangerous shark
4. Passover staple
5. Nonnational
6. Bit of paronomasia
7. Scrawny one
8. Tilling tools
9. Skip by
10. Lady of La Mancha
13. Occult figure
19. Long, thin musical instrument
21. Drone
24. Merchandise ID
25. Cal.'s ocean
26. Show showers
27. Robbery
28. Prevail
29. Commercially popular
30. Designer's monogram
32. Stick up for
33. Place for a finger?
35. Chronic critic
37. Calibrate anew
38. Beauty queen's crown
39. "Vamoose!"
40. Arabic "A"
41. Sol-do bridge
42. Lofted shots
44. Maturing agent
45. Scotsman
46. Moose relatives
49. Minor player

Solution on page 338

Puzzle 112

Across

1. Lemon and lime drinks
5. Comedian Sahl
9. Hans of Dadaism
12. Fully satisfy
13. Cantata melody
14. Weed digger
15. Helper
17. Comedian Bernie
18. Singer ___ King Cole
19. Knights' horses
21. Palestinian ascetic
24. "Evil Woman" rock group
25. Hangmen's needs
26. French lawmakers
29. Latin art
30. Cry to a calf
32. Cafe container
36. Escalator alternative
39. Train stop: Abbr.
40. Sheets and pillowcases
41. Bowling lanes
44. In addition
45. Poetic meadow
46. Trash-can ignorer
51. Auctioneer's quest
52. 1986 Peace Nobelist Wiesel
53. German "a"
54. Pronounce
55. Bambi and others
56. "___ the Man" Musial

Down

1. Happy ___ lark
2. Prosecutors, for short
3. UFO navigators
4. Nets
5. Dull finishes
6. "Are you a man ___ mouse?"
7. Gets the soap out
8. Spill the beans
9. "Alas"
10. Hope/Crosby title word
11. They're above the abs
16. "Compos mentis"
20. Extremely long time
21. Doe in "Bambi"
22. Put in alphabetical order
23. Cubs slugger Sammy
27. Parisian girlfriend
28. Having a hard time deciding
31. Covert WWII org.
33. Opposite dir. from NNW
34. Arranged, as hair
35. Store, as grain
36. Roofing pro
37. Fork prong
38. Guitarist Segovia
41. Church robes
42. Luke Skywalker's sister
43. Gentlewoman
47. Come out even
48. Took the bait
49. Article in Acapulco
50. ___-Xers (boomers' kids)

Solution on page 338

Puzzle 113

Across

1. Escape clauses
5. Association: Abbr.
8. Quarterback's option
12. Author Austen
13. Sunbeam
14. Part of a Latin conjugation
15. Paving stone
16. Point at the target
17. "Ali ___ and the 40 Thieves"
18. Squeals, so to speak
20. Not ajar
21. Pretend to be
24. Sombrero, e.g.
26. "For goodness ___!"
27. Pregrown grass
28. Tijuana uncle
31. Make angry
32. Cosmetics queen Lauder
34. Letter insert: Abbr.
35. Opposite NNE
36. Inc., in England
37. Get to work
39. Ukr. or Lith., once
40. Vampire slayers
41. "The Thin Man" canine
44. Change the hemline
46. Happiness
47. Afternoon hour on a sundial
48. Polite term of address
52. Work hard for
53. Spike TV's former name
54. NYPD alerts
55. Batters' stats
56. Downward bend
57. "___ la vie"

Down

1. Breakfast drinks, briefly
2. Persian Gulf fed.
3. Big blast maker
4. Small sofa
5. Ph.D. exams
6. Banister
7. Sneaker
8. Big name in brewing
9. Indian nurse
10. "Elephant Boy" boy
11. Baseball-card info
19. Studio stands
21. Letters before omegas
22. Propels a canoe
23. Veer off course
25. " ___ Fideles"
27. Not irregular: Abbr.
28. Boat wood
29. Concerning, in memos
30. Fall mos.
33. Narrow waterways
38. Airport surface
39. Composer Camille Saint-___
40. Bee's defense
41. Golden ___; older retired person
42. Bacon quantity
43. Polo or Hatcher
45. Filmmaker Wertmuller
49. Chimp or gorilla
50. Stomach muscles, briefly
51. Winter hrs. in the Rockies

Solution on page 338

Puzzle 114

Across

1. Clumsy one
4. "___ Good Men"
8. Boost
12. EMS procedure
13. Get going
14. "Lucky Jim" author Kingsley
15. Was on the brink
17. Fancy fur
18. Type of number
19. Abhor
20. Like some martinis
21. Rebuke
23. On a liner
26. Palmer of baseball
27. Buddy
28. Many August births
29. Yak
30. Bone parallel to the radius
31. Kilmer of "The Doors"
32. Kids' card game
33. Fuss over one's feathers
34. Lacking ethics
36. Glutton
37. Demeanor
38. Pinkish hue
42. Fastener
43. Popular fund-raiser
44. Klemperer
45. Cote d'___
46. Not a lot
47. Student's hurdle
48. Skirt bottoms
49. Household sets

Down

1. Eight: Prefix
2. Takeoff specialist
3. Astaire
4. Supreme Egyptian god
5. Quick raid
6. Stunt biker Knievel
7. Marry
8. University in Beaumont, Tex.
9. Worthy of copying
10. Tweak
11. Sound of disappointment
16. Ebb and neap
19. Sewn edge
21. Lobster eater's need
22. Abba of Israel
23. Menlo Park middle name
24. One on the same side
25. Featured players
26. Place for pennies
29. Sal of song
30. Lobbies for
32. Pallid
33. Tough questions
35. Transfer, as a houseplant
36. Balderdash
38. Completely demolish
39. Huck's craft
40. Height: Abbr.
41. Morning moistures
42. Trendy
43. Scrooge exclamation

Solution on page 339

Puzzle 115

Across

1. Exercise system from India
5. Use a keyboard
9. Three-way circuit
12. Midterm or final
13. Bar brew
14. Suffix with solo
15. Showy display
16. Big name in fairy tales
18. Bumbles
20. "Lost Horizon" director Frank
21. Snake charmers' snakes
24. Bouquet-delivering org.
25. On ___-to-know basis
26. Stumble
30. Watch pocket
31. Sly one
32. E. Lansing campus
33. Built
36. Narrow valleys
38. Use an oar
39. Queens of France
40. More timid
43. Tiresome one
44. Decisive downfall
46. Tip, as one's hat
50. Suffix with lion
51. "Terrible" czar
52. Kite stablizer
53. Jungle ___
54. Extreme
55. Gumbo goodie

Down

1. Cowboy's assent
2. Nonwinning tic-tac-toe line
3. Leg, slangily
4. Electrical unit
5. Skiers' lifts
6. Yearnings
7. ___ XING (road sign)
8. Raises
9. Trace of smoke
10. River of Belgium
11. Italian volcano
17. X-ray units
19. "Groovy!"
21. Eatery
22. ___ about: roughly
23. Neuwirth of "Cheers"
24. Pickle
26. Like bell-bottoms
27. Certain government agents
28. Feudal laborer
29. "___ in Boots"
31. Not very many
34. Alberta native
35. Oppressively hot
36. From Frankfurt: Abbr.
37. Deceived
39. ABC executive Arledge
40. Gulp from a flask
41. Vague, as a recollection
42. Agenda particular
43. Guy in a sty
45. 56, to Flavius
47. Sturdy tree
48. Pine family tree
49. Orlando's state: Abbr.

Solution on page 339

Puzzle 116

Across

1. Meatloaf serving
5. Mother ptarmigan
8. Chest protector
11. Muscle quality
12. Tender
13. Top fighter pilot
14. Fine or liberal follower
15. Saline drop
16. Sunburned
17. Wobble
19. Accentuate
21. "Thy Neighbor's Wife" author Gay
23. Jungle danger
26. Gobbled up
27. Vamp Theda
31. Swiss range
33. Additionally
35. Luge, for one
36. Head of France
37. 4:00 gathering
39. GI's address
40. Singer John et al.
43. Karate teacher
46. Give a pounding
51. Hasten
52. Henry VIII's second or fourth
54. Supermodel Macpherson
55. Govt. 1040 auditor
56. Urgent want
57. College official
58. Caress
59. Got the picture
60. Gets firm

Down

1. "Immediately," in the O.R.
2. Handed-down stories
3. The "A" in A.M.
4. Numero uno
5. Weeder's tool
6. Rub out with rubber
7. "The heck with it!"
8. One in a million
9. Mouth-cooling treats
10. Resting places
12. Shale features
18. Airport abbreviation
20. Confederate soldiers
22. Slowly, in music
23. Winged mammal
24. Response to a cape flourish
25. Suitable
28. Chicken-king connection
29. Account exec
30. Fuss and feathers
32. Meets, as a bet
34. Damaged, as a fender
38. Campfire leftover
41. Shows partiality
42. Ringworm
43. Use FedEx, say
44. Enya's homeland
45. Robin's domain
47. Wine-list choices
48. Skipper's direction
49. Part of a venetian blind
50. Farm females
53. Just hired

Solution on page 339

Puzzle 117

Across

1. Places for plaques
6. 1980's White House nickname
9. Meandering road shape
12. ___ a time (individually)
13. Before, to a bard
14. "NOW I get it!"
15. Nary a person
16. Actress Ruby
17. Wilt
18. Corn pieces
20. Horne or Olin
21. Ice skater Midori
24. Fade away
25. Hay bundles
26. Dapper fellow?
27. Hombres' homes
29. All wound up
32. Westerns
36. Burr or Copland
38. More than stretch the truth
39. Land maps
42. Little bite
44. Paramount workplace
45. The best
46. General Motors subsidiary
48. Morning riser
49. Pub draft
51. Flows slowly
55. Deadlock
56. Thus far
57. Casual good-byes
58. Suffix with Taiwan
59. UFO passengers
60. In regard to

Down

1. Took the gold
2. "That's ___-brainer"
3. Author Buscaglia
4. Lois of "The Daily Planet"
5. Word with home or bed
6. Exodus crossing
7. Assayer's material
8. Born, in the society pages
9. Painting holder
10. Alan Ladd Western
11. Epic stories
19. Potato press
20. Stay to the finish
21. Words that end bachelorhood
22. Beach acquisition
23. Early afternoon
25. Herd word
28. Actress Braga
30. Determine the age of
31. Petrol
33. Building extension
34. Copacabana city
35. Two of a kind
37. Beginnings
39. Adhesive substance
40. Chemist Pasteur
41. French year
43. Rice alternative
47. Lima or kidney
49. Vote in favor
50. Net-touching serve
52. French summer
53. Criticize
54. Former Atl. crosser

Solution on page 339

Puzzle 118

Across

1. Mid-11th-century date
4. "The Time Machine" leisure class
8. Noah's eldest
12. Wrigley's product
13. Wire thickness units
14. Gridiron kick
15. Slugger's stat.
16. Forest gaps
18. Hearing or sight
20. Farm animal
21. Comic strip scream
23. Puts on the market
27. Soothing application
30. Marshal Wyatt
33. Commercial suffix with Water
34. One of a Freudian trio
35. Ancient reptiles, for short
36. Bearded creature
37. Harbor craft
38. Grps.
39. Head-over-heels
40. President Rutherford B.
42. Software program, for short
44. Quantity of paper
47. Wheelchair-accessible routes
51. Lockheed Martin field
55. Scatter seed
56. Designer Saint Laurent
57. Conceited people have big ones
58. Fed. property manager
59. Campbell of "Scream"
60. Frees (of)
61. Your, of yore

Down

1. Dugout VIPs
2. Mechanic's grease job
3. Poker declaration
4. Banquet host
5. Capp's ___ Abner
6. Designer to Jackie
7. Aoki of the PGA
8. Malice
9. Attila the ___
10. Our lang.
11. Andes, e.g.: Abbr.
17. Carpentry tools
19. Religious sch.
22. Actor Dullea
24. Women's golf org.
25. Ding-a-___
26. Arctic bird
27. "Little Women" character
28. Water, in Madrid
29. Lethargic
31. "Hulk" director Lee
32. Civil-rights activist Parks
35. Medicinal measures
39. Transcript fig.
41. Having an irregular edge
43. Use a steam iron on
45. One who mimics
46. Travelers to Bethlehem
48. High-ranking NCO
49. Deluxe
50. Move in the breeze
51. "The Fountainhead" author Rand
52. December 24 or 31
53. Gun, as an engine
54. Massachusetts fish

Solution on page 339

Puzzle 119

Across

1. Parts of a play
5. Delta rival
8. Show-offish dance maneuver
11. Churn up
12. Poet's planet
13. Walk to and fro
14. ___ of ethics
15. Caustic substance
16. Shortly, to the Bard
17. Icy downpours
19. Cases for insurance detectives
21. King in a Steve Martin song
22. Some parents
23. Rubber ducky's spot
26. Mercury or Mars
28. Sticky substances
32. Commando attack
34. Vote of support
36. Oxford, e.g.
37. Pressed for
39. Wolf Blitzer's employer
41. "___ 'em, Fido!"
42. Scotsman's cap
44. Swe. neighbor
46. "For Your Eyes Only" singer Easton
49. Modifies
53. Places for pints
54. Catch in the act
56. Canaanite god
57. Latin I conjugation
58. Preceding night
59. Utah ski center
60. Finder of secrets
61. Penn. neighbor
62. Overflow (with)

Down

1. Lob trajectories
2. "Neato!"
3. Neap, e.g.
4. Falling ice pellets
5. "War and Peace" author
6. Like ironic humor
7. Nautical position
8. Soap star Linda
9. Bit of Windows dressing?
10. Ballpoints
13. Author John Dos ___
18. Yank
20. Dustcloth
23. Play about Capote
24. Nasser was its pres.
25. Popular
27. Yr.-end month
29. Sounds of surprise
30. Luau dish
31. Champagne designation
33. Opposite of adore
35. Poe's "___ Lee"
38. Vice president Quayle
40. Agree silently
43. Having hair like horses
45. Morocco's capital
46. Relaxing spots
47. Camel feature
48. Online auctioneer
50. Like some ales
51. Actress Sharon
52. Cutting criticism
55. Hail to Caesar

Solution on page 339

Puzzle 120

Across

1. Inc. in the U.K.
4. Emulate Salt-N-Pepa
7. Neighbor of Aus.
10. Femur, e.g.
12. Beethoven's "___ to Joy"
13. New Haven university
14. Tailor
16. Oscar winner Kazan
17. "Xanadu" grp.
18. Run in the wash
19. Mimicry
22. False god
24. Helen of Troy's mother
25. Horizontally
28. Go bankrupt
29. Bank pymt.
30. Pound sound
32. Made over
34. Make yawn
35. Printers' supplies
36. Allotted
37. Feeling of anxiety
40. "___ Darlin'" (jazz standard)
41. Singer Diamond
42. Hollywood hopefuls
47. "Canterbury" episode
48. "China Beach" setting
49. Anniversary unit
50. Sp. Mrs.
51. Pitcher part
52. Gloomy fellow

Down

1. Scala diva.
2. Part of a sock
3. Form of evidence, these days
4. Old newspaper section
5. Suffix with lime or lemon
6. ___ capita
7. Battering wind
8. Novelist Wiesel
9. Try for a part
11. Ireland's nickname
13. Coward
15. Foxy
18. Happy hour hangout
19. ET from Melmac
20. Alligator ___ (avocado)
21. Singer/actress Adams
22. Poisons
23. Do film work
26. Chimney deposit
27. Like poor losers
29. India ___
31. Served dinner to
33. Can. province
36. Former Russian space station
37. Aardvark food
38. Within reach
39. Desert "monster"
40. Item beside an easy chair
42. NBC weekend comedy
43. Mai ___ cocktail
44. Brain scan letters
45. Shape of St. Anthony's cross
46. Prom attendees: Abbr.

Solution on page 340

Puzzle 121

Across

1. Stately tree
4. George Bernard ___
8. Puts the kibosh on
12. Take legal action
13. Mexican sandwich
14. Female friend, in France
15. Assistance
16. "Not to mention . . ."
17. Coin with Lincoln's profile
18. Familiar with
20. Lawyer's load
21. Relaxing
24. Like highways
27. Put back in office
31. Deuce
32. Actress West
33. Peas holder
34. Dubbed anew
37. Louvers
39. Siren luring sailors to shipwreck
41. Item in the plus column
44. Writer Jong et al.
48. Bert who played a lion
49. Big Ben sound
51. Dickens protagonist
52. Gershwin's "___ Rhythm"
53. Not on time
54. Jack Horner's last words
55. Scatters seed
56. W.B.A. calls
57. Tax ID

Down

1. Genesis hunter
2. "The Bridge of San ___ Rey"
3. Ancient Iranian
4. Averred
5. Heavenly rings
6. Rm. coolers
7. Seek the affections of
8. Mrs. Bogart
9. Home of the Iowa State Cyclones
10. Workday start for many
11. Match units
19. Rap's Dr. ___
20. Billiard stick
22. Wall Street transaction
23. Agent's 15%, e.g.
24. P.O. box item
25. Leave dumbstruck
26. The "N" in NCO
28. Clean-air org.
29. Place for a nap
30. QB's scores
32. French sea
35. Gives a heads-up
36. Witty saying
37. Twilled fabrics
38. XXVI doubled
40. Slow, in music
41. Muhammad and others
42. Pudding starch
43. Broadway production
45. Tax experts: Abbr.
46. Points at the target
47. ___ the bottle
49. Sandwich order, briefly
50. Acorn bearer

Solution on page 340

Puzzle 122

Across

1. Ball
4. "60 Minutes" network
7. Sound of relief
11. Links numbers
13. ___ Grande
14. Where Japan is
15. Springsteen's "___ Fire"
16. 20's dispenser
17. PlayStation 2 maker
18. Letting up
20. Lamb's mom
22. Congregation leader
24. Tool for McGwire
27. Stengel of baseball
30. Unspecified one
31. Blanche in "The Golden Girls"
32. Clumsy one's remark
33. Commit perjury
34. Piece of glass
35. ___ roll (lucky)
36. Actor Kingsley
37. Uncles' mates
38. Ballpoint, e.g.
39. Really bothers
41. Maple syrup source
42. Some Russians
46. Gardner of mysteries
49. Proper
51. Jannings or Gilels
52. Cheer for your team
53. Egyptian serpent
54. Ready to harvest
55. Barbecue offerings
56. "Count me in!"
57. Compass pt.

Down

1. Andy Taylor's son
2. Hindu hero
3. Abbr. in many business names
4. Rugged rocks
5. Comedy routine
6. "___ to watch over me"
7. Enclosure to an ed.
8. Prefix with metrics
9. Beefeater product
10. Horse course
12. Takes potshots
19. Dissenting vote
21. Sardonic
23. Pollute
24. Healthful grain
25. First cousin's mom
26. Golf props
27. Chickens' home
28. Jim-dandy
29. Extend over
33. February 29
34. Miniature golf club
36. Arthur of "The Golden Girls"
37. Motorists' org.
40. Stair parts
41. Adjusts, as a clock
43. Author Martin
44. Tears apart
45. Gobs
46. Bo incorrect
47. "Vive le ___!"
48. Slow throw
50. Take habitually

Solution on page 340

Puzzle 123

Across

1. Supply weapons to
4. Artist Jean
7. Challenging
11. Encountered
12. Revivalists
14. Natural burn remedy
15. Bartender's requests, maybe
16. Buttermilk's rider
17. Not prerecorded
18. Follow, as advice
20. Took home after taxes
22. Red-wrapped cheeses
24. Poker-game starter
25. Singing Mama
26. Villain, at times
29. Away from home
30. Light bulb units
31. Tic ___ (mint)
33. Batter's success
35. Like a desert
36. They're split for soup
37. People
38. For mature audiences
41. Chums
42. Ancient Greek coin
43. Going ___ (fighting)
45. Elevator compartment
48. Pickle flavoring
49. "___ of your business!"
50. Before the present
51. Electrified swimmers
52. Senator Kennedy
53. Actor Beatty

Down

1. Friend in France
2. Stop signal
3. Peak north of Redding, Calif.
4. Peruvian heights
5. "___ my lips!"
6. Rep. or Sen.
7. Summer top
8. Came to earth
9. Travel randomly
10. Do-gooder's doing
13. Keystone Kops creator
19. Dash units
21. French seasons
22. System starter?
23. Paint amateurishly
24. Opposing group
26. Dry as a desert
27. Ancient Italian
28. Fence piece
30. Dandelion, for one
32. LPs' successors
34. Incantations
35. Time Warner merger partner
37. Filled up
38. Went by bus
39. Rose's Broadway beau
40. Bridge-crossing fee
41. Tree with cones
44. Youngster
46. Grow older
47. Fishing pole

Solution on page 340

Puzzle 124

Across

1. Banned pesticide
4. Well-suited
7. "Not guilty" is one
11. Piercing locale
12. Fall fruit
14. "WKRP" actress Anderson
15. Get ___ for effort
16. Wise person
17. Like peas in ___
18. Red-tag events
20. Magritte and Descartes
22. Profs' helpers
23. Spy
24. Got off a horse
26. "You've got mail" co.
27. "Sort of" suffix
30. Wks. and wks.
31. Bus. aides
33. Pop singer Peeples
34. Oft-stubbed digit
35. Live and ___ live
36. Quite a few
37. Cats and dogs
38. It's frozen in Frankfurt
39. Genealogy charts
41. Fee schedule
43. Castle fortification
44. MacGraw and Baba
46. Teachers' gp.
48. "Say Anything . . ." actress Skye
49. Dial ___
50. Caesar of comedy
51. Hgts.
52. '60s protest grp.
53. Letter after ar

Down

1. Narcs' org.
2. Rather and others
3. Dissertation
4. Altar sites
5. Like two ___ in a pod
6. "You're it!" game
7. 747, e.g.
8. Long, easy stride
9. Baseball Hall of Famer Slaughter
10. Grant-in-___
13. Transplant
19. Long, opposite
21. Building additions
23. Sail supports
24. Check fig.
25. British john
27. To some extent
28. Preacher's subject
29. Stable diet?
31. On the calmer side, at sea
32. Assaults
36. Sch. near Harvard
37. Rose and Fountain
38. Smooths the path
39. Saw or hammer
40. Emulate Dennis Miller
41. Fruit peel
42. Six, in Seville
43. Actress Farrow
46. ___ Angeles
47. Commercials, for example

Solution on page 340

Puzzle 125

Across

1. Annoying child
5. Solmization syllables
8. Adam and Eve locale
12. Speed competition
13. Ltr. holder
14. Richness
15. Class that's for the birds
16. Stage actress Caldwell
17. 1999 movie about a reality show
18. Morning haze
19. Ancient Cuzco resident
21. Betray boredom
24. Comics kid
28. Slip-on shoe, briefly
31. Small bed
32. High shoes
33. "One ___ Jump"
35. Attic
36. City in northern Japan
37. Good friend
38. L-P connection
39. Spanish appetizers
40. "Born Free" lioness
42. Gull-like bird
44. Cut out, as coupons
48. Jupiter's wife
51. Some market moves
53. Chanel of fashion
54. Petri-dish stuff
55. Cartographer's product
56. 1982 Disney film starring Jeff Bridges
57. Reporters' questions
58. Work at, as a trade
59. Does wrong

Down

1. "Dracula" author Stoker
2. Sitar master Shankar
3. Top cards
4. In a bad mood
5. Moroccan topper
6. Make sacred
7. Cinematographer Nykvist
8. Mrs. Roosevelt
9. Fizzling firecracker
10. Request to a switchboard oper.
11. Ariz. neighbor
20. Intrigues
22. Point a finger at
23. Chinese cooker
25. Cliff's pal on "Cheers"
26. Major Calif.-to-Fla. route
27. This, in Tijuana
28. No longer worth discussing
29. Eight: Prefix
30. Applaud
34. Public speakers
35. 128 oz.
37. Letter-writing friend
41. Bank holdings: Abbr.
43. Roast cut
45. Actress Loughlin
46. Computer screen symbol
47. Operatic Lily
48. Mandible
49. "That's horrid!"
50. Yea's opposite
52. James Bond, for one

Solution on page 340

Puzzle 126

Across

1. Merry old king
5. British big shot
8. Do slaloms
11. Kadett automaker
12. Irene of "Fame" fame
13. Iranian holy city
14. Pipe problem
15. Opposed to, in the backwoods
16. G-man's employer
17. Like llamas
19. Defeated
21. Metamorphic rock
23. Hanes competitor
26. Cowboy singer Ritter
27. Attention-getters
31. "Just the Two ___"
33. Big ___, California
35. Epic story
36. Blue Triangle org.
37. Cotillion girl
39. Stir
40. Adjusts, as a clock
43. African expedition
46. Calif. barrio locale
51. Opposite of vert.
52. Altar vows
54. Awkward person
55. Eisenhower nickname
56. Blood blockage
57. Sacramento arena
58. Kid-___ (children's shows)
59. Half a devious laugh
60. Traveling type

Down

1. Carbonated drink
2. Unseal
3. Be in front
4. Golden Globe winner Sommer
5. Remind too often
6. Small antelope
7. Afflictions
8. Floor space meas.
9. City near Osaka
10. "You can't bluff me out!"
12. Film festival site
18. G-man: Abbr.
20. African snakes
22. Give forth
23. Lad
24. Ex-G.I.'s grp.
25. French nobleman
28. TV reporter Donaldson
29. ___ Friday's: restaurant chain
30. "Wailing" instrument
32. ___ Lee (cake company)
34. Give a makeup to
38. Jamboree grp.
41. Novelist Segal
42. Walk laterally
43. Gangster's blade
44. Golfer Isao ___
45. A Flintstone
47. Smelter residue
48. Bullfight bull
49. "Time" founder Henry
50. Comment ending
53. Amazed exclamation

Puzzle 127

Across

1. Hole puncher
4. Bottle cover
7. Border
11. T'ai ___
12. Wild way to run?
14. Tied, as a score
15. Headlight setting
16. Bygone cinema bonuses
18. Blockhead
20. Tiny bit
21. Not to mention
22. Exact retribution for
26. Maxims
29. Phone button
30. Exuberance
31. Quadri- minus one
32. Seas
36. Wanders off
39. Iced drink brand
40. Cloak-and-dagger org.
41. Part of M.Y.O.B.
42. Plant pests
46. Racer's edge
50. "___ to worry"
51. Hungry for more
52. River to the Ligurian Sea
53. Ostrich's kin
54. Makes a getaway
55. Honorarium
56. Last letter in London

Down

1. "Dirty Deeds Done Dirt Cheap" band
2. Sound like a fan
3. Lemon go-with
4. Type of tooth
5. Changes
6. Wham!
7. Sowed
8. "Now ___ seen everything!"
9. N.J. neighbor
10. Coast Guard rank: Abbr.
13. Relatively cool sun
17. Thumbs-up, and then some
19. Place for a price
23. Naldi of silents
24. Actor Cooper
25. Connecticut Ivy Leaguers
26. Bard of ___
27. Vegas cubes
28. Iowa State city
33. In disagreement
34. Fresh information
35. North Pole resident
36. Card game expert John
37. Be stealthy
38. Stadium cheer
43. "Il Trovatore" soprano
44. Bowl-shaped roof
45. Small earring
46. Actor Holbrook
47. A Gabor
48. "Ready" follower
49. Sandy's bark

Solution on page 341

Puzzle 128

Across

1. Mythical monsters
5. Rowboat needs
9. Mini-glob
12. Caron title role
13. Diamond imperfection
14. Id's counterpart
15. Glum
16. "Look what I did!"
17. Meadow
18. Control the wheel
20. Sugar sources
22. "My kingdom for ___!"
24. Part of a baseball uniform
27. "___the season . . ."
28. Eschew
32. "The magic word"
34. Like some angles
36. Sluggers' stats
37. Distant
38. Stranded motorist's need
39. Golf shot
42. Highest-ranking
44. Files
49. Reclined
50. "Voice of Israel" author Abba
52. Theda of silent films
53. Barely manage, with "out"
54. Type of disco dancer
55. Backup cause
56. Put down; in the 'hood
57. One-dish meal
58. Uses needle and thread

Down

1. Early automaker
2. Urban disturbance
3. Whodunit board game
4. Filly's father
5. Frequently, to Keats
6. Cottonwoods
7. Airplane tracker
8. Makes a trade
9. Strike from a manuscript
10. Stone and Iron
11. Feathery scarf
19. Charlie Brown exclamation
21. "___ we forget"
23. Make haste
24. Class for EMTs
25. Church vestment
26. Mile High Center architect
29. Simple shelter
30. "For the Boys" grp.
31. Like a crescent moon
33. Part of NCAA
34. Furniture wood
35. Title for a rabbit
37. Search for food
40. Supermodel Cheryl
41. Mechanical man
42. Pseudonym of H. H. Munro
43. Potato features
45. Kindergarten learning
46. Bargain hunter's delight
47. Ship's front
48. Loses tension
49. Took the reins
51. This instant

Solution on page 341

Puzzle 129

Across

1. Slight downturn
4. Dell products
7. Jazz variation
12. Fertility clinic stock
13. "Now I see!"
14. Actress Palmer
15. Tranquilized
17. Not from Earth
18. Victory
19. Transplant, as a plant
20. Valuable fur
23. "Gosh!"
24. King Kong, for example
25. Lymph ___
28. Fictional sleuth Wolfe
32. Tierra ___ Fuego
33. Albacore and
    yellowfin
35. "I do," for one
36. Eden resident
38. Quite uncommon
39. Countless years
40. Satisfied sighs
42. Checks for fingerprints
44. Houston baseballer
47. Dory need
48. Ring-shaped coral reef
49. Gone forever
53. Catherine's "Chicago"
    costar
54. Just-passing grade
55. Words of understanding
56. Was nosy
57. Light switch positions
58. Have some tea

Down

1. Hairstyles
2. "___ Got You Under My
   Skin"
3. Pen partner
4. Like Job
5. Joan of "Twin Peaks"
6. Despondent
7. Be loud, as a radio
8. Oscar-winner Heckart
9. Radar screen spot
10. Skillet lubricant
11. Pub portion
16. Leatherworking tool
20. Thompson of "Pollock"
21. Mimicked
22. Lugosi of horror films
23. Camping stuff
26. Not theirs
27. Genetic code letters
29. December 24 and 31
30. ___ canal
31. Holds the title to
34. Calms
37. Oscar-winner Matlin
41. Sank, as a putt
43. Alleged psychic Geller
44. Seniors' grp.
45. Suffix with hip or quip
46. Tennille or Morrison
47. Yoked animals
49. Former name of
    Tokyo
50. Tel. book contents
51. The Bears, on
    scoreboards
52. Cookbook meas.

Solution on page 341

Puzzle 130

Across

1. Candy shapes
5. Polish, as shoes
9. Papa
12. Spanish water
13. Singer Guthrie
14. Electronics brand
15. Yuletide song
16. Foundry refuse
17. Ultimate in degree
18. Stores, as grain
20. Bucks' mates
21. Rorom or Boatty
22. The Beatles' "___ Love You"
24. Casts a ballot
27. Rehab treatment
31. Mrs. Peron
32. Step in a flight
34. Inc., in London
35. Striking scene
37. Out of proper order
39. Gender
40. Bean counter, for short
41. Dressed
44. Loses it
48. One of Lee's men
49. Newspaper's ___ page
51. "I've Got ___ in Kalamazoo"
52. ___ Aviv, Israel
53. Spade, to Bogart
54. Umlaut elements
55. Cloud locale
56. Retrieves
57. Ottoman title

Down

1. Source of ruin
2. Literary conflict
3. Regrets
4. Like seawater
5. Situated
6. Web addresses
7. Neighbor of Ga.
8. Visibility problem
9. James Bond adversary
10. Entr'___ (theater break)
11. Morse code dashes
19. Apartment dweller
20. S, E, or SE
22. Upsilon's successor
23. Mexican shawl
24. Nov. 11 honoree
25. Eggs, to Caesar
26. Treater's pickup
27. Greek consonant
28. Boxer nicknamed "The Greatest"
29. Quart divs.
30. NFL advances
33. Payroll deduction
36. Timothy Leary's turn-on
38. Dead Sea fortress
40. Ciphers
41. PC screens
42. Onion's cousin
43. In a competent manner
44. Moola
45. Entranced
46. Hiker's trail
47. Famous lioness
49. Common URL ending
50. "The Raven" poet

Solution on page 341

Puzzle 131

Across

1. Princess' dad
5. Charlie Rose's network
8. Dermatologist's concern
12. "An apple ___ . . ."
13. Kennel cry
14. "The ___'Clock News"
15. In general
17. Give a longing look
18. Aunt or uncle: Abbr.
19. "___ Dream" ("Lohengrin" aria)
20. Allow in
24. Season to be jolly
26. Sonnets and such
27. Edit
30. ___ Rabbit (Harris character)
31. Wray of "King Kong"
32. Chesapeake bay?
34. Like a cloudless night
36. Bearlike mammal
37. Org. overseeing fairness in hiring
38. Boxer Mike
39. Where hair roots grow
42. Peruvian singer Sumac
44. Actress Singer of "Footloose"
45. High military muck-a-muck
50. Fake: Abbr.
51. Tampa Bay NFLer
52. Nutmeg St.
53. Stag or stallion
54. Command in a library
55. Hall of Fame pitcher Wilhelm

Down

1. Okla. neighbor
2. Chapel words
3. Not wide: Abbr.
4. Sock hop locale
5. "Gomer ___, U.S.M.C."
6. "Achy Breaky Heart" singer
7. Snoop (on)
8. Sneaked off
9. Frat party containers
10. "To Live and Die ___" ('85 film)
11. Thumbs-down votes
16. Pretentiously showy
19. Antiquity, formerly
20. Police dept. alert
21. British bombshell Diana
22. Make the acquaintance of
23. Exodus participant
25. Auto reversal, slangily
28. Pros and ___
29. Big fuss
31. To's counterpart
33. Ceiling appliance
35. Agent: Abbr.
36. School grps.
39. Thin
40. Robin Cook bestseller
41. Seed protector
43. Speed-of-sound number
45. Kids' ammo
46. Educ. institution
47. "Yoo-___!"
48. "___ port in a storm"
49. Explosive ltrs.

Solution on page 341

Puzzle 132

Across

1. Ante matter
4. Fence stake
8. Hurry
11. From the U.S.: Abbr.
13. Wild animal's home
14. Pilot's prediction, for short
15. Resting place
16. Mount in Sicily
17. Good name for a cook
18. Revered Mother
20. Binges
22. Removes
23. Look without blinking
24. Fast flyer
25. Grooves in the road
28. Lanchester of film
29. Ram of the zodiac
31. Exhausted
35. "___ on Down the Road"
36. Conscription agcy.
39. Facilitates
41. Upholstered piece
43. Appearance
45. Nonreactive gases
46. Cause for overtime
47. Nautical prefix?
49. Actor Damon
50. Deighton or Dawson
51. Having little fat
52. Mound
53. Triage sites, briefly
54. Summer drinks
55. Gross minus taxes

Down

1. Moistens, as meat
2. Arab rulers
3. Try to rip open
4. Delight
5. Horse's tidbit
6. Transgresses
7. Golf hazards
8. Close up again
9. Puts into words
10. Queasy feeling
12. AAA recommendations
19. Infection fighters
21. A.A.A. suggestion: Abbr.
26. Acapulco aunt
27. Congressional periods
30. Visualized
31. Paul or Ringo
32. Less difficult
33. Fluttering trees
34. Pigskin's perch
36. Exertion
37. Avoid a trial
38. Group of six
40. La ___ (Milan opera house)
42. Office sub
44. Readied a golf ball
48. "Norma ___" (Sally Field film)

Solution on page 342

Puzzle 133

Across

1. "Wheel" buy
4. Unusually smart
7. Holy ones: Abbr.
10. Cabbage Patch Kid, e.g.
12. Sign before Virgo
13. Party game pin-on
14. Court game
16. Like some shoppes
17. Cauldron
18. Spirited mount
19. Valuable thing
22. Ayatollah preceder
24. True
25. Flip chart holders
28. Parakeet's home
29. Billboard displays
30. Tardy
32. Annoy
34. periods of history
35. Arena level
36. Actors' surface
37. "Annie Hall" director
40. Curiosity victim
41. Pinocchio, at times
42. Intended for a select few
47. Some donations
48. Golf goal
49. Deception
50. Bawl
51. Fill with wonder
52. Milne marsupial

Down

1. Toil and trouble
2. ___ sequitur
3. Land in the Seine
4. Thanks ___
5. Enclosure
6. Stubbed thing
7. Shopper's lure
8. It ebbs and flows
9. Snow transport
11. Billets-doux
13. Precisely
15. ___ King Cole
18. Scandinavian airline
19. Rainbow's shape
20. Predecessor of Roger and Pierce
21. Wise man
22. Passover event
23. Possesses
26. Croft of video games
27. Party for men
29. Darker-than-beer brew
31. Suffix with Japan or Sudan
33. Malleable metal
36. Settled on the sofa
37. "Sorry to say"
38. "___ & Stitch"
39. Ewe's offspring
40. Apple throwaway
42. Clean air grp.
43. Carpenter's cutter
44. Play about robots
45. Equal: Prefix
46. Corp. bigwig

Solution on page 342

Puzzle 134

Across

1. ___ Bones (Ichabod Crane's rival)
5. J. Edgar Hoover's org.
8. ___ Romeo (imported auto)
12. Lubricates
13. Gridiron official, for short
14. Corporate heads: Abbr.
15. Paints like Pollock
17. French peak
18. Cleveland hoopster, for short
19. Beer barrel
20. Fronton basket
21. Bullfighters
23. Eight, in Spain
26. Fall mo.
27. Toupee
30. Catherine of ___
33. Shakespearean "Get lost"
35. Busy co. on Valentine's Day
36. By way of
38. Plastic building block
39. Italian port
42. Rug fiber
45. Sailor
46. Corp. bigwigs
49. Egyptian fertility goddess
50. Response
52. Short-lived fashions
53. Evil
54. "Whatever ___ Wants" ("Damn Yankees" tune)
55. Good lowball card
56. Election winners
57. Remove, as a coupon

Down

1. Popular pear
2. Kelly of morning TV
3. King of Norway
4. Denver clock setting: Abbr.
5. Less restrained
6. Norwegian port
7. Qualifiers
8. Crowning points
9. Most August births
10. Style of type
11. Dashiell Hammett dog
16. Bout outcome, in brief
20. Yacht haven
21. ___ up (dress finely)
22. Steal
23. Clumsy sort
24. PC hookup
25. Was ill with
27. Tale of ___
28. Gerund suffix
29. Former Prizm automaker
31. Shape of the president's office
32. Nothing at all
34. Mop & ___ (floor cleaner)
37. Cyclades' sea
39. Fresh-mouthed
40. Freeways
41. Brokaw's network
42. Prepare flour
43. River to the Danube
44. Pro or con, in a debate
46. Bowed instrument
47. ___ sci (coll. major)
48. Brittle cookie
50. Clean-up hitter's stat
51. Pampering, for short

Solution on page 342

Puzzle 135

Across

1. Fad disk
4. D-H connection
7. Poetic saga
11. The Cubs, on scoreboards
12. Soaks hemp
14. Aviation word starter
15. Most overbearing
17. Meat and vegetable dish
18. Loki's daughter
19. Points the finger at
21. Locations
24. Code carrier
25. Southwest art center
26. Hits the roof
29. Boxing match div.
30. ___-wreck
31. Dignitary, for short
33. Takes for granted
35. Kingsley et al.
36. Japanese sashes
37. Stops for a breath
38. Mariners
41. Hammarskjold of the UN
42. "___ delighted!"
43. 1949 Tracy/Hepburn classic
48. ___-do-well
49. Catch, as calves
50. "It ___" ("Who's there?" reply)
51. Calls it a day
52. AOL alternative
53. Rank below Sgt.

Down

1. Chem. contaminant
2. Taunting shout
3. U.S. soldiers
4. Some native New Yorkers
5. Grope
6. Some sports cars
7. Spring holy day
8. Domesticated animals
9. Bestselling cookie
10. Scattered
13. Thoroughfares
16. "___ a Lady" (Tom Jones tune)
20. Anatomical loop
21. Narrow waterway: Abbr.
22. Ending for Louis
23. Bushy clumps
24. Heredity carriers
26. Study group
27. Nights before holidays
28. By ___ of: due to
30. Unsophisticated sort
32. Letter addenda: Abbr.
34. Suzanne of "Three's Company"
35. Pleads
37. Nagano noodles
38. Trig term
39. Adam and Eve home
40. Under the covers
41. Drops bait
44. Comic DeLuise
45. Rock's Ocasek
46. AOL, e.g.: Abbr.
47. Puppeteer Baird

Solution on page 342

Puzzle 136

Across

1. Was introduced to
4. ___ and cons
8. It may be certified
12. Give it a shot
13. Songstress Horne
14. Verdi work
15. Big shot
16. Excellent server
17. Furrowed part of the head
18. Penn of "I Am Sam"
20. Flank
22. Communications conglomerate
24. One-named Tejano singer
28. Participatory
32. Killed, as a dragon
33. Injury soother
34. Wane's partner
36. Larry King's TV home
37. Court case
40. Instructs
43. Smell and taste
45. Chip go-with
46. Riverbed deposit
48. Male sheep
51. Like a ___ in the woods
54. Calla lily, e.g.
56. Burger roll
58. Hertz rival
59. Not yours
60. Muhammad ___
61. Chatters
62. Shortly
63. Have a late meal

Down

1. Cable rock station
2. Goddess of discord
3. Category
4. Gardener's charges
5. Answering machine button
6. Billfold stuffers
7. Hindu garments
8. Old phone company nickname
9. What you breathe
10. Altar avowal
11. Order's partner
19. Helping hand
21. ___ Moines
23. Haul a trailer
25. Per person
26. Cloud number
27. Miller and Sothern
28. Top 40 songs
29. Farm fraction
30. No in Nuremberg
31. Rebel Turner
35. Struck (out)
38. Review
39. Hawaiian necklace
41. Military pilots
42. P. & L. preparer
44. Shuts with a bang
47. Group of three
49. Corp. execs' degrees
50. "Star Trek" officer
51. Suitcase
52. Gardner of "On the Beach"
53. It's usually served with lobster
55. Lively card game
57. Tiny bite

Solution on page 342

Puzzle 137

Across

1. Was in session
4. Aspen equipment
8. "Thirty days ___
   September . . ."
12. Gorilla
13. The Emerald Isle
14. Not aweather
15. Football's Dawson
16. Sax man Getz
17. Sly Foxx
18. Fancy digs
20. Flippant
21. Scolds
24. Beauty's beloved
27. Oven pan
31. Donkey's cousin
32. Allow
33. Oils and watercolors
34. Iran's capital
37. Drunkard
39. Say another way
41. Concerning Benedict
   XVI
44. "The Far Side" cartoonist
   Gary
48. "Too bad!"
49. Keep ___: persist
51. Soissons summer
52. Got threadbare
53. IX
54. Heavy weight
55. Bridge defeats
56. Heroic exploit
57. Bray beginning

Down

1. Bargain event
2. "Planet of the ___"
3. Jamboree shelter
4. Six-line poem
5. Check falsifier
6. Lyricist Gershwin
7. Capitol Hill VIP
8. Bother continually
9. Malt beverages
10. Danson and Kennedy
11. Lamarr of Hollywood
19. Tummy muscles
20. Ross or Bering
22. "___ You Glad You're
   You": Crosby song
23. Moppet
24. Sosa's stick
25. Opposite WNW
26. Volcanic coating
28. Symbol for torque
29. Hesitant sounds
30. Map abbreviation
32. Carol syllables
35. Obliterates
36. Seminary subj.
37. Said
38. "___ the ramparts we
   watched . . ."
40. Draw ___ in the sand
41. Furry feet
42. Emollient ingredient
43. Parcel's partner
45. Adam's third son
46. Nebraska tribesman
47. State bird of Hawaii
49. "So . . . ?"
50. Suit accessory

Solution on page 342

Puzzle 138

Across

1. "Quiet, please!"
4. President after HST
7. Sills song
11. Evian or Perrier
12. Infuriates
14. Air-condition
15. N.Y.C.'s ___ of the Americas
16. Nair rival
17. Perth pal
18. Interlocks
20. Sports venues
22. Bradley and Sullivan
23. Fuel at the pump
24. Intimidates
27. Wimbledon segment
28. Motorist's org.
31. Word before code or rug
32. Ship's plea
33. Planets, to poets
34. "___ so fast!"
35. Mason's field
36. Yearn for
37. Bro's kin
38. Lunched, e.g.
40. Has a bite of
43. Company avoiders
47. Dublin's home
48. Spew
50. Black or Red
51. Jocular Johnson
52. German's neighbor
53. Pekoe, for one
54. Arctic barker
55. Years in a decade
56. Altar garb

Down

1. Sewing line
2. Contain
3. Colors
4. Ate fancily
5. Frock or gown
6. Extra-wide, at the shoe store
7. Summits
8. Mottled horse
9. Greek "I"
10. Quaffs at dart tournaments
13. Old Wells Fargo vehicles
19. "For ___ jolly . . ."
21. Hamelin pest
24. Soup container
25. ___ y plata
26. Moisten
27. Miss Piggy, e.g.
28. Jackie's second spouse
29. Stomach muscles, for short
30. Pompous type
32. Gave lip to
33. The groundhog seeing its shadow, say
35. Untruth
37. "Stainless" metal
38. Skirt type
39. On a scale of one ___
40. Herbal brews
41. Billion follower
42. Miss, in Mex.
44. Spaniard's "this"
45. Fishing-line holder
46. Swedish auto
49. Gym pad

Solution on page 343

Puzzle 139

Across

1. Org. for Annika Sorenstam
5. Classic Ford
8. Halt
12. Rowboat equipment
13. Biblical affirmative
14. Recommend
15. Seller's caveat
16. Nightmare street of film
17. Late civil rights activist Parks
18. Grandparent, perhaps
20. Finds
22. Unused
24. Zany sort
25. Kodak founder
29. "Amazing" magician
33. Couple
34. Beaver's creation
36. Currency in Kobe
37. Wrinkly fruits
40. Hand warmers
43. ___ Jones
45. Unedited
46. Saved
50. Coke rival
54. Whale of a movie
55. Comic's scream
57. Classic autos
58. Bygone Russian despot
59. Letter after chi
60. Llama's land
61. Buffalo bunch
62. TV news hour
63. Staircase part

Down

1. Put ammo in
2. El___, Tex.
3. "True ___" (Wayne film)
4. Say yes
5. Caustic chemical
6. Swiss archer
7. Pal of Pythias
8. Geologic layers
9. Traffic sound
10. Any of three English rivers
11. Sch. orgs.
19. Dreamy acronym
21. Junkyard dog
23. Gum glob
25. College web address ending
26. Mo. without a holiday
27. Spain's Costa del ___
28. '60s war zone, for short
30. Carrie of "Creepshow"
31. Scout unit
32. Elected ones
35. Former Russian orbiter
38. Security checkpoint item
39. Old French coin
41. Faucet
42. Pipsqueaks
44. Sobs
46. Writer Philip
47. Celtic dialect
48. Sign of an old injury
49. Bandleader Arnaz
51. Amanda of "The Whole Nine Yards"
52. Holding a grudge
53. "The jig ___!"
56. Spherical cereal

Solution on page 343

Puzzle 140

Across

1. She married Mickey, Artie, and Frank
4. "What's ___ for me?"
8. Male sheep
11. "Sticks and Bones" playwright
13. Venus de___
14. Words before sec or jiffy
15. "This must weigh ___!"
16. Tennis serving whiz
17. "___ on your life!"
18. Sweater style
20. Gives an autograph
22. Fight grime
24. "Aeneid" queen
26. Laugh syllable
27. Hot dog server
29. Abel's father
32. Palindromic "before"
33. Shuts with force
35. Stevedores' org.
36. Paper repairer
38. Deep ___ bend
39. Neither's counterpart
40. Leveled, in Leeds
42. "Shucks!"
44. Actor George C.
46. Outmoded
48. Stephen of "The Crying Game"
49. Seed case
51. Barbecue favorites
54. Gumshoe
55. Put the finger on
56. Hall of Famer Slaughter
57. Wood stove residue
58. Poor grades
59. Fam. doctors

Down

1. Palindromic constellation
2. Brewery tank
3. Unassailable
4. Un-PC computer?
5. Trivial
6. Spot in the mer
7. Upper bodies
8. 1961 Sinatra album
9. Author unknown: Abbr.
10. Wrestling surfaces
12. Sicilian resort
19. Pass receivers
21. "This ___ test . . ."
22. Newscaster Huntley
23. "Doctor Zhivago" heroine
25. Citrus fruit
28. Sommer of films
30. Skin-lotion additive
31. Stallion's mate
34. Chair part
37. Gobble up
41. Rise from a chair
43. "While You ___ Sleeping"
44. Young lady of Sp.
45. Middling grades
47. British brews
50. "Norma___"
52. Hit on the head
53. Snaky sound

Solution on page 343

Puzzle 141

Across

1. In the ___ of luxury
4. Angel dust, for short
7. Liver secretion
11. Dockers' org.
12. Boat paddles
14. Give ___ (care)
15. Tape speed abbr.
16. Per item
17. Hebrew letter
18. Hollandaise, e.g.
20. Clarinet parts
22. Morse code sound
23. Rolodex nos.
24. Life-or-death matter: Abbr.
26. Lamb's dad
27. Actor Thinnes
30. Not pro
31. Hotel employees
33. Scratch (out), as a living
34. College transcript no.
35. Corporation abbr.
36. Pedro's house
37. Clearasil's target
38. Coupe or convertible
39. French avenue
41. Home Depot competitor
43. Ink problem
44. Ancient Greek contest
46. Queue before Q
48. The gray wolf
49. The ___ Ranger (Tonto's pal)
50. 551, to Caesar
51. Mon. follower
52. Accomplished
53. ___'wester

Down

1. 52, in old Rome
2. European mountains
3. Rose Bowl site
4. Prepare an egg
5. ___ Canaveral
6. Tennis instructor
7. Uncovers
8. Really steamed
9. Highlands girl
10. Book between Gal. and Phil.
13. Bed cover
19. Former Mideast alliance: Abbr.
21. Shady giants
23. Brief moment
24. Heart printout, for short
25. Floor-washing implement
27. Hits from behind
28. Gives a thumbs-up
29. Senatorial affirmative
31. Cheese nibblers
32. Temper, as steel
36. Crow sound
37. Low voices
38. Funnel-shaped
39. Major League brothers' name
40. Earring's place
41. "WKRP in Cincinnati" actress Anderson
42. Song for one
43. Sandwich letters
45. The Almighty
47. More, in music

Solution on page 343

Puzzle 142

Across

1. In great shape
4. Surf and ___
8. Purchases
12. Perry Mason's field
13. Ostrichlike bird
14. Julia of "The Addams Family"
15. Ethan's costar in "Gattaca"
16. Like hand-me-downs
17. Like a night bird
18. Toward the right, on a map
20. New Jersey university
22. The Trojans of the N.C.A.A.
25. Be jubilant
29. Test subject
34. Bronx attraction
35. "Everybody Hates Chris" network
36. German wine valley
37. Post-op stop
38. Tut's relative?
39. On the way
41. Bird's name in "Peter and the Wolf"
43. Bach's Mass ___ Minor
44. Cry of concern
47. Scoundrels
51. Video-store rentals
54. Be an omen of
57. Belly
58. Jacket
59. I.O.U.
60. Effort
61. "Picnic" playwright
62. Frosh, next year
63. Clinton's instrument

Down

1. Chimney passage
2. "___ Rock": Simon and Garfunkel hit
3. "___ brillig and the slithy toves . . ."
4. Nickname for Capote
5. Sounds of hesitation
6. Really smell
7. Become dim
8. Big Apple borough
9. Motor City gp.
10. Brynner of "Westworld"
11. Subtle
19. Wine cask
21. Arm of the Mediterranean
23. Soap opera, for example
24. "All the Way" lyricist Sammy
26. Submachine guns
27. Mathematical points
28. Brag about
29. Courage, so to speak
30. "___-daisy!"
31. Fluids in wells
32. Cherry seed
33. Letters at Calvary
40. "The Office" network
42. Alacrity
45. Kindergarten basics
46. Big Apple gallery district
48. Ten percenters: Abbr.
49. ___ mater (brain cover)
50. River to the underworld
51. 601, to Caesar
52. German name starter
53. Statesman Hammarskjold
55. Short swim
56. Biblical verb suffix

Solution on page 343

Puzzle 143

Across

1. "___ no kick from Champagne"
5. Capitol Hill figure
8. Players in a play
12. $.37 for the first ounce, e.g.
13. Bi- halved
14. Pisa's river
15. Business letter abbr.
16. Pi-sigma go-between
17. Getz or Kenton of jazz
18. "All You ___ Is Love"
19. Received
20. Use a word processor
21. British sheepdog
24. "I've ___ Be Me"
27. Rather of CBS
28. Blubber
31. "Keep ___ head!"
32. With speed
34. Pigpen
35. TV hookup
38. Actor Lloyd ___
39. More calm
41. Have a long face
44. Versatile vehicle, for short
45. As a result
49. 1997 Peter Fonda role
50. Bill Clinton's instrument
51. Actor James ___ Jones
52. Spearhead
53. Morse Tony-winning role
54. Fashion pioneer Gernreich
55. Election defeat
56. Football distances: Abbr.
57. Squalid neighborhood

Down

1. Its capital is Teheran
2. Garden entrance
3. Kitchen suffix
4. Looks after
5. Political housecleaning
6. In phone limbo
7. Ray of "GoodFellas"
8. Kind of system
9. Pretentious, in a way
10. Break sharply
11. Inflection
22. Cut in two
23. Lacking any point
24. Pump product
25. Autumn mo.
26. Trifle
28. Iron man Ripken
29. ___ Victor
30. Japanese moolah
33. Baggage handlers
36. Like a baguette
37. Delay progress
39. Plant starters
40. Means of connection
41. Ponder
42. Bogus butter
43. Soup morsels
46. Carry by truck
47. Language of Pakistan
48. Svelte

Solution on page 343

Puzzle 144

Across

1. "___ was going to St. Ives . . ."
4. "Chicago Hope" network
7. Alan of "The West Wing"
11. Can material
12. ___ and aahs
14. Fly sky-high
15. Hectic hosp. areas
16. "Just the facts, ___"
17. Legal aide, briefly
18. Halt an assault
21. Periodontist's org.
22. Fanciful story
23. Presses for payment
25. Cardinal cap logo
26. Nightmare street
29. Env. stuffer
30. French seaport
32. Farrow of films
33. Quilting event
34. Seek office
35. Not at all spicy
36. Was on the ballot
37. Writer Fleming
38. Sensitive to criticism
43. Female deer
44. Sunbathers' goals
45. Teachers' org.
47. Concerning, to a lawyer
48. ___ upon a time
49. Auto part
50. Potato parts
51. Do lacework
52. Ems followers

Down

1. Had a meal
2. Dear follower
3. Example
4. Punctuation mark
5. Water craft
6. Deposed Iranian ruler
7. Easy ___ (simple)
8. Laundry batch
9. Take risks
10. Mr. Parseghian
13. Refines, as ore
19. Asner and Bradley
20. Pinball infraction
23. Society gal
24. French one
25. Six-yr. term holder
26. High repute
27. Small, in Dogpatch
28. Insane
30. Raisin ___ (cereal)
31. Seeks solace from
35. ___ Friday
36. Ascends
37. Corner map
38. Cereal box tiger
39. ___ and now
40. German philosopher Immanuel
41. Peruvian
42. Student overseer
43. Vegas cube
46. Mornings, for short

Solution on page 344

Puzzle 145

Across

1. WWII female
4. ". . .___ the cows come home"
7. G-man or T-man
10. Pierre's pals
12. Quoits target
13. Quicksand
14. Some recyclables
16. Prince Charles' sister
17. Milk source
18. War horse
19. Hall of Fame pitcher Warren
22. IOU
24. Keep ___ on (watch)
25. Coarse-toothed tool
28. 601, in old Rome
29. Kasparov's game
31. Shoot the breeze
33. Little laugh
35. Hair on a horse's neck
36. Pie pans
37. Female horses
38. Exams for attys.-to-be
41. Combine
42. Southwestern stewpot
43. Reed instrument
48. First claim, slangily
49. Sound of a punch
50. Papa's mate
51. The "I" in T.G.I.F.
52. Capek play about automatons
53. Derelict

Down

1. "What ___ I thinking?"
2. "I love," to Livy
3. Spanish hero
4. Defrost
5. It may have an extra electron
6. There are 2.2 in a kg.
7. Speeder's penalty
8. Sea eagle
9. Ownership document
11. Goldman's Wall Street partner
13. Damon and Lauer
15. Pull a scam
18. Drinks slowly
19. Part of PST: Abbr.
20. Negotiated agreement
21. His Rose was Irish
22. Canadian Indians
23. Not hers
26. Partially open
27. Grow faint
29. Greek X's
30. Barnyard clucker
32. Film director Craven
34. James and Kett
35. Proverb
37. Space station
38. New Jersey city
39. Narrow cut
40. Ecclesiastical vestments
41. Bryn ___, Pa.
43. Lifesaving technique: Abbr.
44. Singer Rawls or Reed
45. Seize
46. Flightless bird from Down Under
47. Scottish cap

Solution on page 344

Puzzle 146

Across

1. Speedometer abbr.
4. Eng. network
7. Nail
11. Protein source
12. The ___ McCoy
14. Strong rope
15. Title role for George Burns
16. Off from work
17. Dogmas
18. Not interfere with
20. Greetings at sea
22. Evergreen
23. Noise
24. Northern Scandinavians
27. Pal
28. N.Y.C. airport
31. Henri's thought
32. Thin out, as branches
33. Pato do ___ grao
34. Snoring sound
35. Half a bray
36. Did nothing
37. Crash sound
38. Christmas's mo.
39. Hold responsible
41. "And ___ grow on"
44. Grassy fields
45. Cpl. and sgt., e.g.
47. Pussycat's partner
49. Let it all out
50. Dial sound
51. Tiny bit, as of cream
52. Actress Swenson of "Benson"
53. Marked wrong
54. Hoopster Erving, familiarly

Down

1. Chinese food additive
2. Hustler's game
3. Fictional Mr.
4. Buys off
5. Make misty
6. Ripken of baseball
7. Grafting shoot
8. Flower in a pocketful?
9. Prepares for battle
10. Dentist's deg.
13. Precede, with "to"
19. Variety
21. Stayed out of sight
24. Actress Taylor
25. Wood-shaping tool
26. Dispenser candy
27. Theatrical finale
28. Write down quickly
29. Bit of baloney
30. Piano part
32. Bewail
33. Watch part
35. Amateur radioer
36. Had a feeling
37. "Enough!" to Enzo
38. Blackmore's "Lorna ___"
39. "___ there, done that"
40. Lana of Smallville
42. Mary ___ Lincoln
43. Man ___ (racehorse)
44. XIV x IV
46. Tricia Nixon's married name
48. Pres. with a ranch

Solution on page 344

Puzzle 147

Across

1. "It's c-c-cold!"
4. Ho Chi ___
8. Opposite of ecto-
12. Feel sorry about
13. Prefix with logical
14. "Oh, sure"
15. Kuwaiti export
16. Shrew
18. Trapper's trap
20. Remove from a manuscript
21. Legal wrong
23. Light refractor
27. Like many dorms
29. "Get out of ___!"
32. Old Olds
33. City reg.
34. Greek island
35. Sounds of meditation
36. Household animal
37. Chart toppers
38. Agitated mood
39. Skiing surface
41. Spanish half-dozen
43. Every's partner
46. Roasting rods
49. Comfort stations
53. Hoover ___
54. Armbone
55. Where the Mets played
56. Summer, in Strasbourg
57. Invoice
58. "O ___ Night"
59. Fix a seam

Down

1. Warner ___
2. Wrack's partner
3. Associated with
4. Cut at a 45-degree angle
5. Ox tail?
6. Bookworm, perhaps
7. "Fourth base"
8. "The ___ Sanction": Eastwood film
9. Lakers' org.
10. Cozy hideaway
11. Baseballer Mel
17. French peaks
19. Wand
22. Spicy Asian cuisine
24. Old ___: historic warship
25. Tractor-trailer
26. Maximum
27. Police
28. Baseball's Hershiser
30. Ambulance attendant: Abbr.
31. Flagmaker Betsy
34. Get wool from sheep
38. Not guzzle
40. Part of a flower
42. English-class assignment
44. Brit's blackjack
45. Syllables from Santa
47. Noted gallery
48. Eurasian duck
49. Chafe
50. Pharmaceutical giant ___ Lilly
51. Weekend TV program
52. Director Brooks

Solution on page 344

Puzzle 148

Across
1. Fruity desserts
5. Cable film channel
8. Old Iranian ruler
12. Long-division word
13. Sea, to Debussy
14. Actress Spelling
15. Onetime Yugoslav leader
16. Confusion
17. Korean soldiers
18. Takes the helm
20. Sports numbers
22. Word of assent
23. Wino
24. Divining device
27. Kitten call
29. Hardwood tree
33. German conjunction
34. ___ double take
36. Sept. follower
37. Schnozzes
40. Kind of humor
42. Byrnes of "77 Sunset Strip"
43. Summer coolers, briefly
45. Private eye, slangily
47. Nautical pole
49. Summer ermines
53. Goatee location
54. Turkish chief
56. Mailbox opening
57. All's opposite
58. 1960 chess champion Mikhail
59. "___ the mornin'!"
60. Must-have
61. It takes in the sights
62. "Watch your ___!"

Down
1. Racetrack stops
2. Monogram unit: Abbr.
3. Suffix for kitchen
4. Farm call
5. Piled up
6. Club ___ resort
7. Grumpy
8. Layers of rock
9. Owl's call
10. Clumsy boats
11. "___ Girl Friday"
19. Sleep phenomenon: Abbr.
21. Homeland Security director Ridge
24. Campaign (for)
25. Musical Yoko
26. Cavity filler: Abbr.
28. "I'm impressed!"
30. Edgar Allan ___
31. Watch display, for short
32. LAX monitor info
35. Gallery event
38. Was worthy of
39. Chem. or biol.
41. All the same
44. Maine or Montana
46. Prices
47. Mule or moccasin
48. Cone-bearing tree
50. Gazillions
51. Imbibe to excess
52. "Halt!"
53. Larry King employer
55. Like old Paree

Solution on page 344

Puzzle 149

Across

1. Persuade
5. Four-footed friend
8. Neck and neck
12. Do roadwork
13. Maui garland
14. Young Guthrie
15. Currier and ___
16. Chalet site
17. Endure
18. Orkin target
20. Hawaiian honkers
21. "___ Rae"
23. Raises
27. To the rear, at sea
32. Prepared for printing
34. Cheap cigar
35. "___ Mr. Nice Guy!"
36. Smell
37. Mall bags
40. Wears well
44. Poor movie rating
49. Norwegian capital
50. Niagara Falls' prov.
51. Retired Italian money
52. Genoa greeting
53. Part of MPH
54. Slaughter of baseball
55. Dove's opposite
56. Give it a whirl
57. Have an itch for

Down

1. Rotisserie part
2. Undulation
3. Say confidently
4. Polite backwoods affirmative
5. "The Republic" philosopher
6. Specialist in fishing
7. Word of advice
8. Tall story
9. Teheran's country
10. Other than
11. Connect the ___
19. Extra leaves
20. Ilie of tennis
22. Pas' partners
23. Lobster lady
24. Altar words
25. Actress Basinger
26. WWII arena: Abbr.
28. Rocky hilltop
29. "I" strain?
30. Outer edge
31. Educators' org.
33. ___ volente (God willing)
38. Laser printer powder
39. Sweepstakes submission
40. Scottish lake
41. Where China is
42. Shredded cabbage
43. Filched
45. Large quantity
46. Louise or Turner
47. Elvis follower
48. Part of R&R
50. Withdraw, with "out"

Solution on page 344

Puzzle 150

Across

1. Prickly seed case
4. Bigwig
7. Push-up lingerie item
10. Any doctrine
11. Willie of "Eight Is Enough"
13. Sinbad's bird
14. Ship-to-shore connection
16. Israel suffix
17. "It's ___ to tell a lie"
10. Medicinal plants
20. Rubbernecked
23. Prince Hirobumi
24. Hard to hang on to
25. Boxing venues
28. Mao ___-tung
29. Boot attachments
31. ___ Alamos, N.M.
33. Fish features
35. Some children
36. Porky or Babe
37. "The Prince and the ___"
39. One of the five senses
42. Riot queller
43. Cereal bristle
44. Infield position
49. 6 on a phone
50. "Soap" Family
51. Ump's call
52. Salt Lake City-to-Las Vegas dir.
53. Reverse of NNW
54. Zadora of "Butterfly"

Down

1. 1988 Hanks film
2. Stars and Stripes land
3. LBJ follower
4. Authenticated
5. David Bowie's wife
6. Writing instrument
7. Spirit
8. Fixed procedure
9. Fighter pilots
11. Vaulted church recess
12. Does figure eights, e.g.
15. "The Far Side" cartoonist Larson
19. First name in horror films
20. Stage background
21. D'Urberville lass
22. Guinness or Baldwin
23. Like some verbs: Abbr.
25. "The Sound of Music" setting: Abbr.
26. Unbalanced
27. Volume unit
29. Most clever
30. Cribbage piece
32. Bygone map letters
34. Appropriate
35. Litigates
37. French city, in song
38. Nightclub routines
39. Scottish caps
40. Plant appendages
41. Frosty's makeup
42. Zingers
45. "My dog ___ fleas"
46. Spinning toy
47. Yes, to Yves
48. 1968 hit "Harper Valley ___"

Solution on page 345

Puzzle 151

Across

1. Keats poems
5. 100 cts.
8. Words after shake or break
12. Skye of "Say Anything . . ."
13. Lea bleater
14. Lavish affection (on)
15. Bone connector
17. Gershwin's "___ Plenty o' Nuttin'"
18. Cut off, as a branch
19. Outfield material
21. Leaves port
23. ___ Flow (Scottish channel)
26. River of France
27. Dinner course
29. Jamaican liquor
30. Norma ___ (Sally Field role)
31. ___ de Janeiro
32. One who scoffs
35. Watch again
37. Actor Lew
38. Wise people
39. Become mature
40. Part of USDA: Abbr.
41. Thousands, to a hood
44. Meaningless words
49. Alpine river
50. Owed
51. Helen of ___
52. Heartstring stimuli
53. Polite word
54. After-Christmas event

Down

1. ___ and vinegar
2. "___ know you?"
3. Subj. including grammar
4. Protect, as freshness
5. Oceans
6. Hold the deed to
7. "Hmmm . . ."
8. Nike competitor
9. Nautical journal
10. D.D.E.'s command in WWII
11. Wreak vengeance on
16. Burrowing mammal
20. ROTC relative
21. Spot for sweaters
22. Majority leader Dick
24. In and of itself
25. Astrological Ram
26. "Is it Miss or ___?"
27. Historic women's gp.
28. Sock front
30. Faxes again
33. Clears the blackboard
34. Gas pump spec.
35. Tatters
36. Wading birds
38. Less crazy
41. Gangster's gun
42. Water: Fr.
43. Bit of energy
45. Yes, in Paris
46. Org. for gun owners
47. Note after fa
48. Cyclops had one

Solution on page 345

Puzzle 152

Across

1. Spreads seed
5. It may be put out to pasture
8. Sedan or coupe
11. Excellent, in modern slang
12. "Gimme ___!" (start of an Iowa State cheer)
13. Guardianship
14. Razor brand
15. Brooks or Gibson
16. Prayer end
17. Christina Crawford memoir
20. Golfer's goal
21. Mrs. in Madrid
22. Gridiron units: Abbr.
25. Calf's call
27. Put off
31. Iron corrosion
33. Train stop: Abbr.
35. "Fly away!"
36. Begin
38. Bit of a joule
40. Tree liquid
41. Puff Daddy's genre
43. Pedro's aunt
45. Literary sobriquet
52. "When I was___. . ."
53. Smallish batteries
54. ___ and hearty
55. Sheet of glass
56. PC screen
57. Slave girl of opera
58. Circle ratios
59. Summer, in Nice
60. Depots: Abbr.

Down

1. Computer junk mail
2. "___ be in England": Browning
3. Heat up
4. Post office purchase
5. Kodaks, e.g.
6. Having only length
7. Beguiling behavior
8. Put in an appearance
9. War god on Olympus
10. Housing fee
13. Gem measures
18. "___ the Walrus" (Beatles song)
19. "___ Gratia Artis" (MGM motto)
22. 12-mo. periods
23. Payable now
24. Retired airplane: Abbr.
26. Had dessert
28. Relieved sounds
29. Mauna___
30. Cut off, as branches
32. Vehement speech
34. Theatrical pro
37. Slangy negative
39. Tonic's partner
42. Timeless Christmas wish
44. Turkish titles
45. New York Shakespeare Festival founder Joseph
46. Asian range
47. Partner of pots
48. Shopping outlet
49. "Just a sec!"
50. Hawkeye player on "M*A*S*H"
51. Nays' opposites

Solution on page 345

Puzzle 153

Across

1. Franken and Sharpton
4. Golf legend Snead
7. Having no company
12. Apollo vehicle
13. Novelist Levin
14. Third-party candidate of 2000
15. Poet's before
16. Fries or slaw
18. Lassie, for one
20. Pig-poke connector
21. Metric weight
22. Terhune dog
24. Venetian blind part
28. Busy month for the IRS
30. Retrieve
32. I, to Claudius
33. Sound receiver
35. Egyptian capital
37. "i" completer
38. Doc's org.
39. "Wherefore ___ thou Romeo?"
40. "Honest" President
42. Trike riders
44. File folder feature
46. Egyptian threats
49. Easy as ___
51. Summer cottage, perhaps
53. Huge quantity
57. "Sail ___ ship of state"
58. "You've got mail" addressee
59. Wish one hadn't
60. Classic beginning
61. Choreographer Agnes de ___
62. Actress Jillian
63. Mind reader's ability

Down

1. Smart ___ (wise guy)
2. "Vive ___!": "Long live the king!"
3. Suspect dishonesty
4. Emphatic assent in Acapulco
5. Disney's "Little Mermaid"
6. "___ About You"
7. Soon, to a poet
8. "___ Theme" ("Doctor Zhivago" tune)
9. Unmatched, as a sock
10. Maiden name signaler
11. Be mistaken
17. Down-yielding duck
19. Trim
23. Aggravation
25. Magnetic mineral
26. ___-win situation
27. Vietnamese holiday
29. Panasonic competitor
31. Burnt ___ crisp
33. Ingest
34. Latin "I love"
36. Soviet co-op
41. Legally stop
43. Hawker's pitch
45. Rocket engineer Wernher von ___
47. Glazier's units
48. Single-masted vessel
50. Concerning, memowise
52. Genesis garden site
53. Highland cap
54. King, in France
55. Winner's take
56. Mouths, in Latin

Solution on page 345

Puzzle 154

Across

1. Killer whales
5. U.S./U.K. divider
8. Dairy herd
12. Pillager's take
13. Mr. Gershwin
14. Slangy greeting
15. Home of the Blue Devils
16. Round Table knight
18. Golfer's pocketful
20. Scoundrel
21. Remove from copy
23. Bacon piece
28. Long-distance letters
31. Teacup handles
33. Old autos
34. Many Wayne films
36. Little green men
38. Dilbert coworker
39. "Will be," to Doris Day
41. Aug. clock setting
42. Exposed
44. Money in Milano
46. Cathedral city
48. Young socialites
51. Race winner of fable
56. A way in
58. Vegetable-oil spread
59. Tilly or Ryan
60. Lake near Niagara Falls
61. Undulating
62. Panhandle
63. Slave of yore

Down

1. Part of GOP
2. Defeat decisively
3. Pepsi rival
4. Noble mount
5. Be sick
6. Shipping inquiry
7. Sweater girl Turner
8. Revolutionary Guevara
9. Vinegar partner
10. First baseman of comedy
11. Tippler
17. Music purchases
19. Soothsayer
22. Aberdeen miss
24. Prefix with cycle
25. Oboe or bassoon
26. Physics particles
27. Sibilant attention getter
28. Ancient kingdom near the Dead Sea
29. Madre's home
30. "Like ___ not"
32. Indian dress
35. Barely make, with "out"
37. Kitchen fat
40. French president's palace
43. ___ volente
45. Dangerous mosquito
47. An arm or a leg
49. Tiresome speaker
50. Evening, to Yves
51. Pull along
52. Pay follower
53. Gun an engine
54. Kind of poodle
55. Sunny-side-up item
57. Ump

Solution on page 345

Puzzle 155

Across

1. "Quiet!"
4. Diver's tank
9. Alphabetical trio
12. Golden Rule pronoun
13. Rover
14. Caesar's seven
15. Yule quaff
16. First letter
17. Ovum
18. Small spot
20. ___ Saud
22. Amusement, for short
24. Virtuoso
27. Sailor's shout
30. The WB rival
32. "___ us a son is given"
33. Society newcomer, for short
34. Comic's bit
35. ___-Xer
36. Pinochle combination
38. Leather worker's tool
39. Culp/Cosby series
40. Verve
42. S.A.S.E., e.g.
44. Chicle product
45. George Burns film
49. Links org.
51. Accelerator or brake
55. Egypt and Syria, once: Abbr.
56. Makeshift shelter
57. Rejoice
58. Fri. preceder
59. Recolor
60. Window sill
61. Second-stringer

Down

1. Dict. entries
2. Basketballer's target
3. Mammoth
4. Cobra or copperhead
5. Army VIP
6. Diamond authority
7. Exclamation of annoyance
8. Firefighter Red
9. Going-out times
10. Pear-shaped fruit
11. Band booking
19. Weep
21. Heat measure: Abbr.
23. He married Charo
24. Protractor measure
25. Ladder rung
26. Stage award
27. Nav. officers
28. Dickens's Uriah
29. Commit
31. Ferret's foot
37. Actress Joanne
39. I, in Emden
41. Spur
43. Actor Nick
46. Nerve
47. Pearl Harbor's site
48. Beat soundly
49. Grad student's goal, perhaps
50. Fellow
52. Program file extension
53. Fizzler
54. H.S. math class

Solution on page 345

Puzzle 156

Across

1. Enemies
5. Hang loosely
8. Did a takeoff on
12. "___ Wanna Do" (Sheryl Crow hit)
13. Lord's Prayer opening
14. Equestrian sport
15. American patriot Nathan
16. A/C unit
17. Toll road, for short
18. Cannon of Hollywood
19. Village Voice theater award
21. Crackpot
24. Dashboard devices
28. Apply pressure to
31. Knock for ___
32. Bounder
33. Leopard markings
35. Crucial
36. Egg-shaped
38. Wealth
40. South Pacific island
41. Chinese chairman
42. Meat loaf serving
45. Performs in a play
49. Profs, usually
52. Track action
54. Agitate
55. Lover of an Irish Rose
56. Water under the pont
57. Copperfield's bride
58. Male turkeys
59. Illumination unit
60. From ___ to stern

Down

1. Saudi Arabian king
2. Skin care brand
3. Raines of filmdom
4. "Burnt" color
5. Cry out loud
6. Jalopy
7. Vittles on the trail
8. Sex ___
9. Luau paste
10. Antlered animal
11. "Unknown" surname
20. Lake that's a source of the Mississippi
22. Open, as an envelope
23. Shirt or sweater
25. Fountain order
26. Garden tools
27. Engage in espionage
28. Volcano's output
29. Netherlands cheese town
30. Neither fish ___ fowl
32. Fortune 500 orgs.
34. "Meet the Press" host Russert
37. Lobs
39. Stockpiles
43. Biblical murder victim
44. Belle's man
46. Crotchety one
47. Michelin product
48. Shut loudly
49. Stroke gently
50. "Deadwood" network
51. Lower the lights
53. Groom's garb

Solution on page 346

Puzzle 157

Across

1. Entre ___ (confidentially)
5. Glove compartment items
9. Humble home
12. "If it ___ broke . . ."
13. Ardor
14. One ___ kind
15. Ballerina's bend
16. El ___ (weather problem)
17. Negative conjunction
18. "Como___usted?"
19. Corp. bigshot
20. Sixth sense, for short
21. Parcel out
24. Yo-yo, e.g.
26. Chinese menu letters
29. Stinging insect
31. Probability quote
34. Tea type
36. Old anesthetics
38. When tripled, et cetera
39. Coal-rich German region
41. Opposite of ENE
42. Soak (up)
44. "Confound it!"
46. Greek piper
48. Cup lip
50. Grade school basics
54. Id companion
55. Ireland, in poetry
57. Oscar winner Kedrova
58. They have Xings
59. "The World According to ___"
60. Nickel or dime
61. Plum's center
62. Jim-dandy
63. Walk with difficulty

Down

1. Back of the neck
2. Some paintings
3. The "U" in I.C.U.
4. Stand in good ___ (be useful to)
5. Tom, Dick and Harry
6. "___ Restaurant"
7. Window section
8. Nose, slangily
9. Winter melon
10. Sci-fi fliers
11. Ball field covering
22. Have the deed to
23. Slips behind
25. "Golly!"
26. Disorderly crowd
27. The Sun
28. Gorbachev policy
30. Brandy fruit
32. ER staffers
33. Compass reading
35. "What have we here?"
37. "La la" preceder
40. Think highly of
43. Pasta sauce brand
45. After-bath powders
46. Criminal, to a cop
47. Prefix with culture
49. Shah's land
51. High school subj.
52. Ad award
53. Performed an aria
56. "Car Talk" airer

Solution on page 346

Puzzle 158

Across

1. Suffix with flex
5. Triumphant exclamation
8. Connection
12. Tournament exemptions
13. Mineo
14. Jai-___
15. Take a crack ___ (try)
16. Cardinals' home: Abbr.
17. Gratuities
18. Secondhand transaction
20. Choir members
22. Kind of foil
23. Linden of "Barney Miller"
24. Ornamental flower shape
28. Vandyke or goatee
32. "How nice!"
33. Jeanne d'Arc, for one: Abbr.
35. Happy hour locale
36. One of the Allman Brothers
39. Sonnet endings
42. "Alley ___"
44. ___ Bravo
45. Outpouring
47. One way to pay
51. Excellent, in slang
52. Numbered highway: Abbr.
54. No-cholesterol spread
55. Store of knowledge
56. Out of date: Abbr.
57. Marquand's Mr.
58. In days of ___
59. King Cole
60. Coup d'___

Down

1. Letter-shaped girder
2. Computer term
3. Hawaiian neckwear
4. Monticello, for one
5. Agrees
6. Derby, e.g.
7. Moslem Almighty
8. Fight
9. Mixture
10. Afternoon snoozes
11. Put down, on the street
19. Ignited
21. Chemist's workplace
24. Old piano tune
25. Rowing need
26. "Steady as ___ goes"
27. Martians, e.g.
29. President Lincoln
30. Traitor
31. E.R. workers
34. Most uncanny
37. Small beard
38. Obtained
40. Envy or sloth
41. Still ahead
43. Evita's surname
45. Word to a fly
46. Young salmon
48. Considerably
49. ___ poor example
50. Gibson of oaters
51. Carry on, as a trade
53. Unfilled, on a TV sched.

Solution on page 346

Puzzle 159

Across

1. Profs.' degrees
5. Bread with a pocket
9. Talk idly
12. In high style
13. "Iliad" or "Odyssey"
14. Flow's counterpart
15. Whaler's adverb
16. Jr.-to-be
17. Necessary: Abbr.
18. Some turns
20. Some German autos
22. Liquid measures
24. Sly animal
25. Like some piano keys
26. Army affirmative
29. Mark, as a ballot square
30. Fall bloomer
31. Election Day mo.
33. Spoofed
36. Believer's confidence
38. London forecast
39. Social classes
40. Mythical cave dweller
43. Raccoon kin
44. Lew Wallace's "Ben-___"
45. McGregor of "Down With Love"
47. Spice-jar holder
50. Timber-dressing tool
51. Funnyman Carvey
52. Building block of matter
53. Cheyenne's state: Abbr.
54. Bovine beasts of burden
55. Table supports

Down

1. %: Abbr.
2. LBJ's veep
3. Cell phone's lack
4. Storm-door insert
5. Annoyers
6. N.Y.S.E. debuts
7. Waiter's reward
8. Sneeze sounds
9. Richard of "Unfaithful"
10. Adam's second son
11. Backyard parties, for short
19. Young fish
21. Mil. stores
22. Superman foe ___ Luthor
23. Wader with a curved bill
24. Opposite of masc.
26. Nope's counterpart
27. Kick off
28. Mechanical routine
30. Coffee cup
32. Videotape format
34. Gridiron org.
35. Ohio port
36. Airport overseer: Abbr.
37. Starry
39. ___ the Barbarian
40. Take out of the freezer
41. Former mayor Giuliani
42. Petite pasta
43. Chaplin trademark
46. Tussaud's medium
48. Machine tooth
49. Metric distances: Abbr.

Solution on page 346

Puzzle 160

Across

1. Legendary Peter or piper
4. Gasp
8. House top
12. AP competitor
13. Eros, to the Romans
14. Longest river entirely in Spain
15. Craggy height
16. Spanish affirmatives
17. Engine noise
18. Other half, so to speak
20. Some saxes
21. Six-stanza poem
24. Opera solos
27. Disentangle
31. Basinger of "Batman"
32. Ancient
33. Bit of sun
34. Adds on
37. Secret stash
39. Traitors
41. Three-star officer: Abbr.
44. Appropriating
48. Sporty Camaro
49. Rams' mates
51. Sheep's bleat
52. Navel buildup?
53. Went fast
54. Swift-running Aussie bird
55. Getup
56. Tricks
57. Hairstyling goop

Down

1. Sets (down)
2. Each, informally
3. Robert De ___
4. Free tickets
5. Gallic girlfriends
6. Negative replies
7. Angle starter
8. Go back to the drawing board
9. "In memoriam" item
10. Whether ___
11. Airport dangers
19. UN Security Council member
20. Solution: Abbr.
22. Oklahoma city
23. Not Rep. or Dem.
24. Letters before a pseudonym
25. Tombstone inscription
26. Little demon
28. Parabola
29. Cheerleader's cheer
30. Bleaching solution
32. Weird
35. Kicks out
36. Sally Field TV role
37. Discontinues
38. Interview
40. Iron-fisted
41. Cheerful tune
42. Peter, Paul, and Mary, e.g.
43. Chinese percussion instrument
45. "___ to differ!"
46. Partner of rank and serial number
47. France, to Caesar
49. And so on: Abbr.
50. "Face/Off" director John

Solution on page 346

Puzzle 161

Across

1. Potato
5. Feds who catch counterfeiters
9. Thanksgiving side dish
12. Intent look
13. Plasm starter
14. Hosp. scan
15. Speaker of Cooperstown
16. Serving with chop suey
17. A quarter of M
18. Carrier to Amsterdam
20. ___ apso (dog)
22. Entrepreneur's deg.
25. Place side by side
28. "___ la la!"
29. Tip off
30. Former Mach 2 fliers: Abbr.
34. Rosalind Russell role
36. Butter square
37. Oxford or pump
38. Jeanne d'Arc et al.
39. OE letters
41. Salamander
42. Avenue
44. "How silly of me!"
45. Ulan ___, Mongolia
48. "Morning Edition" airer
50. Alas, in Augsburg
51. Arsenal inventory
54. Poses a question
58. Which person
59. "Daily Planet" reporter Lane
60. Hop-jump intervener
61. Moon lander, for short
62. Adept
63. Sprite

Down

1. Police dept. rank
2. What golfers try to break
3. Israeli gun
4. Classroom furniture
5. School assignment
6. Sprint rival
7. And so forth: Abbr.
8. Caroler's tunes
9. Community gym site
10. Circle parts
11. "___ 18" (Leon Uris book)
19. Perry Mason's profession
21. Dame Myra
22. Pops' partners
23. Ketch or yawl
24. "Alas!"
26. Chatter idly
27. Exactly
31. Home for a mower
32. Japanese cuisine ingredient
33. First name in clocks
35. A gas from the past
40. Popular oil additive
43. Song syllables
45. Cry out loud
46. Result of overexercise
47. ___ McAn shoes
49. Wood file
52. Unruly crowd
53. Wire measurement
55. Glide on snow
56. "Kid-tested, mother-approved" cereal
57. CIA employee

Solution on page 346

Puzzle 162

Across

1. Cartoonist Silverstein
5. Plato's P
8. Tub with a whirlpool
11. Sandwich bread
12. Fly like an eagle
13. Escape clause
14. Sciences' partner
15. European volcano
16. Explosive letters
17. Waver
19. Like some stares
21. Slants
23. Bake sale org.
26. Night spot
27. Take third
31. Dinghy propellers
33. Respectful title
35. Picador's target
36. Russian legislature
37. Koppel of "Nightline"
39. It's a drag
40. Country singer Yearwood
43. Lands' End competitor
46. One-celled creatures
51. Volleyball filler
52. Apiary residents
54. Hang around
55. It's uplifting
56. "Little Women" woman
57. Italian resort area
58. Give in to gravity
59. Altar oath
60. Light punishment

Down

1. Small fight
2. Put on staff
3. Luncheon add-on
4. Bringing up the rear
5. Poppycock
6. Puts up, as a painting
7. Papal cape
8. Boozehounds
9. Ogden Nash specialty
10. Mem. of the bar
12. Best of seven, e.g.
18. Abate
20. Like some profs.
22. Mine entrances
23. Okra unit
24. Greek T
25. Quarterback's asset
28. Sexy
29. Gaucho's gold
30. "Holy moly!"
32. Cloy
34. Go over again
38. Beaver's work
41. Synagogue leader
42. "___ a drink!"
43. Chem classes
44. Old Milan money
45. Blow one's horn
47. Additions
48. Seethe
49. Alan of "Manhattan Murder Mystery"
50. Meal fit for a pig
53. WWII theater

Solution on page 347

Puzzle 163

Across

1. Fancy marble
4. End of some URLs
7. Bausch & ___
11. Where Switz. is
12. "No ifs, ___ or buts!"
14. Football shutout line score
15. Indian honorific
16. Pretext
17. Cleansing agent
18. Spuds
20. Animal that beats its chest
22. Gaming cube
23. Throw again
27. Analyzes grammatically
30. "That's enough!"
31. ___ jiffy (quickly)
32. Suffix with Paul
33. Cylindrical
37. Least loco
40. Lenin successor
41. Airport screening org.
42. Adolescent boy
43. Forewarns
47. Check datum
50. Real-estate unit
52. Homer Simpson expletive
53. "___ Flux" (Charlize Theron movie)
54. Carryall bag
55. "Star Wars: The Phantom Menace" boy
56. Money players
57. Sixth-sense letters
58. Thesaurus listing: Abbr.

Down

1. Examination
2. Surrounding glow
3. Habeas corpus, e.g.
4. Stephen King's first novel
5. Burdens of proof
6. Prescription writers: Abbr.
7. Be bested by
8. Winning tic-tac-toe row
9. Extinct kiwi relative
10. '40s jazz style
13. Cataloguer of yore
19. Asner and Wynn
21. Buddy or Socks
24. Bee's nephew
25. Breaks a commandment
26. Editor's "keep it"
27. Peach centers
28. Work without ___ (take risks)
29. ___ avis
34. Burstyn and Barkin
35. Aunt in Madrid
36. "This foolishness must ___ once!"
37. Begins
38. Dozing
39. Scottish negative
44. Suggestions on food labels: Abbr.
45. Broadway award
46. Leg part
47. One way to fish
48. ___ Lingus: Irish carrier
49. Furthermore
51. Iowa college

Solution on page 347

Puzzle 164

Across

1. ASCAP rival
4. Genetic molecules
8. Wood-dressing tool
11. A.k.a. Bruins
13. Sphere lead-in
14. Sundial topper
15. Clucking sounds
16. Beat to a froth
17. Dr.'s graph
18. Neighbor of Ill.
20. Sunglasses
22. "Old Folks at Home" river
25. Not square
26. Kipling lad
27. Baby's bawl
29. Songwriters' grp.
33. Not ___ many words
35. Oil or grease: Abbr.
37. Isle of exile for Napoleon
38. Hybrid garment for women
40. Dict. offering
42. "Monday Night Football" network
43. Lobster eater's wear
45. Scolds
47. Epoch of 50 million years ago
50. Neb. neighbor
51. ATM maker
52. Queen of Carthage
54. Anatomical sac
58. Half a Latin dance
59. New York City archbishop
60. Go on foot
61. Easy throw
62. Cherry and carmine
63. Movies, for short

Down

1. Except
2. Game-show hosts: Abbr.
3. Sort
4. Short end of the stick
5. Ultimate ordinal
6. Some Mennonites
7. Actress Loren
8. Gave the boot
9. Flood prevention structure
10. Sharp turns
12. T ___ "Tom"
19. Not used
21. Notre Dame niche
22. Glides on snow
23. One-eyed flirtation
24. Playground retort
28. 1963 Paul Newman film
30. Bedecked
31. Clerical title
32. Campaign funders, for short
34. Kill ___ killed (law of the jungle)
36. Summons
39. Fire starter
41. Loan org.
44. Brown shade
46. Ruler unit
47. Abbr. on a business letter
48. Dos times cuatro
49. Lobster relative
53. Father
55. Bitty bark
56. Glide down an Alp
57. Singing cowboy Ritter

Solution on page 347

Puzzle 165

Across

1. Governess Jane
5. Jamaican exports
9. Recyclable item
12. Leaves the premises
13. Completely paired
15. Blast of wind
16. Muzzles
17. "Be silent," musically
19. Imperfections
20. Position
22. Calendar box
23. Private pupil
24. Relation
25. Chitchat
28. Change for a five
29. Puppy's cry
30. 1996 also-ran
31. Joined
32. Mania
33. Army vehicles
34. Eggs go-with
35. Rodeo ropes
36. ___ Pendragon (King Arthur's father)
39. Musical paces
40. "I dunno"
42. Me, myself ___
45. Highly regarded
46. "Bring ___!"
47. "Quiet down!"
48. Princes, e.g.
49. College military org.

Down

1. Omelet ingredient
2. "___ rang?"
3. Paraphrased
4. Subjects of wills
5. Romantic gift
6. The U of "Law & Order: SVU"
7. Country singer Tillis
8. Edberg of tennis
9. "Your Show of Shows" regular
10. Yet another time
11. Loch ___ monster
14. One and ___: soul mate
18. Stage prompt
20. Pack (away)
21. Song
22. Dance move
24. Tot
25. Enters
26. Brand for Bowser
27. Porgy's mate
29. Starchy tuber
30. Hopelessness
32. Mockeries
33. Traffic tie-up
34. At this spot
35. City north of Sheffield
36. Does drugs
37. John of New Age music
38. "What ___ God wrought?"
39. Some govt. agents
41. Medical plan, for short
43. Speck
44. Business abbr.

Solution on page 347

THE EVERYTHING GIANT BOOK OF EASY CROSSWORDS

Puzzle 166

Across

1. Hair coloring
4. Historical spans
8. Money
12. Multivolume ref.
13. Neighbor of Ida.
14. Toward shelter, nautically
15. Campbell's container
16. ___ fide
17. Cave dwellers
18. Reporter's asset
21. One side in checkers
22. Pavement material
23. Der ___ (Konrad Adenauer)
25. Doberman's doc
26. Anti-ICBM plan
29. Eventually
33. Creepy Chaney
34. Competed in a marathon
35. Country byway
36. Small bird
37. Swiss river to the Rhine
38. Like a native
43. Greater quantity
44. Came apart
45. Baltic or Bering
47. Pier
48. Rat chaser?
49. One hundred percent
50. Compass point
51. Clothes
52. Kids' running game

Down

1. One of the Seven Dwarts
2. Bear young, as a sheep
3. Ralph Kramden's pal
4. Surround tightly
5. Santa's landing area
6. The A of A.D.
7. Track official
8. Pole tossed by Scots
9. "There oughta be ___!"
10. Hardens, as cement
11. "___ a real nowhere man . . ."
19. "You ain't ___ nothin' yet!"
20. Part of NBC: Abbr.
23. Communication for the deaf: Abbr.
24. London lav
25. Actor Max ___ Sydow
26. Ogles
27. Bear's abode
28. Angry feeling
30. Ireland nickname
31. Tommy gun noise
32. Having wings
36. Pick up the tab for
37. Helps in wrongdoing
38. Reward for Rover
39. Table scraps
40. Say ___ (deny)
41. Haul
42. Designer Oscar ___ Renta
43. Gaping mouth
46. High-school math course: Abbr.

Solution on page 347

Puzzle 167

Across

1. Son ___ gun
4. Where swine dine
7. Zap
11. Genre
12. Enraged
14. Mock words of understanding
15. Daily Planet reporter
17. Nobelist Walesa
18. Meddlers
19. Put into service
21. Inquire
22. Barcelona abodes
25. Go without food
28. "L.A. Law" actress Susan
29. Luau garland
31. "Famous" cookie man
32. Faux ___
33. Part of U.S.A.: Abbr.
34. "The Simpsons" grocery owner
35. Farm food
36. Atlas contents
37. Secret agents
39. "Respect for Acting" author Hagen
41. Harvest goddess
42. Most rational
46. Sportscaster Gowdy
49. Switchboard worker
51. Thailand's continent
52. Of ships: Abbr.
53. Wed. preceder
54. Attire
55. AWOL hunters
56. Moose cousin

Down

1. Greasy
2. Floating ice sheet
3. Related (to)
4. Marner of fiction
5. "East of Eden" family name
6. Japanese coin
7. Comic Soupy
8. Not just "a"
9. The Trojans
10. Stylized Japanese drama
13. Tennis ties
16. Box score numbers
20. Put into words
23. Diva Gluck
24. Fall through the cracks?
25. Air-safety org.
26. Bandstand boxes
27. Minestrone, e.g.
28. Dennis or Doris
30. Apr. 15 addressee
32. Send along
33. Maytag competitor
35. With it
38. Minuscule amounts
39. Run out of
40. Fruit desserts
43. Suffix for leather
44. James Brown's music
45. Tough journey
46. Pussy
47. Troop entertainment sponsor: Abbr.
48. 18-wheeler
50. Bobby's wife on "Dallas"

Solution on page 347

Puzzle 168

Across

1. "___ homo" (behold the man)
5. Mark O'Meara's org.
8. Gave dinner
11. In ___ land: spaced-out
12. Task
13. Capuchin monkey relative
14. Lesage's "Gil ___"
15. Weep
16. "Sesame Street" skills
17. High point
18. English channel, with "the"
20. Florida's Miami-___ County
23. Butterfly relatives
27. Lobbying org.
30. Word on a gift tag
31. French painter Jean
32. Frasier's ex
34. Covet
35. Deteriorate
36. Stick for Minnesota Fats
37. Brand of cooking spray
38. Moving slightly
39. Little Joe's brother
41. Norway's most populous city
43. O.K. in any outlet
47. Military stronghold
50. Suffix of approximation
52. Ah follower
53. Fills with wonder
54. Tappan ___ Bridge
55. Brinker with silver skates
56. ___-Mex
57. Not a particular
58. Go after a gnat

Down

1. Napoleon's home, briefly
2. Coll. math course
3. ___ up (be quiet)
4. Reduced, as pain
5. Bedwear, briefly
6. Peanut, in Dixie
7. Lane who sang with Xavier Cugat
8. Little white lie
9. And so forth
10. Insult, in the 'hood
13. No-nos
19. Roasts' hosts
21. Dessert, to a Brit
22. Cry from Homer Simpson
24. Excursion
25. Israeli dance
26. Blossom's support
27. Not guilty, for one
28. Publicizes
29. Blood vessel obstruction
33. Dolts
34. Dynamic ___
36. Appointed
40. Nobel-winning poet Nelly
42. Actress Minnelli
44. Mouthful of tobacco
45. Lady of Portugal
46. Retail price
47. The 2% in 2% milk
48. Be indebted to
49. Stout of whodunits
51. Casual greeting

Solution on page 348

Puzzle 169

Across

1. Dr. No, to Bond
4. Talk back to
8. Barn attachment
12. Psychic Geller
13. Edenite
14. Donkey pin-on
15. Bang up
16. Tie, as shoes
17. Poker-hand starter
18. Opt
20. Religious group
22. DDE's predecessor
24. Syrian president
28. Gentle, as a horse
31. Nile slitherers
34. Amount past due?
35. Palette selection
36. Nonpoetic writing
37. Chem. classroom
38. Wedding vow
39. Criminals break them
40. Young male horse
41. Moses' mountain
43. Ascot
45. Lanky
48. Trucker's expense
52. Exxon predecessor
55. Baby holders
57. "Black gold"
58. Running behind
59. Fabric colorings
60. 1949 film noir classic
61. Don of talk radio
62. Memo words
63. Coll. major

Down

1. Show anger
2. Preacher Roberts
3. Ireland
4. Epsom ___
5. Toothpaste raters' org.
6. Pouchlike structures
7. Captain Hook's henchman
8. Sports figures
9. Author Fleming
10. Afire
11. Spanish cheer
19. Fidel's friend
21. Job for Perry Mason
23. Scarlett O'Hara's home
25. D-Day battle site
26. Russian inland sea
27. Money you owe
28. "Now hear ___!"
29. German carmaker
30. "You're putting ___!"
32. Piglet's mother
33. "Hey . . . over here!"
36. Ballet movement
40. Company VIP
42. Burn soothers
44. "___ Easy" (Ronstadt song)
46. Swit costar
47. Thumbs-down votes
49. Comstock, for one
50. King of beasts
51. Smelter waste
52. Connecticut Ivy Leaguer
53. Detective Spade
54. V preceders
56. Vet's patient

Solution on page 348

Puzzle 170

Across

1. Big gobblers
5. Illuminated
8. Cage's "Leaving Las Vegas" co-star
12. Brief quarrel
13. Promissory initials
14. School session
15. Lamp fuel
17. Tenant's expense
18. Pasty-faced
19. Travel on snow
21. Seethes
23. Windshield sticker
26. Bothersome ones
27. Wrestling pair
29. Turkish title of respect
30. Hardly gregarious
31. "___ in the bag!"
32. Bargain hunter's stop
35. Imelda's collection
37. Comb backward
38. ___ d'Alene, Idaho
39. Follower of sigma
40. Vitamin bottle info
41. Phi ___ Kappa
44. Bridge supports
49. Long time
50. Go quickly
51. Patriot Nathan
52. Austrian peaks
53. Greenskeeper's supply
54. Part of ASAP

Down

1. Tut's cousin
2. Reveal, in verse
3. Scuff up
4. "Shut up!"
5. Bank claims
6. Charged particle
7. Payback time for Wimpy
8. Exacting
9. Bit of a bray
10. Large vase
11. Ambulance worker, for short
16. Mineo et al.
20. Frat party staple
21. Sired, Biblically
22. Native American
24. Vowel quintet
25. Afterward
26. Bit of butter
27. U.S. Constitution's first article
28. Orig. texts
30. Gumshoes
33. "___ Cheerleaders" (1977 film)
34. Fit ___ fiddle
35. Does lawn work
36. Overgrown wastelands
38. Church doctrine
41. Ewe's call
42. Snakelike fish
43. Apex
45. ___ de la Plata
46. Vientiane native
47. "Hold On Tight" band
48. Cong. member

Solution on page 348

Puzzle 171

Across

1. Home of the Braves: Abbr.
4. Senate output
8. Psychic reader
12. Tic-tac-toe win
13. Hymn "Dies ___"
14. Rock singer Turner
15. Chair part
16. Hawaii's ___ Coast
17. Culturally pretentious
18. Vodka cocktail
21. "Atlas Shrugged" author Rand
22. Suffix with hero
23. Big brass instrument
25. Brian of ambient music
26. Fuse word
29. Yarn-making device
33. Wrestling win
34. Metal to be refined
35. River through Florence
36. ___-Cone (summer snack)
37. School zone sign
38. Moon material, supposedly
43. Fishhook attachment
44. Two fives for ___
45. La la lead-in
47. Opera that debuted in Cairo
48. June celebrant
49. "Just ___ suspected!"
50. Cut with light
51. Right angle shapes
52. Meth. or Cath.

Down

1. It merged with Time Warner
2. "Little piggies"
3. Lincoln's birthplace
4. Compare
5. ". . . pretty maids all in ___"
6. Harry Potter prop
7. Very hot
8. Part of a barrel
9. Irish Republic
10. ___'acte (intermission)
11. Actor Walston
19. Actress Meg
20. "___ pronounce . . ."
23. Baking meas.
24. Wire service inits.
25. Opposite WSW
26. Former Ford minivan
27. Fraternity members
28. West Bank org.
30. Second to ___
31. Archaeological period
32. Hearty's partner
36. Caterpillar hairs
37. Mails
38. Earth goddess: Var.
39. Clears (of)
40. Computer keyboard key
41. Get well
42. Scottish Gaelic
43. Dance, in Dijon
46. Be unwell

Solution on page 348

Puzzle 172

Across
1. Little lie
4. Pt. of speech
7. 1950, in copyrights
11. Here, in Paris
12. Put down
14. "Horton Hears ___"
15. Floor covering
16. Parasites
17. Load cargo
18. Dove or love murmurs
20. Kwik-E-Mart owner on "The Simpsons"
22. Jigger of whiskey
23. Gawking sort
26. Stairway parts
27. Witch's spell
28. ___ Mahal
30. Makes haste
31. "It's freezing!"
32. German mister
33. Many months: Abbr.
34. "___ pasa?"
35. Fathers
36. In a chair
38. Newcastle-upon-___, England
39. Amer. seagoing force
40. Movie-rating org.
41. Jazzman Herbie
44. Former sneaker brand
46. Inc., in Britain
49. Loretta of "M*A*S*H"
50. In ___ (properly placed)
51. Roman 56
52. Letter carriers' grp.
53. Gibson of film
54. Shrill bark

Down
1. Certain evergreen
2. Hospital area: Abbr.
3. Head honcho
4. Dishes out
5. Table of honor
6. Old ___ (London theater)
7. Conductor Kurt
8. 100 lbs.
9. Conductance unit
10. Almost empty
13. More tidy
19. "How clumsy of me!"
21. Bellum's opposite
22. Uses a swizzle stick
23. Rip up
24. Forever
25. Carnival show
26. Timid
29. Some namesakes, for short
31. "___ noches"
32. "Howdy!"
34. Fourths of gals.
35. Capital of Minnesota
37. Mom's sisters
40. Tiny amount
41. Sch. in East Lansing
42. Sounds of disappointment
43. Bite like a pup
45. Vigor's partner
47. Dam building org.
48. Immerse

Solution on page 348

Puzzle 173

Across

1. John of England
4. Hive dweller
7. Apexes
11. Mushy food
12. Many N.Y.C. dwellings
14. Irish Rose's guy
15. Most strict
17. ___ Raton, Florida
18. Citrus beverage
19. Most washed out
21. Sail holders
24. Proofreader's word
25. Looks at
26. Takes turns
29. Narc's employer
30. ___ of Troy
31. Grassland
33. Rip Van Winkle, notably
35. ___ dunk
36. Ladies of Sp.
37. Telescope sights
38. Gets cheeky with
41. Trumped-up story
42. Lamb's sobriquet
43. Send
48. Redcoat supporter
49. Bone-dry
50. Man-mouse connector
51. Rainbow features
52. Sponsor's spots
53. ___ Zedong

Down

1. Turntable turners, briefly
2. Bit of grain
3. Unlatch, to bards
4. Rock groups
5. Safe sword
6. UFO occupants
7. Writing pad
8. Musical instrument
9. Snapshots
10. Couch or chair
13. Noted gatekeeper
16. Pied Piper's followers
20. Arkin or Alda
21. Kind of school
22. Certain votes
23. Make airtight
24. Metes (out)
26. Feasts
27. Grammy winner Fitzgerald
28. Brown quickly
30. Roll-call call
32. Morning times, for short
34. Literary pieces
35. Fr. Holy women
37. Trigonometric functions
38. A brother of Cain
39. Felipe or Moises
40. Part of an equine pedigree
41. Shortening
44. Stephen of "V for Vendetta"
45. Popular tattoo
46. Levin or Gershwin
47. Lao-tzu's philosophy

Solution on page 348

Puzzle 174

Across

1. Altar locale
5. Axis villain
9. Get the chair
12. Cut, as a lawn
13. Carousing
15. Tartan-wearing group
16. Court summons
17. They're shown to a novice
19. Chopper's blade
20. Light-footed
22. Excellent, in slang
23. With aloofness
24. Spring time
25. Scene-ending shout
28. Citizen of film
29. Wing it, musically
30. Aria, e.g.
31. H.S. requirement
32. Interval
33. "The Merry Widow" composer Franz
34. Bale contents
35. Shining
36. Some jazz
39. John Fowles novel, with "The"
40. Haifa residents
42. Milieu for Lemieux
45. In working condition
46. Pop singer Sands
47. Scatter, as seed
48. Nicholas or Ivan
49. Seductive

Down

1. Rambler mfr.
2. D.C. dealmaker
3. Bee activity
4. Dignify
5. "We're off ___ the wizard . . ."
6. Unpleasant task
7. Bowe blow
8. Fish-eating hawk
9. Stew (over)
10. Las Vegas rival
11. January to December
14. Magician's sound effect
18. Layer
20. New Balance competitor
21. Sammy Davis Jr.'s "Yes ___"
22. Beavers' project
24. Weatherman's backdrop
25. Unified
26. ___ bator
27. Civil wrong
29. First Chief Justice John
30. Makes safe
32. Watch in disbelief
33. Drag
34. Kind of frost
35. "Star Wars" weapon
36. Life stories, for short
37. Hockey great Phil, familiarly
38. Make tea
39. "___ 18" (Uris novel)
41. Scale abbr.
43. Prohibit
44. Important

Solution on page 349

Puzzle 175

Across

1. Italian wine center
5. Price of admission
8. Unconsciousness
12. Restful resorts
13. Table part
14. Really impressed
15. Capital of American Samoa
17. Rip apart
18. Implore
19. ". . . and nothing but the truth?" response
21. "___ all, folks!"
23. "___ Marner"
26. Takes wing
27. Took the wheel
29. "___ Not Unusual"
30. Curved letter
31. Stutz Bearcat contemporary
32. Take back
35. Cripples
37. Tries to find
38. Antiquated
39. Tanner's tub
40. Giant great
41. Fairy-tale opener
44. In the end
49. Kazakhstan sea
50. W. C. Fields persona
51. Lunch box treat
52. Rooters
53. "I'd be happy to!"
54. Revue unit

Down

1. Reptile of the Nile
2. Restorative resort
3. Price marker
4. Barometric line
5. United Nations display
6. Head lines?: Abbr.
7. "Me" types
8. Actress Lombard
9. Be obliged
10. Fathers and grandfathers
11. Use an abacus
16. Teachers' favorites
20. Reno roller
21. Carries
22. Quickness
24. "Mrs. ___ Goes to Paris"
25. Teacher's request
26. Galahad's title
27. JFK arrival
28. Coifs
30. Rapture
33. Makes merry
34. Wanted poster abbr.
35. Pal, Down Under
36. Houston nine
38. "Designing Women" actress Annie
41. Dolt
42. Shooters' grp.
43. Something to recycle
45. Hostile force
46. Biblical boat
47. Waikiki welcome
48. Building site

Solution on page 349

Puzzle 176

Across

1. Mexican cheers
5. NBC rival
8. Rudely abrupt
12. Electric unit
13. Food cooker
14. Prefix meaning "both"
15. Fitzgerald of scat
16. Beam of light
17. Not of the cloth
18. Boss Tweed's lampooner
19. Put up on eBay
21. List abbr.
24. State of India
28. Malos
31. Court wear
34. Comic Costello
35. G.I.'s mail drop
36. Fictitious name
37. Prefix with verse
38. Sales agent, for short
39. Al ___ (firm)
40. Teut.
41. Note from the boss
43. Opposite of NNE
45. Pendulum paths
48. Mgr.'s aide
52. Cutlass or Delta 88
55. Scraggly horse
57. ___-fly pie
58. Looting-in-the-streets event
59. Victoria's Secret item
60. Bartlett or Bosc
61. Tampa footballers, for short
62. Mushroom topper
63. Japanese rice drink

Down

1. Baking appliance
2. Falana or Albright
3. Some building additions
4. ___ of the art
5. EMT expertise
6. Feathery scarves
7. Eye inflammation
8. Rings up
9. Thurman of "Dangerous Liaisons"
10. Stat for a slugger
11. Sign of nerves, perhaps
20. Maidens
22. Wall Street employee
23. ___ slaw
25. Phony coin
26. Topnotch
27. "The Ghost and Mrs. ___"
28. The fourth planet
29. Olympics sword
30. Slangy denial
32. Coal holder
33. Truck-stop offering
42. A ketch has two
44. Big stingers
46. "Closing Bell" airer
47. Mystery author Paretsky
49. Was the Met's stadium
50. Saturate
51. Skedaddled
52. Scepter accompanier
53. Actress Lucy
54. Med school grad
56. Clothing store, with "The"

Solution on page 349

Puzzle 177

Across

1. Mugger stopper
5. Pulled the trigger
9. Bundle of bills
12. Subsides, as the tide
13. Vaulter's tool
14. Suffix with cash
15. Boss Tweed nemesis
16. Inventor's flash
17. Tofu source
18. Kipling's "Gunga ___"
20. British guns
22. Deuce, in tennis
25. More tranquil
28. Bon ___ (witticism)
29. Romanian-born Wiesel
30. Sieben follower
34. Premed course
36. ___ man: unanimously
37. Grimace
38. "Tiny" Archibald
39. Prefix for freeze
41. Schnozz ending
42. Falls into disuse
44. 60's war zone, briefly
45. "___ in Toyland"
48. Capone and Capp
50. Bruins' Bobby
51. Forget to include
54. Anent
58. Mincemeat dessert
59. "Just do it" sloganeer
60. How not to run
61. The "p" in m.p.g.
62. Broadway diva Linda
63. Baseball bases

Down

1. Fellows
2. Lawyers' org.
3. Dan Rather's network
4. Abbr. on a cornerstone
5. Band in a 1984 film parody
6. Mason's trough
7. Bullring cry
8. Make fun of
9. All-knowing
10. Extremely long time
11. Prohibition supporters
19. Drink cooler
21. Overhead transportation
22. Fed. agent
23. College in New Rochelle, N.Y.
24. State, to Pierre
26. Kings of beasts
27. T. Rex, notably
31. Masked critter
32. Hippy dance
33. Group of players
35. Conference opening?
40. Cuba or Aruba: Abbr.
43. In sync
45. Comet Hale-___
46. Indy winner Luyendyk
47. Uncle Remus address
49. Swedish car
52. Prefix with life or wife
53. '50s White House nickname
55. Diminutive, in Dundee
56. Dress up, with "out"
57. Gives the go-ahead

Solution on page 349

Puzzle 178

Across

1. Telecom giant
4. Gore and D'Amato
7. Not appropriate
12. Berlin bar need
13. Word before "I told you so!"
14. Singer Mariah
15. Ending with absorb
16. Greyhound stop: Abbr.
17. Shed ___: cry
18. Mink wrap
20. Charlotte ___ (dessert)
21. NYC zone
23. ___ Lingus (Irish carrier)
24. Monkey relatives
27. Cereal grain
29. This, south of the border
33. Summer hrs.
34. Places for MDs
35. Chess champion Mikhail
36. Knife wound
38. Maiden name lead-in
39. Narrow street
40. Hesitation sounds
42. The travel people
44. Very, to Verdi
47. Iranian coins
51. Kitchen protectors
52. WNW's reverse
54. Wetland
55. Bless
56. Western alliance since '48
57. Certain grandson
58. Copy-machine powder
59. D.D.E.'s WWII command
60. Water faucet

Down

1. Thousands, in slang
2. Pale color
3. This, to Jorge
4. Bubbleheads
5. Suffix for book
6. One of 100 in D.C.
7. Words of compassion
8. Inherent character
9. Greek war god
10. Pod denizens
11. Brit's radial
19. Gene Kelly's "___ Girls"
22. Animated characters
23. In between ports
24. Magazine fillers
25. L.A. clock setting
26. Second letter after epsilon
28. "Who ___ we kidding?"
30. Amtrak listing: Abbr.
31. Beach bum's shade
32. Pub beverage
37. John, Paul, George, or Ringo
39. My ___, Vietnam
41. Chorus platform
43. Playground retort
44. Amo, amas, ___
45. Chinese: prefix
46. British submachine gun
48. Throw ___ (get angry)
49. Han Solo's love
50. Small scissor cut
52. Help wanted ad abbr.
53. Didn't move off the shelves

Solution on page 349

Puzzle 179

Across

1. "Made in the ___"
4. Harbor boat
7. Wheaton of "Star Trek: The Next Generation"
10. Sardine cans
12. Troy, New York sch.
13. First baseman Martinez
14. Attractive
16. Makes a goof
17. Doublemint, e.g.
18. Linen item
19. Papas' partners
22. Jane's role in "Klute"
24. Hubbubs
25. Nook
28. Fruity spread
29. Knife wounds
31. "That'll show 'em!"
33. Cosby costar Phylicia
35. Back part
36. Spinning toys
37. Kiddie-lit trio
38. Count with an orchestra
41. Sammy Sosa, for one
42. Rival of "Vogue"
43. Cute
48. Its capital is Vientiane
49. Ullmann or Tyler
50. Intl. business accord
51. Recipe abbreviation
52. "Bah!"
53. Initials for Elizabeth II

Down

1. Sport ___ (all-purpose vehicle)
2. Defy a Commandment
3. Film director Lee
4. Quick haircut
5. WB competitor
6. Band date
7. Metal thread
8. Concerning, on memos
9. Didn't win
11. Drawn-out tales
13. Snicker sound
15. Gloomy ___
18. Min. components
19. Rank below Lt. Col.
20. Sixth Jewish month
21. N.Y.C. gallery
22. Wire nails
23. Yank's war foe
26. New York stadium
27. German valley
29. Loafer or moccasin
30. Beer keg insert
32. Mins. and mins.
34. Porcine pads
35. Pack again, as groceries
37. Prickly seed casing
38. Slug
39. Sigher's word
40. Sow's supper
41. Small bay
43. Sitcom alien
44. CCLI doubled
45. Scrooge's cross word
46. Envelope enclosure: Abbr.
47. Ordinal suffix

Solution on page 349

Puzzle 180

Across

1. ___-Cone (icy treat)
4. Happy hour stops
8. Airline to Stockholm
11. Cry from Charlie Brown
13. Skin care additive
14. Legal grp.
15. Words before date and record
16. Fill fully
17. Famous oversleeper
18. Marvin or Majors
20. Castle protectors
22. Plus item
25. Ballpark in Queens
27. "___ Walks in Beauty"
28. Inter ___ (among others)
30. Rocking Turner
34. Paving material
35. Composer Erik
37. Tic follower
38. Roadside refreshers
40. Boy or man
41. Serpent's tail?
42. Seating level
44. Bonet and Kudrow
46. Leveled, in London
49. Atlantic crosser
50. "What a good boy ___"
51. Just in case
54. No-no for Mrs. Sprat
58. "Ode ___ Nightingale"
59. Small: Suffix
60. The Beatles' "Penny ___"
61. Prepare to shoot
62. Sofa or stool
63. Likewise

Down

1. 12th graders: Abbr.
2. Scot's refusal
3. Hall-of-Famer Mel
4. Military headquarters
5. Pie ___ mode
6. "Hogwash!"
7. "If they could ___ now . . ."
8. Lee of cakes
9. "This won't hurt ___!"
10. Drains of energy
12. December 26 event
19. Greek H's
21. Horse's morsel
22. "The Thin Man" pooch
23. Food fish
24. Like the Gobi
25. Indian stringed instrument
26. Hard rain?
29. Fabric with metallic threads
31. Medical suffix
32. Zola courtesan
33. High cards
36. Sea wrigglers
39. Canonized Mlle.
43. Just hangs around
45. "___ have to do"
46. Pro ___ (proportionally)
47. Mine, in Marseille
48. Thailand, once
49. Proofreading notation
52. Summer, on the Somme
53. RR terminal
55. Have lunch
56. Spanish year
57. New: Prefix

Solution on page 350

Puzzle 181

Across

1. Muscle spasm
4. Name in plus-size modeling
8. Rifles and such
12. ___ -mo camera
13. Lima or garbanzo
14. Water around a castle
15. Barbie's beau
16. Wife of Geraint
17. "Julius Caesar" garb
18. Sex determinant
21. Wagon track
22. P, on a fraternity jacket
23. Cake finisher
25. Code-breaking org.
26. Where antes go
29. Deeply hurt
33. Rocky Mountain Indian
34. French dance
35. "Just say ___ drugs"
36. Trucker's truck
37. Loud noise
38. Explained away
43. Dairy airs?
44. "Amo, ___, I love a lass"
45. Suffix with musket
47. Bronte's Jane
48. Queue
49. Confederate soldier
50. Wanders (about)
51. February 14 figure
52. Compete in a slalom

Down

1. Sound of disapproval
2. Holly
3. Tangible
4. Film reviewer Roger
5. "Tell ___ lies"
6. Hurt badly
7. Support, as a candidate
8. Playground retort
9. ___ and board
10. Wizard, old-style
11. RR depot
19. William of "The Doctor"
20. Cager O'Neal, familiarly
23. Post-O.R. stop
24. Slice
25. Gretzky's grp.
26. Trailblazers
27. Halloween's mo.
28. Fight ender, for short
30. Kimono ties
31. Place to buy bric-a-brac
32. Part of UCLA: Abbr.
36. Kentucky Derby flowers
37. Prescription amounts
38. Spanish painter
39. British nobleman
40. Moslem ruler
41. Soap actress Linda
42. Smell awful
43. Ryan of "Sleepless in Seattle"
46. Stat for A-Rod

Solution on page 350

Puzzle 182

Across

1. Farmland
5. Hawaii, e.g.: Abbr.
8. Englishman, for short
12. Victims of the Morlocks
13. Doo-wop syllable
14. At any ___ (nevertheless)
15. Breathe quickly
16. Actor Herbert
17. "Grapes of Wrath" character
18. Ivan, for one
20. Country singer Buck
21. Russian range
24. Bird on a beach
26. "Like a Rock" singer Bob
27. Convent leader
30. ". . . happily ___ after"
31. ESE's reverse
32. Slangy agreement
34. Trawled
36. Territory in northern India
37. Cows chew them
38. Allan-___ (Robin Hood cohort)
39. Japanese beer brand
42. "The World of Suzie ___" (1960 movie)
44. Latvian seaport
45. Boeing 747, e.g.
46. Colorful Apple product
50. Unique thing
51. Ending with cash or bombard
52. Portnoy creator Philip
53. Opposite of sud
54. '60s muscle car
55. "___, from New York . . ."

Down

1. Aug. follower
2. Suffix with scram
3. Electrically charged atom
4. "Long Tall Sally" singer
5. Majorca, for one
6. Concise
7. On the ___ (fleeing)
8. 1967 Van Morrison hit
9. Leaf-gathering tool
10. "Put ___ writing!"
11. Collarless shirts
19. Kazakhstan, once: Abbr.
20. Crystal ball, e.g.
21. Deplete, with "up"
22. Guns, as a motor
23. Onetime "Time" film critic James
25. "Charlotte's Web" author's monogram
28. Ward of the screen
29. Comedian Mort
31. Unite in marriage
33. Hotfoot it, old-style
35. Rapa ___ (Easter Island)
36. Anchorman Rather
39. Elvis ___ Presley
40. ___-Japanese War
41. Golden-___ (senior citizen)
43. Another, south of the border
45. It's up when you're caught
47. Pronoun for Miss Piggy
48. Off-road goer, briefly
49. Guerrilla Guevara

Solution on page 350

Puzzle 183

Across

1. Mil. mail depot
4. Impress deeply
7. Native American group
12. Exemplar of little worth
13. Knightly title
14. Artist's cap
15. Certifies by oath
17. Appliance manufacturer
18. Critic's pick?
19. Relaxes
20. Horse relatives
23. NNW opposite
24. School zone caution
25. Faucets
28. Like most cagers
32. Drunk
33. Foldout bed
34. Large body of water
35. 1994 film "Guarding ___"
37. Part of R and R
39. Prime-time hour
40. Primate
42. Clear the chalkboard
44. Way up?
47. Augusta National members
48. Fine thread
49. Desertlike
53. "___ of Old Smoky"
54. Sampras serve, often
55. WWII area
56. River dams
57. Barely passing grade
58. Dieter's concern

Down

1. "___ matter of fact . . ."
2. Kitty
3. Not at home
4. Help out
5. Skater Katarina
6. Hosp. sections
7. Ski lifts
8. Convene after a break
9. Savings plans, for short
10. Flexed
11. Greek vowels
16. Suffix with benz
20. Admin. aide
21. Wild plum
22. Tosspots
23. Retired planes: Abbr.
26. One of the "north forty"
27. "The Tell-Tale Heart" writer
29. Film canine
30. Grant and Majors
31. Sprinter's path
36. Expert on spars and stars
38. Giggle
41. Gets ready for surgery
43. Genetic carrier
44. Tortoiselike
45. Fork feature
46. Sparkling wine center
47. Defensive spray
49. In the doldrums
50. Gridiron zebra
51. ___ moment's notice
52. Ready alternative

Solution on page 350

Puzzle 184

Across

1. Bad habit, so to speak
5. Pool sticks
9. Incorrect
12. Altar assurances
13. Strongly recommend
14. Ghostly greeting
15. Quitter's word
16. Billboard
17. Quick punch
18. Psychic power
20. European autos
22. Clip-on communicator
25. Picture card
27. Threader's target
28. Heavy burden
30. Sharp side of a blade
33. Tear apart
35. Back, on a ship
36. Impair
37. Meat inspection org.
38. Male deer
40. Stat for a DH
41. Chirac's states
43. Aromatic chemical
45. Stop, in France
47. Soaked
48. Purse
49. Elizabethan instrument
52. Poet Pound
56. Fin. adviser
57. Not guaranteed
58. Hammerhead part
59. Popular fuel additive
60. Religious offshoot
61. Arousing

Down

1. London's Old ___
2. Neighbor of Wyo.
3. Swindle
4. Cosmetician Lauder
5. Zodiacal border
6. "Psychic" Geller
7. Over-easy item
8. Sir, in Seville
9. Curio
10. Mare's offspring
11. Watch chains
19. Sellout sign letters
21. Limerick, e.g.
22. South American country
23. Affirmative votes
24. Differences between men and women
25. Massachusetts university
26. "The Thin Man" pooch
29. Political cartoonist Thomas
31. Taunting remark
32. Mideast potentate
34. Fruit from a palm
39. "How about that!"
42. Mythical world lifter
44. Phases
45. Basic skills
46. In a trance
47. Toward the sunset
50. Avail oneself of
51. Involuntary muscle movement
53. Zuider ___
54. Tyrannosaurus ___
55. Unspecific number

Solution on page 350

Puzzle 185

Across
1. Related, as a story
5. Square footage
9. Strawberry, once
12. Melville effort
13. "Darn it!"
14. Tree feller
15. Boys
16. Actress Hartman
17. Perfect gymnastics score
18. Straighten up
20. Midterm, e.g.
21. Stove fuel
22. Clean air org.
24. Folkways
27. Russian empress
31. "Wheel of Fortune" purchase
32. ___ and true
34. Dime novelist Buntline
35. Evening get-togethers
37. Copenhagen residents
39. Do arithmetic
40. Part of ATV
41. "Hey there!"
44. Skirt features
47. Part of a G.I.'s address
48. Part of a deck chair
50. Actor Dillon
52. Gullible person
53. Prefix with dynamic
54. Sandwich cookie name
55. Graduating class: Abbr.
56. Money rolls
57. Indefinite amount

Down
1. Young'un
2. Arabian Peninsula land
3. Miner's bonanza
4. Medicinal amount
5. Van Gogh home
6. Reason for postponement
7. Klingons, e.g.
8. Naked ___ jaybird
9. Life partner
10. Spot markers
11. Campsite sight
19. Sampled, as soup
20. Driveway stuff
22. Opposite of WNW
23. Table tennis racket
24. Rainey and Barker
25. Artist Yoko
26. Title for Louis XIV
27. "Deck the Halls" contraction
28. Hostel
29. Born, in bridal bios
30. Product pitches
33. Checkers side
36. Stool pigeon
38. Southwestern poplars
40. Chorus members
41. Football throw
42. Box for practice
43. Dips in gravy
44. Cowpoke's buddy
45. Root in Hawaiian cookery
46. Flower stalk
48. Tool with teeth
49. Herd's hangout
51. Little piggy

Solution on page 350

Puzzle 186

Across

1. Female pigs
5. "Gunsmoke" network
8. Spaniard's six
12. Intestinal sections
13. Bray starter
14. Stick ___ in the water
15. Not messy
16. ___ room (den)
17. ABA members
18. Clinton's vice president
19. Nasdaq debut: Abbr.
20. Arthur and Benaderet
21. Ancient ascetics
24. "It ___ been easy"
27. Nutritional inits.
28. Propel a boat
31. ___ of one's own medicine
32. From the time of
34. High, aroing shot
35. "Far out"
38. Growing out
39. Weeping
41. Floor-washing implements
44. Indent key
45. Dutch artist Frans
49. "The Clan of the Cave Bear" author Jean
50. Wall St. whiz
51. "Here ___, there . . ."
52. Cat-o'- ___ -tails
53. Co., in France
54. Day laborer
55. Radiator sound
56. Attention-getting word
57. Scots Gaelic

Down

1. Carry a tune
2. Dairy-case buy
3. Wash's partner
4. Glossy fabrics
5. Rock or Evert
6. Paging device
7. Support, as a motion
8. Swedish autos
9. Novel suffix
10. Letter before kappa
11. Meeting: Abbr.
22. Back of a ship
23. Soother
24. Computer in "2001"
25. Noisy commotion
26. Cry audibly
28. Genetic material: Abbr.
29. Busy mo. in politics
30. Very small
33. Physically fit
36. Fasten
37. Honeybunch
39. Maui and Kauai
40. Friar's home
41. Staffs
42. French affirmatives
43. Writing tools
46. Part of N.A. or S.A.
47. Novelist Anita
48. Acoustic measure

Solution on page 351

Puzzle 187

Across

1. "I smell ___"
5. Swiss peak
8. ___ Hari
12. Nuclear reactor
13. Indy 500 month
14. Et ___
15. CPR experts
16. Tot toter
18. Stops fasting
20. Circus structure
21. New Haven institution
23. Scroll in an ark
27. "Play It Again, ___"
30. Midterm or final
32. Reduced-price event
33. Plaza Hotel heroine
35. Tarzan, for one
37. Revivalists, briefly
38. ___ survivor
40. ___ longa, vita brevis
41. Grand ___ National Park
43. Former Miss America host Parks
45. Danish physicist Niels
47. Skyscraping
50. Dressing ingredient
54. Town NNE of Santa Fe
56. Polish border river
57. Agreeable reply
58. Nile snakes
59. Black and Red
60. Industrious insect
61. Let stand, in editing

Down

1. Gorilla or chimp
2. Winter coating
3. Utah ski spot
4. In a peeved mood
5. Morning hrs.
6. Some coffee orders
7. Flammable pile
8. Sugar type
9. 100 percent
10. Garbage bag securer
11. Lungful
17. Ottawa's prov.
19. Srs.' exams
22. Directors Spike and Ang
24. "___ Lama Ding Dong" (1961 hit)
25. Controversial apple spray
26. Egg producers
27. Placed in the mail
28. Nautical position
29. Not worth debating
31. "Canterbury" story
34. Weather map lines
36. Flippant
39. Leno follower
42. Silent bid
44. Bye-byes
46. Georgetown athlete
48. Final
49. Easy gait
50. Maritime message
51. Citrus drink
52. Grassy area
53. D-Day craft: Abbr.
55. Retired fast plane: Abbr.

Solution on page 351

Puzzle 188

Across

1. Jokester Johnson
5. Anatomical pouches
9. High-speed Internet letters
12. Highway
13. Ernie or Gomer
14. Suffix for schnozz
15. Homeowner's payment: Abbr.
16. TV producer Norman
17. Infant fare
18. King: Fr.
20. Bowling alley buttons
22. Ski lodge
25. Son of Judah
26. Dissuades
27. Astronomer Carl
29. Foolish fellow
30. Culture-supporting org.
32. Boy Scout group
36. Openings
39. Essayist Lamb
40. Dark brews
41. Fords that failed
43. Dentists' org.
44. Golf pro Trevino
45. List ender, briefly
47. Fork part
51. Suffix for velvet
52. Move, in Realtor lingo
53. Smooth the way
54. Wt. or vol.
55. Shut with force
56. Hosiery problem

Down

1. Lever on a casino "bandit"
2. Decay
3. Children's game
4. Noted channel swimmer
5. Divvies up
6. Sailor's affirmative
7. Mild cigars
8. Williams of tennis
9. Atone
10. Narrow board
11. Racetrack circuits
19. On top, to poets
21. Lose tautness
22. S. & L. offerings
23. Winter budget item
24. Now
28. At no time, in verse
31. Long-eared equine
33. Cheer
34. Crude carriers
35. Subdued color
36. Zigzag skiing event
37. Hippie home
38. Striped stones
41. Zeno's birthplace
42. Have an opinion
46. In the style of, on a menu
48. Bond creator Fleming
49. Govt. code crackers
50. Brain-wave test: Abbr.

Solution on page 351

Puzzle 189

Across

1. Prefix for light
4. Freshly made
7. Display
11. Cries of dismay
12. "Grand" ice cream brand
14. Farewell, in Florence
15. Japanese money
16. Not on shore
17. Business-letter letters
18. ___ voce (softly)
20. Drakes and boars
22. Nancy Reagan's son
23. Fruit-filled dessert
24. Author ___ Stanley Gardner
27. Lawyer's deg.
28. Wintertime bug
31. Type of sonnet
35. Watergate prosecutor Archibald
36. Coffee-break time
37. Decorative evergreens
38. Auto Club offering
39. L.B.J.'s successor
41. French river
43. Old MacDonald refrain
46. "Good heavens!"
47. Curtain supports
49. Defense advisory org.
51. Kind of ad
52. Salty sauces
53. One-tenth of MDX
54. Soapmaking substances
55. Hardly macho
56. Brick carrier

Down

1. Christmas purchase
2. Ex followers
3. "Money ___ object!"
4. Marvy
5. Pele's first name
6. Penultimate letter
7. Butcher's device
8. Writer Shere
9. Feed bag contents
10. Took the pennant
13. Taste
19. "Star ___: The Next Generation"
21. Verdi title character
24. Emergency PC key
25. Letter between pi and sigma
26. Lenient
27. Hosp. employee
28. Lawyer's charge
29. Attorney's field
30. Young'___ (kids)
32. British prep school
33. Seamstresses
34. Sandberg of Cooperstown
38. Honks
39. Change back to brunette
40. Hip-hop artist Elliott
41. Light carriage
42. ___ Boleyn
44. Fraction of a foot
45. Norway's capital
46. Night bird
48. Punch-in-the-stomach reaction
50. Spanish hero El ___

Solution on page 351

Puzzle 190

Across

1. First word of "The Aeneid"
5. Curved line
8. Grade-school basics
12. French kings
13. Affectedly modest
14. Johnny Carson predecessor
15. Some PTA members
16. Is the owner of
17. Paul who sang "Puppy Love"
18. Make more precipitous
20. Someone ___ (not mine)
21. "Citizen Kane" director Welles
23. Catchers' gloves
27. King of the Huns
32. Most scarce
34. Disorderly disturbance
35. Holds responsible
36. Have ___ on one's shoulder
37. Philosopher Kierkegaard
40. H.S. juniors' exams
44. Main courses
49. Apex
50. "The ___ Squad"
51. Coat-of-arms border
52. Police assault
53. Op. ___ (footnote abbr.)
54. "Crazy" bird
55. Rustic lodgings
56. ___-mo (instant replay feature)
57. Millions of years

Down

1. Sleeve fillers
2. Show team spirit
3. Marcel Marceau
4. Caama
5. One who's sore
6. Horses of a certain color
7. Songwriter Coleman et al.
8. "Be ___!" ("Help me out!")
9. Forbids
10. Birthday-party dessert
11. Spanish ladies: Abbr.
19. Have
20. Contest hopeful
22. Boor
23. Hazel's boss, to Hazel
24. Suffix with president
25. La-la prelude
26. President pro ___
28. Middle X of X-X-X
29. German "I"
30. Medieval poem
31. Poisonous snake
33. General on a Chinese menu
38. Lubricate again
39. Put an ___ (stop)
40. ___-mutuel (form of betting)
41. CAT ___
42. Idi of Uganda
43. Kennedy and Turner
45. Acting job
46. Slangy suffix with switch
47. NC college
48. D.C. 100: Abbr.
50. Banquet hosts: Abbr.

Solution on page 351

Puzzle 191

Across

1. ___ Lee of Marvel Comics
5. The past, in the past
8. Overconfident
12. Italian cash
13. ___ Schwarz
14. Top-rated
15. Spheres
16. Sr.'s test
17. Graceful bird
18. Wagon-train direction
19. "___ Death" (Grieg work)
21. Stage of a journey
24. Adjust, as sails
28. Devise
31. "A Bell for ___"
32. Merry month
33. Paving stones
35. Tiny amount
36. Research money
38. Kind of salad
40. Princess of India
41. Calif. clock setting
42. Mouse-catching device
45. Alphabetical start
49. Litter's smallest
52. Kiltie's cap
54. Tie up in the harbor
55. Nutmeg covering
56. Philosophical ideal
57. Father
58. Fr. Miss
59. Wall Street whiz
60. For males only

Down

1. Snail-like
2. Bike wheel
3. Wall St. traders
4. Cozy up
5. Three after D
6. Dr. Zhivago's love
7. Accomplishes
8. Answered impudently
9. Cut the grass
10. A, in Acapulco
11. O.T. opener
20. Wipes clean
22. Day to wear a bonnet
23. Communications giant
25. Hindu prince
26. "___ out?" (pet's choice)
27. Caught
28. Singer Irene
29. Pitcher Nolan
30. Cousin of et al.
32. Baseball VIP
34. Touch on the shoulder
37. Irk
39. Post-office purchases
43. Encouraging word
44. Old TV host Jack
46. Canoe or kayak
47. Nightclub in a Manilow tune
48. Pull from behind
49. Lamb's father
50. Internet address, briefly
51. Diddly
53. Rioting group

Solution on page 351

Puzzle 192

Across

1. Over-the-hill horse
4. Folk singer Phil
8. Mane makeup
12. 12 months in Madrid
13. Flyspeck
14. Teenage woe
15. Driveway surface
16. Bye-bye, in Brighton
17. Hood's knife
18. Pilfer
20. Enlarged map segments
22. Newsman Koppel
24. Costa ___ Sol
25. African nation since 1993
29. Opposing sides
33. ATM access code
34. Music buys
36. Scrooge's shout
37. "___ which will live in infamy": F.D.R.
40. German thoroughfare
43. "___ the fields we go . . ."
45. Spy novelist Deighton
46. Tex-Mex snack
49. Put on ___ (pretend)
53. Dismounted
54. "Dragnet" force: Abbr.
57. Pooh pal
58. Succeed on a diet
59. Mellowed
60. Arroz ___ pollo
61. Buttonlike?
62. Bears' hands
63. It's over your head

Down

1. Turner and Cole
2. Med. school subject
3. Bloodshed
4. Horse handler
5. CFO, perhaps
6. Like some peppers
7. Sedately dignified
8. Inconvenience
9. Muscle pain
10. Monogram ltr.
11. Guns the engine
19. LL.D. holder
21. Tennis court divider
23. Boxing Day mo.
25. Mileage rating org.
26. Free from, with "of"
27. One ___ million
28. Some mag pages
30. Sit-ups strengthen them
31. More, to Miguel
32. That woman
35. Arch city: Abbr.
38. Perfectly
39. Moray, e.g.
41. Double-checks the math
42. Raggedy ___
44. Pass again, in a race
46. Bath-powder ingredient
47. Ballplayer Moises
48. "Gorillas in the ___"
50. Circle segments
51. Chuck wagon VIP
52. Theater award
55. Turkish VIP
56. Worshiper's seat

Solution on page 352

Puzzle 193

Across

1. Tea-set pieces
5. Monk moniker
8. "Herzog" author Bellow
12. Aruba or Maui
13. Summer Games org.
14. Aborigine of Japan
15. Within view
16. "___, humbug!"
17. Naval hoosegow
18. Birds at sea
20. Dislike with a passion
22. ___ and tuck
24. Golden, in Grenoble
25. Arsonist
29. "Oh, come on!"
33. Web address ender
34. Campaign contributor, maybe
36. Be in hock to
37. Japanese noodles
40. Flashing lights
43. Core
45. Cheerleader's word
46. Brief arguments
49. Grand parties
53. Cook cookies
54. Minivan alternative, briefly
56. Hindu melody
57. Yankee or Oriole, briefly
58. 151, in old Rome
59. Islamic prince
60. Turner and Danson
61. Have an evening meal
62. Went under

Down

1. Film, in France
2. Techie's customer
3. Architect's design
4. Cool and calm
5. Stretch the truth
6. Street
7. Was in pain
8. Cavalry weapons
9. Ventilates
10. Fixed quantity
11. Clumsy guy
19. Sis or bro
21. Pinnacle
23. Young seal
25. Chemin de ___ (casino game)
26. State west of Mont.
27. Pirate's drink
28. Mobil product
30. Fireplace shelf
31. Reverent respect
32. Thriller director Craven
35. Middle: Abbr.
38. Makes an appearance
39. Cashew, for one
41. Dusting aid
42. Tara family
44. Pear varieties
46. Discount event
47. ___ out a living (barely got by)
48. "Enterprise" helmsman
50. Dalai ___
51. Opposed to, in dialect
52. Cutty ___: Scotch brand
53. Step to the plate
55. Big shot, for short

Solution on page 352

Puzzle 194

Across

1. Plant pockets
5. ___ glance (quickly)
8. Currier partner
12. Large continent
13. Enero or julio
14. Hawaiian honker
15. Rustic film couple
18. Brief memo
19. Drink by the dartboard
20. Hash house sign
23. Brewers' needs
27. FDR opponent Landon
30. Shakespearean king
32. Carrot or turnip, e.g.
33. Speckled horse
35. "We ___ not amused!"
36. Of sound mind
37. Dust bunny particle
38. Sally or Ayn
40. Insult, in slang
41. High-spirited horse
43. Works in the garden
45. Suffix with star or tsar
47. Syllables in "Deck the Halls"
50. Daydreaming
56. "Rule Britannia" composer
57. "It's clear now!"
58. Sask. neighbor
59. Get snippy with
60. Ship's call for help
61. Have the lead role

Down

1. American Uncle
2. Slippery ___ eel
3. Italian farewell
4. A votre ___: to your health
5. Electrical unit
6. Crumpets go-with
7. "___ silly question . . ."
8. All broken up
9. Dobbin's doc
10. Photog. service
11. Have a look
16. Start a card game
17. Shade tree
21. Drop from the eye
22. Opera's Caldwell
24. Fill, as a camera
25. Grammy-winner Braxton
26. French holy women. Abbr.
27. Up in ___ (outraged)
28. Thief's take
29. Karma
31. Nevada city
34. Teases
39. Editor's "take out"
42. Hound
44. Teasdale et al.
46. Author Peter
48. Light, happy tune
49. Pilaster
50. Once existed
51. ". . . man ___ mouse?"
52. Come-___ (inducements)
53. Nevertheless
54. "Elvis ___ left the building"
55. Long-jawed fish

Solution on page 352

Puzzle 195

Across

1. Points (at)
5. Dr. Seuss's Sam-___
8. Tagged along
12. H.S. junior's test
13. Hosp. test
14. Steinbeck migrant
15. Like auto shop floors
16. Everything considered
18. Jamboree housing
20. Long periods of time
21. Make, as money
23. Got by with difficulty
27. Cleanse (of)
30. Movie critic Pauline
32. Kid's building toy
33. Gotten up
35. Some Oldsmobiles
37. Type of tide
38. Auctioneer's last word
40. Article in Arles
41. Loafed around
43. Pod veggies
45. Ice unit
47. Knife
50. Military units
54. Valentine's Day cherub
56. Part of Superman's costume
57. Labor Day mo.
58. Mideast's ___ Strip
59. Whiskey drink
60. Have a bawl
61. Third place

Down

1. Part of a milit. address
2. "What time ___?"
3. Buck or bull
4. Composer Jule
5. "___ monkey's uncle!"
6. "What's My Line?" panelist Francis
7. "Venus de ___"
8. Give comfort to
9. Alias initials
10. A thousand thou
11. "Electric" fish
17. Corporate abbr.
19. "___ it or leave it!"
22. Phoned
24. Lima's country
25. Designer von Furstenberg
26. Two caplets, say
27. Sari wearer
28. Plenty mad
29. Obsolescent phone feature
31. Country path
34. Phantom
36. Grassy pastures
39. First game of a series
42. Twosome
44. Men-only parties
46. Kind of pear
48. Oriental nurse
49. Old TV clown
50. Desktop items, for short
51. Neighbor of a Vietnamese
52. Kwik-E-Mart proprietor on "The Simpsons"
53. CIA operative
55. Like sushi

Solution on page 352

Puzzle 196

Across

1. Equal
5. Alternatives to Macs
8. Pyramid scheme, for one
12. Wall St. newsmakers
13. Louis XIV, for one
14. O'Hara homestead
15. Horn sound
16. Mich. neighbor
17. Amo follower
18. Unanimously
20. Clobber
21. Christian of Hollywood
24. Photo ___ (publicity events)
26. Buenos___
27. Santa ___, California
28. Businesses: Abbr.
31. Acquire
32. Weight deductions
34. Once ___ while
35. Bring to court
36. Psychic ability
37. Spot on a tie, say
39. Scoreboard fig.
40. Seer's decks
41. Apple leftover
44. Milton's Muse
46. Verdi solo
47. Prot. or Cath.
48. Sci-fi author Frederik
52. Telescope part
53. Sigma follower
54. "Dies ___" (liturgical poem)
55. Theater section
56. '60s radical grp.
57. Kind of salmon

Down

1. "Take a load off!"
2. Military address: Abbr.
3. Bovine bellow
4. Manor
5. Before, with "to"
6. State south of Mass.
7. Half an LP
8. Wild guesses
9. Arrived
10. Shrinking Asian sea
11. Sail holder
19. Last six lines of a sonnet
21. Loses rigidity
22. In ___ of (rather than)
23. Museo contents
25. VW model
27. Dada daddy
28. Farewell in Florence
29. "Don't bet ___!"
30. ___-serif
33. Declares
38. ___ of Capricorn
39. "___ Porridge Hot"
40. Anklebone
41. Ring up
42. Best-selling cookie
43. Wagner cycle
45. Pore over
49. Mexican metal
50. "Take that!"
51. Heavenly lion

Solution on page 352

Puzzle 197

Across

1. Thick mane
4. Stupefy
8. Kitchen basin
12. Non's opposite
13. Sit, as for a portrait
14. Egyptian queen, for short
15. Family nickname
16. Last of a Latin trio
17. Jungle sound
18. Nonverbal affirmation
20. Mexican's nap
22. Looked lecherously
25. Reveal
26. Higher than
27. Of the mouth
30. Roofing material
31. Gloss target
32. Comedy revue since '75
35. Kings and queens
36. Striker's anathema
37. Turkey topper
41. Draws with acid
43. More ethereal
45. Jr.'s junior
46. Frosts, as a cake
47. Prayer's end
50. "___ semper tyrannis"
53. Carryall
54. Territory
55. 6, on a phone
56. "___ a Lady" (Tom Jones hit)
57. Turns sharply
58. Hog home

Down

1. Kind of scene
2. "Days of ___ Lives"
3. Trailblazer
4. Gardener's tool
5. Male cat
6. Made in the ___
7. Shrimpers' needs
8. Mountain debris
9. Pauline Kael's "___ It at the Movies"
10. Super-duper
11. Islamic text
19. Hockey great Bobby
21. "___ Be Seeing You"
22. Developer's land unit
23. Sister of Zsa Zsa and Magda
24. Ration (out)
28. Free (of)
29. Church alcove
32. Splits
33. Scot's turndown
34. Weigh-in abbr.
35. "See ya"
36. Biol. or chem.
37. Trot and canter
38. Canon competitor
39. Mountain crest
40. Squeezers
42. Fork prongs
44. Heckle
48. French pronoun
49. School subj.
51. Part of IRS
52. Coquettish

Solution on page 352

Puzzle 198

Across

1. Theater offering
6. What a swish shot doesn't touch
9. Brat
12. On ___ (counting calories)
13. "Strangers ___ Train"
14. Aussie hopper
15. Finger-pointer
16. Amin of Uganda
17. Demented
18. Price stickers
20. "___ what you think!"
22. Ukrainian city
25. Capote, on Broadway
26. Temporary fashion
27. Shows contempt
30. The one nearby
32. Coffee, slangily
33. Bulletin board sticker
36. First born
38. 4 on a phone
39. Scrap of food
40. Videotaped over
43. Sheriff's star
46. Liverpudlian, e.g.
47. 1051, to Nero
48. Sgt.'s mail drop
50. Katey of "Married . . . With Children"
54. Out of date
55. Coffee container
56. Kevin of "A Fish Called Wanda"
57. Union inits.
58. Superstation letters
59. "Ready, ___!"

Down

1. Former veep Quayle
2. Nutritional initials
3. Align the crosshairs
4. Track contests
5. Gillette razors
6. 18 Louises
7. Hoosier st.
8. ___ d'
9. "___ la Douce" (1963 film)
10. Castle's protection
11. Places for peas
19. Stove nozzle
21. Injured
22. Frequently, in poems
23. Lah-di-___
24. Mrs. Ernie Kovacs
25. Ride a seesaw
28. Dissenting votes
29. Gives in to gravity
31. Walk heavily
34. Revolutionist Guevara
35. Grade-schooler
37. Fantasized
41. Perils
42. Dickens title opener
43. Campus VIP
44. "___ Want for Christmas . . ."
45. Prank
46. Marshes
49. Alehouse
51. "Vamoose!"
52. "Brokeback Mountain" director Lee
53. August zodiac sign

Solution on page 353

Puzzle 199

Across

1. Russian parliament
5. Asian arena, for short
8. ___-nine-tails
12. Barbell material
13. Birth control option, briefly
14. ___ Ben Adhem
15. Something very funny
16. Library fillers: Abbr.
17. Has an evening meal
18. Bygone gas brand
19. Spanish artist
21. Its cap. is Sydney
24. Spritelike
28. "Is that so?"
31. Pee Wee of Ebbets Field
32. "Piece of the rock" company, informally
33. Stock market transaction
35. Brooklyn campus: Abbr.
36. Red deer
38. Responds to stimuli
40. Estuary
41. Pharmaceutical watchdog grp.
42. Bursts, as a balloon
45. Explosion sound
49. Riot spray
52. Basketball position: Abbr.
54. Arsenal contents
55. ___ one's time: wait
56. ___ choy (Chinese green)
57. Sitcom producer Norman
58. Author Martin or Kingsley
59. ___ Paulo, Brazil
60. Florentine river

Down

1. Rock music's ___ Straits
2. "Mila 18" novelist
3. Cow sounds
4. Cleopatra's love
5. Pen tip
6. Arctic birds
7. Store goods: Abbr.
8. Royal home
9. ___ Simbel
10. Blouse or shirt
11. Humor finale?
20. Enjoy a book again
22. Begins, as work
23. Major conflict
25. Pool table cover
26. Goddess pictured in Egyptian tombs
27. Recent, in Germany
28. Algerian city
29. Toss
30. One of two hardy followers
32. ___ Beta Kappa
34. Telephonic 3
37. Conical shelters
39. Occult doctrine
43. Banned pollutants, briefly
44. Plato's promenade
46. Hebrew dry measure
47. Arabian Sea adjoiner
48. Italian statesman Aldo
49. CEO's degree, maybe
50. Order between "ready" and "fire"
51. 401, in old Rome
53. "It's a Wonderful Life" studio

Solution on page 353

Puzzle 200

Across

1. Iwo ___
5. Cleanse
9. Dunce
12. Well ventilated
13. Hardly any
14. Expire
15. Get up
16. Singer Turner
17. Conclusion
18. Help a crook
20. Ketch's pair
22. Grace, e.g.
25. Young socialite
26. Dressed as a judge
27. Mail again
30. Rowboat propeller
31. Prefix with profit
32. Shipping magnate Onassis
34. Made an incursion
37. Turkic speaker
39. Vintage wheels
40. Insertion marks
41. Poet Teasdale et al.
44. Invited
45. Have bills
46. Unsatisfactory
48. Chicago paper, informally
52. "Ode on a Grecian ___"
53. Slender woodwind
54. Listen to
55. Deli loaf
56. Cookie containers
57. Bullets, for example

Down

1. Food container
2. "Richard ___"
3. Ms. alternative
4. Reply to the captain
5. In a little while
6. Keep ___ (persist)
7. Handyman's vehicle
8. Mingo player on "Daniel Boone"
9. Poems of tribute
10. "___ Misbehavin'"
11. Government agents
19. Four-poster, e.g.
21. Bart's grandfather
22. PGA member
23. Lion's sound
24. Magician's start
25. ___ of iniquity
27. Fishing gear
28. Basketballer Archibald
29. "Doggone it!"
31. Classic opening?
33. Form 1040 org.
35. Nest egg component, briefly
36. Autocrat
37. Small child
38. Singer Franklin
40. Anxieties
41. Become disillusioned
42. Out of whack
43. Painter Magritte
44. Unexpected advantage
47. ___-Wan Kenobi of "Star Wars"
49. Radiation unit
50. "Take me as ___"
51. Pal in the 'hood

Solution on page 353

Puzzle 201

Across

1. '30s boxing champ Max
5. Mom's mate
8. Knighted Guinness
12. Like the storied duckling
13. Pesticide-regulating org.
14. Zilch, to Zapata
15. Chose
17. Prohibitionists
18. Decade divs.
19. That woman
20. Flirt with
21. Diatribes
23. Roman emperor
26. White ___
27. Beatles adjective
30. As yet
33. Actress Stevens
35. Grog ingredient
36. Criticize, slangily
38. Barn area where hay is kept
39. With anticipation
42. In a germane manner
45. "___ gratias"
46. Pep
49. Feather scarves
50. September birthstone
52. "Livin' La Vida ___" (Ricky Martin hit)
53. Small guitar
54. Any day now
55. The "E" of B.P.O.E.
56. Old horse
57. Mafia bosses

Down

1. In use
2. Stress, perhaps
3. Right-angled shapes
4. Sandwich bread
5. Actor Ustinov
6. Musical dramas
7. Inflate, as a bill
8. Mountains in Chile
9. Julie's "Doctor Zhivago" role
10. "Grand" brand
11. Detective's job
16. T'ai ___ ch'uan
20. Printed material
21. Coal delivery unit
22. Author John ___ Passos
23. Above, in poems
24. Capote, to friends
25. Haw's companion
27. "Alice" spin-off
28. TV extraterrestrial
29. Louisville Slugger
31. Anita of jazz
32. Artificial locks
34. "Tarzan" star Ron
37. Pop singer Neil
39. "___ Dream" (Wagner aria)
40. Fasten anew, in a way
41. Remove, as branches
42. Ready and willing's partner
43. Combine, as resources
44. Bulletin-board fastener
46. Italian wine
47. De-wrinkle
48. Haberdashery department
50. Great ball o' fire?
51. Possessed

Solution on page 353

Puzzle 202

Across

1. Does better than
5. Fond du ___
8. Spanish house
12. Diva's melody
13. Yvette's "yes"
14. Emcee Trebek
15. Conks on the head
16. Bi- + one
17. Kind of curve, in math
18. "___ real nowhere man ..."
20. Cancels a dele
21. Is concerned
24. Get moving
25. Elite guest roster
26. Cowboy ropes
29. ___ Moines, Iowa
30. Collision sound
31. Paint carefully
33. Part of S.W.A.K.
36. Quotable catcher Yogi
38. ___ King Cole
39. Walking ___: ecstatic
40. Put ___ to (end)
43. Teen's bane
45. Pencil filler
46. "See ya!"
47. Evening, in Paris
51. Female horse
52. Wide shoe specification
53. Dear, to Donizetti
54. Tsp. and tbsp.
55. Welby and Kildare: Abbr.
56. ___ bucco

Down

1. Restaurant bill
2. Tijuana treasure
3. Spot on a playing card
4. Obis
5. Land parcels
6. Mystical glow
7. XXXIV tripled
8. Social groups
9. "It's a Sin to Tell ___"
10. Telegraphed
11. X and Y on a graph
19. N.Y. wintertime
20. Bro's sibling
21. Ungentlemanly sort
22. Brewpub offerings
23. Move up
24. Sandwich meat
26. Terhune title character
27. Polish border river
28. New Delhi dress
30. Put money on
32. Saloon
34. Battery poles
35. Drink like a cat
36. "___ voyage!"
37. Romanian composer Georges
40. Gluck of opera
41. Line of stitches
42. Fruit pie
43. Philosopher A.J. ___
44. Average grades
46. Fourposter, e.g.
48. Western alliance: Abbr.
49. Tax agency: Abbr.
50. Aussie jumper

Solution on page 353

Puzzle 203

Across

1. Sauna sounds
5. Call at the net
8. Discard
12. Achievement
13. Suffix with east
14. Bullring figure
15. Part in a play
16. Gloppy stuff
17. Too
18. Beginning stage
20. Take long steps
22. Install, as carpeting
24. Suffix for mountain
25. Entered gradually
29. 1964 Elvis song
33. However, briefly
34. Dad
36. Particle with a charge
37. Latin dance
40. Got going
43. High peak
45. Beer relative
46. Flyer Earhart
49. Metabolism descriptor
53. Dreadful
54. Columnist Landers
56. Dear, to Luigi
57. Angered
58. Mai ___ (rum drink)
59. Laced up
60. Prescriptions, for short
61. Part of D.A.
62. Do in, as a dragon

Down

1. Frizzy hairdo
2. Ages and ages
3. Dutch portraitist Frans
4. Brosnan TV role
5. Table support
6. Love's inspiration
7. CD alternative
8. Elevator alternative
9. "___ your horses!"
10. Irish Gaelic
11. Scooby-___
19. Youngster
21. Actor Stephen of "The Crying Game"
23. Sharp bark
25. Aviators in tabloids
26. Cry of discovery
27. Impresario Hurok
28. Negatives
30. Model builder's buy
31. Howard of slapstick
32. ___ of the line
35. Harper Valley gp.
38. Arabs
39. One way to the WWW
41. Mass robe
42. Responds to a stimulus
44. Gaucho gear
46. Suffix with billion
47. TV's talking horse
48. Premed course: Abbr.
50. Go to sea
51. Surroundings
52. Lord's mate
53. Poorly lit
55. Louse egg

Solution on page 353

Puzzle 204

Across

1. Spoon-bender Geller
4. Part of B&B
7. Flabbergast
11. Got together
12. New Haven collegians
14. Simplify
15. Zero-star review
16. Ring weapon
17. Selected, as straws
18. Exactly right
20. Ecol. watchdog
22. "___ y plata" (Montana's motto)
23. Idaho product
27. Rubbernecker
30. Active volcano, e.g.
31. Kind of sister
32. Coast Guard officer: Abbr.
33. Most loyal
37. Doesn't consent
40. "Amen!"
41. Land in la mer
42. ___ Arbor, Mich.
43. Plays for time
47. Victories
50. Solemn vow
52. Reaction to a mouse
53. Teen's torment
54. Run away
55. No matter which
56. Requisite
57. Victoria's Secret product
58. Bambi's mom, for one

Down

1. Baseball officials, for short
2. Gather up crops
3. Pay ___ mind
4. Prior to
5. Donahue of "Father Knows Best"
6. Put down, slangily
7. Cool and calm
8. Driveway covering
9. Put to work
10. Just minted
13. Instruction segments
19. Rocky pinnacle
21. Burst open
24. Knocks for a loop
25. Volunteer State: Abbr.
26. Ballpark expression
27. Fast flyers: Abbr.
28. Corrida critter
29. Adjoin, with "on"
34. Wiped away
35. Daily riser
36. ___ seven: 6:50
37. Many a bridesmaid
38. Tennis great Gibson
39. Thumbs-up vote
44. X-ray vision blocker
45. TV host Jay
46. Type of terrier
47. Washed-out
48. Skating surface
49. Opposite of SSW
51. Liturgical vestment

Solution on page 354

Puzzle 205

Across

1. Type of poem
4. Lays down a lawn
8. "Durn it!"
12. First-aid box
13. Lieutenant Kojak, to friends
14. Race in "The Time Machine"
15. Coward
17. Reclined
18. Deep down
19. Corn throwaways
20. "I ___ Rock": Simon and Garfunkel
21. Tiled art
23. Spring plantings
26. Walkman batteries
27. "___ culpa"
28. JFK listings
29. Ave. crossers
30. Yacht spar
31. Cries of delight
32. Go out, as a flame
33. ___ and raves
34. Maker of popular "pieces"
36. ___ Remo, Italy
37. Places for patches
38. Feldspar, e.g.
42. Counting-out starter
43. Tedious
44. The Green Hornet's aide
45. General Robt. ___
46. "Yabba dabba ___!"
47. College in North Carolina
48. ___ out: barely makes
49. A, in Aachen

Down

1. Creole cuisine staple
2. Losing effort?
3. Carve in stone
4. Cooks, in a way
5. "Gone with the Wind" surname
6. Fender ding
7. Boozer
8. Site of an oracle of Apollo
9. Mobile resident
10. Most raucous
11. ___ and tonic
16. Enjoys a book
19. Funnyman Bill, familiarly
21. Pas' spouses
22. Long-running Broadway show
23. Burn the surface of
24. Heavenly
25. Gradually become part of
26. Gulped down
29. Lisa, to Bart Simpson
30. Thick heads of hair
32. ___ Moines
33. Rajahs' wives
35. Watch secretly
36. "Yes ___ Bob!"
38. Half of half-and-half
39. Went by taxi
40. Mine, in Marseilles
41. Writer Uris
42. Barely earn, with "out"
43. Golf-ball platform

Solution on page 354

Puzzle 206

Across

1. Little brat
4. Shed tears
7. Circle the Earth
12. Evergreen
13. Covered up
14. Blackbird
15. Guile
17. Opted for home cooking
18. Mouse-spotter's cry
19. Parts to play
20. Talons
23. Shiverer's sound
24. Stage show-off
25. "On the Waterfront" director Kazan
28. Period in office
32. Hawaiian instrument, for short
33. Mails away
35. Batter's stat
36. Polite fellow
38. From a fresh angle
39. Cosmonaut's home
40. Psyche segments
42. Clean the chalkboard
44. Runway vehicle
47. Z, to a Brit
48. King or emperor
49. Leave port
53. Church keyboard
54. "The Sopranos" station
55. Nemesis
56. Is afraid of
57. Fifth-century warrior
58. Promgoer's rental

Down

1. "No ___ ands or buts!"
2. .001 of an inch
3. Meddle
4. American and Swiss
5. Take a chance with
6. QB's gains: Abbr.
7. Astrologer Sydney
8. Sharp comeback
9. Composer Jacques
10. Bjorn rival
11. Change for a 20
16. Partner of improved
20. Gulp down
21. Erie or Huron
22. Prayer finale
23. Expressed, as farewell
26. Meadowlands
27. Country stopover
29. First name in household humor
30. Stats for Bonds
31. Slough
34. Fond of
37. Musical ineptitude
41. Laura and Bruce
43. Routes: Abbr.
44. Grad student's mentor
45. Angler's purchase
46. Stagnant water problem
47. Indian ox
49. "No whispering!"
50. To the rear, at sea
51. Letters on a chit
52. ___ Luthor

Solution on page 354

Puzzle 207

Across

1. Lb. and kg.
4. ___ de la Cit
7. Kemo ___ (the Lone Ranger)
11. Own, in Scotland
12. Gear teeth
14. ". . . and to ___ good night!"
15. Toronto's loc.
16. Asian nurse
17. ___ St. Laurent
18. Calypso cousin
19. Prepared
21. Part of a hammer head
23. Atmosphere
24. "___ my wit's end!"
26. Knox and Dix: Abbr.
27. Postpone, with "off"
30. Proverbial sure thing
34. Bon ___; witticism
35. Not happy
36. Enzyme suffixes
37. Opposite of max.
38. Lions and tigers
40. Storyteller
44. Mil. jet locale
47. Chops down
48. Outside: Prefix
49. Lamb's cry
50. A ___pittance: very little
51. Branch of Islam
52. K-O filler
53. "Liberal" studies
54. Above, in poetry
55. Mouse hater's cry

Down

1. "___ on first?"
2. Armored vehicle
3. Isolate
4. Part of Caesar's boast
5. Arthur Miller's salesman
6. Old-fashioned expletive
7. Pop singer Leo
8. Thomas ___ Edison
9. Ran in the wash
10. Not hard
13. Close-fitting dress
20. ___ and shine
22. Airport info: Abbr.
24. Apple competitor
25. "O Sole ___"
26. 1-800-FLOWERS rival
27. Adequate
28. One: Fr.
29. Football scores: Abbr.
31. "Beauty ___ the eye . . ."
32. Port in the Loire Valley
33. Stetson, e.g.
37. Exodus leader
38. ___ pie (sweetheart)
39. Loud, as the surf
40. "___ Lama Ding Dong"
41. Downsizer
42. "Dead ___" (Dick Francis novel)
43. Sound in a cave
45. Hall of ___
46. Check point?

Solution on page 354

Puzzle 208

Across

1. Broadway star Verdon
5. Letter-shaped fastener
9. Doctrine: Suffix
12. San ___: Riviera resort
13. Chosen one
15. Scottish port
16. Aardvark
17. Iridescent button material
19. Sporty car roofs
20. Memorable sayings
22. Place a wager
23. "Cry, the Beloved Country" author
24. Gymnastics device
25. Digital readout, for short
28. Make smooth
29. Foot the bill
30. Dullard
31. Illiterates' signatures
32. Limb
33. Star in the constellation Cygnus
34. Unkind remark
35. Extends a subscription
36. Covers with concrete
39. Theater sections
40. Krypton, for one
42. Verne hero
45. Broadway opening
46. Nagy of Hungary
47. Cool, in the '50s
48. Yuletide drinks
49. Okla. or La., once

Down

1. Miracle-___ (garden brand)
2. "Charlotte's ___"
3. Flows forth
4. Nine-sided figure
5. Former Russian rulers
6. Hawaiian state bird
7. Max.
8. Move unsteadily
9. "Leave ___ Beaver"
10. Leak slowly
11. French seas
14. Suffragist Carrie
18. One hundred yrs.
20. Uppermost point
21. Jay's competitor
22. San Francisco/Oakland separator
24. "Paper or plastic?" item
25. In need of company
26. Racing team
27. Society newbies
29. Cribbage marker
30. Fund-raiser
32. Pay attention
33. Ph.D., e.g.
34. Bruce or Laura of Hollywood
35. Valentine flowers
36. "Oh, nonsense!"
37. Suffix with utter
38. Prez's backup
39. Singer k. d. ___
41. Yucky stuff
43. Doberman's warning
44. Berlin's country: Abbr.

Solution on page 354

Puzzle 209

Across

1. Fair
5. Mischievous children
9. Guy
12. "The Grapes of Wrath" figure
13. Not carefully considered
14. Woodsman's tool
15. Strong urges
16. Lyons friend
17. Boeing product
18. "Of ___ I sing"
20. Copper-zinc alloy
22. Capital of Tibet
25. Dear old ___
26. Solemn pledge
27. Clinton Attorney General
30. Easy marks
34. Ailing
35. Ill-kempt
37. Greek X
38. Wee
40. Hera's mother
41. Claiborne of fashion
42. Mind reader's claim
44. Put out, as a fire
46. Dress fold
49. Quick look
51. Jar topper
52. Cooking pot
54. Wound cover
58. E.T.'s ship
59. Neighbor of Cambodia
60. Lay eyes on
61. Small wonder
62. Office phone nos.
63. Gross minus net, to a trucker

Down

1. Elation
2. Luau strings
3. One of the seven deadlies
4. Proctor's handouts
5. Dies___
6. Broadway aunt
7. Pitchfork-shaped letter
8. Biblical queen's home
9. Goya's "Naked ___"
10. Chopping tools
11. Tennis court dividers
19. Poet Crane
21. Country rtes.
22. 57
23. Romance novelist Victoria
24. Hole-punching tools
25. Be overly fond
28. Gunfighter Wyatt
29. High degree
31. Legal rights grp.
32. Key letters
33. Medium or extra-large
36. Part of a Seinfeld catchphrase
39. Pro's vote
43. Filched
45. Day one
46. Outlet insert
47. "Not on your ___!"
48. Ancient region bordering Palestine
49. Coin entry
50. Big Mama
53. Negligent
55. 1860s abbr.
56. Fourth mo.
57. "So long"

Solution on page 354

Puzzle 210

Across

1. Electric power network
5. G-man's org.
8. "Do ___ others as . . ."
12. Repose
13. Operate
14. Dresden denial
15. One of Columbus' fleet
16. N.Y. clock setting
17. Scotsman's wear
18. Main order in a restaurant
20. Verdi opera based on a Shakespeare play
22. Robinson or Doubtfire
23. Beer source
24. London's Royal ___ Hall
27. Production
31. Washington and ___ University
32. Chemical ending
33. Afternoon nap
37. Emceed
40. Ridge in Washington
41. "___ to Billy Joe"
42. Dahl or Francis
45. City on the Black Sea
49. Immodest look
50. Murphy, for one
52. Literary pen name
53. Wings' measure
54. Many moons ___
55. Ugandan exile
56. Sounds of amazement
57. Swelled head
58. Whipping memento

Down

1. Hereditary factor
2. Wet forecast
3. Doesn't exist
4. "Heavens to Betsy!"
5. Least restrained
6. School transport
7. Lock, stock, and barrel
8. Given away
9. Playwright Simon
10. Cash register
11. Latch ___ (get)
19. Make a mistake
21. Upsilon preceder
24. Hirt and Hirschfeld
25. Floral necklace
26. Domesticated insect
28. Indy stop
29. Sport-___ (off-road vehicle)
30. One of the Kennedys
34. Howard and Isaac
35. Whole bunch
36. Lab slide subjects
37. Bad luck
38. Unusual
39. Teeter-totter
42. Part of a.k.a.
43. Bank takeback, for short
44. Actress Remini of "The King of Queens"
46. "Ditto"
47. Black & Decker competitor
48. "___ Too Proud to Beg" (1966 hit)
51. Poultry product

Solution on page 355

Puzzle 211

Across

1. He preceded JFK
4. NBC show since 1975
7. Bachelor parties
12. Craving
13. "The Gold Bug" writer
14. Golfer Palmer's nickname
15. Run longer than expected
17. Jessica of "Tootsie"
18. Before, to a poet
19. Connection
20. Wood strips
23. Concorde
24. Actor Hunter
25. Sporting sword
28. "The Forsyte ___"
32. Wallet item
33. Writer Dahl
35. Train component
36. Tree in Miami
38. Adjudicate
39. Shoebox letters
40. Vigoda of sitcoms
42. MasterCard alternatives
44. Spy novelist John Le ___
47. Place to park
48. One of "The Honeymooners"
49. Stressful position
53. September bloom
54. Gibbon or orang
55. 66, for one: Abbr.
56. Christmas carols
57. Diocese
58. It's not gross

Down

1. Batiking need
2. Family room
3. Football lineman
4. Less dense
5. Pitch indicator
6. Dixie general
7. Preserves, as pork
8. Qualities
9. Stuart queen
10. Lerner and Loewe musical
11. "Now I've ___ everything!"
16. Give the green light
20. Word on an octagonal sign
21. Actress Turner
22. Son of Adam
23. Auction off
26. Mull (over)
27. Seine contents
29. Passes easily
30. Greek Mother Earth
31. Bellicose Olympian
34. Fan
37. Mime Marceau
41. Brewskis
43. "___ a deal!"
44. "Misery" costar James
45. In addition
46. Solemn ceremony
47. Canter's cousin
49. Keeps
50. East end?
51. Broke the fast
52. Hanoi New Year

Solution on page 355

Puzzle 212

Across

1. "The Greatest" in the ring
4. Braun and Gabor
8. Bryn ___, PA
12. Piece of turf
13. Fender flaw
14. Most-draftable status
15. Parisian summer
16. Direction from which el
    sol rises
17. Property right
18. State with confidence
20. Furry companions
22. Windy City trains
23. Former coin of Spain
26. Woolen fabric
29. Meet a poker bet
30. Business card no.
31. Tavern mugfuls
32. Carrier from Stockholm
33. Sicily's highest point
34. Stein contents
35. Voided tennis shot
36. Paradisiacal places
37. Lease signer
39. Senate vote
40. Amount of space
41. Like many tuxedos
45. Churchill Downs event
47. Vessel for Jack and Jill
49. Conquistador's
    treasure
50. Western ski resort
51. Highland dialect
52. Light bite
53. Lickety-split

54. Alteration canceler
55. "Golly!"

Down

1. On the Atlantic
2. Oodles
3. Fateful day in March
4. English Channel swimmer
   Gertrude
5. Guarantees a pension
6. Aardvark's morsel
7. Treeless plains
8. Drops feathers
9. Licorice-flavored cordial
10. Pint-sized
11. Competed in a 10K
19. Brain scans, for short

21. Extra-wide shoe size
24. Where Nashville is: Abbr.
25. Word of sorrow
26. German industrial region
27. French fashion magazine
28. Plays over
29. Took a break
32. Pancho's ponchos
33. Home for Adam and Eve
35. Brenda or Peggy
36. Hole in a sneaker
38. Dog's reward
39. Wake up
42. Chinese secret society
43. City north of Pittsburgh
44. Idiot
45. U.K. fliers

46. Neighbor of Miss.
48. High school elective

Solution on page 355

Puzzle 213

Across
1. Trucker with a transmitter
5. "Comprende?"
8. "Take ___ your leader"
12. Calla lily family
13. Gene material, in brief
14. Flying: Prefix
15. Scores 72 on a 72 course
16. Cleo's bane
17. Trough fare
18. Tokyo, to shoguns
19. Science guy Bill
20. Purchase prices
21. Historic beginning?
23. Hatfields or McCoys, e.g.
25. Imitators
27. Paving goo
28. Speaks, informally
31. Pleasantly warm
33. Gambler's milieu
35. Degree div.
36. E-mail guffaw
38. Seabees' motto
39. Ex-Secretary Federico
40. Cleaving tool
41. Strong winds
44. Elevs.
46. Iowa hrs.
49. Drooling dog of the comics
50. Opponent
51. Maui dance
52. Nair competitor
53. Bruin legend Bobby
54. Valentine's Day figure
55. Serf
56. London's Big ___
57. Kitty cries

Down
1. Superhero's garment
2. Actor Pitt
3. Old-world
4. Apt. units
5. Haulage cart
6. Bug
7. Generation ___
8. Stoneworker
9. Electrified fish
10. Harness-race pace
11. Clumsy one's cry
19. Gets cozy
20. Capital of Venezuela
22. Monopoly purchases: Abbr.
24. Varnish resin
25. 24-hr. cash source
26. Luau food
28. Cushy job
29. Dead-___ street
30. Animal house
32. Over there, old-style
34. Jazz instrument
37. Pakistani city
39. Pro golfer Calvin
41. "___ with the Wind"
42. Summer beverages
43. Mortgage
45. Gull cousin
47. Like molasses
48. Soviet news source
50. Palm (off)
51. ___ and haw

Solution on page 355

Puzzle 214

Across

1. Basketball official
4. Lower, as headlights
7. Army cops: Abbr.
10. Woodchopper's tool
11. Library device
13. Dot-com's address
14. Andrew Jackson's home, with "The"
16. Beetle
17. Great server on the court
18. Fountain drinks
20. Turning points
23. Felt cap
24. Physics units
25. Party attendees
28. Designer initials
29. Archaeological fragment
31. Ad ___ committee
33. Group of five
35. Dunce
36. Paper holder
37. "Julius ___" (Shakespeare play)
39. Quick-witted
42. Change residences
43. Experimentation room
44. Tour outline
49. Eye, to Eduardo
50. Kitchen gadget
51. Except for
52. Price add-on
53. In a merry mood
54. Charisse of "Singin' in the Rain"

Down

1. Pep-rally word
2. English river
3. ___-de-lance
4. Palm tree fruits
5. ___-Tass (Russian news agency)
6. Ryan of "When Harry Met Sally"
7. Newsman Roger
8. Malay boat
9. Some cameras, briefly
11. Monopoly rollers
12. Do some lawn repair
15. Bach's "___ in B Minor"
19. Liq. measures
20. "Eureka!" is one
21. Sound hoarse
22. Just sitting around
23. Mink or sable
25. Roam (about)
26. The one close by
27. Body of an organism
29. Radio interference
30. Was in possession of
32. EMT's technique
34. "Fresh Air" network
35. Crystal ball user
37. ___ Island, N.Y.
38. Swear to
39. Kind of car or machine
40. Goya's "The Naked ___"
41. "Life is like ___ of chocolates"
42. Oscar winner Sorvino
45. ___ out (dress up)
46. "Nightline" network
47. Chess's ___ Lopez opening
48. Balance sheet abbr.

Solution on page 355

Puzzle 215

Across

1. Nincompoop
5. Pushrod pushers
9. Move diagonally
12. Traveler's document
13. Something detested
15. Swine's supper
16. Party hearty
17. Russian Revolution leader
19. Bartletts
20. Actor Omar
22. Future flower
23. Lab glove material
24. Hole in the green
25. Slangy refusal
28. Picked out of a lineup
29. ___ Tolkien
30. "Livin' La Vida ___": Ricky Martin hit
31. CD players
32. Boston Red ___
33. Observer
34. Artist Vermeer
35. "The Clemency of Titus" composer
36. Side road
39. Choreographer Champion
40. Red Riding Hood's rescuer
42. Teeny bites
45. Ran in
46. Computer nerd
47. Japanese currency
48. Give the eye to
49. Get a glimpse of

Down

1. Boob tubes
2. Actor Wheaton
3. Sequesters
4. Came to a point
5. Ariz. neighbor
6. Have ___ (be connected)
7. Dallas cager, for short
8. Increase, as production
9. Greek "Z"
10. Manchurian border river
11. Empty spaces
14. Left in a hurry
18. Decide against
20. Glided
21. Trip to Mecca
22. Prickly husk
24. '80s-'90s Honda sports car
25. Document certifiers
26. Perfect server
27. Witch's blemish
29. Actor Voight
30. Cough drop
32. Insists
33. "This instant!"
34. Green mineral
35. Paris newspaper, with "Le"
36. NYC theater district
37. Old times
38. In need of patching
39. Critic Greene
41. Bus. get-together
43. Kind of rally
44. Cloud's place

Solution on page 355

Puzzle 216

Across

1. Bridge distance
5. Grill partner
8. Baseball's Say Hey Kid
12. Word before ranger or wolf
13. Adam's mate
14. Right away, in memos
15. Chooses (to)
16. Yahtzee cube
17. Frost-covered
18. Attention-getting sound
19. Bustles
21. Coin opening
24. "Of course," slangily
28. Potpie veggie
31. Struggle to make, with "out"
32. Secretary of State Root
33. Coves
35. Introduction
36. ___ home (out)
37. "By the way . . ."
38. Go on and on
39. Cussed
40. Beame and Burrows
42. Monorail unit
44. Moon goddess
48. Foot fraction
51. Haul into court
53. "Pretty Maids All in ___"
54. Mane area
55. Part of AT&T: Abbr.
56. Colt's mother
57. Printer's color
58. Class
59. Lost one's footing

Down

1. Pig food
2. Boston orchestra
3. Household pests
4. Snug spots
5. Stream bottom
6. Pilot a plane
7. Riverbank growth
8. Sicilian port
9. "___ was saying"
10. Thanksgiving tuber
11. Espionage agent
20. Cyclops feature
22. A, B, or C
23. Approvals
25. Neat
26. ___ Pet
27. Head turner at the beach
28. Bowler's target
29. Sufficient, in poetry
30. Kind of saxophone
34. Made of clay
35. Research room
37. Prophet who anointed Saul
41. Criticizes
43. Piedmont wine area
45. Eurasia's ___ Mountains
46. "Me neither"
47. Wowed
48. Bus. abbr.
49. Voice vote
50. H&R Block employee
52. Tundra wanderer

Solution on page 356

Puzzle 217

Across

1. Chopping tool
4. Med. sch. course
8. Migration
12. ___ Alamos
13. "Beowulf," e.g.
14. Casanova
15. Urban vehicle
16. Chick sound
17. "Give it ___!"
18. British unit of weight
20. "___ 'em!"
22. Tiny hill dwellers
25. Sports data
29. Cellar dweller's position
32. "___ your disposal"
34. When doubled, a dance
35. French friends
36. Born: Fr.
37. Poker token
38. Goose egg
39. 2001, e.g.
40. Roosters' mates
41. Feel blindly
43. Acting part
45. "Say ___!"
47. Stable compartment
51. Boring routines
54. Taj Majal site
57. Abba's "Mamma ___"
58. Trapped like ___
59. Narrow aperture
60. Handful
61. Chimney duct
62. The Boston ___
63. What eds. edit

Down

1. Priestly garb
2. Strike through
3. Former gas name
4. Colorado ski town
5. Scottish denial
6. Get mellower
7. Bugler's evening call
8. Expanse of land
9. Decompose
10. Part of E.U.: Abbr.
11. Very important
19. Cole and Turner
21. Adherent's suffix
23. Trident prong
24. Do finger painting
26. Post-workout symptom
27. "The ___ Man"
28. Chuckleheads
29. "Auld ___ Syne"
30. Eastern prince
31. Farm storage building
33. Prefix for space
37. Guitarist Atkins
39. Nay's opposite
42. Adhesive
44. Atty.-to-be exams
46. Lock holder
48. Two-band, as a radio
49. Untruths
50. Statutes
51. WWII heroes
52. Hi-tech bookmark
53. Letter after sigma
55. Day-___ paint
56. Tear up

Solution on page 356

Puzzle 218

Across

1. Sense of humor
4. ___ offensive (Vietnam War event)
7. Swedish soprano Jenny
11. ___-ha
12. Do harvesting
14. ___ account (never)
15. Year, south of the border
16. Estranges
18. Snarl
20. President after Jimmy
21. Suffix with bombard
22. Put in a pleat
26. Cleans the slate
29. More difficult
30. Tennessee footballer
31. Ottoman official
32. Stick on a stick
36. Colorful fishes
39. Reduce
40. John's Yoko
41. Grass mat
42. Levels of society
46. Backward
50. Mohawk-sporting actor
51. Restrooms, informally
52. Elk relative
53. Drill insert
54. Not as much
55. Bride's title
56. Debt letters

Down

1. Reporter's query
2. New Rochelle school
3. Cel character
4. Rose's home, in song
5. Certain anglers
6. Mai ___ (cocktail)
7. Repair shop substitute
8. Bank account amt.
9. SSW's reverse
10. Partners of don'ts
13. Birdcage feature
17. Nick Charles' wife
19. PX customers
23. Month after Shebat
24. Electronic game giant
25. Time periods
26. Foul doings
27. Capital of Italy
28. Swiss mountains
33. Appraise
34. Pope after Benedict IV
35. All through
36. Salad maker
37. Comes in
38. "High ___" (Anderson play)
43. Prefix with dexterity
44. Threesome
45. One of the Aleutians
46. Not feeling well
47. Scot's negative
48. Campers, briefly
49. Sleep stage, briefly

Solution on page 356

Puzzle 219

Across

1. Kibbutz dance
5. Make, as tea
9. Rx watchdog
12. The White House's ___ Office
13. Water-skiing locale
14. Alley-___ (basketball play)
15. Very observant
17. Dollar bill
18. Outdated
19. The sun is one
21. Hangs in there
24. Be a burglar
26. Paramedic: Abbr.
27. Daisy or Fannie
28. Noted nightclub
31. Ancient kingdom east of the Dead Sea
33. Kind of verb: Abbr.
34. Catch the wind under one's wings
35. Construction location
36. Urban music
37. Chem., for one
38. They, to Monet
40. Knight's mount
42. Menu
44. Homer Simpson outburst
45. "Long ___ and Far Away"
46. Ideals
52. Fifth sign of the zodiac
53. River in Hesse
54. Astronaut Armstrong
55. Moon vehicle, for short
56. Italy's capital
57. Bloody

Down

1. Gardening tool
2. Egg cells
3. Scott Joplin tune
4. Apportion
5. Ran, as colors
6. Flat fish
7. Just manage, with "out"
8. Pie slice
9. Unencumbered
10. Lady of Lisbon
11. One who imitates
16. Raised railways
20. Baglike structures
21. Moon vehicles
22. "Help!" in France
23. Cruise lodging unit
24. Lee and Teasdale
25. Maryland collegian
27. Tract of wet ground
29. Walk back and forth
30. Mojave-like
32. Suspenders alternative
39. Shunned one
40. Outfield surface
41. Person, place, or ___
42. Use the phone
43. "The Morning Watch" writer James
44. "You wouldn't ___!"
47. "Without further ___ . . ."
48. "What's the Frequency, Kenneth?" band
49. Prefix with thermal
50. Fallen space station
51. Like a fox

Solution on page 356

Puzzle 220

Across

1. Metros and Prizms
5. Finder's reward
8. Moon valley
12. Not at all polite
13. Minister, slangily
14. Expression of understanding
15. Seeing red
16. Dick was his veep
17. Online journal
18. Synagogue scrolls
20. Three-toed birds
22. Make a collar
23. Recite
24. Outlaw
27. Rooster's mate
29. Loved ones
33. Massage
34. Cataract site
36. J. Edgar Hoover's gp.
37. Once more
40. Taxi
42. Twitch
43. Cut off
45. Key above caps lock
47. Stockholm resident
49. FBI employees
53. Not at all nice
54. Burglarize
56. Take a gander
57. Mean person
58. Barn bird
59. "Mon Oncle" star Jacques
60. Tea holders
61. Opposite SSW
62. Visit a store

Down

1. Courage
2. Money in Italy
3. Czech river
4. Four-door
5. "Flying" toy disk
6. Response to a rodent
7. "Tinker to ___ to Chance"
8. Steakhouse offering
9. Mallorca, por ejemplo
10. Some summer babies
11. Race segment
19. "So there!"
21. Fooled
24. Playtex product
25. Hot mo.
26. L.A. Clippers' org.
28. MoMA's home
30. Not fore
31. Stat for Sosa
32. Incite to attack, with "on"
35. Fit for consumption
38. Actresses Graff and Kristen
39. Nonverbal agreement
41. Bellhop's burden
44. Eva or Juan
46. Hits hard
47. Bell-shaped lily
48. Toad feature
50. Webster of dictionaries
51. Dorothy Gale's dog
52. Leave out
53. Floor cleaner
55. Possess

Solution on page 356

Puzzle 221

Across

1. Andalusian aunts
5. All het up
9. It's south of Eur.
12. Help a hoodlum
13. Opera highlights
14. Caribbean, for one
15. Father: Fr.
16. Aspirin target
17. Member of Cong.
18. Boulder
20. Oktoberfest vessels
22. Makeup exam
24. Stop-sign color
27. Scale starts
28. Metric work units
32. Destroys slowly
34. More meddlesome
36. Cause of distress
37. Minuscule amount
38. Scoreboard postings: Abbr.
39. Quaking in one's boots
42. Roofed-in gallery
44. Venetian blind parts
49. ___-K (toddlers' school)
50. Actress Cameron
52. ___ gin fizz
53. Have dinner
54. Repetitive learning method
55. Hightailed it
56. Resident ending
57. Existence: Lat.
58. D.C. pols

Down

1. Army "lights out" tune
2. "Not bloody likely"
3. Prefix with -nautics
4. WWII submachine gun
5. AOL or MSN
6. Facetious tributes
7. Exclusive group
8. Enjoys an elegant meal
9. Special-interest grp.
10. Professional charges
11. Made tracks
19. Earth, in Essen
21. Residents: Suffix
23. Goddess of the dawn
24. Confederate soldier, for short
25. Period of history
26. Put on, as clothes
29. Make a tear in
30. Garner
31. Fourth-yr. collegians
33. Family tree abbr.
34. Glasgow veto
35. Racetrack postings
37. Picks up the check
40. Leadership group
41. Lone Ranger's farewell
42. Smell ___ (be wary)
43. Neural network
45. D-Day craft: Abbr.
46. Shaving-cream ingredient
47. Ripped apart
48. Looks at
49. Architect Ieoh Ming ___
51. Last letter

Solution on page 356

Puzzle 222

Across

1. Merely
5. Wall St. debuts
9. "Zip-A-Dee-Doo-___"
12. Billion-selling cookie
13. Tennis champ Sampras
14. Gardner of "The Night of the Iguana"
15. Dog barks
16. Colander
18. Italian writer Umberto
20. It's west of Que.
21. Moved in a circular path
24. Hindu social group
28. "Well, ___-di-dah"
29. Thin mud
33. Ca++ or Cl-, e.g.
34. Hawaiian paste
35. Ram's cry
36. Family
37. Sing wordlessly
38. ___ and Cher
40. Israelite judge
41. Advil competitor
43. Double-curve letters
45. Greece neighbor: Abbr.
47. Org. that keeps an eye on pilots
48. "The Flintstones" setting
52. Old Ford models
56. Waiter's payoff
57. PC monitors
58. Marionette man Tony
59. Agt.'s take
60. Boxing results: Abbr.
61. Stuck in ___

Down

1. Happiness
2. Spoonbender Geller
3. Autumn mo.
4. ". . . off ___ the wizard"
5. ___ facto
6. Cat or dog
7. Another, in Andalusia
8. Medium's medium
9. Dapper ___
10. "___ Maria"
11. Kramden laugh syllable
17. "Ain't ___ shame?"
19. LP's successors
21. First Greek letter
22. "High Sierra" director Walsh
23. Doorbell sound
25. "Oliver Twist" villain
26. Sheer cotton
27. Singer Skinnay
30. Wall St. maneuver
31. James Bond creator Fleming
32. Homo sapiens
38. Choose
39. Congressional vote
42. Mover's truck
44. Spicy chip dip
46. Trunk cover
47. Parker who played Daniel Boone
48. Gas-additive letters
49. Facial spasm
50. Make a choice
51. Classic Pontiac
53. Road topper
54. Joanne of film
55. Rank above Cpl.

Solution on page 357

Puzzle 223

Across

1. Soused
4. Home of Arizona State
9. Holiday in Hue
12. "___ Maria"
13. "This Was ___ Nice Clambake"
14. Stop ___ dime
15. Bear's home
16. Skate's kin
17. "The Star-Spangled Banner" preposition
18. ___ Lauder
20. Wee bit
22. Pound sound
24. Small shot
27. Subtle alert
30. Actress Charlotte
32. Lugosi of film
33. "The Hairy ___" (O'Neill play)
34. Bleating beast
35. Sculler's implement
36. Weathercock
38. Royal flush card
39. Mama's boys
40. Halts legally
42. Opposite of NNW
44. "___ pig's eye!"
45. Reindeer herders
49. "The Gold-Bug" writer
51. Old Ford model
55. "All the Things You ___" (Kern tune)
56. Dashed
57. "___ you ashamed of yourself?"
58. Lobster eggs
59. Mel in Cooperstown
60. Riga natives
61. Pop the question

Down

1. Put on cargo
2. Folk singer Burl
3. Camper's cover
4. Bronco buster
5. Hurler's stat.
6. Stag attendees
7. Butter unit
8. Gratify
9. "Bye!"
10. WSW's opposite
11. Finish the road
19. Have supper
21. Priest's vestment
23. Guitar ridges
24. Hammer parts
25. Pizzazz
26. Paves
27. Macadamize
28. Health resorts
29. Conscious
31. Veneration
37. Years and years
39. The Aegean, e.g.
41. Of the Holy See
43. Casino machines
46. Legal lead-in
47. Major-leaguers
48. Look for
49. Old hand
50. Cheerios ingredient
52. Hot temper
53. Kind of profit
54. Explosive inits.

Solution on page 357

Puzzle 224

Across

1. Kilmer of "Batman Forever"
4. "Oh yeah? ___ who?"
7. Roman poet
11. "I Like ___"
12. Impoverished
14. Bundle
15. Coq au ___
16. Chills, as a drink
17. Tasting of wood, as some wines
18. Hang in there
20. DVD player ancestor
22. Z ___ "zebra"
23. Fertilizer ingredient
27. Significant
29. Erratic
30. Hustle
31. Drink cat-style
32. Citrus fruit
36. Literary spoof
39. For this reason
40. "Moby-Dick" captain
41. Arafat's org.
42. Chinese noodle dish
45. Old Testament scribe
48. Black: Fr.
50. Writer Serling
51. Loathsome
52. ___ souci
53. PanAm rival
54. Tennille of the Captain and Tennille
55. Agent's amount
56. Shoot the breeze

Down

1. On the qui ___
2. Closely related
3. Pay attention
4. Enthusiasm
5. Epoch in the Cenozoic Era
6. Pulitzer playwright Akins
7. City north of Lisbon
8. Itinerary preposition
9. Type
10. Actress Susan
13. Answers an invitation
19. GI entertainment sponsor
21. One with a beat
24. Free
25. Leading actor
26. Big buildup
27. "Yikes!"
28. Give the axe
33. Himalayan denizen
34. Guy's date
35. British jackets
36. Kind of Solution
37. What Richard III offered "my kingdom" for
38. Cap with a pompom
43. Des Moines is its capital
44. Bismarck's state: Abbr.
45. Small salamander
46. Chaotic scene
47. Sprint
49. Bumpkin

Solution on page 357

Puzzle 225

Across

1. DDE predecessor
4. Part of a dehumidifier
7. Lie in the sun
11. Sailor's "yes"
12. Summers in France
14. Toward the sheltered side
15. Dynamite relative
16. London farewell
17. Scattered, as seed
18. Certain fisherman
20. Red vegetables
22. Onassis
23. Took command of
24. Chairs
27. Look at
28. Six-pointers, for short
31. Daytona 500, for one
32. Opposite of 'tain't
33. Combustion byproduct
34. Paintings
35. Stimpy's sidekick
36. Dove houses
37. Pod vegetable
38. Duffer's goal
39. Mattress supports
41. Microscopic swimmer
44. Sock parts
45. Mystery writer Gardner
47. Rope-a-dope boxer
49. The ___ have it
50. Towering
51. Sum total
52. Like Mother Hubbard's cupboard
53. Submissions to eds.
54. 180 degrees from NNW

Down

1. Stovepipe
2. "Auld Lang ___"
3. Head, to Henri
4. Dwindles, with "out"
5. Early video game name
6. Fisherman's profit?
7. Headquartered
8. Bushelfuls
9. Puts in a hem
10. Barbie's former beau
13. Expensive furs
19. Behind schedule
21. Wide shoe width
24. Mallorca Mrs.
25. Barber's obstruction
26. Circus routine
27. Transgression
28. Kindergartner
29. Anonymous surname
30. D and C, in D.C.
32. Afternoon service
33. Achy
35. Collecting Soc. Sec.
36. Desert ruminants
37. Out-of-date
38. Becomes tiresome
39. Tofu source
40. Nasty look
42. Calls to a shepherd
43. "___ well that . . ."
44. Bill at the bar
46. St. Louis footballer
48. Suffix with percent

Solution on page 357

Puzzle 226

Across

1. Island of Napoleon's exile
5. Mom's partner
8. Hits, slangily
12. Duffers' goals
13. Believer
14. Ended in ___: drew
15. Biblical pottage purchaser
16. Without company
18. Brain-scan letters
19. Hard worker
20. Basic version: Abbr.
21. Happy feeling
23. Three times, in a prescription
25. Degrader
27. The Wizard of Menlo Park
31. Prefix meaning trillion
32. "Psycho" actress Miles
33. Milliner
36. Pep
38. Dallas school: Abbr.
39. "Mona ___"
40. Computer storage acronym
43. Encompassing everything
45. Family drs.
48. Pizza portion
50. "Guilty" or "not guilty"
51. Basketball targets
52. ATM-making co.
53. Flamingo color
54. Imminently
55. Hogs' home
56. All finished

Down

1. Blunt sword
2. Give off coherent light
3. Blowhard
4. Tempe campus: Abbr.
5. Rotary phone user
6. Hun leader
7. X out
8. Dance, in France
9. Oklahoma Indians
10. Half a quart
11. Bird food
17. Not worth ___ cent
19. ___ Wee Reese
22. Exams for would-be attys.
24. Splits
25. Olympics participant: Abbr.
26. Arthur who played Maude
28. Harem
29. Part of NATO: Abbr.
30. Aye's opposite
34. Olympic track champion Zatopek
35. Disagreeable encounters
36. Mystery author Queen
37. None at all
40. Reagan and Howard
41. "___ 'Clock Jump"
42. "Get ___ the Church on Time"
44. Bank no.
46. Sean or William
47. "For Pete's ___!"
49. ID with two hyphens
50. Mail order abbr.

Solution on page 357

Puzzle 227

Across
1. Mrs. and Mrs.
5. Walter Raleigh's title
8. Singer Lane
12. English river
13. Sun Devils' sch.
14. Rip up
15. Have concern
16. Male offspring
17. Shakespearean epithet
18. Proof-of-age items, for short
20. On a deck, perhaps
21. Moisten, as a turkey
24. Subtle "Hey!"
27. The Monkees' "___ Believer"
28. Mystery writer Marsh
30. Tic-___-toe
33. Pull apart
34. Estonian city
35. "Long, Long ___"
36. Hosp. employees
37. Do a tailor's job
38. Stimpy's cartoon pal
39. Despondent comment
40. Group of students
42. USMC enlistees
45. Govt. narcotics watchdog
46. Fibs
47. JFK preceder
49. Open-and-___ case
53. "It's ___ misunderstanding"
54. Unit of time
55. Corrida competitor
56. Began, with "off"
57. USN officers
58. Rod at a pig roast

Down
1. ___ and cheese
2. Hamm of soccer fame
3. To do this is human
4. "Try to ___ my way . . ."
5. Fresh talk
6. Prefix with -metric
7. Campaign for office
8. Hitter's turn
9. Actress Arthur and others
10. Undecorated
11. "Das Rheingold" role
19. Kind of floss
21. Whirring sound
22. Dictator Idi
23. Tree fluids
24. Labor's partner
25. Locale
26. Reporter's contact
29. Elaborate party
30. The O'Hara homestead
31. Mellows, as wine
32. Hoodwinks
39. Syrian president Bashar al-___
41. Endures
42. Subdivision of land
43. Repulsive
44. Prompter's beginning
45. Cozy hideaways
47. Dover is its cap.
48. Period, in web addresses
50. School dance
51. Self-proclaimed psychic Geller
52. Infant

Solution on page 357

Puzzle 228

Across

1. Current style
6. Mo. city
9. Actor Mineo
12. Ancient Aegean land
13. Suit ___ T
14. Command to a horse
15. "Play ___ for Me"
16. Actress Brenneman
17. Pedal digit
18. 50% off event
20. Personnel data: Abbr.
21. Seed case
24. Hosiery fabric
26. Wallach of "The Misfits"
27. Did a marathon
28. Hagar's dog
32. Brand of peanut butter cup
34. Bit of body art
36. German industrial city
36. Tosspot
37. Raggedy doll
38. Conger hunter
40. Yield to gravity
41. Young woman
44. Sport ___ (modern vehicles)
46. Essen exclamation
47. Wrestler's need
48. Ancient Greek marketplace
53. Ruby or Sandra
54. Scheduled to arrive
55. Defense acronym
56. Leaky tire sound
57. Opposite NNW
58. Bordered

Down

1. "A Christmas Carol" boy
2. Louis XVI, e.g.
3. USNA grad: Abbr.
4. Complaint that's "picked"
5. Calendar boxes
6. Yalta participant
7. Big books
8. ___ of the land
9. Bilko et al.. Abbr.
10. Very long time
11. Grant and Marvin
19. Poet's plaint
20. Mailed out
21. Paris papa
22. Bullring cries
23. Fizzles (out)
25. Future attorney's exam: Abbr.
27. Mathematician Descartes
29. Letters from Athens
30. Gossip queen Barrett
31. Secret society
33. Envisages
34. Came apart at the seams
36. Sofa
39. Hawaiian feasts
41. Young men
42. One-spots
43. "___ Gotta Have It" (Spike Lee film)
45. Having one's marbles
47. ER VIPs
49. Apollo or Ares
50. Nonprofit's URL suffix
51. Comic actress Charlotte
52. Build (on)

Solution on page 358

Puzzle 229

Across

1. It begins in Mar.
4. New Orleans summer hrs.
7. Average marks
11. Small: Suffix
12. Ventilates, with "out"
14. In re
15. Container for peas
16. Comedienne Martha
17. Half a ticket
18. No ifs, ands, or ___
20. Band equipment handler
22. Animal snarers
24. Chi-Town daily
25. His and ___
26. Ocean condiment
29. Yoko of music
30. Al ___ (not too soft)
31. Org. overseeing quadrennial games
33. ___ cordiale
35. Angel's topper
36. Landers and Miller
37. Sensitive spots
38. Speak highly of
41. "___ be a cold day in July . . ."
42. Represent in drawing
43. A fisherman may spin one
45. Art or novel add-on
48. Curriculum division
49. Kitchen flooring piece
50. NASA approval
51. Dept. bosses
52. Psychedelic drug
53. Australian hopper, for short

Down

1. Break bread
2. Arafat's group: Abbr.
3. Snoopy's foe
4. Fairway vehicles
5. "Buenos ___"
6. Make an attempt
7. Yellow melon
8. Founded: Abbr.
9. Carrier for needles and pins
10. "___ it!" ("Amen!")
13. Saw-toothed
19. Downs' opposite
21. River of northern France
22. Notwithstanding that, briefly
23. Russo of films
24. Camp shelters
26. Keystone Kops creator Mack
27. 1997 Jim Carrey film
28. Enameled metal
30. Family rooms
32. Fortune 500 listings: Abbr.
34. Contaminates
35. Jan. 1, e.g.
37. Knight's horse
38. Cushy job
39. It often comes with a proposal
40. Mideast chief: Var.
41. Aches and pains
44. Be bedridden
46. Michigan's ___ Canals
47. Bout ender, briefly

Solution on page 358

Puzzle 230

Across

1. Bumbling one
4. Coke, for one
8. Guys' partners
12. Producer Ziegfeld
13. Related by blood
14. Online auction site
15. Birds do it
16. Newborn
17. Harness strap
18. Rope fiber
20. Defeats
21. Change the title of
25. Athlete
28. ___ empty stomach
29. Stanley Cup gp.
32. ET's transport
33. "Tiny" Albee character
34. Army off.
35. April payment
36. Quote authoritatively
37. Enamored (of)
38. Poked fun at
40. NCOs two levels above cpl.
44. Hyde Park carriages
48. Jewish wedding dance
49. Home loan: Abbr.
52. Arrow shooter
53. Norse Zeus
54. Off Broadway award
55. Air conditioner meas.
56. Clammy
57. Cosmo and GQ, e.g.
58. Sweet potato

Down

1. Murders, mob style
2. "___ Ever Need Is You"
3. Noted vaudeville family
4. TV signal carrier
5. Russian river
6. Women's ___
7. "Press ___ key to continue"
8. "Pretty Woman" actor
9. Lincoln and Vigoda
10. Brest milk
11. Thesaurus entries: Abbr.
19. "Raiders of the Lost ___"
20. The "B" of N.B.
22. "Truly!"
23. Loos or Ekberg
24. Medieval weapons
25. Protrude
26. Birds ___ feather
27. Courteney of "Friends"
29. Cpl. or sgt.
30. Darlin'
31. Attorney's deg.
33. Circus routines
37. WWII pres.
39. Rapiers
40. Wearing sandals, say
41. Scotch mixer
42. Sort of smile
43. Army vehicle
45. Noted adviser
46. Manny of the Dodgers
47. Gone across a pool
49. Apple pie partner?
50. "TV Guide" notation
51. Musician's job

Solution on page 358

Puzzle 231

Across

1. Calendar doz.
4. Puts the collar on
8. Doctors' group: Abbr.
11. ___ Spumante (wine)
13. The "E" in QED
14. ___ favor: please (Sp.)
15. Spanish artist Joan
16. Gillette razor
17. Tire pressure meas.
18. Nastier
20. Tampa neighbor, informally
22. Songlike
23. Madame de ___
24. WWII transport
25. Pack (down)
28. "___ right with the world!"
29. Willow tree
31. Rocks that are mined
35. Cherry or chestnut
36. Physique, briefly
39. Of the kidneys
41. Look up to
43. More ridiculous
45. Andean beasts
46. Very old: Abbr.
47. Lighten, as a burden
49. Designer Chanel
50. Hoops tourney, for short
51. Numbered roads: Abbr.
52. Common condiment
53. D.D.E. opponent
54. Fast fliers: Abbr.
55. Prefix meaning "new"

Down

1. Bear or hare, e.g.
2. Willow trees
3. Bering, for one
4. Region including Lebanon
5. Craft or skill
6. Taverns
7. Data, for short
8. Legal motion
9. Zero of "The Producers"
10. Durant and Sharon
12. Prefix with sphere
19. This, in Mexico
21. School support org.
26. Russian for "peace"
27. Without equal
30. Fishing line holder
31. Journalist Fallaci
32. Actor Michael
33. Passes, as a law
34. ___ Diego, CA
36. Lament
37. Soothsayer
38. Explorer Hernando
40. Nasty looks
42. Dust busters, for short
44. Lab animals
48. Harden, as cement

Solution on page 358

Puzzle 232

Across

1. Aquatic mammal
5. Farm father
9. Actress Barbara ___ Geddes
12. Folk knowledge
13. Singing syllables
14. Mideast inits.
15. Radiation measures
16. "Play it ___ lays"
17. Rockies, e.g.
18. "Leaving ___ Vegas"
20. Brazilian dances
22. Actress Danes
25. Etc. kin
26. Copy-machine supplies
27. Tennis rival of Hingis
29. Drunkard
30. Try for apples
32. "For ___ sake!"
36. Overdue payment
39. Have the courage
40. Has the helm
41. Motive
43. R.E. Lee's org.
44. Three-strikes result
45. "It's clear now!"
47. Hindmost
51. It's north of Calif.
52. Hokey acting
53. Stable mom
54. Fight enders, briefly
55. Smell ___ (be leery)
56. Encl. with a manuscript

Down

1. Popular camera type, for short
2. Help-wanted abbr.
3. Elbow's place
4. Actor Nielsen
5. Positions of equilibrium
6. April 15 addressee
7. Elevates
8. Jefferson's Monticello, e.g.
9. Busy buzzer
10. "Do I dare to ___ peach?": Eliot
11. More or ___
19. Departure's opposite: Abbr.
21. ___ de mer (seasickness)
22. Dollar parts: Abbr.
23. Airshow stunt
24. Comes before
28. Emulate an eagle
31. Apt. features
33. Helpers for profs
34. Beethoven's third symphony
35. Detection device
36. Upward movement
37. ACLU concerns: Abbr.
38. Kingdoms
41. Piece next to a knight
42. French money
46. Big Band or Disco period
48. Motor-club letters
49. Former jrs.
50. Golf ball support

Solution on page 358

Puzzle 233

Across

1. Folk tales and such
5. Summit
9. Edge
12. River of Russia
13. Truth stretcher
14. College website suffix
15. Burns and Berry
16. Cover a road
17. "Slippery" tree
18. Perfume compound
20. Secret languages
22. Artificial
26. Psyche parts
29. Breton, for one
30. Helgenberger of "CSI"
34. Call it a day
36. Clamp shape
37. Verdi masterpiece
38. Second-year student
39. "Jabberwocky" starter
41. Full circle, on the track
42. Major record label
44. Count of jazz
47. Teacher's charges
52. Env. insertion
53. Moby Dick seeker
57. "___ take arms . . ."
58. Baseball's Gehrig
59. Stadium feature
60. Sharp blow
61. Demolition stuff
62. Festoon
63. Hula hoops and yo-
    yos

Down

1. New Testament book
2. Miner profits?
3. Rave's partner
4. "Will there be anything
    ___?"
5. Mont Blanc e.g.
6. Intelligence grp.
7. Dallas player, in headlines
8. Build, as a building
9. Riverside plant
10. Not doing much
11. "___ the word"
19. Kind of room
21. Baum princess
23. Prefix with linear
24. Lots and lots
25. Bothered no end
26. Mensa stats
27. The Righteous Brothers,
    e.g.
28. Wine tasting?
31. Be under the weather
32. Nutritional abbr.
33. Interstice
35. Neighbor of a Laotian
40. Baglike structure
43. Pores over
44. Boxer's trophy
45. Soon, to the bard
46. Rabbit's tail
48. Came in second
49. Guthrie with a guitar
50. Remain
51. Soaks (up)
54. In what way
55. Doctors' grp.
56. Beseech

Solution on page 358

Puzzle 234

Across

1. Printers' measures
4. Antitoxin sources
8. Kid's transport
12. Outback hopper
13. New Mexico art center
14. Siren's sound
15. Do damage to
16. Inning sextet
17. The "A" in ABM
18. On ___ (rampaging)
20. Novelist Amy
22. First lady before Mamie
25. Padlocked fasteners
29. Judge's garment
32. Elevator name
34. "A likely story!"
35. Levin and Gershwin
36. . . .—. . .
37. Brummell or Bridges
38. Actor Aykroyd
39. Chimney accumulation
40. Be worthy of
41. Vote in
43. Get beaten
45. Pirate's potable
47. Snares
51. Local theater
54. "Dancing Queen" quartet
57. Medic
58. Cutting tools
59. ___ of approval
60. Logical beginning
61. Track happening
62. Give a hoot
63. Miss Piggy, for one

Down

1. Humorous Bombeck
2. Castle protector
3. Painful
4. Boutique
5. Yvette's water
6. Become compost
7. Man Fri.
8. Safari boss
9. Actor Ziering
10. First-aid ___
11. Gin maker Whitney
19. Lincoln and Burrows
21. Sounds of relief
23. Middlin'
24. Milker's support
26. Was Mets' home
27. Carson's predecessor
28. Keep away from
29. Carousel, e.g.
30. Rev. Roberts
31. Ruination
33. "What ___ become of me?"
37. Stein beverage
39. Actor Erwin
42. Wave's high point
44. Like hard bread
46. Fem. opposite
48. Fruit drinks
49. Slightly, in music
50. Garbage boat
51. Where many vets served
52. Hew-man resource?
53. Spelling competition
55. "___ Clown"
56. Happy hour site

Solution on page 359

Puzzle 235

Across

1. Feasible
7. Impassive
13. Bone-related
14. Journalist Greeley
15. Mucho
16. Lacking energy
17. No, to Nikita
18. "Little Women" sister
19. Sugar amts.
22. Sonata section
26. Stressful spots
30. Oscar winner Patricia
31. Single: Prefix
32. Salary max
33. Brief letters?
34. Uncle ___ rice
36. Living it up
39. Surfeits
41. Hair colorer
42. Machine part
44. Robe for Caesar
47. Grapefruit kin
50. When there's darkness, in a Koestler title
52. Restrain
53. Shoot the scene again
54. Drive-in feature
55. Play friskily

Down

1. Tennessee athlete, for short
2. "The heat ___!"
3. Bar association member: Abbr.
4. Attacks on all sides
5. Chinese philosopher
6. Magical being
7. Deception
8. Copy-machine need
9. Eugene's state
10. Flee hastily
11. Here, at Les Halles
12. Christmas mo.
20. Fashion designer Rabanne
21. Get to one's feet
23. S. Dak. neighbor
24. Pulitzer-winning humorist Barry
25. Kind of shoppe
26. Major airports
27. Suitable to serve
28. Add some color to
29. Neuter, as a pet
35. Withdraw (from)
37. Irish or English dog
38. In nothing flat
40. French explorer La ___
43. Big name in faucets
45. Gretzky score
46. Golfer Isao
47. "Sesame Street" sta.
48. Killer whale
49. Russian village
50. Kennel comment
51. Japanese computer co.

Solution on page 359

Puzzle 236

Across

1. Elvis's record label
4. Oink pad?
7. Loud thud
10. 1947 Oscar winner Celeste
11. Hat, in slang
12. Ireland's nickname
14. French friend
15. Chicago trains
16. Pitchfork part
17. Prepare for printing
19. Pigtail
20. Sen.'s counterpart
21. Sheep's cry
22. Greyhound transport
25. It's good for a laugh
30. Monogram pt.
32. Neckline shape
33. Poker variety
34. Bluenose
37. Bride's new title
38. Orbiter until 2001
39. Last letter in Leeds
41. "The Sound of Music" family name
44. "Amahl and the Night Visitors" composer
48. Table staple
49. Keyboard key
50. "Get a load of that!"
51. Paper-and-string flier
52. Ostrich kin
53. Unaccompanied
54. Silent O.K.
55. Girl at a ball
56. Wily

Down

1. Actress Schneider
2. Cut, as nails
3. Arab ruler
4. Pajama party
5. Pinball foul
6. Gridiron gains: Abbr.
7. Sells out
8. Diva's performance
9. Skimpy skirt
10. Bowler or boater
13. "Waking ___ Devine" (1998 film)
18. "Hold on a ___"
19. Sinister
21. Old Nick
22. Storage unit
23. Cycle lead-in
24. [Not my mistake]
26. Singer Tillis
27. It requires a PIN
28. Mutt
29. QB's stats
31. Played the siren
35. Puppy's bite
36. Strong desire
40. Guys' partners
41. Cluck of disapproval
42. April forecast
43. Countertenor's counterpart
44. Broadway Auntie
45. Hammer, for one
46. Singer Bennett
47. Presidential nickname
49. Danson of "Cheers"

Solution on page 359

Puzzle 237

Across

1. I-70, e.g.
4. Desire
8. Hide's companion
12. Openly displayed anger
13. Letters for Jesus
14. Filmmaker Jacques
15. Philosopher ___-tzu
16. Be a gadabout
17. ___ and crafts
18. Ran the show
20. Argentine plains
22. Fruit drink suffix
23. Peak for Heidi
24. Pub staples
27. Hour after noon
28. ___ first-name basis
31. Mail destination
35. Sturgeon eggs
36. Butter serving
37. Bit of dialogue
38. Garage contents
39. ___ Cruces, N.M.
41. Free conditionally
44. Frightens
48. Bullfight cries
49. Jason's ship
51. Spanish uncle
52. Mailed
53. Snick-a-___
54. Ike's WW II command
55. Alimony receivers
56. Does road work
57. ___ Francisco

Down

1. Anger, with "up"
2. Mine vehicle
3. Fed. job-discrimination watchdog
4. Did electrical work
5. Cathode's counterpart
6. Gun rights org.
7. Kettledrums
8. Post-office purchase
9. Wyatt of the Old West
10. Blues singer ___ James
11. Chocolate candy
19. The Orient
21. Actor Guinness
24. Busy mo. for CPAs
25. London lavatory
26. Ship heading: Abbr.
27. Frequently, in poetry
28. Kimono tie
29. Oui's opposite
30. Logger's tool
32. Whitish gem
33. China, Japan, etc.
34. "Born Free" heroine
38. Expenses
39. Light-colored beer
40. Lotion ingredients
41. Prepare to be photographed
42. Trebek of "Jeopardy!"
43. Lacoste of the courts
45. Blvds. and rds.
46. Big name in copiers
47. In the near future
50. "Messenger" molecule

Solution on page 359

Puzzle 238

Across

1. Start of the 16th century
4. Lather
8. Macbeth trio
12. Bit of wordplay
13. Tropical fever
14. Highest draft rating
15. Republicans, for short
16. Goatee's locale
17. Husband or wife
18. ___ Nabisco
20. Stan Musial's nickname
22. Eisenhower Center city
26. "Golden Boy" dramatist Clifford
27. Flintstones pet
28. Computer-screen image
30. Highway sign abbr.
31. Comic book punch sound
32. Letter holder: Abbr.
35. Copenhagen resident
36. Breakfast-in-bed need
37. "I didn't do it!"
41. Like some soap
43. Highway entry
45. Violin-string material
46. Hawaiian garlands
47. Give ___ for one's money
50. Climbing vine
53. Have a chat
54. Climbing plant
55. Heart of a PC
56. Building annexes
57. Betting info
58. Make inquiries

Down

1. Fuel efficiency abbr.
2. Simon and Garfunkel, e.g.
3. Available, as a book
4. Start of a French oath
5. Sound of discomfort
6. It makes MADD mad
7. Faxed, perhaps
8. Zeroed (in)
9. "What's in ___?": Shak.
10. Imply
11. "Danse Macabre" composer Saint-___
19. Selena portrayer, familiarly
21. Sweetums
22. Modifying word: Abbr.
23. Lighter brand
24. Indian palm
25. Commercial prefix with Lodge
29. "The Virginian" author Wister
32. Blue books?
33. Get a little shuteye
34. Eustacia of "The Return of the Native"
35. Rep. foe
36. Capote's nickname
37. "Cape Fear" star
38. Shaq of basketball
39. Warbling sound
40. Halloween disguises
42. Actress Moorehead
44. Peacock constellation
48. Disencumber (of)
49. Sturm ___ Drang
51. Corp. execs
52. Loud laugh

Solution on page 359

Puzzle 239

Across

1. Ukr. and Lat., once
5. Deli option
8. Persia, after 1935
12. Plumber's concern
13. Wriggly fish
14. Prefix with physical
15. 1862 Maryland battle site
17. Be in the game
18. Mom-and-pop org.
19. Does electrical work
21. Check-cashing needs
22. Glass container
23. Paddy crop
25. Resistant
28. Dark suit
31. Carpenter's fastener
32. Papal tribunal
33. Go AWOL
36. Short snooze
38. Warm up in the ring
39. St. crosser
40. Toy gun "ammo"
42. Blackjack player's request
44. "Oz" network
47. Salacious glance
49. Force
51. Yes-___ question
52. Critical campaign mo.
53. Jeans color
54. Mike who married Liz Taylor
55. Ring decision, briefly
56. Chronic imbibers

Down

1. Response to a rude advance
2. Used E-mail
3. Pro ___ (proportionately)
4. Enjoy the slopes
5. Stop working
6. Two semesters
7. Fudd and Gantry
8. Mischief-maker
9. Swore by
10. Not very much
11. Dissenting votes
16. McGregor of "Star Wars" films
20. Tiny taste
22. Minty drink
24. ___ blanche
25. Neither Rep. nor Dem.
26. Screen siren West
27. Squander
29. Pilot's prediction: Abbr.
30. Schlemiel
34. Stadium roar
35. Worsted cloth
36. Regained consciousness
37. Attest
40. Thicken
41. Prefix with -naut
43. Tick-___
44. Aloha State port
45. Boxing match
46. Bills with George on them
48. Fishing need
50. Letterman's network

Solution on page 359

Puzzle 240

Across

1. Moo goo gai pan pan
4. NYPD alert
7. Farmer's sci.
10. Allies foe
12. Dernier ___ (last word)
13. ___' Pea ("Popeye" kid)
14. "Cheers" habitue
15. First of three-in-a-row
16. Make repairs to
17. Opposed to, to Li'l Abner
19. Doesn't just diet
20. London length
23. Alcatraz unit
25. Mediterranean island
26. Jumps for joy
29. "Don't go"
30. D.D.E.'s predecessor
31. Army food
33. Glimpses
35. Sedimentary rock
36. Scored 100 on an exam
37. Tree with pods
38. Like Kansas in August?
41. Score after deuce, in tennis
43. "Don't count ___!"
44. "Charlie's Angels" costar Lucy
45. Sound of fright
49. Dict. entries
50. AOL, for one
51. "Within" word form
52. Comic-strip bark
53. "See you later"
54. Actor Brynner

Down

1. Pale
2. Losing tic-tac-toe line
3. Cassis-flavored aperitif
4. Broadway start
5. Judith Krantz novel
6. Paper Mate rival
7. Astounds
8. Mannerly man
9. Cincinnati baseballers
11. Wise guy
13. Nickels and dimes
18. "How about that?!"
19. Grippe
20. Show hosts, for short
21. Noted Art Deco illustrator
22. Earl Grey and oolong
24. Business card abbr.
27. Start of a whaler's cry
28. Song for one person
30. Half a giggle
32. Internet
34. Sleet-covered
35. ___-fi
38. Concluding passage
39. Unique individual
40. Repeated musical phrase
42. Make a fool of
44. A little freedom?
46. At ___ rate
47. R-V link
48. DC figure

Solution on page 360

Puzzle 241

Across

1. Peat sources
5. Bedwear, informally
8. Duffer's cry
12. Barbecue rod
13. Spicy
14. Wide-spouted pitcher
15. ___spumante
16. Not Dem. or Rep.
17. Charitable contributions
18. Acapulco abode
20. Davis of "Dr. Dolittle"
21. Soaks up sun
24. Carpenter's fastener
26. Beatnik's "Got it"
27. Long-necked birds
30. It follows 11
31. Brief craze
32. Move quickly
34. Arrives, as darkness
36. Media workers' union
37. Skater Brinker
38. Long-winded
39. Had supper
42. "Pow!"
44. K-6: Abbr.
45. Entertainer Zadora
46. Prefix with -logue
50. Japanese aborigine
51. Frequently, poetically
52. One of Asta's owners
53. Brave act
54. Follower
55. Souffle needs

Down

1. Youth org.
2. Photo ___(camera sessions)
3. "Shoo!"
4. Fuddy-duddy
5. Greek consonants
6. Gulliver's creator
7. Yardstick: Abbr.
8. No middle ground, successwise
9. Nocturnal birds
10. Notes after do
11. Gaelic language
19. Egyptian snake
20. "___ Town" (Thornton Wilder play)
21. Storage container
22. Famous cookie man
23. Loafer, for example
25. Beatty or Rorem
28. Filberts and pecans
29. Lith. and Ukr., formerly
31. Bygone auto ornament
33. Grass in a loft
35. Crestfallen
36. Titled Turk
39. Not working, as a battery
40. Tennis great Nastase
41. Oahu goose
43. Can't stomach
45. Hawaiian dish
47. Follow persistently
48. Bit of work
49. W. Hemisphere grp.

Solution on page 360

Puzzle 242

Across

1. Gab or song ending
5. Blunder
9. Order to attack, with "on"
12. Easter egg colorer
13. "___ Rock" (Simon & Garfunkel hit)
14. Blood-typing letters
15. Mr. Fixit
17. Gratuity
18. "___ been robbed!"
19. Rebuke
21. Histories
24. Fire-setting crime
26. Top left PC key
27. Arthur or Lillie
28. Part of HEW: Abbr.
31. Kind of rug
33. Curved path
34. Red flower
35. Guam, e.g.: Abbr.
36. Perfect, at NASA
37. "___ Abner"
38. Satiates
40. C sharp's equivalent
42. Shipping container
44. Bit of baby babble
45. Sot's sound
46. Vanilla-flavored drink
52. Southwestern Indian
53. To the ___ (completely)
54. Leveling device
55. Club ___ (resort chain)
56. Ben and Jerry's alternative
57. Television award

Down

1. New Deal monogram
2. Potato feature
3. End-of-summer mo.
4. Characteristic
5. Cannoneer's command
6. Get away
7. Thurman of film
8. Judges' seats
9. Ellington tune
10. As before, in footnotes
11. Make do
16. Hosp. hookups
20. Weed whacker
21. Annoyer
22. Late tennis V.I.P.
23. Like Capone
24. Akron Class AA ball team
25. Ruin's partner
27. Phoenician deity
29. Voice of Amer. overseer
30. Boston hoopster, for short
32. Stick-to-itiveness
39. Milk, in Madrid
40. ___ Perignon
41. "All That Jazz" director Bob
42. Buddy
43. Religious ceremony
44. Gangsters' guns
47. Eliminate
48. English cathedral site
49. Electrical unit
50. Lower, as the lights
51. "Little Women" woman

Solution on page 360

Puzzle 243

Across

1. How to address a Fr. lady
4. "Exodus" protagonist
7. General region
11. "Boy, am ___ trouble!"
12. McNally's map partner
14. Actor Grant
15. Command to a dog
16. Modus vivendi
18. Like a wedding cake
20. Military mail drop: Abbr.
21. Ancient alphabetical character
22. Kidnapper's demand
26. Rag
28. "The Spectator" essayist
29. Edible tuber
30. Brownish
31. Mushroom stems
35. Quaking trees
38. Part of Congress
39. "Don't move, Fido!"
40. Sp. woman
41. Iroquoian language
44. Prison guard?
48. "My gal" of song
49. Soprano Berger
50. Ireland's ___ Fein
51. Run-of-the-mill: Abbr.
52. ___ out a living (just gets by)
53. Avenue crossers: Abbr.
54. Govt. code breakers

Down

1. Light fog
2. 1003, in old Rome
3. Amuse
4. Dahl in the movies
5. Oakland athlete
6. Like Beethoven's Symphony No. 6
7. Start of a play
8. Bit of sunshine
9. Schubert's "The ___ KIng"
10. Favorable vote
13. Sweetie pies
17. Petty argument
19. Boring routine
23. Look at
24. "The Good Earth" wife
25. Kind of room
26. Light throw
27. Part of a French play
32. Ziti and spaghetti
33. To be, to Satie
34. Penn and Connery
35. Concurrence
36. Backs of boats
37. Tin ___ Alley
42. Detroit products
43. Alan of "Jake's Women"
44. Average mark
45. Orson's planet
46. Compass pt. opposite SSW
47. Malign, in slang

Solution on page 360

Puzzle 244

Across

1. Annoys
5. L times VI
8. Sporting sandals
12. Miami basketball team
13. E.T.'s transport
14. Islands dance
15. Fairy-tale bad guy
16. Lap dog, for short
17. ___ 500 (auto race)
18. Barbershop emblem
19. Breadth
21. La ___, Bolivia
24. Antitoxin
28. "Anna Karenina" author
32. Fruit container
33. Nonstandard: Abbr.
34. "Peg Woffington" author Charles
36. Wind dir.
37. Burn ___ in one's pocket
39. Goes back (on)
41. Desert features
42. Handheld computer, briefly
43. Crash-probing agcy.
46. One of 16 in a cup: Abbr.
50. "SOS" pop group
53. Golfer Se Ri ___
55. Dino's tail?
56. Field's yield
57. Kind
58. High: Prefix
59. Elias or Julia
60. Suffix with beat or peace
61. Those over there

Down

1. Breakfast restaurant chain
2. ___ Park, Queens
3. Malden or Marx
4. Marinates
5. Soup order
6. Corp. money managers
7. Casino freebie, e.g.
8. Black eye
9. Attila follower
10. Elderly
11. 24 hours
20. Climb up
22. Not moving
23. Actress Caldwell
25. Summoned the butler
26. Alternative magazine
27. Kittens' cries
28. Sitcom interruption
29. Honolulu's locale
30. Scientologist ___ Hubbard
31. Shostakovich's "Babi ___" Symphony
35. Bank acct. entry
38. Delaware tribe
40. Bothers greatly
44. Twirl
45. Island east of Java
47. Composer Johann Sebastian
48. Kind of bet or thing
49. High-school dance
50. Teutonic exclamation
51. Sibling, for short
52. Gift decoration
54. "The Birth of a Nation" grp.

Solution on page 360

Puzzle 245

Across

1. Metallic deposit
5. Apply gently
8. Wise
12. Beginning blossoms
13. Historic age
14. Memorable time periods
15. Leave in, as text
16. Play on the radio
17. Audition
18. Finis
20. Make another recording
22. Avoids an F
25. Poetic word
26. Future flounder
27. Poet's "eternally"
29. Gaucho's lasso
33. End __ high note
34. Be ill
36. Howard of "Happy Days"
37. Sharp argument
40. Kind of nut or brain
42. Bilk
43. Exists
45. "Seward's Folly" purchase
47. Egg roll time
50. Checkers color
51. Coin place
52. "___ overboard!"
54. ___ bomb
58. Survey
59. Orange or lemon drink
60. Law assistant, for short
61. Unclothed
62. It thickens the plot
63. Wrongful act

Down

1. Barbell abbr.
2. No longer chic
3. Ike's initials
4. Colorado's ___ Park
5. World's lowest lake
6. "Kate & Allie" actress Meyers
7. Wilkes-___, PA
8. Medium-sized sofa
9. General vicinity
10. Sound of astonishment
11. Noble It. family
19. Hillary Clinton, ___ Rodham
21. Make a blunder
22. Golf instructors
23. First-rate
24. Straphanger's lack
28. Tear apart
30. Curved paths
31. Snatched
32. "The King and I" heroine
35. Found out
38. Snitch
39. Silver container
41. Hearty draught
44. Humorist Bombeck et al.
46. Modify to fit
47. Sports cable channel
48. Baseball's Matty or Felipe
49. Real-estate sign
53. Hue and cry
55. Confucian way
56. #4 of the Bruins
57. "Welcome" site

Solution on page 360

Puzzle 246

Across

1. Opposite of neg.
4. Small lizard
7. Bering Sea island
11. Feel regret over
12. Limp as ___
14. Have the looks of
15. Airport posting: Abbr.
16. Carty of baseball
17. Catches sight of
18. Mood
21. Sounds of doubt
22. ___ Yutang
23. But: Ger.
26. Solo in "Star Wars"
27. Tues. preceder
30. Sherlock Holmes
    portrayer
34. Commercials, e.g.
35. Alley-___ (basketball
    maneuver)
36. Not home, on a sports
    schedule
37. Elevations: Abbr.
38. Seattle clock setting:
    Abbr.
40. Keep cool
45. Hoses down
46. ___-tat-tat
47. Plant seeds
49. Boggy material
50. Blue Jay or Oriole
51. Money for old age: Abbr.
52. Intro for boy or girl
53. Part of TGIF: Abbr.
54. Half a tuba sound

Down

1. Before: Prefix
2. The triple in a triple play
3. Airplane assignment
4. The third planet
5. Drive-thru side order
6. Mexican food
7. Guilty ___
8. High schooler, probably
9. ___ off: angry
10. Speakers' hesitations
13. Lose air, as a tire
19. Ethereal: Prefix
20. Ho Chi ___ City
23. Lawyers' gp.
24. Not behaving well
25. Double-curve letter
26. Prefix for hazard
27. Cut the lawn
28. "Put ___ Happy Face"
29. Napoleonic general
31. Mississippi senator Trent
32. Spots for speakers
33. Make less intense
37. "___ la vista!"
38. "___ and the Wolf"
39. Puppeteer Lewis
40. Red vegetable
41. State: Fr.
42. 50/50 share
43. Take ___ (try some)
44. ___ Bora (Afghan region)
45. Depression-era prog.
48. Crib cry

Solution on page 361

Puzzle 247

Across

1. Siamese or Persian
4. Popular pets
8. Sacramento-to-Santa Cruz dir.
11. Old-fashioned verses
13. "Garfield" dog
14. Yale player
15. Situated by itself
16. Round roof
17. Blow the ___ off (expose)
18. Mr. Kefauver
20. Abounding
22. Give (out) sparingly
24. Cash on the Ginza
25. Hair goop
28. Gossip, slangily
30. Puff of smoke
33. Tarzan, e.g.
35. Give a guarantee
37. Statistical info
38. Pop singer Amos
40. Miss Piggy's question
41. Doubtfire's title
43. Await
45. Railroad bridge
48. Dance in Rio
52. Word on a towel
53. Military status
55. Watch's face
56. Flying expert
57. First part of a play
58. Soviet ballistic missile
59. Common article
60. Unskilled worker
61. Old name for Tokyo

Down

1. "Merry old" king of rhyme
2. Hullabaloos
3. Camping gear
4. Massachusetts Cape
5. Cherishes
6. It marches on
7. Tending to ooze
8. Element #34
9. Use a letter opener
10. Like EEE shoes
12. Gardener's spring purchase
19. Fizzy drink
21. Ayres and Wallace
23. Fabric fuzz
25. Wander (about)
26. Govt. air-quality watchdog
27. "Hmmm . . ."
29. Cocky Aesop character
31. Sign at the Bijou
32. Architect I. M.
34. Roman war god
36. Pride and envy, e.g.
39. Willing to try
42. Purse handle
44. Moms' mates
45. "How do you like ___!"
46. Well-to-do
47. Tie, as a shoe
49. Cursor controllers
50. Modem speed unit
51. Actor Ray of "Battle Cry"
54. Relative

Solution on page 361

Puzzle 248

Across

1. Convenience store convenience
4. Rosemary or basil
8. Guy's counterpart
11. Breakfast, lunch, or dinner
13. Verbal
14. ___ Lilly and Co.
15. Persian elf
16. Bread for gyros
17. Oslo's land: Abbr.
18. Big beer buy
20. Glossy alternative
22. Less green
25. The Beatles' "And I Love ___"
26. Juan's gold
27. Home for la familia
30. Degrees held by many CEOs
34. Warm the bench
35. Milk mishap
37. Shred
38. PTA part: Abbr.
40. ___ Stanley Gardner
41. Lupino of Hollywood
42. Say more
44. Visored helmet
46. Moisten the turkey
49. Logical
51. 108-card game
52. Songwriter Jacques
54. Carpentry class
58. Cell material
59. Frog's relative
60. Hawaiian tuber
61. Tot's time-out
62. Grain storage area
63. Cycle starter

Down

1. Sound booster
2. Golfer's prop
3. Scratch or dent
4. Brewing ingredient
5. Canal to Buffalo
6. Inform (on)
7. Point one's finger at
8. Urbane fellow
9. Zillions
10. Italian coins
12. Cooties
19. Rainbow shapes
21. Ulna's locale
22. Parks of civil rights
23. Spring bloom
24. Lobster traps
25. School corridor
28. Made like
29. Madam's mate
31. Cup lip
32. Capitol Hill worker
33. To-do
36. Like Jack Sprat's diet
39. Insurrectionist Turner
43. IOUs
45. Take a breather
46. Scorch
47. Teacher in Siam
48. Dove or Dial
49. Aquarium performer
50. Tough-guy actor ___ Ray
53. Louis XIV, par exemple
55. Derby or bowler
56. Hockey Hall of Famer Bobby
57. Luau treat

Solution on page 361

Puzzle 249

Across

1. Seemingly limitless
5. Responses to amasseur
8. Barn bundle
12. Moisturizer additive
13. Shelter bed
14. Indigo dye
15. Basis of a suit
16. Number-crunching pro
17. ___-serif (type style)
18. Not dense
20. Loveseat
22. ___ in "Able"
23. Suffix with chlor- or fluor-
24. Young women
27. Takes it all off
31. ___ man out
32. Big name in China
33. Talks back to
37. Extremely
40. Actress Long or Peeples
41. Point opposite WNW
42. Most wise
45. Cellist Pablo
49. Ancient Greek city
50. Author Le Shan
52. Yours, in Ypres
53. Sausage unit
54. Suffix with north
55. Hard on the ears
56. Domino or Waller
57. Cashew or filbert
58. Massachusetts's motto start

Down

1. Vintners' vessels
2. Off center
3. Carolina rail
4. Aquarium fish
5. Means of approach
6. Jump on one foot
7. Equilibrium
8. Turkey moistener
9. Med.-school course
10. Fishing cord
11. If things change
19. Ms. enclosure
21. Savannah summer hrs.
24. The "L" of L.A.
25. Dentists' grp.
26. 1960's radical grp.
28. "___ Mine" (George Harrison book)
29. Bosom buddy
30. Dim sum sauce
34. Moves furtively
35. "___ for Evidence" (Grafton novel)
36. Lustrous cotton fabric
37. Trigonometry ratio
38. Explorer Johnson
39. Thrift-shop transaction
42. Egotist's love
43. Inter___
44. Dude
46. Lots and lots
47. Costello et al.
48. "Them" or "us"
51. Joanne of "Abie's Irish Rose"

Solution on page 361

Puzzle 250

Across

1. Hoopsters' org.
4. Come in first
7. Queen of Scots
11. Canoe paddle
12. Inhabitants: Suffix
14. Suffix with convert
15. Dr. who discovered Eminem
16. Like some evening gowns
18. Alaska or Hawaii
20. Actress Cannon
21. Baseball iron man Ripken
22. Spews out
26. Animal advocate Cleveland
28. ___ - Magnon
29. Happened upon
30. Lassies' partners
31. Juilliard subj.
32. Window glass
33. Communications co.
34. Slight amount
35. Lahr and Parks
36. Beset
38. Disappoint, with "down"
39. Electrical units
41. No longer together
44. Mishaps
48. ___ -Tzu: Taoist philosopher
49. Billiards relative
50. Just so
51. Environmental prefix
52. D.C. bigwigs
53. Derek and Jackson
54. Piece of animation

Down

1. Nonverbal O.K.'s
2. "The Simpsons" son
3. Long-distance callers' needs
4. With good judgment
5. Hairy TV cousin
6. Bookish one
7. Eeyore's creator
8. Lincoln or Vigoda
9. "Treasure Island" inits.
10. Affirmative answer
13. Lord Peter Wimsey's creator
17. When doubled, a Samoan port
19. Old mariners
23. Wise guy
24. Camp shelter
25. Jeanne d'Arc and others: Abbr.
26. Bit of pond vegetation
27. "Welcome" sites
28. Cow chew
31. Croquet need
32. Chick's sound
34. Made a knot
35. Explosions
37. Seed covers
40. Patronizing person
42. Competition
43. Hammer or chisel
44. Computer program, for short
45. Dove's sound
46. Rank above maj.
47. Lao-tzu principle

Solution on page 361

Puzzle 251

Across

1. Hebrew month
5. Cat's cry
9. Groupie
12. Mrs. Dithers, in 'Blondie'
13. ___ Cod
14. Cagers' org.
15. Bulletin board fastener
16. "Now it's clear"
17. Silent
18. Valuable Possession
20. Administer the oath of office to
22. Not quite spherical
24. Sandwich initials
27. Install, as a carpet
28. Lymph bump
32. Workers' rewards
34. Squanders
36. Partner of ready and willing
37. Part of Ascap: Abbr.
38. U.K. channel
39. Endured
42. "Maybe"
45. Starts to fish
50. Wall climber
51. Take down ___ (humble)
53. Come in third
54. Sine qua ___
55. Ivory Coast neighbor
56. Falafel bread
57. Kinsey subject
58. "___ a song . . ."
59. Singer Wooley

Down

1. Official proceedings
2. "___ I say, not . . ."
3. Curved lines
4. Yard tool
5. Long distance letters
6. With little effort
7. ___ can of worms
8. Most minuscule
9. Low-cost home loan org.
10. Be adjacent to
11. Tattle on
19. Painted metalware
21. Change for a $20 bill
23. ___ -relief
24. Maidenform product
25. Science class
26. Up to, for short
29. Handicapper's hangout: Abbr.
30. Society girl
31. PC bailout key
33. Do a clerk's job
34. "___ is me!"
35. Electrical letters
37. TV's "Remington ___"
40. "Me too"
41. Part of a flower
42. Finishes first
43. Bacchanalian cry
44. Short-tailed wildcat
46. Poisonous snakes
47. ___ Tzu
48. Large bag
49. Sailor's mop
52. "Scoot!"

Solution on page 361

Puzzle 252

Across

1. Country music's McEntire
5. Tarzan's raisers
9. Thoroughfares: Abbr.
12. Old furnace fuel
13. Cadence
14. Hugs, in letters
15. Ben Stiller's mom
17. Inc. alternative
18. Lawyer's thing
19. Attempts
21. They may be checkered
24. "My Heart Skips ___"
26. Pub draught
27. Mets stadium
29. Address for a lady
32. Fiber fluff
34. Parseghian of Notre Dame
35. Variety of fine cotton
36. ___ Hari (spy)
37. Swell, as a river
39. Chihuahua on TV
40. Decree of a Muslim ruler
42. Peewee or Della
44. Less feral
46. Blasting material
47. Cheer for a matador
48. San Francisco transport
54. Yet, in poems
55. Metallic rocks
56. Tiptop
57. Fast plane
58. Barbershop call
59. Chimney dirt

Down

1. "His Master's Voice" co.
2. Very long time
3. Make taboo
4. Conscious
5. Vigoda and Lincoln
6. Vegetable that rolls
7. A barber has to work around it
8. Michigan or Minnesota
9. Card game for one
10. Carrying bag
11. Puts in a lawn
16. Sloppy situation
20. Highway entrance
21. Coconut tree
22. Et ___ (and others)
23. Feeling
24. Eagle's retreat
25. Sheep sounds
28. Brain-busting
30. Ed of "Daniel Boone"
31. Lion's hair
33. Empty truck's weight
38. Seabird
41. Criminal conflagration
43. Singer James et al.
44. Pedal digits
45. Pub drinks
46. Final or midterm
49. Uno + due
50. Mystery author Stout
51. Whisper sweet nothings
52. Yucatan year
53. Collecting a pension: Abbr.

Solution on page 362

Puzzle 253

Across

1. Speeder stopper
4. Priest's robe
7. City of India
11. Shake up
13. Nearly worthless coin
14. Set of socks
15. Tolstoy's "___ Karenina"
16. Plaything
17. Mail-chute opening
18. Skin art
20. Fence uprights
21. On-line company for investors
24. Silent artists
27. Boy
28. However, informally
31. Mediterranean seaport
32. "My country, ___ of thee"
33. Pronounced
34. Always, in sonnets
35. Split ___ soup
36. Sheep shelters
37. ___ tunnel syndrome
39. Helpers: Abbr.
43. In the center of
47. Hourly wage
48. Score 100% on
50. Boxer Oscar ___ Hoya
51. Art sch. class
52. Physicians: Abbr.
53. "Get lost, kitty!"
54. Prefix with factor
55. Bee follower
56. Sit-up targets

Down

1. Ending for auto or pluto
2. Wife of Charlie Chaplin
3. Pub measure
4. Fur magnate
5. Card game
6. Purchase
7. Lhasa ___ (dog)
8. Some square dancers
9. Civil uprising
10. Carney and Garfunkel
12. Triangular sail
19. Tiebreakers, briefly
20. ___ XING (street sign)
22. "Are you calling me ___?"
23. Court figures, briefly
24. One of the Three Stooges
25. Furious feeling
26. St. Patrick's Day mo.
28. Make doilies
29. Step on it, old-style
30. Some ER cases
32. Orange pekoe, e.g.
33. Three-dimensional objects
35. Mac alternatives
36. Wheel projection
38. Bel ___ (cheese)
39. Saudi citizen, for one
40. Not crazy
41. Baseball's ___ the Man
42. French head
44. Ten: Prefix
45. Hunk of bacon
46. Makes doilies
48. HBO rival
49. Alphabetic sequence

Solution on page 362

Puzzle 254

Across

1. Private or captain
5. Auto for hire
8. "And giving ___, up the chimney . . ."
12. Amo, amas, ___ . . .
13. Victrola company
14. "I never ___ man I didn't like"
15. Department store department
17. Young horse
18. Verb suffix
19. Oregano and basil
21. Bill ___, TV's Science Guy
22. ___XING, crosswalk sign
23. McEntire of music
25. Angry looks
28. "Am not!" retort
31. "La Boheme" role
32. Period of office
33. Tree of the mimosa family
36. Wild animals
38. Package of paper
39. They, in Calais
40. 901, in old Rome
42. Prefix with vitamin
44. Clerical garb
47. Close friends
49. Releases
51. Good for what ___ you
52. Abel's mom
53. ___ Vista: Internet search engine
54. Road-sign warning
55. U.A.R. member
56. Chimney dust

Down

1. Branches
2. Congregation's response
3. Da ___, Vietnam
4. Gold measures: Abbr.
5. Beliefs
6. Rent-___
7. Ms. Streisand
8. Big letters in bowling
9. Newborns
10. Our Gang affirmative
11. Roy Rogers' wife
16. Sled rider's cry
20. Sunday address: Abbr.
22. Cost
24. Alphas' followers
25. "Today" rival, initially
26. Permit: Abbr.
27. Texas city
29. Uneaten morsel
30. Mantra chants
34. "___ a Rock": Simon and Garfunkel
35. Makes laugh
36. Resentful
37. Yale players
40. IRS experts
41. Letters and packages
43. Impose, as a tax
44. Folk singer Guthrie
45. Mother of Apollo and Artemis
46. Cop's route
48. Wind direction: Abbr.
50. Notes after mis

Solution on page 362

Puzzle 255

Across

1. Dutch airline
4. On the disabled list
8. Bivalve mollusk
12. Whole wheat alternative
13. From a distance
14. Georgetown player
15. Apr. tax collector
16. Part of DMZ
17. Not yet risen
18. Bobby of the Black Panthers
20. Summer shirts
22. Prefix with tonic
24. "I cannot ___ lie!"
28. Snow structure
31. Pyramid bottom
34. Cry of delight
35. De Maupassant's "___ Vie"
36. Midwest Indians
37. Flapper accessory
38. Go astray
39. Views
40. Coop moms
41. Great buy
43. Biol., e.g.
45. Not fem.
48. Enjoys a novel
52. Mirthful sounds
55. Belfast's land
57. Salon stiffener
58. Freudian subjects
59. New Mexico art community
60. Prefix with hazard
61. Some coniferous trees
62. Cries uncontrollably
63. Pen pal?

Down

1. Songwriter Kristofferson
2. Ancient stringed instrument
3. High plateau
4. Visibility problems
5. Spooky sighting
6. Go ape
7. Maple or mahogany
8. Run after
9. Arcing shot
10. "Yes, Captain!"
11. Hot under the collar
19. Inebriated
21. French summers
23. Double reed
25. Earring holder
26. Large diving bird
27. Cries of discovery
28. Ado
29. "Put a lid ___!"
30. It's put before Descartes
32. Profound respect
33. Back talk
36. Cuba, por ejemplo
40. Hurry
42. Gather up
44. Green garnish
46. Coagulates
47. "See you later!"
49. Matures
50. Art ___: geometric style
51. Like a tortoise
52. "Listen up!"
53. Have another birthday
54. Question for Sherlock
56. Rip off

Solution on page 362

Puzzle 256

Across

1. "___ bodkins!"
4. Dry as a desert
8. Austen heroine
12. Smidgen
13. Big truck
14. Resorts with springs
15. Baden-Baden, for one
16. Pre-1917 Russian ruler
17. Use UPS, e.g.
18. End of a New Year's song
20. Persian of old
22. Metal in rocks
24. Provide
28. Scrams
32. About to cry
33. Salad-dressing ingredient
34. Louse-to-be
36. Chaney of horror films
37. Garbage
40. Blue-eyed cat
43. Medal recipients
45. Code-cracking org.
46. "All ___ are off!"
48. Corn holders
51. Pie a la ___
54. Shout of understanding
56. Cigarette's end
58. Safari sound
59. Cop's patrol
60. Get on in years
61. High peaks
62. Lumberjacks' tools
63. RR depot

Down

1. Delivery docs, for short
2. Ballroom dance maneuvers
3. Admonition to Fido
4. Fall bloomers
5. ___ judicata
6. Moslem leader
7. More urgent
8. Dead Sea Scrolls writer
9. NASCAR measure
10. ___ tai
11. Type of cobra
19. "Wayne's World" negative
21. Investigator: Abbr.
23. "Ich Bin ___ Berliner": JFK
25. Roy's cowgirl partner
26. Greek love god
27. Sandberg of the Cubs
28. The two together
29. Gaelic republic
30. Winglike
31. "___ the season . . ."
35. Component of bronze
38. Gets serious
39. Haw lead-in
41. Neckwear
42. China's Chairman ___
44. Knifes
47. The Mets' old stadium
49. Sheep cries
50. Army drill instructor, often: Abbr.
51. "The A-Team" star
52. Hugs, in a letter
53. Patriotic org. since 1890
55. Carpentry tool
57. Barnyard cackler

Solution on page 362

Puzzle 257

Across

1. "The West Wing" network
4. Corp. leaders
8. "Jumbo" plane
11. ___ chi (Chinese discipline)
12. Latin learner's verb
13. Bubbly beverage
14. Smash
15. Microwave, slangily
16. Internet address starter
17. Angry, with "off"
19. "Jungle Book" actor
21. Corn unit
23. "Psycho" setting
26. Election loser
30. Fur trader John Jacob ___
32. Toddler's break
33. November veggie
35. Leather-punching tool
36. Tumbler
39. Abs and pecs
42. Take ___ in the right direction
44. Month after avril
45. Leather-punching tools
47. Disparities
50. With adroitness
53. Woeful words
55. Sock ___
57. "The Haj" author Leon
58. Southwestern art center
59. Cable modem alternative, briefly
60. Keystone ___
61. Took a photo of
62. Utter

Down

1. To the ___ degree
2. Fisherman's lure
3. Quote from
4. Frankness
5. Australian bird
6. Hardwood trees
7. Water vapor
8. Write hastily
9. N.Y.C. summer clock setting
10. Water spigot
13. Closes tightly
18. Environmentalist's prefix
20. Long scarf
22. Hound sound
24. And others
25. "The West Wing" actor
26. "The Ice Storm" director ___ Lee
27. Words after fa
28. Baths
29. '60s war zone
31. "Kidnapped" monogram
34. It's "the word"
37. Death row reprieves
38. Do some tailoring
40. Most judicious
41. Espionage org.
43. City maps
46. Former ruler of Iran
48. Highest degrees
49. Slugger Sammy
50. Arctic bird
51. Sis's sibling
52. Place for gloss
54. Cow comment
56. Tire layer

Solution on page 362

Puzzle 258

Across

1. Oklahoma Indian
4. Expel, as from power
8. "The Nazarene" novelist
12. Gen-___ (boomer's kid)
13. Not tied down
14. Big Dipper unit
15. Popeye's Olive ___
16. Sanyo competitor
17. Prefix with masochism
18. Hard-boiled item
20. Broadcasts again
22. Aspen abode
25. Queues
26. Pre-stereo sound
27. Nautical shout
30. Beetle and Golf, briefly
31. Apt. ad abbr.
32. Cpl.'s inferior
35. 24-hr. cash sources
36. Duet plus one
37. With regret
41. Add on
43. Final words
45. Abbr. before an alias
46. Rice-A-___
47. Bacon partner
50. Toronto Argonauts' org.
53. Not a duplicate: Abbr.
54. Sullen expression
55. Prefix for goblin
56. Alan Alda series
57. Baking utensils
58. Interjections from
    Rocky

Down

1. Kitchen gadget company
2. "Brat Farrar" author
3. City saved by Joan of Arc
4. Mature
5. Alleged spoon-bender
   Geller
6. Replace a button
7. Drop from Niobe
8. Very, in music
9. Dry cleaner's challenge
10. Group of officers
11. Perot of politics
19. Day-___: pigment brand
21. Ron of "Tarzan"
22. 905, in old Rome
23. "___ do you do?"
24. Fruity pastry
28. "Let me think . . ."
29. Bones, to a doctor
32. Tediously didactic
33. $5 bill
34. How some packages are
    sent
35. Author Rand
36. Hwy. with tolls
37. Sen. Thurmond
38. Now, in Nogales
39. France's patron saint
40. Janet of "Psycho"
42. Former times
44. Johnny of "Pirates of the
    Caribbean"
48. ___ long way
49. Rev, as an engine
51. Rock music's ___
    Fighters
52. Dieters' units: Abbr.

Solution on page 363

Puzzle 259

Across

1. Western Indians
5. ___ Butterworth's
8. Spawning fish
12. Old Norse character
13. Deteriorate
14. Office assistant
15. Pour like crazy
16. Paris's ___ de la Cite
17. Writer Hubbard
18. Late actor Davis
20. Most spooky
22. Craggy hill
24. Howard or Reagan
25. Italian for "to the tooth"
29. Admirer of Beauty
33. Five-spot
34. U.F.O. crew
36. Baby bear
37. At ___ (in any case)
40. Son of Agamemnon
43. Tic-toe connector
45. Food morsel
46. Sound reproduction
    systems
50. Israeli native
54. Czech river
55. ___ culpa (my fault)
57. Golden Pond bird
58. Big Apple baseballers
59. Shea Stadium player
60. Walk the earth
61. Optometrist's concerns
62. Elbow's site
63. Did in, as a dragon

Down

1. "___ take arms against .
   . ."
2. Mardi Gras, e.g.: Abbr.
3. White Monopoly bills
4. Israeli, e.g.
5. Hosp. procedure
6. Performer's part
7. Animal in a roundup
8. Briny
9. Add staff
10. Big fusses
11. Fender-bender result
19. Long period of time
21. Steal from
23. Map line: Abbr.
25. 1960s gridiron org.

26. Be untruthful
27. Genetic stuff
28. WWII battle zone
30. Perform on a stage
31. Bring an action against
32. Atlanta network: Abbr.
35. Broadway hit sign
38. Type A's concern
39. Menlo Park initials
41. Speech hesitations
42. Drags one's feet
44. Pause indicator
46. A portion of
47. Group's pronoun
48. Old Harper's Bazaar
    artist
49. Crystal-ball user

51. Bring to 212 degrees
52. Meander
53. From the start
56. 24-hr. bank feature

Solution on page 363

Puzzle 260

Across

1. Tiny
4. Auntie of Broadway
8. High schooler's woe
12. Strong insect
13. Inland Asian sea
14. Wooden wedge
15. Vitamin bottle no.
16. Lengthy footrace
17. NaCl
18. Probate concern
20. Overstuffs
21. Address book abbr.
22. Awful
23. Alan of "M*A*S*H"
26. LAX watchdog
27. Physician, familiarly
30. "Little Orphan Annie" character
34. Caesar's hello
35. Furniture mover
36. MasterCard alternative
37. "___ Miserables"
38. Top poker card
40. Author Gardner et al.
43. Can't stand
47. Role for Carrie
48. Highlands family
50. Charged atom
51. Low voice
52. Tibia or clavicle
53. Young child
54. Russian-born designer
55. Order to Fido
56. "Who am ___ say?"

Down

1. Suffix with silver or glass
2. Brings to a halt
3. "L'___ c'est moi": Louis XIV
4. Not glossy
5. Tottering
6. "You da ___!"
7. Caribou relative
8. Syria's Hafez al-___
9. Informal talk
10. Cairo's waterway
11. Paramedics, for short
19. Tiny bit
20. Stockholm sedan
22. Tavern
23. Orthodontists' org.
24. W.C.
25. J.F.K.'s predecessor
26. Ceiling fixture
27. 601, to Nero
28. Gives the green light
29. The Gray: Abbr.
31. The "Y" of Y.S.L.
32. Existed
33. Eye layer
37. Car financing option
38. George Hamilton's ex
39. Brooklyn's ___ Island
40. North Sea feeder
41. Derriere
42. Inventory
44. S.A. monkey
45. Catcall
46. Within: Comb. Form
48. Letterman's employer
49. Parking area

Solution on page 363

Puzzle 261

Across

1. Summer hrs. in N.Y.
4. Serene
8. Run with the football
12. Life lines?
13. Pulitzer author James
14. Twin of Jacob
15. Track transaction
16. Gossip columnist Barrett
17. Fleshy fruit
18. Penn or Connery
20. Prefix with meter
22. Apollo mission craft, briefly
24. "Return to ___"
28. Stockpiled
32. Patriot Silas
33. Argon or neon
34. Homer Simpson's neighbor
36. Summit
37. Negatively charged atom
40. Blue feeling
43. Use one's noodle
45. Maude portrayer Arthur
46. Spin like ___
48. Dermatologist's concern
51. Naval jail
54. Dermal opening
56. Research site
58. Wingless parasites
59. Great flair
60. Debunked mentalist Geller
61. Playpen items
62. Cushiony
63. "How the Grinch Stole Christmas" director Howard

Down

1. Wane
2. Goes out, as a fire
3. Shopper's bag
4. "Bette Davis Eyes" singer Kim
5. Long, long ___
6. ___ the Hyena
7. Breakfast, lunch, and dinner
8. Fret
9. WWII entertainers
10. Famous Uncle
11. Artist's decision
19. Hirt and Gore
21. Kennedy or Koppel
23. "Of Mice and ___"
25. Go steady
26. Baseballer Slaughter
27. Sales agents, briefly
28. Lab culture
29. Neck hair
30. Where Borneo is
31. ___ Plaines, Illinois
35. Pat gently
38. Some oranges
39. "___ in a million years!"
41. Not half bad
42. Aye canceler
44. Slangy turndowns
47. Prince Charles' game
49. Disparaging remark
50. Poi ingredient
51. Diner sandwich
52. "Blame It on ___"
53. Slippery
55. British WWII fliers
57. Trash collector

Solution on page 363

Puzzle 262

Across

1. Parts of qts.
4. Pulls from behind
8. "I ___ Grow Up" ("Peter Pan" song)
12. Intense anger
13. Grocery list item
14. Ever and ___
15. Word in most of the Commandments
16. Underestimate
18. Follow as a result
20. Japanese zither
21. Get in a stew
23. Valentine's Day gift
27. Ending with tele-
29. Three-toed bird
32. Paid player
33. "___ Gang"
34. Serta competitor
35. Orthodontist's org.
36. "West Side Story" gang member
37. Cries of surprise
38. Pipe section
39. Irish-born actor Milo
41. To be, in Paris
43. Seize
46. Letter after gee
49. Priestly garments
53. Debt acknowledgment
54. Hawk's opposite
55. Sarcastic response
56. Johnny ___
57. Fatty treat for birds
58. Fellow, slangily
59. Mag. workers

Down

1. Yearn (for)
2. 1982 sci-fi film
3. Describes
4. "We're off ___ the Wizard"
5. Bullfight cheer
6. Bubbly bandleader
7. Virtuoso performance?
8. Large mackerel
9. Noted resident of the Dakota
10. Neither hide ___ hair
11. Blaster's need
17. Wander off
19. Keats praised one
22. Locust or linden
24. Trunk item
25. Earth goddess
26. It's seen in bars
27. Axis leader
28. Tints
30. It's cut and dried
31. "What ___ is new?"
34. Ventriloquist Lewis
38. Prefix with angle
40. Heron
42. Take a sip of
44. Battery fluid
45. Hindu gentleman
47. Sorority member
48. Centers of activity
49. Music store purchases
50. Hall of Famer Brock
51. New Year's ___
52. Had followers

Solution on page 363

Puzzle 263

Across

1. Pvt.'s boss
4. "Kapow!"
7. Close at hand
11. Prefix with Asian
12. One: Prefix
13. Knickknack
14. Attempt
15. One behind bars
16. Lower-leg joint
17. Primitive home
18. Half-moon tide
20. Conciliatory gift
22. Fashionable initials
23. Spigot
26. Descartes's conclusion
28. Hat with a curled brim
31. Cartoonist Goldberg et al.
34. Warm and snug
35. Indifference
37. Needing a refill
38. Take the cake
39. "Son ___ gun!"
41. 76ers' org.
44. Doozie
45. "20/20" network
47. Lie in store for
51. Gerund maker
53. Seek the hand of
54. Poet Ezra
55. Zenith competitor
56. Designer Claiborne
57. Asks for alms
58. Your of yore
59. On the ___: secretly

Down

1. Adam's youngest
2. Mentors
3. "___ Remember" (1960 song)
4. Tampa Bay player, for short
5. Assumed name
6. Explosive devices
7. Woman of habit?
8. Vex
9. Former Mets manager Hodges
10. Garden tool
13. Head covering
19. Furry TV alien
21. Dutch artist Mondrian
23. Male turkey
24. Cartoon bark
25. Compensation
27. Fire remnant
29. Novelist Umberto
30. Low in spirits
31. Like sashimi
32. News agcy.
33. Prohibition
36. "___ don't say!"
37. Cape Canaveral event
40. Coquette
42. Cries one's eyes out
43. Bubbling, as hot water
44. Co. alternative
46. Snug
47. LAPD alert
48. Hardship
49. Holiday-free mo.
50. Elected officials
52. Not straight

Solution on page 363

Puzzle 264

Across

1. Victory signs
5. P. and L. preparer
8. Cut short
11. Courtroom promise
12. "Ben-___"
13. Hors d'oeuvre spread
14. Novello of old films
15. Pres. Lincoln
16. To be, in France
17. Declares untrue
19. Plays the role of
21. Butterfly catcher's need
22. IV x XIII
23. Claims without proof
27. Oklahoma Indians
31. Word form for "earth"
32. Cornhusker State: Abbr.
34. Use a crowbar
35. Fit for a queen
38. Furniture wheels
41. Uncooked
43. Title for Churchill
44. Make an accusation
47. Rascals
51. Choo-choo's sound
52. Suffix with lemon or orange
54. Hawaii's "Valley Isle"
55. Toe the ___ (obey)
56. Slow down, in music: Abbr.
57. Cotton cloth
58. Gerund's end
59. Printer's spaces
60. Close loudly

Down

1. Invalidate
2. Icicle hangout
3. Type of collar or jacket
4. Pilgrim's goal
5. Punish
6. Tavern
7. Of a region
8. Cave-dwelling fliers
9. Oaxaca "other"
10. Quilters' parties
13. Small: Fr.
18. Brain scan, briefly
20. A.F.L.'s partner
23. Farming: Abbr.
24. Summer zodiac sign
25. Myrna of the movies
26. Part of a min.
28. Unlock, in poetry
29. Prove one's humanity?
30. Part of DOS: Abbr.
33. Droopy-eared hounds
36. Sharp-crested ridge
37. Time delay
39. [Intentionally so written]
40. Hobos
42. "___ the World"
44. Hun king, in Scandinavian legend
45. Meat cut
46. Before ___ (soon)
48. Postal delivery
49. Fast feline
50. "The King and I" country
53. Not well lit

Solution on page 364

Puzzle 265

Across

1. Belted out, as a tune
5. Newspaper notice
9. Cable network
12. "That's clear"
13. Critical warning
15. Person, place, or thing
16. "Messiah," for one
17. Argue against
19. 5 1/2-point type
20. Toasting word
22. Bawl
23. Change, as a clock
24. City vehicle
25. Cul-de-___
28. Singletons
29. Army bed
30. Toy blocks brand
31. Guitarist Montgomery
32. Long March VIP
33. Eagle claw
34. Diamond or emerald
35. Power failure
36. Not domesticated
39. Pays for poker
40. Stuffs oneself
42. Alphabet run
45. Stage anew
46. Gives a hand
47. Come to a close
48. Closed
49. To a smaller extent

Down

1. Gluttony, for one
2. Mil. hangout
3. Emotional disorders
4. Beginnings
5. "Are you in ___?"
6. Friend of Ernie
7. Sweet-as-apple-cider girl
8. Dwellers along the Volga
9. Sister and wife of Zeus
10. "I say!" sayer
11. Missouri River tribe
14. Sluggish
18. Small part
20. Front of a boat
21. Director Clair
22. Director's cry
24. Halloween cry
25. Ethiopia's Haile ___
26. Eyes-a-poppin'
27. Ice-cream holder
29. Pushrod pusher
30. Sideways
32. Brawls
33. Egyptian boy king
34. Teri of "Mr. Mom"
35. First appearance, as of symptoms
36. Golfer's cry
37. Smooth out
38. Invoice abbr.
39. Westernmost of the Aleutians
41. Ooh's partner
43. Gridiron stats
44. Letters at sea

Solution on page 364

Puzzle 266

Across

1. Flow's partner
4. Travel rtes.
7. Shows flexibility
12. Loving murmur
13. Hurricane center
14. Farewell, in France
15. Pay or Cray ending
16. Churchillian gesture
17. Giant of myth
18. Fat
20. You, Biblically
22. Hairpin curves
24. "I've been ___!"
25. Overalls part
28. Lily family plants
30. Out ___ limb
31. Knight with Pips
34. Readily available
37. Atop, poetically
38. Capital of Yemen
40. Big lug
41. Feel unwell
42. Brighton baby buggies
46. Author Harte
47. Horse gait
48. Board, as a trolley
51. Simone's sea
54. Sign of stage success
55. Piece of the pie
56. "The Greatest" boxer
57. Acorn, eventually
58. After-bath need
59. Small drink of liquor
60. SSW's opposite

Down

1. Jules's school
2. Gauchos' weapons
3. Male swine
4. Accelerate, with "up"
5. Go blonde, say
6. Be boiling mad
7. With ___ breath: tensely anticipatory
8. Entertainer Adams
9. Lousy egg?
10. Narc's org.
11. Early riser?
19. In need of recharging
21. Is wearing
23. Stallone, to pals
25. Constrictor
26. Wayside stopover
27. Mischievous
29. Davis of "Jungle Fever"
31. Moo ___ gai pan
32. Place to graze
33. Rover's remark
35. Catch forty winks
36. Kaufman collaborator
39. Director Robert
41. Synthetic fiber brand
43. Malicious burning
44. Gangster Bugs
45. Feed, as a fire
46. Cause to yawn
48. FDR successor
49. Exclamation of surprise
50. Fido's foot
52. Wallach of film
53. Mr. Van Winkle

Solution on page 364

Puzzle 267

Across

1. Maple product
4. Pecan and pumpkin
8. Spy Mata
12. Leave slack-jawed
13. Entr' ___
14. Sufficient, slangily
15. House member: Abbr.
16. Religious splinter group
17. Fruity drinks
18. St. Francis' home
20. Rant's partner
22. Oscar winner Kingsley
23. Tips off
26. Couches
29. Fuel additive
30. Take to court
31. Banned orchard spray
32. Optometrist's interest
33. Ice cream holder
34. Feb. follower
35. Response to a ques.
36. Improved one's muscles
37. Hole for a lace
39. Command to Fido
40. Became frayed
41. Be on the brink
45. Help hoods
47. Feels remorse
49. It's bottled in Cannes
50. Become liquid
51. Cubemaster Rubik
52. Suffix for southeast
53. Look at lasciviously
54. Pop singer Celine
55. Colo. clock setting

Down

1. "___ Smile" (1976 Hall & Oates hit)
2. Makes one's jaw drop
3. Livens (up)
4. Doesn't fail
5. Isolate during the winter
6. And others: Abbr.
7. Fixed charge
8. "___ ho!"
9. "Father Knows Best" family name
10. Feel remorse for
11. Maybes
19. Building girder
21. Austrian peak
24. Jukebox choice
25. Caraway or sunflower
26. Unchanged
27. Rival of Nivea
28. Parting word
29. Network: Abbr.
32. Went in
33. Pigeon's home
35. Aviation prefix
36. Attaches, as a rope
38. Ms. Lenya
39. Dictation pro
42. Be abundant (with)
43. Roasting items
44. Smallest of the litter
45. ___, amas, amat
46. Entreat
48. "Mentalist" Geller

Solution on page 364

Puzzle 268

Across

1. Internet letters
4. Abbr. on a shingle
7. Compaq products
10. Colorado ski spot
12. Classic Jaguar model
13. Look surreptitiously
14. Too stylish, perhaps
15. El ___ (Spanish hero)
16. Noblewoman
17. Program listing, briefly
19. "Breaking Away" director Peter
20. Pistol's kickback
23. Corpulent
24. Praise highly
25. Charlatans
28. 14, in old Rome
29. Nine-to-five activity
30. Elsie's chew
32. Women's shoe fastener
35. Pilot light
37. Wheel's center
38. Like trombone music
39. Boris Badenov's boss
42. Auto racer A.J.
43. Business-school subj.
44. Church bench
45. Downs of "20/20"
49. Cookiemaker Wally
50. High-speed connection, for short
51. Fencing blade
52. Hosp. worker
53. Ice cream amts.
54. 160, to Caesar

Down

1. Allegheny Mts. state
2. Armed conflict
3. Quipster
4. Do well (at)
5. Slide on ice
6. Letters after a proof
7. Bog product
8. Give up rights to
9. "The ___ the limit!"
11. Disinfectant brand
13. Batter's position
18. Caboodle's partner
19. Tibetan ox
20. Critic Reed
21. Sign over a door
22. Cleveland cagers, briefly

23. ___ Four (Beatles)
25. Vain sort
26. Some DVD players
27. Addition problems
29. Boxer's punch
31. Susan of "The Partridge Family"
33. Adds turpentine to
34. Shampoo target
35. Cook in hot oil
36. Carpenter's machine
38. Cereal servings
39. Breakfast or brunch
40. Ottawa-based law enforcement gp.
41. Windfall
42. Celebratory suffix

44. ASAP kin
46. Checkout bars: Abbr.
47. Hair stiffener
48. Put a spell on

Solution on page 364

Puzzle 269

Across

1. "Rushmore" director Anderson
4. Dusting cloth
7. Plant's beginning
11. Bowler, for example
12. Is in debt
14. ___ the line (behaved)
15. Appraise
17. Designer Klein
18. More macabre
19. Cole nicknamed "King"
21. Moreover
22. Winter gliders
25. Get the wrinkles out
28. Apt., e.g.
29. Sighs of content
31. Intl. relief org.
32. Exaggerate, as expenses
33. Toward shelter
34. Preposition in poetry
35. A Smothers brother
36. Various: Abbr.
37. White-plumed wader
39. Supply with weapons
41. Airport listing, for short
42. Lathered
46. Vigoda and Fortas
49. Tokyo farewell
51. French father
52. "Stop!"
53. Country lodge
54. Canvas shelter
55. "Rumor ___ it . . ."
56. Word before a maiden name

Down

1. Carnival ride cry
2. Roof edge
3. Polaris, e.g.
4. Where Joan of Arc died
5. Tony or Emmy
6. Obtain
7. One of fifty
8. Time out of mind
9. Bard's nightfall
10. H.S.T.'s successor
13. Perceived
16. Vine
20. Pacino and Hirt
23. Painter Salvador
24. Cheerleaders, often
25. Rink surface
26. Steak preference
27. Wash. neighbor
28. Ewe's mate
30. Dry, as wine
32. Soap ingredient
33. Jordan's capital
35. Vietnamese New Year
38. Furnace button
39. Refuges
40. Genealogy
43. Ache
44. Fish-eating bird
45. Niels Bohr, for one
46. Fitting
47. Honey maker
48. Fish-eating bird
50. "That feels so good!"

Solution on page 364

Puzzle 270

Across

1. Atty.'s degree
4. Hypodermic amts.
7. Actress MacGraw et al.
11. "___ Got the World on a String"
12. Farmer, at times
14. Popular teen hangout
15. Wire diameter measure
16. Comic Johnson
17. Cheese on crackers
18. "Lady Sings the Blues" autobiographer
21. Suffix with drunk or tank
22. Game show host Sajak
23. Tennis pro Lendl
26. Actor Gazzara
27. Playing card spot
30. Petty
34. Big wine holder
35. PC linking acronym
36. ___ instant (quickly)
37. Atlas item
38. "Huh?"
40. Best Actress Oscar nominee for "The Collector"
47. Just ___ (slightly)
48. Mrs. Charlie Chaplin
49. "May ___ of service?"
50. Stubborn animal
51. Classmate
52. Basketball hoop
53. Summers, on the Riviera
54. Insecticide banned since 1973
55. Susan of "Looker"

Down

1. Tree branch
2. Roman 57
3. Steeple feature
4. Run, as a meeting
5. Prepared apples
6. Brother of Cain and Abel
7. Boundary
8. Cooking fat
9. Hipbones
10. Weaver's reed
13. Investigate again, as a case
19. Long and slender
20. Come to earth
23. Storekeeper's stock: Abbr.
24. Rome's ___ Veneto
25. Nightclub routine
26. Test-___ treaty
27. Sewing-basket item
28. "___ Yankee Doodle dandy"
29. Animal enclosure
31. Dashing style
32. Portable computer
33. Corner-to-corner: Abbr.
37. Spouses
38. Died down
39. Valentine decoration
40. Identical
41. Lie adjacent to
42. 1/500 of the Indianapolis 500
43. Broke some ground
44. Encircle with a belt
45. Guy with an Irish Rose
46. ___ Martin (cognac brand)

Solution on page 365

Puzzle 271

Across

1. "Anything but ___!"
5. Painter Jean
8. Male voice
12. Dell
13. Sheep sound
14. Purina competitor
15. FBI employees
16. Recycling receptacle
17. Thailand's former name
18. Snow glider
20. Ditto
21. Nostalgic songs
24. ___-tzu (Taoism founder)
26. French topper
27. Tree with needles
28. Columbus Day's mo.
31. Where Boise is: Abbr.
32. Mezzo Frederica Von ___
34. "___ cool!"
35. Observed
36. Director Van Sant
37. Heavy French weight
39. Corn holder
40. Contacts, e.g.
41. "Kiss Me, ___"
44. Submission encl.
45. Ethereal glow
46. Elvis' first label
47. Landers and Sothern
51. Numbered hwys.
52. One, to Pierre
53. In ___ of (replacing)
54. Small carry-on
55. Writers' submissions: Abbr.
56. Come to a halt

Down

1. Rural power org.
2. Witch
3. Key near Ctrl
4. Entertainer O'Shea
5. French clergymen
6. Surprise police tactic
7. Wok, e.g.
8. Low voice
9. Inter ___ (among other things)
10. Unsolicited e-mail
11. "___ Like It Hot"
19. "Come on!"
21. Kimono sashes
22. Helen's mother, in Greek myth
23. Make a sketch
24. Jar top
25. Rugged ridges
27. Notes before sols
28. Holds the deed on
29. Walking stick
30. Nautical chains
33. Clumsy vessel
38. Ryan and Tatum
39. ___ and desist
40. Road divisions
41. Miniature racer
42. Prefix meaning "self"
43. Weight allowance
44. Solar-system centers
46. I am, to Caesar
48. Tiny criticism
49. Modern: Prefix
50. Have dinner

Solution on page 365

Puzzle 272

Across

1. Menlo Park inits.
4. Video maker, for short
7. Capital of Yemen
11. Birmingham's state: Abbr.
12. Oka River city
14. Et___
15. "I tawt I taw a puddy ___!"
16. Poll category
18. Shoe part
20. EarthLink alternative
21. Second notes of the scale
22. Pull into, as a station
26. Lowers in rank
29. Vocalist Brewer
30. Small rug
31. 19th letter of the Greek alphabet
32. Lyric poets
36. Not in class
39. Make good as new
40. ___ tai (drink)
41. Amount after expenses
42. Picks from the menu
46. Onetime Gidget portrayer
50. 1950 Edmond O'Brien classic thriller
51. ___' fixe (obsession)
52. Sounds of sorrow
53. "Do ___ say, . . ."
54. Amorous gaze
55. Have breakfast
56. Angry

Down

1. "Mr. Hulot's Holiday" star
2. Former Fed chief Greenspan
3. Gobbles down
4. Grand ___ Dam
5. "Gunsmoke" star James
6. Club ___ (resort)
7. Popeye, e.g.
8. City official: Abbr.
9. Never, in Nuremberg
10. Pitch in for
13. Minimum amount
17. Dove's home
19. Hospital areas: Abbr.
23. St. ___ (city near Tampa)
24. Straight ___ arrow
25. Having no slack
26. Love, Spanish-style
27. Expressed, as a farewell
28. Eagerly expecting
33. Carpenter's tool
34. Wedding-cake feature
35. Span. misses
36. One-celled being
37. Least furnished
38. Comic Caesar
43. Cheese from Holland
44. Civil-rights leader Parks
45. Articulated
46. The "S" in R.S.V.P.
47. Suffix with lemon or lime
48. Jacqueline Kennedy ___ Bouvier
49. Bambi's mother

Solution on page 365

Puzzle 273

Across

1. '50s presidential monogram
4. Datebook entry: Abbr.
8. Nincompoop
12. Jazz legend Kid ___
13. Squeezing snakes
14. Nest-egg accts.
15. "So long!"
16. City in SW Russia
17. Damon of "Good Will Hunting"
18. Comforter
20. Yellow fever mosquito
21. Ancient Scandinavian
23. Difficult duty
25. Bard of ___ (Shakespeare)
26. Pesky bug
27. "The Lord of the Rings" monster
30. "Song of the South" song
33. Driver's lic. and such
34. Tabula ___ (clean slate)
35. Pricey theater section
36. 50-and-over org.
37. Meet official
38. Commandments verb
41. ___ Janeiro
43. "Get over here, Fido!"
44. Clothes-dryer buildup
45. Boy King of ancient Egypt
48. In ___ (bogged down)
49. Noted plus-size model
50. Comic Phillips
51. Silents actress Theda
52. Barely passing grades
53. Engine speed, for short

Down

1. DMV datum
2. Lacking moisture
3. Tears?
4. Higher than
5. Apple or pear
6. Over the hill
7. Tongue-clucking sound
8. Thin coins
9. Toward the Mouth
10. ___ de foie gras
11. Body shop calcs.
19. Annapolis school: Abbr.
20. Coupe or convertible
21. "Schindler's List" villain
22. "Metamorphosis" poet
24. Zilch, to Pedro
26. Drive or reverse
27. Dashboard gauge
28. All the ___: widely popular
29. Sonny and ___
31. "Dang!"
32. Foul-smelling
36. Prince Valiant's love
37. Shopping bags
38. Picket-line crosser
39. Dance at a Jewish wedding
40. Manchurian river
42. "By the power vested ___ . . ."
44. Was in charge of
46. Ballpark official
47. Actor Selleck

Solution on page 365

Puzzle 274

Across

1. Batik artisan
5. It's no bull
8. H followers
11. Deliberate loss
12. Simple rhyme scheme
14. Combatant
15. Snick-or-___
16. Latvian port
17. Witchy woman
18. Constantly find fault with
20. Sorority members
22. ___ dish (lab item)
24. "The X-Files" network
25. Looking at
26. Brings bad luck to
29. Chelsea "Z"
30. Coltrane's instrument
31. Substance partner
33. Change tactics
36. Origami need
38. "Hee ___"
39. Cattle groups
40. Makes the fur fly?
43. Bangor's state
45. Tease playfully
46. Beatnik's "Gotcha!"
48. TV sports award
51. Bird-to-be
52. Orson Welles role
53. Phrase of understanding
54. "How come?"
55. Not pre- or post-
56. Pillow filler

Down

1. ADA member
2. Yang's complement
3. Twilight
4. Win back, as trust
5. "___ Mia" (1965 hit)
6. Memorial news item
7. Move one's tail
8. "___ hollers, let . . ."
9. "The Grapes of Wrath" family name
10. Frat party purchases
13. Breakfast meat
19. Musical engagement
21. Tic-tac-toe loser
22. Dispensable candy
23. One who stares
24. Repair
26. Tenor Peerce
27. Starbucks order
28. Took to court
30. Espied
32. "___ Miniver"
34. Prof's deg.
35. Corrective eye surgery
36. Letter after upsilon
37. Virgil epic
40. Slant unfairly
41. Mighty's partner
42. Innovative and daring
43. Short skirt
44. Got gray
47. Grand Coulee, e.g.
49. Bench with a back
50. Kobe currency

Solution on page 365

Puzzle 275

Across

1. Fuse units
5. America's Uncle
8. Suffered from
11. Longest African river
12. "What Kind of Fool ___?"
13. ___-Japanese War
14. W.C. Fields exclamation
15. Holm of "Chariots of Fire"
16. Marine eagle
17. Submitted by mail
19. NBC sportscaster Bob
21. Feedbag bit
22. Have a hamburger
23. Bill and ___
26. Chess pieces
28. Raises, as children
32. ___ Romeo (Italian auto)
34. The old man
36. Peter, Paul and Mary,
    e.g.
37. Like mesh
39. Classroom favorite
41. Provincetown's cape
42. Herbal ___
44. HELP!
46. Court challenge
49. Muscle twitches
53. Bewail
54. Make stuff up
56. Former Iranian ruler
57. Used a firehouse pole
58. Make a boo-boo
59. Hawaiian seaport
60. "The Star-Spangled
    Banner" contraction

61. "Are we there ___?"
62. Poker-pot starter

Down

1. & & &
2. Deep mud
3. Schedule
4. Sharp fight
5. Holy
6. Internists' org.
7. Cut into tiny pieces
8. Trumpeter Al
9. Magnani or Moffo
10. Fawns' moms
13. Six-line stanza
18. Descartes' conclusion
20. Rower's need

23. When doubled, a dance
24. Flamenco exclamation
25. Frequently, to a poet
27. Time-out of a sort
29. Javelin path
30. "Flying Down to ___"
31. Lawn base
33. Go to, as a concert
35. Baked Alaska, e.g.
38. Parliamentary vote
40. First-rate
43. Tin Pan ___
45. "Peter and the Wolf" bird
46. Playground reply
47. Flag holder
48. Ark unit
50. Climb, in a way

51. ___ liquor
52. Brogue or brogan
55. Anger

Solution on page 365

Puzzle 276

Across

1. Kept out of sight
4. "The Sweetheart of Sigma ___"
7. Reduce drastically, as prices
12. Troy, NY college
13. ___ room (play area)
14. Sal of "Rebel Without a Cause"
15. Witchcraft
17. Historical record
18. Rocket launch site
19. Dominion
20. Crunchy salad toppers
23. School support gp.
24. Continent north of Afr.
25. Caesar's "Behold!"
28. Joke response, informally
32. Trio after R
33. Leaks slowly
35. West Bank initials
36. Lays a new lawn
38. MGM founder Marcus
39. Break, as a balloon
40. Meditative sounds
42. Some Art Deco works
44. La ___ (Italian opera house)
47. ___ volente: God willing
48. Worrier's woe, it's said
49. Raspberry
53. "I'm innocent!"
54. B-F connection
55. Driver's license abbr.
56. Twirls
57. Fivescore yrs.
58. Roast beef au ___

Down

1. "48 ___" (Nick Nolte film)
2. Wall St. launch
3. Corp. board member
4. Folds
5. It's rounded up in a roundup
6. Hardly hospitable
7. Intelligent
8. Of direct descent
9. Fictional Karenina
10. Close, as an envelope
11. Celeste of "Gentleman's Agreement"
16. Sharkey's rank
20. She preceded Mamie
21. Coupe or sedan
22. Gunky stuff
23. ___ Le Pew
26. Cartoon frames
27. "Forbes" profilee
29. Sched. entry
30. Oceanic ice
31. Fancy dressers
34. Add sugar to
37. Very serious
41. Colts' moms
43. Legendary bird
44. Gets a tan
45. Filly's footfall
46. Start of a play
47. Miami's county
49. VI x L
50. Noun modifier: Abbr.
51. Costello or Gehrig
52. Many oz.

Solution on page 366

Puzzle 277

Across

1. Health resort
4. Christmas poem opener
8. Horse-hoof sound
12. Bandleader Kyser
13. Breakfast chain, briefly
14. Robber's haul
15. Brynner of "The King and I"
16. Pepsi competitor
17. Turkish official
18. Carefree episode
20. Ruckus
22. Depletes, with "up"
25. Actor's line
29. Oyster relative
32. Bruce or Laura of film
34. Apple computer
35. Cruet contents, often
36. Think tank products
37. First US capital
38. BTU relative
39. Repairs, as a roof
40. Fire-hydrant attachment
41. . . . miss is as good as ___
43. Annoying e-mail
45. Little scamp
47. Minimum points
50. Cookouts, for short
53. Pond floater
56. Breakfast meat
58. Tightly stretched
59. Completely bollix
60. Uncertainties
61. Salt Lake City collegians
62. Urges (on)
63. Actress Tilly

Down

1. The limit, proverbially
2. One of the Apostles
3. Jean Auel heroine
4. Watch sounds
5. Question starter
6. Hunky-dory
7. Moved quickly
8. Highland families
9. Ship's record
10. Aah's partner
11. School org.
19. Jamaican export
21. Fleming and McKellen
23. Icelandic literary work
24. Fortune-tellers
26. "___ Angel" (Mae West film)
27. Calendar squares
28. Behold, in old Rome
29. ___-Cola
30. Neeson of "Kinsey"
31. "You're ___ Need to Get By"
33. Throaty utterance
36. Thing on a list
40. Med. plan
42. Rosters
44. Arkin and Alda
46. Peel, as an apple
48. Passing fancy
49. Place for valuables
50. A/C stat
51. Stand at the plate
52. Neighbor of Ont.
54. Haul
55. Jazz job
57. "No ___" (menu phrase)

Solution on page 366

Puzzle 278

Across

1. Left, at sea
5. Swine
9. Day-___: pigment brand
12. African fox
13. Step ___ (hurry)
14. Lucy of "Charlie's Angels," 2000
15. Helped to relax
17. Repeatedly, in rhyme
18. Jar cover
19. Haile Selassie follower, for short
21. Involuntary twitch
24. Revealing skirts
26. Solo of "Star Wars"
27. Sound of contentment
28. Was dressed in
31. Curved entryway
33. NYC subway overseer
34. Declare frankly
35. Greek earth goddess
36. Gave a meal to
37. Female sheep
38. Quarterback Phil
40. Exposes
42. Kama ___
44. In need of replenishing
45. Pizzeria ___ (restaurant chain)
46. Mind reading
52. P.O. delivery
53. Book after Gen.
54. "___ a Teen-age Werewolf"
55. Ring decisions
56. Rules, for short
57. Like skyscrapers

Down

1. Mushy stuff
2. The Buckeyes, for short
3. Q-U connection
4. Blue-green shades
5. Whacked weeds
6. Words before roll or whim
7. USO show audience
8. Ship's rear
9. Explain away
10. Brit's elevator
11. "I'm ___ here!"
16. Comedian Conway
20. Panasonic competitor
21. Rug variety
22. Prefix with legal or chute
23. Family tree members
24. Husbands and wives
25. "If ___ a Hammer"
27. Two-band radio
29. T. ___ Price (investment firm)
30. Wool producers
32. Ponytail material
39. Alma ___
40. Dizzy Gillespie's genre
41. Hang around for
42. Mope
43. "Do ___ others . . ."
44. Watch readouts, briefly
47. Computer program suffix
48. Captain's journal
49. Former Pan Am rival
50. "Barney Miller" star Linden
51. High-fashion monogram

Solution on page 366

Puzzle 279

Across
1. They, in Tours
4. DMV document
7. Central street
11. Comics caveman Alley ___
12. "Be ___ . . .": "Help me"
14. Highest point
15. Gun owners' org.
16. Cro-Magnon's home
17. Falling sound
18. Marsh plants
20. Admittance
22. Streets: Abbr.
23. Homer Simpson exclamation
24. Mlle.'s Spanish counterpart
27. "For ___ a jolly good fellow"
28. Packers' org.
31. Fail to attend
32. Former Mideast org.
33. Having no doubt
34. Baseball arbiter
35. Reverse of ENE
36. ___ Penh, Cambodia
37. "Wow!"
38. Pier gp.
40. Long looks
43. Tropical rays
47. Cloth texture
48. ___ Bator, Mongolia
50. "Where did ___ wrong?"
51. "Laugh-In" comedian Johnson
52. Apple or quince
53. Boggy area
54. Walking pace
55. "Acid"
56. Magical, as elves

Down
1. Charged atoms
2. Oral tradition
3. Miner's nail
4. Secured, as a skate
5. "No bid," in bridge
6. Cleveland cager, for short
7. Lighter alternative
8. Post-workout complaint
9. Radio host Don
10. Sparks and Rorem
13. Pacesetter
19. Mardi___
21. Comedian Bill, familiarly
24. Dallas campus: Abbr.
25. What an air ball doesn't touch
26. Cook's abbr.
27. Hee follower
28. Mother Teresa, e.g.
29. To's reverse
30. Moon vehicle
32. Exhausts
33. Wingspread
35. Teeny
37. Meet at the door
38. Muslim leaders
39. Divided, as a freeway
40. Pirate's booty
41. "Gone with the Wind" estate
42. High: Prefix
44. Argument
45. James who wrote "A Death in the Family"
46. Walkman maker
49. Chat room guffaw

Solution on page 366

Puzzle 280

Across

1. Numbered rds.
5. Used a bench
8. Mrs. Colin Powell
12. Suffix with million
13. Flat ___ pancake
14. Symbol of sadness
15. Additional
16. Taxpayer's ID
17. London's ___ Gallery
18. "My country, ___ of thee . . ."
20. Linkletter and Garfunkel
21. Hair stylist's shop
24. Nostradamus
27. Mine matter
28. Five-and-ten, e.g.
30. Sibling, for short
33. "Scream" director Craven
34. Orderly display
35. George's former press secretary
36. Carrier to Stockholm
37. "Nifty!"
38. Tennis-match part
39. So-so marks
40. Like May through August, letterwise
42. Old king of rhyme
45. Start of a bray
46. "East of Eden" brother
47. Take notice of
49. Hand-cream ingredient
53. Payment to a landlord
54. Sot's ailment
55. Sound stages
56. Fireplace fillers
57. The Caribbean, e.g.
58. Head, in Le Havre

Down

1. Computer capacity, for short
2. South-of-the-border uncle
3. "To ___ is human . . ."
4. Be responsible for
5. Impertinent talk
6. Donkey
7. Light brown
8. Perfume ingredient
9. Limerick man
10. Olympic swimmer Biondi
11. Greek Mars
19. Ridiculous
21. Scatters, as seed
22. Polygon measurement
23. "___ is more"
24. Carolina rails
25. QED center
26. Pooh's donkey pal
29. Family-history diagram
30. Enclosure with a MS.
31. Angers
32. Rests for a moment
39. Partner of dollars
41. Fewest
42. Sagan or Sandburg
43. Triple-decker cookie
44. Yearn (for)
45. "___ Rebel" (1962 song)
47. Radical '60s grp.
48. Summer: Fr.
50. Martial arts expert Bruce
51. Giant Hall-of-Famer
52. Reverse of WNW

Solution on page 366

Puzzle 281

Across

1. More than damp
4. Bone in a cage?
7. "The Giving Tree" author Silverstein
11. Center of activity
12. Prefix for social
14. ___ Alto, Calif.
15. Decade parts: Abbr.
16. Wine quality
17. Portland's st.
18. 1982 Meryl Streep film
21. Hard to explain
22. Dearie
23. Spherical starter
26. Go chop-chop?
27. Flag Day grp.
30. Untrustworthy types
34. Crooner Damone
35. Humorously sarcastic
36. Lobster's grabber
37. Thurs. follower
38. Contend (for)
40. 1990 Alan Alda film
47. ". . . way to skin ___"
48. Spelling of "Beverly Hills 90210"
49. Partner of wide
50. "Wizard of Oz" dog
51. ". . . ___ I'm told"
52. Pharm. watchdog
53. Underskirt
54. Gender abbr.
55. "Hurrah!"

Down

1. Reasons
2. It replaced the lira
3. Recipe amount: Abbr.
4. Like a mad dog
5. "The Woman ___" (Gene Wilder film)
6. Air conditioner meas.
7. Cereal utensil
8. Mata ___ (spy)
9. Basic util.
10. Seating section
13. Was restless
19. Horse's foot
20. Serenade the moon
23. Versatile transport, for short
24. Prefix with night or light
25. Soft shoe, briefly
26. "You, there!"
27. Kilmer of "The Saint"
28. ___ Diavolo (seafood sauce)
29. ENE's opposite
31. Cockeyed
32. "The Count of Monte ___"
33. Decorated, as a cake
37. Shutterbug's setting
38. And ___
39. "Talk turkey," e.g.
40. Flying mammals
41. E.P.A. subj.
42. Comic actor Jacques
43. Klingon on the Enterprise
44. In doubt
45. Nothing, in Mexico
46. Battleship shade

Solution on page 366

Puzzle 282

Across

1. Run smoothly
4. Corduroy feature
8. Mezz. alternative
12. Psychiatrist's concern
13. Petri dish filler
14. Sulk
15. Greek consonant
16. Rhino feature
17. Elsewhere
18. Apropos of
20. Campus figure
22. Hoover's org.
25. Foul up
29. Yellow wildflower
34. Mighty tree
35. French article
36. Not restrictive
37. Hardly hale
38. Vitamin bottle abbr.
39. Among others
41. "The Velvet Fog" Mel
43. Gridiron arbiter
44. Worship from ___
47. Dosage amts.
51. Newsman Huntley
54. Old Venetian official
57. Antlered critter
58. Very large
59. Old-fashioned showdown
60. Minuscule
61. Brain tests, briefly
62. ___-help
63. Witnessed

Down

1. Zeus' wife
2. Exclamations of disgust
3. Irrelevant
4. Infant's cry
5. In the past
6. Fat in a can
7. Shore soarer
8. Citizen of Muscat
9. Propel a dinghy
10. Expert on IRS forms
11. Attention-getting shout
19. Many a lime
21. Unit of current
23. Dogma
24. Golf-bag club
26. Potting material
27. Artist Salvador
28. Neighbor of Tex.
29. Lancaster of films
30. Open, as a tie
31. Rip
32. Basic bed
33. Internet patron
40. Opposite of fore
42. Pub pals
45. Does basic math
46. Cad
48. Does some darning
49. Defendant's response
50. Distort
51. Fidel's compadre
52. Peach or plum
53. Easter basket item
55. Goo in a do
56. Santa's helper

Solution on page 367

Puzzle 283

Across

1. If all ___ fails . . .
5. Carol contraction
8. Supercomputer name
12. Christmas season
13. Sony rival
14. Part of a poem
15. Deuce or trey
16. Sushi fish
17. Gibbons
18. Lacking vigor
20. Metal fastener
22. Morse Mayday
23. Vigoda of "Fish"
24. Milky
28. Prepare for a test
32. European peak
33. Unimpressive brain size
35. In low spirits
36. Dish
39. Patriotic songs
42. "___ a girl!"
44. Lao-tzu's way
45. Put ___ to (halt)
47. Shoelace ends
51. Airline to Israel
52. Tax mo.
54. Entice
55. The ___ Ranger
56. Deer lady
57. Explorer ___ the Red
58. Govt. agents
59. Asner and Ames
60. Cordlike

Down

1. Suffix for differ
2. Hang out
3. Medieval worker
4. Firstborn
5. Source of maple syrup
6. Rocks, to a bartender
7. Tex-Mex sauce
8. Red wine
9. Fit for picking
10. Again
11. "Okay"
19. Boot part
21. "60 Minutes" airer
24. Napkin's place
25. Start and end of the Three Musketeers' motto
26. Form 1040 completer
27. Pastoral setting
29. Employ
30. River barrier
31. QB's stats
34. Star in Scorpius
37. Knight, dame, etc.
38. WWII command
40. License plate
41. Shout
43. Digging tool
45. Skin-soothing stuff
46. Grit
48. Money in Madrid
49. Begin a fall
50. Cabinet member: Abbr.
51. North Pole worker
53. Pea holder

Solution on page 367

Puzzle 284

Across

1. Exiled Amin
4. Apple computers
8. Bag
12. Bit of ointment
13. Greenland base
14. Peanut covering
15. Like a ranch house
17. Part of a molecule
18. Triangular sails
19. Medical-insurance cos.
20. Fawn's mother
21. Sign after Aquarius
23. Golf Cup
26. Neon or freon
27. Shad product
28. Afrikaner
29. Despicable
30. Waters: Fr.
31. Theory suffix
32. Metered vehicle
33. Threadbare
34. Appeared to be
36. Easel part
37. Spice made from nutmeg
38. Article supplement
42. KFC piece
43. Scenic view
44. Nebraska Indian
45. Nantes notion
46. Blood, so to speak
47. "___ all in this together"
48. Buntline and Rorem
49. Mouse sighter's cry

Down

1. Admired celebrity
2. Comic Carvey
3. "Yeah, sure!"
4. Shooting star
5. Make amends (for)
6. Sedans and coupes
7. Less than forward
8. Hoaxes
9. Absolute ruler
10. Liquidation sale
11. J-N connector
16. Passover celebration
19. Towel stitching
21. Feline foot
22. Titillating
23. Score-producing stats
24. California national park
25. Behavior
26. Hunk
29. Young chap
30. Chomping at the bit
32. Epcot center?
33. Makes over
35. "Me and Bobby ___"
36. Like notebook paper
38. "No Ordinary Love" singer
39. Put in the oven
40. French girlfriend
41. Corporal or captain
42. "That's incredible!"
43. Brooch

Solution on page 367

Puzzle 285

Across

1. Nick Charles' dog
5. West ender
8. Seal hunter
12. Weed whackers
13. Zodiac lion
14. Prosperous period
15. Baby blues
16. Treasure hunter's aid
17. Chicago area
18. Horses' hair
20. Deserves
22. Kind of dance
24. Sink in the middle
25. Carrot cousin
29. Sign gases
33. Part of a GI's address
34. Done ___ turn
36. Gidget portrayer Sandra
37. Overused, as an expression
40. Implore
43. Consumes
45. Stocking stuffer?
46. Intelligence
49. Treaties
53. Coal stratum
54. Pie ___ mode
56. Codger
57. Zoo fixture
58. Smash into
59. Dog in Oz
60. Makes angry
61. A sister of Zsa Zsa
62. Whole lot

Down

1. Throat clearer
2. Kind of bean
3. Many a Britney Spears fan
4. Desirable traits
5. Shade maker
6. Paper measure
7. Slangy denials
8. Do a favor for
9. Fans do it
10. Talks amorously
11. Fuse rating unit
19. ___ Bernardino
21. Sought public office
23. Racetrack area
25. Soft touch
26. Showery mo.
27. Louis XIV, e.g.
28. Creator of the Ushers
30. Poem of praise
31. PBS funder
32. Matched batch
35. Picnic intruder
38. London's river
39. Lobe locale
41. Do better than
42. Does a double take, e.g.
44. Astonished look
46. Affix a brand to
47. Sorcerer
48. Serb or Croat, e.g.
50. Unruffled
51. Open handbag
52. Put into the hold
53. High school subj.
55. Group of drs.

Solution on page 367

Puzzle 286

Across

1. Post mortem bio
5. ___-o'-shanter
8. Mexico Mrs.
11. Taken care of
12. Pig ___ poke
13. Musical phrase mark
14. Dodge City marshal
15. D.C. type
16. "Penny ___" (1967 Beatles chart-topper)
17. Takes the wheel
19. Since way back when
21. Feast on
22. Manx or Persian
23. Nature's alarm clock
27. Parisian papas
31. Capture
32. Charlotte of "The Facts of Life"
34. Gene ID
35. Greet the day
38. Satisfies
41. Chinese drink
43. 90-degree bend
44. Pedestal parts
47. Punctuation marks
51. Personal flair
52. Feed bag tidbit
54. Sheriff Taylor's son
55. Stag attender
56. Colorado tribesman
57. Grow dim
58. Song from "A Chorus Line"
59. CSA icon
60. Sty food

Down

1. Poetic works
2. Wake maker
3. Concerning, in a memo
4. Conical abodes
5. Racetrack informant
6. Year, in Spain
7. Acid in apples
8. Smelting refuse
9. Mysterious letter
10. Mars' counterpart
13. Party list
18. Spill the beans
20. Doze
23. Genetic info
24. Rower's tool
25. Geisha's sash
26. Sharp knock
28. Map lines: Abbr.
29. Trenton-to-Newark dir.
30. Airline to Sweden
33. November winner
36. Mason's material
37. Wide shoe size
39. "Evil Woman" grp.
40. Lets
42. "Don't tell ___!"
44. Test-driven vehicle
45. Alda of "M*A*S*H"
46. Mrs. Roy Rogers
48. Gem
49. El ___ (Pacific Ocean current)
50. Ooze
53. Filled up on

Solution on page 367

Puzzle 287

Across

1. Baby's first word, sometimes
5. Heavenly bodies
9. Ring result, briefly
12. Delinquent G.I.
13. Pepper partner
14. Reviewer Reed
15. Boor
16. Pronghorn
18. Diana of "The Avengers"
20. Russian president Vladimir
21. Outfit
24. Christmas tree
25. Beverage
26. Grow old
30. Last letter, in London
31. Bar code?
32. "You, over there!"
33. It may be penciled in
36. Crystal-filled stone
38. Manhandle
39. Smoothing tool
40. Peculiar expression
43. Shed, snake-style
44. Bullfighter
46. Supreme Court justice ___ Bader Ginsburg
50. Noah's vessel
51. Bird of peace
52. Farm prefix
53. Audiophile's collection
54. Bullets, in poker
55. ___ Ed.

Down

1. Raincoat, for short
2. Leatherworker's tool
3. Bossy's call
4. Astronaut Buzz
5. Oklahoma Indian
6. Sounded a bell
7. Deli order
8. Take over
9. Moderate gait
10. French military hat
11. Yoke wearers
17. Angler's need
19. Grate on
21. Carpenter's tool
22. Deuce beater
23. Beach washer
24. Small number
26. Toothed tool
27. Did a blacksmith's job
28. Give over
29. Ogler
31. Fan setting
34. Lodge letters
35. Best Western rival
36. "My ___ Sal"
37. Lure into crime
39. Painful spots
40. Type style: Abbr.
41. Hamlet
42. Ticks off
43. Pull up stakes
45. Bespectacled dwarf
47. "That's gross!"
48. Take a shot at
49. That guy's

Solution on page 367

Puzzle 288

Across

1. The "one" in a one-two
4. Trolley
8. Very popular
11. Thumbs-up votes
13. German auto
14. Sci-fi vehicle
15. Measure (out)
16. Machine part
17. Can metal
18. Picked up
20. Central points
22. Skee-Ball site
25. Senate vote
26. Hall & Oates, e.g.
27. Hydroelectric project
29. Ceremonial staffs
33. Big spender's phrase
35. Barker and Bell
37. Numbskull
38. Flower parts
40. Many a Little League coach
42. Chick's mom
43. PC alternative
45. Lamented
47. Tetley competitor
50. Fly-by-night sort
51. Snoop
52. Ancient Peruvian
54. Seek divine guidance
58. Game with "Draw Two" cards
59. Anon
60. Food fish
61. ___ compos mentis
62. Club ___ (resorts)
63. Short order

Down

1. Traffic trouble
2. Popeye's "Positively!"
3. Play the ponies
4. Wrestling duo
5. McClanahan of "The Golden Girls"
6. Rhett's last words
7. Sister of Moses
8. Primitive homes
9. "Think nothing ___"
10. A lot
12. Nintendo rival
19. Uneven
21. Pair
22. Ruckuses
23. Puny pup
24. Tag along
28. "Spy vs. Spy" magazine
30. "Walking in Memphis" singer Marc
31. Blunt-tipped sword
32. Mail out
34. 1816 Jane Austen novel
36. Pago Pago residents
39. Extreme cruelty
41. Part of D.J.I.A.
44. Lake boat
46. Mont Blanc's range
47. Made a web
48. Italian river
49. Sue of "Lolita"
53. New England cape
55. Burgle
56. Last word in the Pledge of Allegiance
57. "Is it soup ___?"

Solution on page 368

Puzzle 289

Across

1. Printer's need
4. Joins in holy matrimony
8. ___ erectus
12. It's heard in a herd
13. Atlanta arena
14. "The Heat ___": Glenn Frey hit
15. Request
16. Crack the books
17. Modeler's adhesive
18. Opt for
20. Reverberations
22. Neth. neighbor
23. Certain computer, informally
24. Punxsutawney groundhog
27. Testing site
28. Surfing area
31. Well-dressed guy
32. Wrestler's goal
33. Military group
34. Milk units: Abbr.
35. Proof-ending letters
36. Wall St. index
37. Blackguard
38. Craze
40. Prohibitions
43. Plains Indians
47. Homecoming attender
48. Mythical meanie
50. Band box
51. Crocus bulb
52. Basketball Hall-of-Famer Archibald
53. Supporting
54. Sandwich fish
55. Imitator
56. Take a crack at

Down

1. Apple computer
2. Snack between meals
3. "Out of the Inkwell" clown
4. More unfavorable
5. Arab chieftain
6. Heredity helix
7. Jazz band member
8. Soprano's note
9. Capital of Norway
10. Pained look
11. Wallet items
19. Look amorously at
21. It's hailed in cities
24. ASAP
25. Primitive abode
26. Driver's lic. et al.
27. Coffee-to-go need
28. Twisted, as humor
29. Dorothy's aunt et al.
30. "Catch ya later!"
32. ___ non grata
33. Forever ___ day
35. Quid pro ___
37. Pause sign
38. Strong point
39. Moslem prince
40. Social asset
41. Felipe or Matty of baseball
42. Incinerate
44. Knife handle
45. Love, in Madrid
46. Light on one's feet
49. Popular clothing store, with "The"

Solution on page 368

Puzzle 290

Across

1. ___-di-dah
4. "Mona ___"
8. Start with boy or girl
12. ___pro nobis
13. One day in March
14. Any minute now
15. Spirit
16. Place to dock
17. Cut, as logs
18. Makes less difficult
20. Highland hillside
22. Rep.'s foe
24. Moffo and Magnani
27. Toscanini and others
31. Pigpens
33. Neckline type
34. Curtain fabric
36. Gun lobby, briefly
37. Chou ___ of China
39. Watered down
41. Put into office
43. Portion of corn
44. Spick-and-span
46. Bills to pay
50. Dig this!
53. NYC museum
55. Use the oars
56. Carpet buyer's calculation
57. Bristol baby buggy
58. Historical period
59. Singer Cole et al.
60. Hill-building insects
61. Install, as carpet

Down

1. Frequent song subject
2. Operatic piece
3. Bad actors
4. Insincere support
5. Terse vow
6. Belgrade native
7. Ad ___ per aspera: Kansas motto
8. Give the OK
9. Grind ___ halt
10. Pull from behind
11. Landers or Lee
19. End of some e-mail addresses
21. Yosemite photographer
23. Cow sound
25. "___ That a Shame"
26. Dried
27. Thoroughfare: Abbr.
28. French statesman Coty
29. Rat (on)
30. Funny Caesar
32. Feeling blue
35. Tell a fib
38. Hero of a Virgil epic
40. Suffix with press
42. Florida port
45. Ripped
47. Belgian songsmith Jacques
48. 1/3 of a WWII movie title
49. Rock back and forth
50. Chesspiece
51. Retirement asset, briefly
52. Tennis-court divider
54. It might say WELCOME

Solution on page 368

Puzzle 291

Across

1. ___-tac-toe
4. Tennis champ Arthur
8. Jazzman Zoot
12. Moviedom's Myrna
13. Avoid deliberately
14. Feeling tense
15. Meet expectations
18. Achy after a workout
19. Jack Sprat's bane
20. The Charles' terrier
23. Run amok
27. Lambs' mothers
30. "This round's ___!"
32. ___ for the course
33. "Guys and Dolls" guy
36. Acne spot
37. Deer moms
38. Ancient laborer
39. Helpful
41. Impudent talk
43. Make a pick
45. Kiln for drying hops
48. Look-alike
54. Maxi's opposite
55. Pet-shop buy
56. Ending for press
57. Silent film star Negri
58. Health retreats
59. Mafia

Down

1. Motherly ministering, for short
2. Promises to pay: Abbr.
3. Cell: Prefix
4. Fireplace flakes
5. Girl's pronoun
6. Motor sound
7. Plenty, informally
8. Bench-clearing incident
9. Boise is its cap.
10. Dugout VIP
11. Pink Floyd guitarist Barrett
16. Dumpster filler
17. Bob of "Full House"
21. Up ___ good
22. Llama locale
24. G.I. addresses
25. ___ in the neck (pest)
26. One-named Art Deco designer
27. Auto maker Ferrari
28. Model persona
29. Rebuke to Brutus
31. Butte relative
34. Capable
35. Convened again
40. Actress Braga of "Kiss of the Spider Woman"
42. Shoe bottoms
44. Involuntary contractions
46. Done laps
47. Novice
48. Mischievous kid
49. God, in Roma
50. Big picture?: Abbr.
51. Beanie
52. Turkish noble
53. Omaha's state: Abbr.

Solution on page 368

Puzzle 292

Across

1. "___ be darned!"
4. Part of USSR: Abbr.
7. Oregon capital
12. Bandleader Lombardo
13. "Curb Your Enthusiasm" network
14. Cape Cod town
15. Including everything
17. Come about
18. Monk's moniker
19. Cobblers' forms
20. Gardener's need
23. Swampland
24. Noticeable opening
25. Went by bike
28. Two-year-olds
32. The first "T" of TNT
33. Not her
34. Deep distress
35. Droops
37. Claire and Balin
39. This minute
40. Sgt., e.g.
42. Houses in trees
44. Barbecue site
47. Boxer Baer
48. Wide open, as a mouth
49. Marsh plant
53. Located
54. Atomic energy org.
55. AK-47 relative
56. Skyrockets
57. The highest degree
58. Cupid's mo.

Down

1. "Here ___ again!"
2. Broadway comedy of 1964
3. Soapmaker's solution
4. Generous one
5. It precedes di or da, in a Beatles song
6. Remote control abbr.
7. No longer fresh
8. Notorious
9. San ___ Obispo, Calif.
10. Formerly, old-style
11. "The Simpsons" tavern
16. "Mayberry ___"
20. Certain NCO's
21. Trooper prefix
22. ___ in a poke
23. Govt. disaster agency
26. Canton's state
27. Lot of noise
29. Possesses
30. Sound the horn
31. Makes clothes
36. Hidden marksman
38. Seize suddenly
41. Some college students
43. No. after a phone no.
44. Avoid an F
45. Money exchange premium
46. "So long!" in London
47. Retail store
49. MSNBC alternative
50. ___ Wiedersehen
51. Verb-forming suffix
52. Freedom, briefly

Solution on page 368

Puzzle 293

Across

1. "The Best Is ___ to Come"
4. "Fourscore and seven years ___ . . ."
7. Oft-swiveled joint
10. Homeowner's document
12. Spies' org.
13. Goods
14. Delta deposit
16. Facial features
17. Actor Sparks
18. Bronco catcher
19. Alda and Ladd
22. Mark with a branding iron
24. Hoops great Archibald
25. Church platforms
28. Court hearing
29. Extra play periods, for short
30. Prefix meaning "billionth"
32. Calm and quiet
34. What icicles do
35. Burrows and Vigoda
36. Leaves in, editorially
37. ___ with faint praise
40. Stinging insect
41. ___ the Red
42. "M*A*S*H" star
47. Chinese side dish
48. Musical notes
49. Caviars
50. Stephen of "Michael Collins"
51. '60s records
52. Computer monitor: Abbr.

Down

1. Fractions of a mi.
2. Wide shoe designation
3. "Nightline" host Koppel
4. Served perfectly, in tennis
5. Martini liquor
6. Feedbag grain
7. Makes bales for the barn
8. Hot tempers
9. Money in Mexico
11. Debutante's event
13. Result of normal use
15. Month, in Madrid
18. Livy's lang.
19. Year in Yucatan
20. "Betcha can't eat just one" chips
21. To ___: perfectly
22. Fills completely
23. Chicago Loop trains
26. Extremely uncommon
27. Grumpy mood
29. Taxonomic suffix
31. Photo ___: publicity events
33. Muscles to crunch
36. Japanese money
37. Author Earl ___ Biggers
38. Indy 500's Luyendyk
39. Translucent mineral
40. Low voice range
42. Part of A&P
43. Kind of service
44. ___ cit. (footnote abbr.)
45. ___ Bingle (Crosby moniker)
46. Nova Scotia clock setting: Abbr.

Solution on page 368

Puzzle 294

Across

1. Of ocean motion
6. Cat's foot
9. Sailor, slangily
12. State, as an opinion
13. Color gradation
14. Sch. in Tempe
15. Goose egg
16. California fort named for a Union general
17. Jury-___ (improvise)
18. ___-American relations
20. ___ Alt
21. Like an antique
24. Neighbor of Leb.
25. ___ or less
26. Library patron
29. "The Simpsons" clerk
31. Theodore of Broadway's "The Sound of Music"
32. Daytime TV fare
36. Abbr. on a rap sheet
38. Pesos
39. Cut, as a log
42. "You don't ___!"
44. Kernel holder
45. Marseille Mrs.
46. Make ready, briefly
48. Son of, in Arabic names
49. That fellow
50. Linen shades
55. R.N.'s forte
56. Family guy
57. A la ___
58. Scornful laugh
59. Above, to a poet
60. Scarecrow filler

Down

1. Dam-building agcy.
2. Debtor's note
3. Cutting remark
4. Rhine whine?
5. "___ Do It" (Porter tune)
6. Counterfeit
7. ___ borealis (northern lights)
8. Hitched, so to speak
9. "Anna Christie" star
10. American dogwood
11. Reveille instrument
19. Netanyahu's land: Abbr.
21. Planet, poetically
22. Hawaiian wreath
23. U.S. territory divided in 1889
25. Atomic particle
27. College head
28. Big game animal
30. Letter before omega
33. Truman's nuclear agcy.
34. Golf instructor
35. Cry loudly
37. Eagerly wish
38. Blonde's secret, maybe
39. Common surname
40. Walk leisurely
41. Strumpet
43. Knight clothing
47. Chest muscles, briefly
49. Cable movie channel
51. Purring pet
52. School basics, initially
53. Hagen of Broadway
54. Do some darning

Solution on page 369

Puzzle 295

Across

1. Elec. bill unit
4. Each, in pricing
8. Easter entree
12. "I kid ___ not"
13. Auto payment default consequence
14. Orchestra woodwind
15. Put another way
17. Buffalo Bill
18. Red-faced
19. Silent greeting
20. Wine cocktail
21. Hay wirers
23. Desert stops
26. Beer holder
27. Cry of disgust
28. Nutritional figs.
29. Toast topper
30. Chess ending
31. A's opposite, in England
32. Muslim pilgrimage
33. Gave a hoot
34. "___ Twist"
36. Deluxe seat
37. ___ yet (so far)
38. Turncoat
42. Type of pasta
43. Way back when
44. "___ it my way"
45. Makes a request
46. Superman foe Luthor
47. Private eyes, for short
48. Cry on a roller coaster
49. Door opener

Down

1. Actress Sedgwick
2. Travails
3. "Be quiet!"
4. Dumas dueler
5. Actor O'Toole
6. Pundit's column
7. Peas' home
8. In the neighborhood
9. Like a bogey
10. Preside over
11. Ottoman Empire governor
16. Film director's units
19. Joker
21. Hobo
22. Backyard structure
23. Ricelike pasta
24. Capital of South Australia
25. Cruel
26. Capt.'s superior
29. Cookie container
30. Long skirts
32. Playboy founder, familiarly
33. Rough
35. Nullifies
36. Slow
38. Former "Entertainment Tonight" cohost John
39. Chat
40. Molding style
41. Popular theater name
42. Clearasil target
43. Go off course

Solution on page 369

Puzzle 296

Across

1. Barbecue offering
5. "Evita" character
8. Game with mallets
12. Most eligible to serve
13. Play a kazoo
14. Commentators' page
15. Nearly all
16. Lawyer's org.
17. Cure start
18. Follows
20. Medicinal syrup
22. Out of service?: Abbr.
23. Minstrel's song
24. Water absorber
27. Like the Grand Canyon
31. Linden or Holbrook
32. One, to Juan
33. Finishes
37. African antelopes
40. Letters between two names
41. Eyeliner target
42. Stereotypical pirate feature
45. Ready to roll
49. Yale students
50. World Series mo.
52. "Tell ___ the judge!"
53. ___ Marie Presley
54. Expected in
55. Shoulder of a road
56. They might be saturated
57. Do simple math
58. Hook's sidekick

Down

1. Forum site
2. Let ___ a secret
3. Good Queen ___
4. Titan orbits it
5. Modest
6. Busy airport
7. Hits the "Send" button
8. Bluto's rival
9. Crude cartel
10. Mother of Castor and Pollux
11. Of Pindar's work
19. Brain test, for short
21. Lobbying grp.
24. Feminine pronoun
25. Bad review
26. Worn out
28. Habit wearer
29. Neither Dem. nor Rep.
30. Comedian Bill, informally
34. Dips for chips
35. Hula accompaniment
36. Chinese temple
37. Filled with joy
38. ___ Abner
39. Off-the-cuff remarks
42. Dirty money
43. Pen name of Charles Lamb
44. Core
46. Flower supporter
47. To be, in Tours
48. Heavy book
51. Bossy's chew

Solution on page 369

Puzzle 297

Across

1. Forbid
4. Army NCO
8. Cadabra preceder
12. Hockey surface
13. Theater section
14. Horn sound
15. ___ of a kind
16. Not ___ eye in the house
17. First-rate
18. Make calm
20. Playbill listings
21. "Gil Blas" novelist
24. Business mgmt.
27. Chinese ideal
28. Police rank: Abbr.
31. Start up a computer
32. Rapper ___ Def
33. Carbonated drink
34. Raven's call
35. The Beatles' "___ the Walrus"
36. Smooths wood
37. Sadat's predecessor
39. Lucifer
43. Wreath
47. Was imitative
48. Flows back
50. Spy's org.
51. Wasn't truthful
52. Fabric texture
53. Slip-___ (pullovers)
54. Okla. neighbor
55. Hurricane centers
56. Computer giant

Down

1. Book jacket briefs
2. Teen's woe
3. Necessity
4. ___ Island Ferry
5. "Us" and "Them"
6. Aus. neighbor
7. Have a go at
8. "Mamma Mia" quartet
9. Hive denizens
10. Everything else
11. Condos and co-ops: Abbr.
19. Reached Dulles
20. Business VIP
22. Parts of molecules
23. Oil alternative
24. Alphabet starter
25. 1988 Dennis Quaid remake
26. Do the lawn
28. Ho of Hawaii
29. Actor Byrnes
30. Profs.' helpers
32. Calf's cry
33. ___ Lee cakes
35. A home away from home
36. Sight and touch
38. Expensive fur
39. Polio vaccine developer
40. Samoa's capital
41. New driver, typically
42. Finds a sum
44. Pesticide brand
45. "___ kleine Nachtmusik"
46. Opposite of fem.
48. Cote denizen
49. Howl at the moon

Solution on page 369

Puzzle 298

Across
1. Periodical, for short
4. Detectives, for short
7. Mulberry bark
11. British rocker Brian
12. "Wanna bet ___?"
14. Emulated
15. "It's ___ for Me to Say"
16. Fixes illegally
17. Stitched line
18. However
21. Morse code message
22. Rocky outcropping
23. Desserts with crusts
25. "Spring ahead" letters
26. Advanced degree: Abbr.
29. Highest card
30. "Psycho" motel owner
32. 1973 Supreme Court decision name
33. But: Lat.
34. The "I" of T.G.I.F.
35. Prepare for a photo
36. ___ gratias: Thanks to God
37. "Boston Legal" fig.
38. Salon stylist
43. Small mountain lake
44. Tunisian titles
45. Theology sch.
47. Decrease gradually
48. Old-style dagger
49. How-___ (instructional books)
50. Simple sugars
51. Tooth pro's deg.
52. Concorde: Abbr.

Down
1. Stag party attendees
2. Of unknown authorship: Abbr.
3. Deteriorate
4. Skin features
5. Part of a monogram: Abbr.
6. Express relief
7. Police weapon
8. Chimps and orangutans
9. Green veggies
10. Naval off.
13. Dangerous African fly
19. Calculator figs.
20. A whole bunch
23. Mas' mates
24. Frozen water
25. Drunk's problem
26. Puts up a fuss
27. Santa's laughs
28. Lousy grade
30. Coffin stand
31. Not seeing eye to eye
35. Quart parts: Abbr.
36. Has an elegant supper
37. Long-eared equines
38. Actor Lukas
39. "Rule Britannia" composer Thomas
40. Sunder
41. Got a good look at
42. '20s autos
43. Duo
46. Wyo. clock setting

Solution on page 369

Puzzle 299

Across

1. Cunning trick
5. Use a microwave
8. Bygone carrier
11. Herr's home
12. One named in a will
13. Towel inscription
14. Leave out
15. Prefix with derm
16. Noah's project
17. Soak up
19. Upper crusts
21. Pencil's end
23. Station that uses veejays
26. Nourished
27. D followers
31. "Battle Cry" novelist
33. Married
35. "Dumb" girl of old comics
36. What gingivitis affects
37. High tennis shot
39. Be a Nosy Parker
40. Soprano Tebaldi
43. California peak
46. Defeat thoroughly
51. Flesh and blood
52. Catcher's base
54. "Render ___ Caesar . . ."
55. Tick off
56. Among
57. Gouda cousin
58. Utmost degree
59. Turn down
60. Belafonte refrain

Down

1. Horse-stopping word
2. Two-syllable foot
3. Director Bunuel
4. "___ perpetua" (Idaho's motto)
5. Kind of Buddhist
6. Executive's staff
7. Worker, informally
8. Not this
9. Electricity carrier
10. Entreats
12. Talmud language
18. Gridiron judge
20. Upset
22. Author ___ Rogers St. Johns
23. Make a face
24. Morse role on Broadway
25. Vitality
28. Clotheshorse
29. Watchdog's warning
30. Cow chow
32. Lith. and Ukr., once
34. Like some lines
38. Ebenezer's exclamation
41. Allen or Frome
42. The elder Judd
43. Epidermis
44. "Java" player Al
45. Egyptian cross
47. Regretted
48. Wing ___ prayer
49. "Don't move!"
50. ___ sapiens
53. Be sociable

Solution on page 369

Puzzle 300

Across

1. Kobe cummerbund
4. Lawyer's grp.
7. Part of a tuba's sound
10. Kisser
12. Lots and lots
14. "What a surprise!"
15. Singer ___ James
16. Senator Trent
17. Not cooked
18. Jefferson Davis was its pres.
20. Buenos ___
22. Gets up
25. Jeff Lynne rock band
26. Tried to get elected
27. Notes after dos
29. Turnpike charges
33. '50s car features
35. Make soaking wet
37. Greek letters
38. Malt brew
40. eBay action
42. Larry King's employer
43. New York ballplayer
45. Giggles
47. Diamond bags
49. ___ constrictor
50. Purview
51. Prefix with second
53. Tug tow
57. Wander idly
58. Madrid Mmes.
59. Prefix with graph
60. Public vehicle
61. Method: Abbr.
62. Pug or boxer

Down

1. Reveal, poetically
2. Excuse starter
3. Follower: Suffix
4. Map collections
5. Derisive cry
6. Pilasters
7. Skin opening
8. Shouts of discovery
9. "___ the West Was Won"
11. Potato bag
13. Clown's prop
19. Sunday talk: Abbr.
21. Underground part
22. Comments from Sandy
23. Cool one's heels
24. ___ Domini
28. Weep loudly
30. Shoe tie
31. Debussy's "Clair de ___"
32. Taxpayer IDs
34. Totals
36. Casino supervisor
39. Kids with curfews
41. ___ gratias (thanks to God)
44. Old Russian despots
46. Door attachment
47. Boyfriend
48. "No ifs, ___ . . ."
50. Putin's former org.
52. Opponent's vote
54. No-goodnik
55. Spanish gold
56. Tail motion

Solution on page 370

Puzzle 301

Across

1. Home utility: Abbr.
5. Overseas network
8. Unopened
12. Raisin rum cake
13. High craggy hill
14. One of Jacob's wives
15. Ink smudge
16. Commando's weapon
17. Off-center
18. "___ a gun!"
20. Flow back
22. Expire, as a subscription
25. Peanut butter container
28. Theatrical travelers
31. Fictional bell town
33. Greeting at sea
34. Center X or O
36. Crooner Williams
37. Royal domain
39. ___ & Noble
41. Made a meal for
42. Russell of "Gladiator"
44. River, to Ricardo
45. Goes on a hunger strike
50. Small child
53. Athena's symbol
56. Practice with Rocky
57. Peace signs
58. "Who, me?"
59. Harbor
60. NCO
61. Last word of the golden rule
62. Ancient Greek colonnade

Down

1. Trails off
2. "Le Roi d'Ys" composer
3. Jet-black, in verse
4. Ancient Roman censor
5. AC capacity measure
6. Dickens pen name
7. Has a bawl
8. Bacon portion
9. Cut down
10. Former Mideast alliance
11. Biblical possessive
19. Winter ailment
21. "Luck ___ Lady"
23. Well put
24. Singer Bryson
25. Tarzan's love
26. No ifs, ___, or buts
27. Singer Orbison
28. You, to the Amish
29. Pothole place
30. Olive in the comics
32. Rather of news
33. Canine cry
35. Crow's cry
38. Sprint competitor
40. Hockey official
43. Hardly cramped
44. Sabbath activity
46. Egyptian biters
47. Dick and Jane's pooch
48. Source of poi
49. Span. miss
50. RCA products
51. Agreeable response
52. Fraternity party staple
54. Go a-courting
55. Lucy of "Kill Bill: Vol. 1"

Solution on page 370

Puzzle 302

Across

1. Novelist Bellow
5. Overhead trains
8. Follow directions
12. Anderson of "WKRP in Cincinnati"
13. "Apocalpyse Now" setting, briefly
14. Gesture of greeting
15. Have ___ with: influence
16. Chinese drink
18. Affirmative responses
20. Jewel
21. Be in hock
23. Leaf aperture
28. Quick swim
31. Tobacco-drying oven
33. Sources of silver
34. Adjusts to fit
36. Musical composition
38. Grape holder
39. H.S. junior's exam
41. Nascar unit
42. Rose-colored dye
44. Prefix meaning "three"
45. Neighbor of Syr.
47. Picket line crossers
52. Forceful
57. Yours and mine
58. Baseball great Ruth
59. ET's craft
60. Israel's Golda
61. Bruce Springsteen, with "the"
62. Flower area
63. Stately shade trees

Down

1. Kill, as a dragon
2. Super-duper
3. Les Etats-___
4. Bus route
5. Chang's Siamese twin
6. Some T-shirts
7. Never Never Land dweller
8. Hold title to
9. Belfry resident
10. December 24th, for one
11. Nay canceler
17. Initials on an ambulance
19. Flue dirt
22. Hornet, e.g.
24. Coal unit
25. Said aloud
26. Prefix with morphosis
27. Right away, in a memo
28. Jay's rival
29. Prefix meaning "peculiar"
30. Gives a bad review
32. Pre-Lenin Russian ruler
35. Architect I. M. ___
37. Elevator inventor
40. Discord
43. Entertainer Peeples
46. Checkbook record
48. Show up
49. "Clan of the Cave Bear" author
50. Sombrero feature
51. Belarus and Ukraine, once: Abbr.
52. Recede
53. Former Chinese Chairman
54. "Mystery!" network
55. "For ___ a jolly . . ."
56. Pkg. with money due

Solution on page 370

Puzzle 303

Across

1. Mingo portrayer
5. Hasty escapes
9. Chapeau
12. Customary function
13. Dripping sound
14. Miner's discovery
15. Campus house
16. Ancient Greek portico
17. Boom box button
18. Touch or sight
20. Marshal Dillon's portrayer
22. Most unusual
24. End of an ___
27. "___ the season . . ."
28. Olympian Lipinski
32. Smelt, e.g.
34. Spooked
36. Not very good
37. Coolio's music
38. 180 degrees from WSW
39. Daughter of Zeus
42. Thoroughfare
44. Baseball card data
49. Deli bread
50. Broadway production
52. Gin flavorer
53. Aardvark's tidbit
54. Nobelist Wiesel
55. Pierre's pop
56. Agent's due
57. Long, long time
58. Mail off

Down

1. Comics barks
2. Oliver Twist's request
3. Liveliness
4. Stage constructions
5. CD precursors
6. Communion tables
7. Actress Demi
8. Bridges
9. ___ d'oeuvre
10. God of war
11. P.I.
19. "Harper's Bazaar" illustrator
21. Ms. Kett of the comics
23. Assist
24. Plural ender, usually
25. Early auto
26. Ques. counterpart
29. Have being
30. Stimpy's TV pal
31. Fruit-drink suffix
33. Rise quickly
34. ___ Luis Obispo
35. Tax pros
37. Keep
40. Indian dwelling
41. Welcoming word
42. New Year's word
43. Place for a beret
45. Recipe measures: Abbr.
46. Protected from the wind
47. In tatters
48. Planter's purchase
49. Brit. fliers
51. Thumbs-up vote

Solution on page 370

Puzzle 304

Across

1. Watering holes
5. Timber wolf
9. Painter Steen
12. "Li'l Abner" cartoonist
13. Five Nations tribe
15. Exaggerated publicity
16. Closet spook
17. Bright-eyed and bushy-tailed
19. Actress Winger
20. Fixed looks
22. Roll of bills
23. Playwright Capek
24. Blue bird
25. Litter member
28. Crossed (out)
29. Windy City team
30. Despise
31. Executed
32. Quaker possessive
33. Pose again
34. Small fish
35. Terrapin, e.g.
36. '1950s candidate Stevenson
39. Discourage from acting
40. Mukluk material
42. Rikki-tikki-___ (Kipling mongoose)
45. Capitol Hill gang
46. "___ the Mood for Love"
47. Toll hwy.
48. Saber cousin
49. Five, in France

Down

1. Aoad.
2. Salary
3. Materialized
4. Grabbed with a toothpick
5. Parts of ears
6. ___ close to schedule
7. Morass
8. Twenty-four hours
9. Door frame part
10. Actor John
11. Snatcher of Peter Pan's shadow
14. Changed the color of
18. Type of toothpaste
20. Agenda, for short
21. Metered vehicle
22. Car wash option
24. Pride partner
25. Deli meat
26. Gas or elec., e.g.
27. Tennis great Sampras
29. Introverted
30. Religious dissenter
32. Sibelius' "Valse ___"
33. Same old grind
34. Presidential pooch
35. Form of a verb
36. Aide: Abbr.
37. Not shallow
38. Long and lean
39. Serious
41. Keystone character
43. Paris potable
44. Govt. investigation

Solution on page 370

Puzzle 305

Across

1. Swiss peaks
5. ___ Jose, CA
8. Bridge declaration
12. Gaucho's gear
13. "Roses ___ red . . ."
14. China: Prefix
15. Paperback, e.g.
16. Gun owners' grp.
17. Glacial
18. Certify
20. Work on a doily
22. Many a John Wayne film
24. Parakeet or poodle
27. Arcade attractions
31. Canada's most populous province
33. Winter Olympics sport
34. Small batteries
35. Theda of 1917's "Cleopatra"
36. Debts
38. Like daisies
39. Courtroom VIPs
40. Type of coffee
42. "Casablanca" pianist
43. Li'l Abner's creator
48. Helper: Abbr.
51. SHO alternative
53. Sheltered from the wind
54. Tribal tales
55. Bic filler
56. British machine gun
57. Head-and-shoulders sculpture
58. Lettuce type
59. Auctioneer's call

Down

1. "Mamma Mia" pop group
2. Burglar's booty
3. Whodunit's essence
4. Drink with sushi
5. Mr. Claus
6. Incoming plane: Abbr.
7. Tidies
8. "Check this out!"
9. Feel badly
10. ___-Cat: winter vehicle
11. Female pig
19. Sinking ship's signal
21. Museum contents
23. Best man's offering
24. Ask for divine guidance
25. Republic of Ireland
26. Frog kin
27. Delighted
28. Mystical quality
29. Dept. heads
30. Unusual shoe width
32. Attorneys' org.
34. Language spoken by Jesus
37. Chicken ___ king
38. Member of the fam.
41. Carpet fasteners
42. Proofer's word
44. Mama of the Mamas and the Papas
45. Voice above a tenor
46. Fruit covering
47. Await judgment
48. Priestly vestment
49. Insignificant amount
50. Grads-to-be: Abbr.
52. 6, on a telephone

Solution on page 370

Puzzle 306

Across

1. City in Mo.
4. Great success
7. ___-CIO
10. Campground letters
11. Newsman Morley
13. AFL affiliate
14. Savings acct. addition
15. First course of action
16. Swiss mountain
17. Believe appropriate
19. Boulders
21. Butter servings
22. Vitality
23. A whole slew
25. ___ stone (hieroglyphics key)
29. Letters before John F. Kennedy
30. Center of a peach
31. Karel Capek drama
32. In the wrong role
35. Punish, perhaps
37. ___ Marie Saint
38. ". . . hear ___ drop"
39. Masseur's application
42. Rental contracts
45. "Gimme ___!" (start of a Rutgers cheer)
46. For any reason
48. 1051, to Caesar
49. R followers
50. Unfamiliar with
51. "This ___ fine how-do-you-do!"
52. "The Murders in the Rue Morgue" writer
53. Spanish king
54. Tartan cap

Down

1. Enjoys Aspen
2. Sound of music
3. Note excusing tardiness
4. Puts a stop to
5. "___ Man Answers" (Sandra Dee film)
6. Sawbuck
7. Open ___ of worms
8. Manicurist's tool
9. Cuts, as branches
11. Barbecue rods
12. Prices
18. Current rage
20. Unclose, poetically
23. Addition result
24. CBS forensic drama
25. Slower, in mus.
26. Broadcast
27. Winery cask
28. Noah creation
30. Prayer book
33. Corporate V.I.P.
34. Bird-related
35. European wheat
36. Actress Zadora
38. Assuage
39. Trunk fastener
40. Well aware of
41. Not false
43. "Born Free" roarer
44. Thailand once
47. Knock the socks off of

Solution on page 371

Puzzle 307

Across

1. "___ you there?"
4. Fancy dance
8. Gore and Sharpton
11. Mrs. Dithers, in "Blondie"
13. Margarine
14. Aegean or Bering
15. Duck in a pond
16. Fido's reward
17. DC figure
18. Latin being
20. Touch or taste
22. Pack animals
25. NNW's opposite
26. Was inactive
27. Siamese
30. Laddie's love
34. Words before carte or mode
35. Circus performers
37. Undercover agent
38. Tennis ace Sampras
40. Guy
41. Geological span
42. Foolish sort
44. Die down
46. Beginning
49. "Nobody doesn't like ___ Lee"
51. Excessively glib
52. Allotment words
54. Alluring skirt feature
58. Shapiro of NPR
59. Lecher
60. Inoculation fluids
61. Turner or Cole
62. Knights' titles
63. Dapper fellow

Down

1. Play a role
2. Anonymous Richard
3. Historical time
4. Short haircuts
5. Burn-soothing plant
6. Grid great Dawson
7. Loamy soil
8. Part of AAA: Abbr.
9. Majors and Grant
10. Rational
12. Toward the sheltered side
19. Grounded fliers, for short
21. Wriggler
22. Without delay: Abbr.
23. Store event
24. Sports fig.
25. Window ledge
28. Skirt lines
29. Small battery size
31. On a cruise
32. Dalmatian mark
33. Seasonal song word
36. Burn quickly
39. Q-Tip target
43. Sky lights
45. Paul McCartney's instrument
46. Stretch of time
47. Scarlett's home
48. Busy, busy, busy
49. Pucker-inducing
50. Earth rulers in a 1968 film
53. Baked Hawaiian dish
55. Was in front
56. Nest-egg letters
57. Leather color

Solution on page 371

Puzzle 308

Across

1. Ambulance grp.
5. Tea times: Abbr.
9. Pickle container
12. Bird's bill
13. "And ___ goes"
14. Have a payment due
15. Penny-___ poker
16. Long sandwich
17. Magazine magnate, familiarly
18. Is unobliged to
20. Twisty-horned antelopes
22. Cleared the boards
24. Intl. clock standard
27. Sal of song, e.g.
28. "Snug as ___ . . ."
32. Oohs' companions
34. Informal affirmative
36. Gooey ground
37. Mangle
38. Sagebrush ST.
40. OPEC measure
41. Sandinista leader Daniel
44. Words to a black sheep
47. Cochise portrayer Michael
52. Breakfast quaffs, for short
53. Varieties
55. Change for $5
56. "___-di-dah!"
57. God, to Gaston
58. Cold and clammy
59. Prefix with acetylene
60. Pronounces
61. Rental units: Abbr.

Down

1. Diplomat Abba
2. Word on a Biblical wall
3. London art gallery
4. Calendar a la "Variety"
5. Site of many flicks
6. Friend's opposite
7. Akron products
8. Took illegally
9. Gospel writer
10. Very impressed
11. Boxing officials
19. Opposite of pos.
21. ___ Clayton Powell
23. Coeur d'___, Idaho
24. Pinup's leg
25. Barnyard sound
26. Wed. follower
29. Baby's neckwear
30. Metropolitan area, briefly
31. Hair application
33. Messy dresser
35. Winged horse of myth
39. Delivery truck
42. Incursions
43. Shire of "Rocky"
44. Machete's cousin
45. "Stronger than dirt" sloganeer
46. Like a fireplace floor
48. Ice cream drink
49. Take ___ (snooze)
50. Apartment fee
51. Proposes
54. Lock opener

Solution on page 371

Puzzle 309

Across

1. It may scare you
4. Catch some z's
7. Unload, as stock
11. Pervasive emanation
13. Geologic time period
14. Healing plant
15. Awful
16. Lacking color
17. New Mexico county
18. ___Sweet: aspartame
20. Hannibal's challenge
21. Arouse
24. Obote's successor
26. Greek nymph
27. Malibu hue
28. Flavor enhancer, briefly
31. Classic laundry detergent
32. See-through
34. Welcome ___
35. Pro-Second Amendment grp.
38. Region of Asia Minor
39. Afternoon parties
40. With regrets
41. Caen cleric
44. Tear in little pieces
46. "Tomb raider" Croft
47. ___ man (unanimously)
48. Distinctive times
52. Bullring cheers
53. Barking sound
54. Reject as false
55. Prefix with conference
56. Collection
57. Coal container

Down

1. Good, in the 'hood
2. Arles affirmative
3. Bobby of the Bruins
4. Congressman Gingrich
5. Ark landfall
6. Kind of hat
7. Devil
8. Airline to Haifa
9. Cloverleaf feature
10. Not as many
12. Trojan War hero
19. Brought to ruin
21. Fish bait
22. Opera solo
23. Superman alias
25. Cut into
28. Heal
29. Leave port
30. Overcast
33. Really rich
36. Haile Selassie followers
37. No longer sailing along
39. Play the coquette
41. "Thanks ___!"
42. Large bundle
43. Belgian composer Jacques
45. Huck Finn's conveyance
49. Fighter in gray
50. "Wheel of Fortune" request
51. Wd. in Roget's

Solution on page 371

Puzzle 310

Across

1. Dickens' pen name
4. Pool tool
7. Osaka sash
10. Bedazzles
12. Tiny crawler
13. Belgrade native
14. Fender mishap
15. [Not my error]
16. Roll-call reply
17. Bartender's "rocks"
19. Catches one's breath
20. Some door locks
23. Chicago daily, familiarly
25. Word form for "twenty"
26. Outback maker
29. Hippie's digs
30. "Oh, brother!"
31. Car loan fig.
33. Expel from the legal profession
36. World Wildlife Fund's symbol
38. Humble homes
39. Par ___ (airmail label)
40. Neap and ebb
43. Swear ___ stack of Bibles
44. Eastern Indian
45. Bare peak
47. Fat-free milk
51. Lease subject
52. Eyeball
53. Rocker Turner
54. Flavor enhancer, for short
55. "___ Doubtfire"
56. Pub fixture

Down

1. Misbehaving
2. "I ___ you one"
3. Buddhist sect
4. Task for Holmes
5. Verse opening?
6. And so on, for short
7. Cheers for a matador
8. Football great Starr
9. "As I was going to St. ___ . . ."
11. Hogs' homes
13. Queen of ___
18. Civil War initials
19. Beef cut
20. Puppy sound
21. Nav. school
22. City near Sacramento
23. Bygone dictators
24. Hose problem
27. Hindu princess
28. High hairstyle
30. Shoe-wiping place
32. Was in charge of
34. Linen sale purchase
35. Greyhound, e.g.
36. Criticize harshly
37. Sailor's "Stop!"
40. Life is a long one
41. More than annoys
42. Small dent
43. Eyeballs
45. He's a turkey
46. Bobby of hockey
48. Do-it-yourselfer's purchase
49. Once ___ lifetime
50. Cartographer's creation

Solution on page 372

Puzzle 311

Across

1. Diarist Anais
4. Hole punching tool
7. Letters on a radio switch
11. Son-gun filler
12. Corp. takeover
13. Queen of Carthage, in myth
14. Prefix with shipman
15. Alan of "Shane"
17. Jeanne ___ (French saint)
18. "Die Fledermaus" role
20. Eliel Saarinen's son
22. Hair-protecting kerchief
23. Open-toed shoe
27. Send again
30. Cabinet dept. since 1965
31. Andean tubers
34. Certain test results
35. Sounds of reproach
36. Fort Worth sch.
37. Long overcoat
39. Galoot
41. Network, e.g.
45. ___ and rave
47. Backbone
48. Proof of pmt.
51. "Newsweek" competitor
53. LI doubled
54. Short-tailed rodent
55. One-fifth of MMMV
56. Atlanta-based public health agcy.
57. 1974 Sutherland/Gould film
58. Yang partner
59. Approximation suffix

Down

1. Wanderer
2. "Don't mind ___!"
3. 2000 candidate Ralph
4. Declare in court
5. Pugilists' org.
6. Gold deposit
7. Computer accessory
8. Actress Sara
9. '40s presidential monogram
10. Soft shoe, for short
16. Cease
19. Unseen "Mary Tyler Moore Show" character
21. Eminem's music
24. Some ALers
25. Northern diving bird
26. Mormon gp.
28. Noiseless
29. Command ctrs.
31. Wagering place: Abbr.
32. 201, in old Rome
33. Sept. preceder
35. Outing
37. ___ tree (trapped)
38. Enter cautiously
40. Comic Johnson and others
42. Designer Nina
43. Bagnold and Blyton
44. Clinton's first Secretary of Labor
46. In order
48. Campers, for short
49. CBer's "bear"
50. Perform diligently, as a trade
52. ___ WorldCom

Solution on page 372

Puzzle 312

Across

1. CIO's partner
4. Smoke, for short
7. Actress Streep
12. Gamble
13. Half of dos
14. "You're in ___ of trouble!"
15. Ltd. cousin
16. P, in the Greek alphabet
17. Replies to an invitation, briefly
18. Cpl., for one
19. Brain tests: Abbr.
21. Shoulder muscle, informally
23. Seedy loaf
24. Not him
27. Tiny Tim strummed one
29. Shinbones
32. Backbreaking dance
35. Showed interest
36. Most unfriendly
38. When repeated, a ballroom dance
39. Deposit
40. Civil ___
42. Large amount
46. Reduce, as expenses
47. TV movie channel
48. Sensational
52. Pigeon patter
54. &
55. Talia of "Rocky"
56. North Pole toymaker
57. Actress Ryan
58. Often ___
59. Rock's ___ Leppard
60. Bo nooy

Down

1. In ___; in trouble
2. Backyard border
3. Maj.'s superior
4. Mongrel
5. Response to "Where are you?," maybe
6. Sticky
7. Planet beyond Earth
8. Questioning interjections
9. Part of IRS: Abbr.
10. Jabber
11. Vinyl records
20. Receive
22. Toothpaste holder
24. Big success
25. ___ de Cologne
26. Workout unit, for short
28. Boxing stats
30. "Sorta" suffix
31. Sounds from the meadow
32. Place to apply gloss
33. Post-op locale
34. Cal Tech rival
37. Howard Hughes's airline
38. New Orleans cuisine
41. Took a circuitous path
43. Titleholder
44. Capp character
45. Evasive
46. Writer of rhymes
48. "Be prepared" grp.
49. Cries of surprise
50. Snorkeling accessory
51. To and ___
53. Not working today

Solution on page 372

Puzzle 313

Across

1. Coastal diving birds
5. Sturdy tree
8. 450, in old Rome
11. Burglar's take
12. Floral welcome
13. "That's ___!" ("Not true!")
14. George W. Bush's alma mater
15. Late columnist Landers
16. St. Paul's state
17. Not much
20. Lille lily
21. Bay area airport letters
22. Biked
26. Debate subject
30. Dermal lead-in
31. Narcs' agcy.
33. St. Louis clock setting
34. Diamond weight unit
37. Cowboy hat
40. ___-Man (arcade game)
42. Medical care grp.
43. Elite clientele
50. Cousin of the bassoon
51. "Vive le ___ !"
52. Blend together
53. Tosses
54. Exxon product
55. 10 C-notes
56. Kiddie
57. Polo Grounds legend Mel
58. Hernando De ___

Down

1. Actor Ron et al.
2. Travel aimlessly
3. Song popularized by Vincent Lopez
4. "A Streetcar Named Desire" woman
5. Went by, as time
6. "Tonight Show" host
7. After-dinner candies
8. Advertising award
9. Eat fancily
10. Part of the eye
13. Response to "Are not!"
18. "___ Abner"
19. Back, at sea
22. Upper-bod muscle
23. MPG raters
24. N, E, W, or S
25. TV host O'Connor
27. Workstation machines, for short
28. "Equal" word form
29. Shipping unit: Abbr.
32. Nonbeliever
35. After, to Antoine
36. Mai ___ (drink)
38. Ambulance driver, for short
39. Bodies
41. Freight
43. Young stallion
44. Peek add-on
45. Gen. ___ E. Lee
46. Barnyard beast
47. "___ added expense"
48. Cut calories
49. Logician's "therefore"

Solution on page 372

Puzzle 314

Across

1. Windows boxes?
4. . . . ___ ___ ___ . . .
7. Bio. or chem.
10. ___-de-France
11. Stitched lines
13. Gas station freebie
14. Soda
15. Bother incessantly
16. Way to get there: Abbr.
17. Typewriter bar
19. Knots again
21. Performs like Ice-T
22. Spot for a first shot
23. Rating units
25. Backslide, medically
29. Hamelin evictee
30. ___ Antonio
31. TV chihuahua
32. Run, as a machine
35. "Fargo" creators Ethan and Joel
37. Dec. 31, e.g.
38. Bathroom rugs
39. Roofer's need
42. Most appropriate
45. Ill temper
46. Back in vogue
48. Virgo preceder
49. Alphabet ender
50. Tarnishes
51. Southeast Asian language
52. Silly one
53. ___-cone (summer treat)
54. Retired airplane

Down

1. Domino spots
2. Hoofbeat sound
3. Split up
4. Scorches
5. Dobbin's nibble
6. Wise (up)
7. Calcutta cover-up
8. Quote with authority
9. Incenses
11. Slips through the cracks?
12. Sword metal
18. Indy 500 entrant
20. Tetley product
23. "Sold out" letters
24. Keg attachment
25. Actress ___ Dawn Chong
26. Takes advance orders for
27. D.C. legislator
28. Naval rank: Abbr.
30. Sound systems
33. Word preceding dog and rover
34. States firmly
35. Mob bosses
36. Mel of the Giants
38. Mrs. Donahue
39. Singer Minnelli
40. Trojan War god
41. Rick who sang "Disco Duck"
43. Huge expanses
44. Tugboat sound
47. Baking container

Solution on page 373

Puzzle 315

Across

1. Decide
4. Deadly poison
8. Calif. neighbor
12. Celeb's life story
13. Brother of Cain
14. Learning system
15. Bank acct. addition
16. Skinny
17. Hokey humor
18. Horse color
20. Lauder of lipstick
21. Sci-fi writer Ellison
23. Meerschaum, e.g.
26. Pilgrim to Mecca
31. Apply balm to
34. False start?
35. Ottoman ruler
36. Chills and fever
37. Went ape
41. Blue Ribbon maker
45. Governor Schwarzenegger
48. "And pretty maids all in ___"
49. Parisians' seasons
50. Province east of N.B.
52. Poker pot primer
53. Similar
54. EU member
55. Architect Ludwig Mies van der ___
56. Suffix with gab or slug
57. Demand, as a price

Down

1. Japanese waistband
2. Bowler's targets
3. In ___ (entirely)
4. Iraq's second-largest city
5. More competent
6. Sam of "The Piano"
7. "A Nightmare on ___ Street"
8. Tolkien beasts
9. Underground plant part
10. To be, in Toulon
11. Hackman of Hollywood
19. Scarlett's spouse
20. Cardinal Slaughter
22. Elec. unit
23. Ltr. additions
24. Letters of debt
25. Party rep
27. Bygone defense grp.
28. Pull with effort
29. University web address suffix
30. Broadway's "Five Guys Named ___"
32. Sentry's "Stop!"
33. Rocker Brian
38. French composer Erik
39. Difficult journeys
40. Map section
41. Carson's TV predecessor
42. Florence's river
43. The two of them
44. ___'pea ("Popeye" kid)
46. Women's links org.
47. Ruby and Sandra
49. North Pole helper
51. Annoy

Solution on page 373

Puzzle 316

Across

1. Owl's question?
4. ___ Lilly and Company
7. Article
10. Female relative
12. Lab-maze runner
13. Bering and Caribbean
14. Poll or trick follower
15. Like Perot's party: Abbr.
16. Atlantic Coast states, with "the"
17. Oscar winner Guinness
19. Lusterless finish
20. Swiftly, to Shakespeare
23. Airline that serves only kosher food
25. Selects
26. OPEC is one
29. NEA member
30. Be greedy
31. Beer topper
33. Farm machine
35. Is overrun
36. Business abbr.
37. Just perfect
38. Kept under one's hat
41. River to the English Channel
43. ___ about: approximately
44. Tijuana gold
45. Curved sections
49. Affectionate
50. Mary ___ cosmetics
51. Fifth-century pope who was sainted
52. Sure-footed work animal
53. Capone and Pacino
54. Cookbook abbreviation

Down

1. "___ it something I said?"
2. "Survivor" shelter
3. Early afternoon hour
4. Cleveland's water
5. Marine rank
6. "___ be my pleasure!"
7. Suckling spot
8. Verb with "thou"
9. From Santiago to Buenos Aires
11. Performance history
13. Shake on it
18. Brown with a Band of Renown
19. Cause damage to
20. Prone (to)
21. Photos, briefly
22. Muscle soreness
24. Word after jet or time
27. Extreme shoe width
28. The Dalai ___
30. Billy Joel's "Tell ___ About It"
32. Hi-speed connection
34. Comic Rickles
35. Metal in pewter
38. Living room seat
39. Years in Spain
40. Cargo weights
42. Rogers and Orbison
44. Volga tributary
46. Not active: Abbr.
47. Corn on the ___
48. ___ boom bah

Solution on page 373

ANSWERS

319

Puzzle 1

Puzzle 2

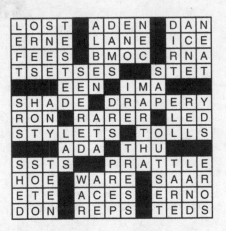

Puzzle 3

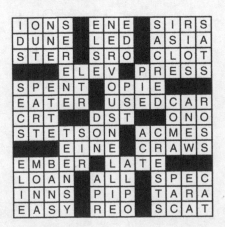

Puzzle 4

Puzzle 5

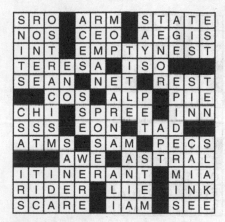

Puzzle 6

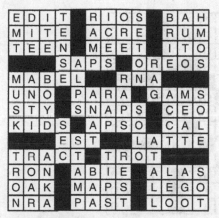

Puzzle 7

Puzzle 8

Puzzle 9

Puzzle 10

Puzzle 11

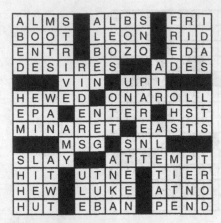

Puzzle 12

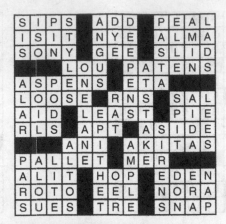

Puzzle 13

Puzzle 14

Puzzle 15

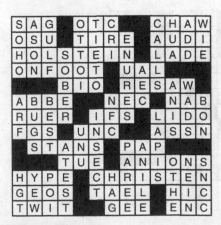

Puzzle 16

Puzzle 17

Puzzle 18

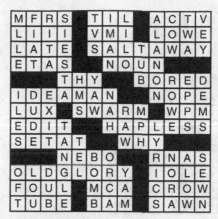

Puzzle 19

Puzzle 20

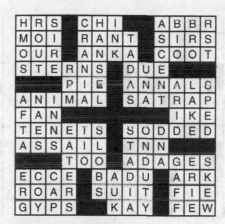

Puzzle 21

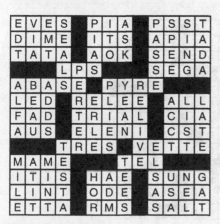

Puzzle 22

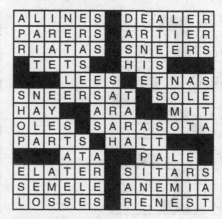

Puzzle 23

Puzzle 24

Puzzle 25

Puzzle 26

Puzzle 27

Puzzle 28

Puzzle 29

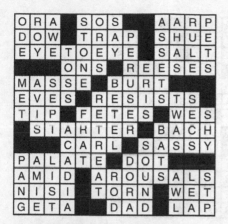

Puzzle 30

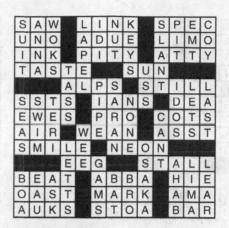

Puzzle 31

Puzzle 32

Puzzle 33

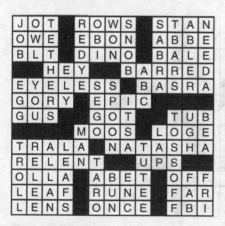

Puzzle 34

Puzzle 35

Puzzle 36

Puzzle 37

Puzzle 38

Puzzle 39

Puzzle 40

Puzzle 41

Puzzle 42

Puzzle 43

Puzzle 44

Puzzle 45

Puzzle 46

Puzzle 47

Puzzle 48

Puzzle 49

Puzzle 50

Puzzle 51

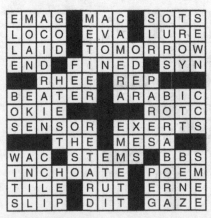

Puzzle 52

Puzzle 53

Puzzle 54

Puzzle 55

Puzzle 56

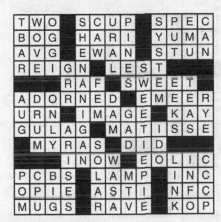

Puzzle 57

Puzzle 58

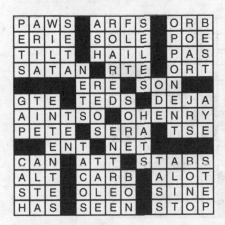

Puzzle 59

Puzzle 60

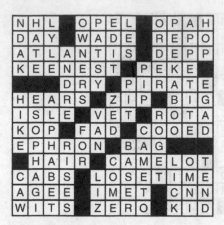

Puzzle 61

Puzzle 62

Puzzle 63

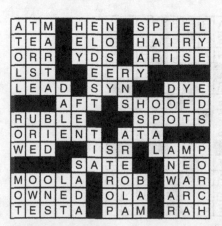

Puzzle 64

Puzzle 65

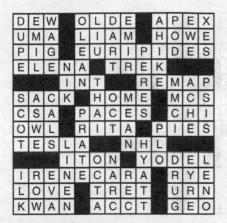

Puzzle 66

Puzzle 67

Puzzle 68

Puzzle 69

Puzzle 70

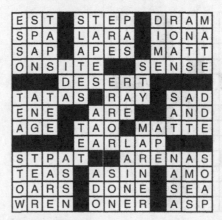

Puzzle 71

Puzzle 72

Puzzle 73

Puzzle 74

Puzzle 75

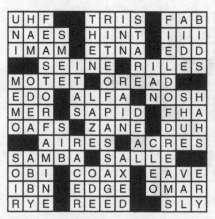

Puzzle 76

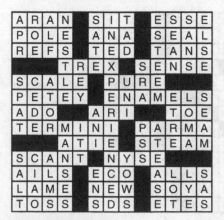

Puzzle 77

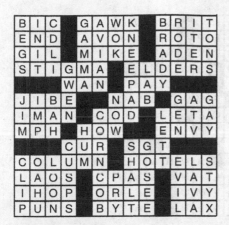

Puzzle 78

```
BIC GAWK  BRIT
END AVON  ROTO
GIL MIKE  ADEN
STIGMA  ELDERS
    WAN PAY
JIBE  NAB  GAG
IMAN COD  LETA
MPH HOW  ENVY
    CUR SGT
COLUMN  HOTELS
LAOS CPAS  VAT
IHOP ORLE  IVY
PUNS BYTE  LAX
```

Puzzle 79

```
ENVS BEBE  TBA
MOIL RIOS  HUP
INSOFARAS  RRR
   PONE  APERS
ASSERT  LYRE
BAT  WISEST
OPES BED  COOK
  SALSAS  MEA
  LAPS ABLEST
ABATE  LIRE
NAW AVALANCHE
DNA KANE  THUD
ICY SCAD  SABU
```

Puzzle 80

```
DEE SPA  ATT
ODES TUT  SLOE
ESEL ASA  HARE
  OATH  TONES
ABLER  ULEE
ROOST  PANDAS
RDS EDT  MOD
 STELLA  START
  MALI  RESTS
APRES  SOSA
AEON TIA  LASS
READ RET  SNEE
ERN  ESS  SAC
```

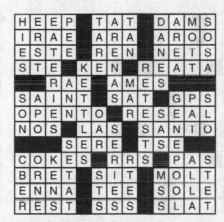

Puzzle 81

```
HEEP TAT  DAMS
IRAE ARA  AROO
ESTE REN  NETS
STE KEN  REATA
  RAE  AMES
SAINT SAT  GPS
OPENTO  RESEAL
NOS LAS  SANTO
  SERE  TSE
COKES RRS  PAS
BRET SIT  MOLT
ENNA TEE  SOLE
REST SSS  SLAT
```

Puzzle 82

```
SLID GLEE  UPS
PARA OONA  MAP
CYAN TUGS  PTA
ASSET  EASED
  ARTIST
HID BORN  MDSE
ELIS WIN  SEAM
SEEK ACID  MCS
  YANKEE
APSES  CLASS
PAT SHAM  ORAL
EVE AUTO  OLIO
DEW MELS  MODE
```

Puzzle 83

```
GRES ZEE  LABS
LIRA IVS  OFME
AVIS GEM  ARIZ
DEKE  NEET
  SAWS  SHIRT
HAW FAO  CEDAR
ONHOLD  CASINO
ONENO PUP  GIT
PINTA  OREM
  OTIC  APBS
OKLA GOB  TOOK
FIGS GNU  CLOY
FRET YOM  HOPE
```

Puzzle 84

Puzzle 85

Puzzle 86

Puzzle 87

Puzzle 88

Puzzle 89

Puzzle 90

```
P E N S   C A R L   E L S
E L E A   I D E O   L A O
L E A N   G O N G   E S O
T E T E   B E A   A T T
      R A R E   N A N
M A T   D E S I   C O R D
A G E N D A   S T E R E O
S O N E   L A N E   A Y E
    A D A   R O N S
P A N   L E E   L U S T
A N T   A T O R   A L T O
N N E   M A L E   P E E R
T E D   O L E O   S E R A
```

Puzzle 91

```
U K E   I B O   R I B
M E R C   R O D   C O R A
A L S O R A N S   H A I R
    M E N D   D E N S E
P A T E N   J O V E
S T A T   A N D R E W S
A L S O   E M S   L A I C
T E S T A T E   E R N O
    E R E S   M A N E T
S A B R E   B R A D
A R A M   L O O S E E N D
T O R S   A N T   R O O S
S O I   C D S   S R O
```

Puzzle 92

```
A G R A   P O D   S A P S
P L A T   E W E   A L O U
B E N T   T L C   D U M P
  E D I C T S   A M P S
    R O Y   P S T
P I L E D   R O T   H O W
T K O   D R A P E   U F O
S E W   L E G   P E E T E
    D E B   C O N
D I V E   C O N T R A
R A I N   T O N   H O S H
A G E S   O T T   A M I E
M O D E   W E E   P A N S
```

Puzzle 93

```
M S S   P E P E   B R A T
T A L   A R A N   A I R E
G R E   G A R S   A T K A
  I D E A T E   B L E S S
      S N O R E R
C H A T   L A S E R S
D E M E A N   L E T S O N
E N I S L E   R O T O
      E L A N C E
C A S A S   T A R P I T
A R A B   D A T A   D O S
S A G E   E L A M   A M C
S L O E   C E L S   S A I
```

Puzzle 94

```
M S G   E L F   D E C I
O A R   N E E R   E L I S
N N E   D R E A M B O A T
K E A T O N   F A R
  T I R E   T R I T E R
T O B E A R   S E S A M E
O P E         K E G
R E A M E R   I D L E R S
E N R A G E   N E S T
    T O N   S A T U R N
F O O T S T O O L   R E O
A O N E   S O L E   N A M
B O O R   P E R   S L O
```

Puzzle 95

```
C B S   G A Y   O F F S
L O G   A D I T   P O L Y
A C T A L O N E   A X O N
P A S T O R   N H L
  W O N   D E S I R E
D O N A T   B O X   R A P
O M E R   N U N   M A N O
N A H   Z E N   R A N D S
T R I B E S   T A J
  J E T   R I A L T O
P U Z O   E M I S S I O N
I G O R   D O N E   F L Y
T H E N   M I D   T U X
```

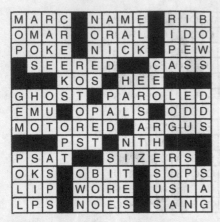

Puzzle 96

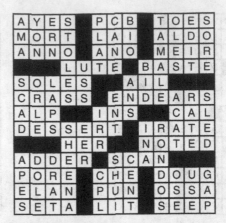

Puzzle 97

Puzzle 98

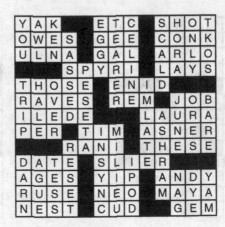

Puzzle 99

Puzzle 100

Puzzle 101

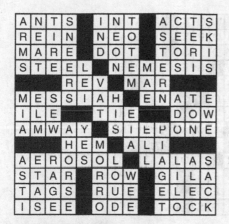

Puzzle 102

Puzzle 103

Puzzle 104

Puzzle 105

Puzzle 106

Puzzle 107

Puzzle 108

Puzzle 109

Puzzle 110

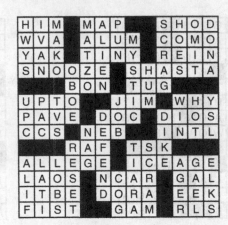

Puzzle 111

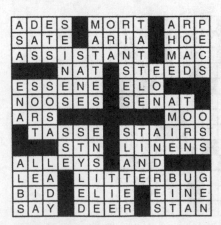

Puzzle 112

Puzzle 113

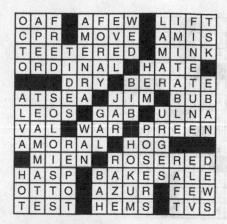

Puzzle 114

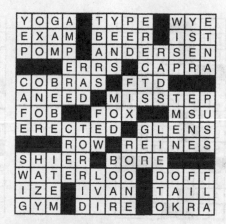

Puzzle 115

Puzzle 116

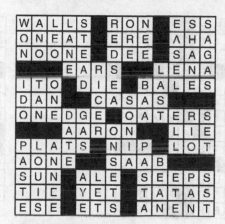

Puzzle 117

Puzzle 118

Puzzle 119

Puzzle 120

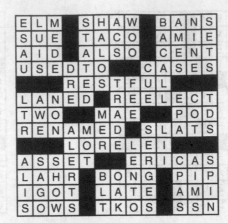

Puzzle 121

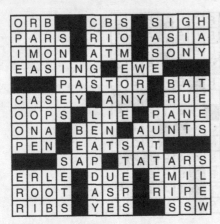

Puzzle 122

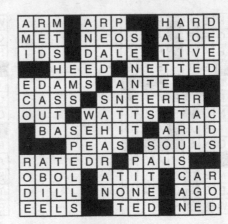

Puzzle 123

Puzzle 124

Puzzle 125

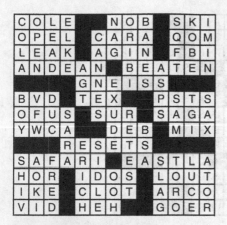

Puzzle 126

```
COLE    NOB   SKI
OPEL  CARA    QOM
LEAK  AGIN    FBI
ANDEAN   BEATEN
     GNEISS
BVD  TEX    PSTS
OFUS  SUR   SAGA
YWCA    DEB  MIX
     RESETS
SAFARI    EASTLA
HOR  IDOS   LOUT
IKE  CLOT   ARCO
VID  HEH    GOER
```

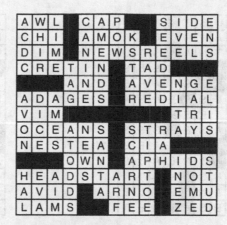

Puzzle 127

```
AWL   CAP    SIDE
CHI  AMOK    EVEN
DIM  NEWSREELS
CRETIN   TAD
    AND   AVENGE
ADAGES    REDIAL
VIM         TRI
OCEANS   STRAYS
NESTEA    CIA
    OWN   APHIDS
HEADSTART    NOT
AVID   ARNO   EMU
LAMS    FEE   ZED
```

Puzzle 128

```
ORCS   OARS   DAB
LILI   FLAW   EGO
DOUR   TADA   LEA
STEER  MAPLES
     AHORSE
CAP  TIS    SHUN
PLEASE   OBTUSE
RBIS   FAR    TOW
     STROKE
 SENIOR   RASPS
LAY  EBAN   BARA
EKE  GOGO   CLOG
DIS  STEW   SEWS
```

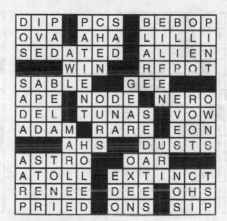

Puzzle 129

```
DIP   PCS   BEBOP
OVA   AHA   LILLI
SEDATED    ALIEN
     WIN   RFPOT
SABLE    GEE
APE  NODE   NERO
DEL  TUNAS  VOW
ADAM  RARE  EON
    AHS   DUSTS
ASTRO     OAR
ATOLL   EXTINCT
RENEE  DEE   OHS
PRIED  ONS   SIP
```

Puzzle 130

```
BARS   BUFF   DAD
AGUA   ARLO   RCA
NOEL   SLAG   NTH
ENSILES     DOES
     NED  PSI
VOTES   THERAPY
EVA  STAIR   LTD
TABLEAU    AMISS
     SEX  CPA
CLAD    GOESAPE
REB  OPED   AGAL
TEL  ROLE   DOTS
SKY  GETS   AGHA
```

Puzzle 131

```
KING   PBS   SKIN
ADAY   YIP   TENO
NORMALLY    OGLE
    REL   ELSAS
ADMIT    YULE
POESY   REDACT
BRER   FAY   WOOF
 STARRY   PANDA
   EEOC   TYSON
SCALP    YMA
LORI  BRASSHAT
IMIT   BUC   CONN
MALE   SSH   HOYT
```

Puzzle 132

Puzzle 133

Puzzle 134

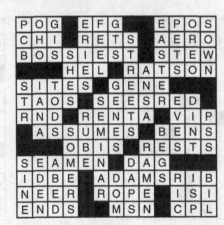

Puzzle 135

Puzzle 136

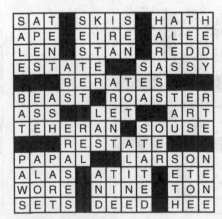

Puzzle 137

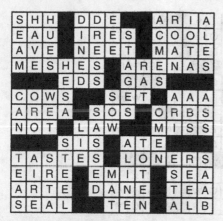

Puzzle 138

```
SHH _ DDE _ ARIA
EAU IRES COOL
AVE NEET MATE
MESHES ARENAS
EDS GAS
COWS SET AAA
AREA SOS ORBS
NOT LAW MISS
SIS ATE
TASTES LONERS
EIRE EMIT SEA
ARTE DANE TEA
SEAL TEN ALB
```

Puzzle 139

```
LPGA LTD STOP
OARS YEA TOUT
ASIS ELM ROSA
DOTER LOCATES
NEW NUT
EASTMAN RANDI
DUO DAM YEN
UGLIS MITTENS
DOW RAW
RESCUED PEPSI
ORCA EEK REOS
TSAR PSI PERU
HERD SIX STEP
```

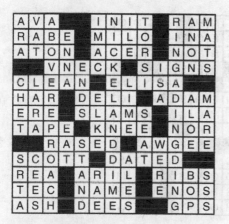

Puzzle 140

```
AVA INIT RAM
RABE MILO INA
ATON ACER NOT
VNECK SIGNS
CLEAN ELISA
HAR DELI ADAM
ERE SLAMS ILA
TAPE KNEE NOR
RASED AWGEE
SCOTT DATED
REA ARIL RIBS
TEC NAME ENOS
ASH DEES GPS
```

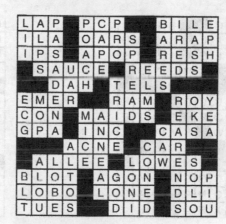

Puzzle 141

```
LAP PCP BILE
ILA OARS ARAP
IPS APOP RESH
SAUCE REEDS
DAH TELS
EMER RAM ROY
CON MAIDS EKE
GPA INC CASA
ACNE CAR
ALLEE LOWES
BLOT AGON NOP
LOBO LONE DLI
TUES DID SOU
```

Puzzle 142

```
FIT TURF BUYS
LAW RHEA RAUL
UMA USED OWLY
EAST KEAN
USC EXULT
GUINEAPIG ZOO
UPN RHINE ICU
TSK INTRANSIT
SASHA INB
ALAS CADS
DVDS BODE GUT
COAT CHIT TRY
INGE SOPH SAX
```

Puzzle 143

```
IGET POL CAST
RATE UNI ARNO
ATTN RHO STAN
NEED GOT TYPE
SHELTIE
GOTTA DAN CRY
ACOOL APACE
STY VCR NOLAN
SERENER
MOPE UTE THUS
ULEE SAX EARL
LEAD TRU RUDI
LOSS YDS SLUM
```

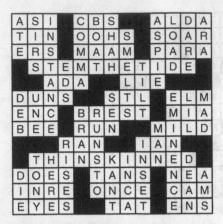

Puzzle 144

Puzzle 145

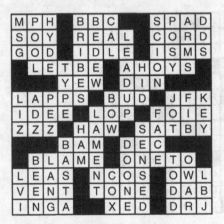

Puzzle 146

Puzzle 147

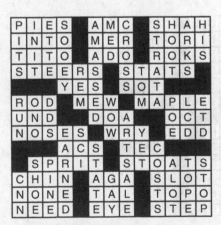

Puzzle 148

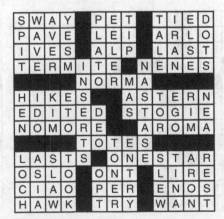

Puzzle 149

Puzzle 150

Puzzle 151

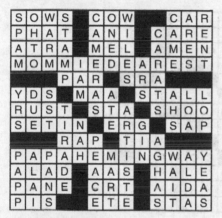

Puzzle 152

Puzzle 153

Puzzle 154

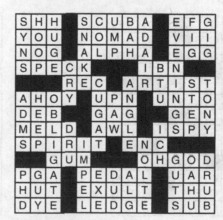

Puzzle 155

Puzzle 156

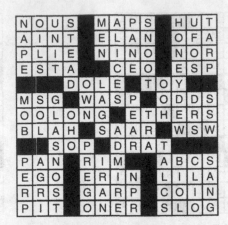

Puzzle 157

Puzzle 158

Puzzle 159

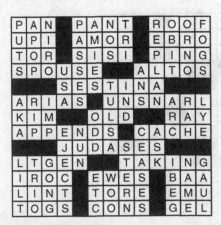

Puzzle 160

Puzzle 161

Puzzle 162

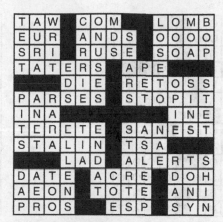

Puzzle 163

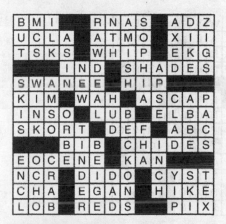

Puzzle 164

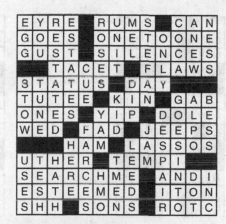

Puzzle 165

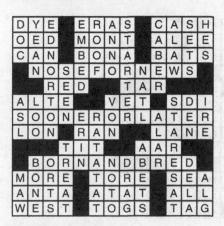

Puzzle 166

Puzzle 167

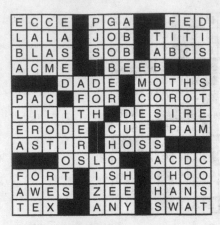

Puzzle 168

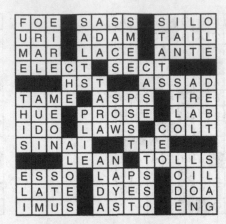

Puzzle 169

Puzzle 170

Puzzle 171

Puzzle 172

Puzzle 173

Puzzle 174

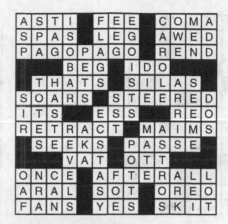

Puzzle 175

Puzzle 176

Puzzle 177

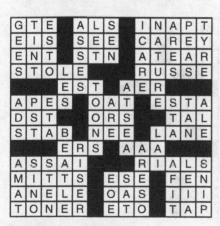

Puzzle 178

Puzzle 179

Puzzle 180

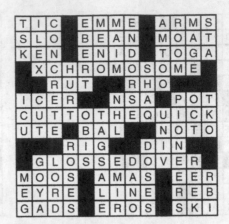

Puzzle 181

Puzzle 182

Puzzle 183

Puzzle 184

Puzzle 185

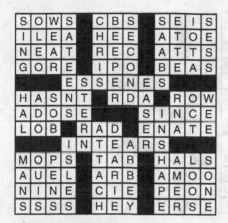

Puzzle 186

Puzzle 187

Puzzle 188

Puzzle 189

Puzzle 190

Puzzle 191

Puzzle 192

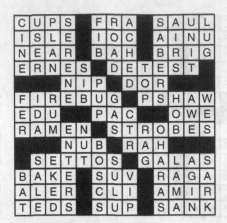

Puzzle 193

Puzzle 194

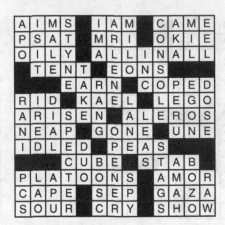

Puzzle 195

Puzzle 196

Puzzle 197

Puzzle 198

Puzzle 199

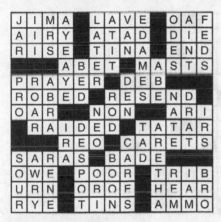

Puzzle 200

Puzzle 201

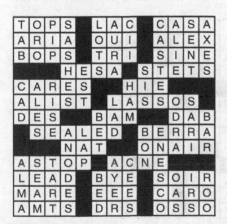

Puzzle 202

Puzzle 203

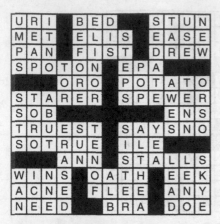

Puzzle 204

Puzzle 205

Puzzle 206

Puzzle 207

Puzzle 208

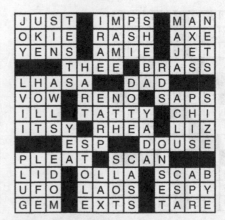

Puzzle 209

Puzzle 210

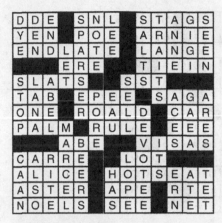

Puzzle 211

Puzzle 212

Puzzle 213

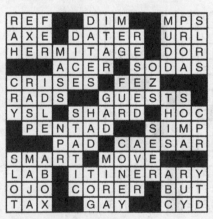

Puzzle 214

Puzzle 215

Puzzle 216

Puzzle 217

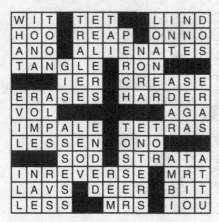

Puzzle 218

Puzzle 219

Puzzle 220

Puzzle 221

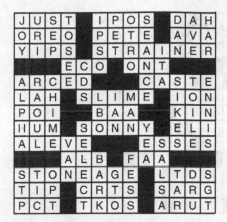

Puzzle 222

Puzzle 223

Puzzle 224

Puzzle 225

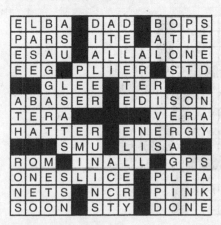

Puzzle 226

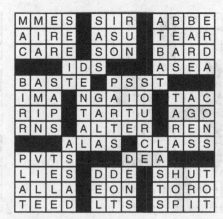

Puzzle 227

Puzzle 228

Puzzle 229

Puzzle 230

Puzzle 231

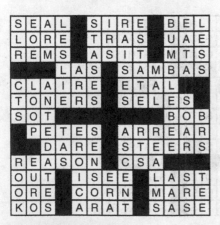

Puzzle 232

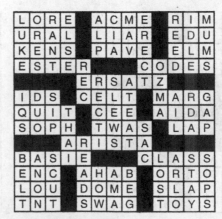

Puzzle 233

Puzzle 234

Puzzle 235

Puzzle 236

Puzzle 237

Puzzle 238

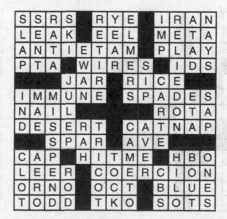

Puzzle 239

Puzzle 240

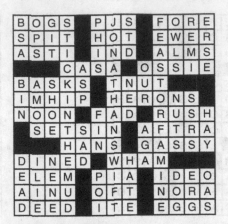

Puzzle 241

Puzzle 242

Puzzle 243

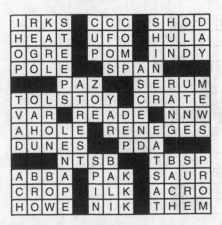

Puzzle 244

Puzzle 245

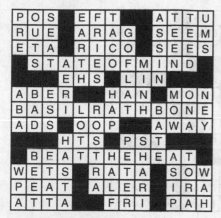

Puzzle 246

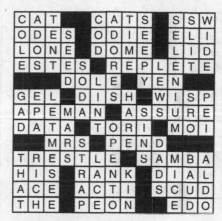

Puzzle 247

Puzzle 248

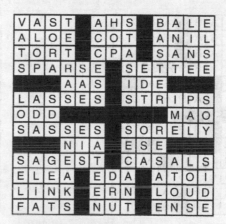

Puzzle 249

Puzzle 250

Puzzle 251

Puzzle 252

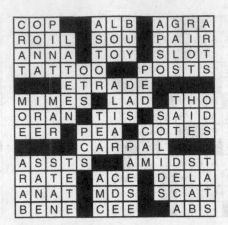

Puzzle 253

Puzzle 254

Puzzle 255

Puzzle 256

Puzzle 257

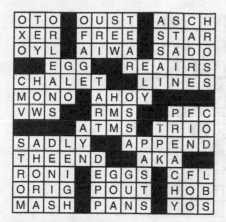

Puzzle 258

Puzzle 259

Puzzle 260

Puzzle 261

Puzzle 262

Puzzle 263

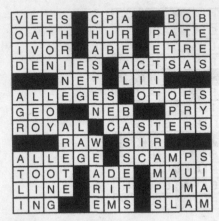

Puzzle 264

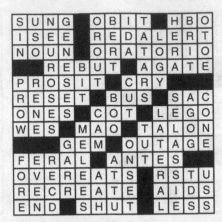

Puzzle 265

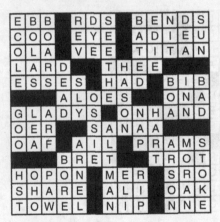

Puzzle 266

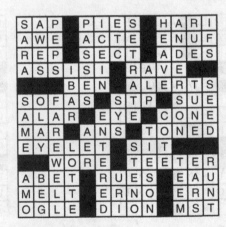

Puzzle 267

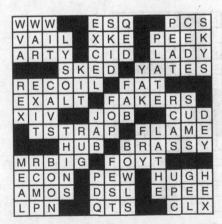

Puzzle 268

Puzzle 269

Puzzle 270

Puzzle 271

Puzzle 272

Puzzle 273

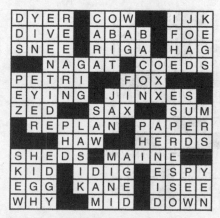

Puzzle 274

Puzzle 275

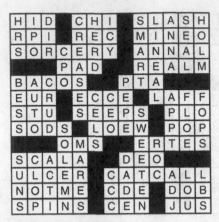

Puzzle 276

Puzzle 277

Puzzle 278

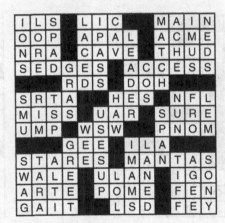

Puzzle 279

Puzzle 280

Puzzle 281

Puzzle 282

```
HUM  WALE  ORCH
EGO  AGAR  MOPE
RHO  HORN  AWAY
ASTO  DEAN
    FBI  MISDO
BUTTERCUP  OAK
UNE  LOOSE  ILL
RDA  INTERALIA
TORME    REF
  AFAR    TSPS
CHET  DOGE  ELK
HUGE  DUEL  WEE
EEGS  SELF  SAW
```

Puzzle 283

```
ELSE  TIS  CRAY
NOEL  RCA  LINE
CARD  EEL  APES
EFFETE  SCREW
   SOS  ABE
LACTEAL  STUDY
ALP  PEA   SAD
PLATE  ANTHEMS
   ITS  TAO
 ASTOP  AGLETS
ELAL  APR  LURE
LONE  DOE  ERIC
FEDS  EDS  ROPY
```

Puzzle 284

```
IDI  MACS  SACK
DAB  ETAH  HULL
ONESTORY  ATOM
LATEENS  HMOS
   DOE  PISCES
RYDER  GAS  ROE
BOER  LOW  EAUX
ISM  CAB  RATTY
SEEMED  LEG
 MACE  SIDEBAR
WING  PANORAMA
OTOE  IDEE  KIN
WERE  NEDS  EEK
```

Puzzle 285

```
ASTA  ERN  ORCA
HOES  LEO  BOOM
EYES  MAP  LOOP
MANES  MFRITS
   TAP  SAG
PARSNIP  NEONS
APO  TOA   DEE
TRITE  ENTREAT
   HAS  IOE
 SMARTS  PACTS
SEAM  ALA  COOT
CAGE  RAM  TOTO
IRES  EVA  SLEW
```

Puzzle 286

```
OBIT  TAM  SRA
DONE  INA  SLUR
EARP  POL  LANE
STEERS  INAGES
   EAT  CAT
ROOSTER  PERES
NAB  RAE   DNA
ARISE  PLEASES
   TEA  ELL
DADOES  COLONS
ELAN  OAT  OPIE
MALE  UTE  WANE
ONE   LEE  SLOP
```

Puzzle 287

```
MAMA  ORBS  TKO
AWOL  SALT  REX
CLOD  ANTELOPE
   RIGG  PUTIN
ATTIRE  FIR
DRINK  SENESCE
ZED  LAW   HEY
EYEBROW  GEODE
   PAW  SANDER
IDIOM  MOLT
TOREADOR  RUTH
ARK  DOVE  AGRI
LPS  ACES  PHYS
```

Puzzle 288

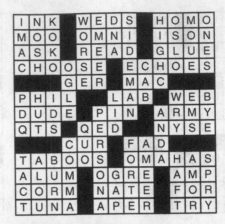

Puzzle 289

Puzzle 290

Puzzle 291

Puzzle 292

Puzzle 293

Puzzle 294

Puzzle 295

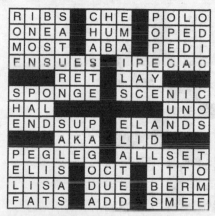

Puzzle 296

Puzzle 297

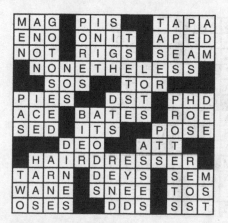

Puzzle 298

Puzzle 299

Puzzle 300

Puzzle 301

Puzzle 302

Puzzle 303

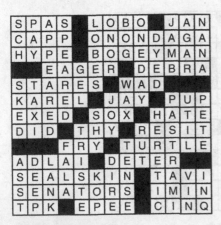

Puzzle 304

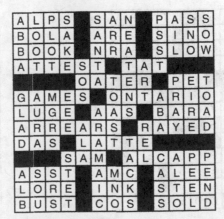

Puzzle 305

Puzzle 306

Puzzle 307

Puzzle 308

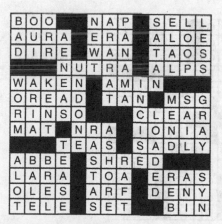

Puzzle 309

Puzzle 310

Puzzle 311

Puzzle 312

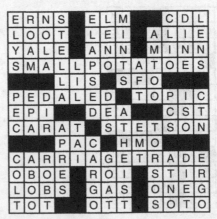

Puzzle 313

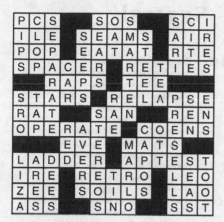

Puzzle 314

Puzzle 315

Puzzle 316

The EVERYTHING Series!

BUSINESS & PERSONAL FINANCE

Everything® Accounting Book
Everything® Budgeting Book, 2nd Ed.
Everything® Business Planning Book
Everything® Coaching and Mentoring Book, 2nd Ed.
Everything® Fundraising Book
Everything® Get Out of Debt Book
Everything® Grant Writing Book, 2nd Ed.
Everything® Guide to Buying Foreclosures
Everything® Guide to Fundraising, $15.95
Everything® Guide to Mortgages
Everything® Guide to Personal Finance for Single Mothers
Everything® Home-Based Business Book, 2nd Ed.
Everything® Homebuying Book, 3rd Ed., $15.95
Everything® Homeselling Book, 2nd Ed.
Everything® Human Resource Management Book
Everything® Improve Your Credit Book
Everything® Investing Book, 2nd Ed.
Everything® Landlording Book
Everything® Leadership Book, 2nd Ed.
Everything® Managing People Book, 2nd Ed.
Everything® Negotiating Book
Everything® Online Auctions Book
Everything® Online Business Book
Everything® Personal Finance Book
Everything® Personal Finance in Your 20s & 30s Book, 2nd Ed.
Everything® Personal Finance in Your 40s & 50s Book, $15.95
Everything® Project Management Book, 2nd Ed.
Everything® Real Estate Investing Book
Everything® Retirement Planning Book
Everything® Robert's Rules Book, $7.95
Everything® Selling Book
Everything® Start Your Own Business Book, 2nd Ed.
Everything® Wills & Estate Planning Book

COOKING

Everything® Barbecue Cookbook
Everything® Bartender's Book, 2nd Ed., $9.95
Everything® Calorie Counting Cookbook
Everything® Cheese Book
Everything® Chinese Cookbook
Everything® Classic Recipes Book
Everything® Cocktail Parties & Drinks Book
Everything® College Cookbook
Everything® Cooking for Baby and Toddler Book
Everything® Diabetes Cookbook
Everything® Easy Gourmet Cookbook
Everything® Fondue Cookbook
Everything® Food Allergy Cookbook, $15.95
Everything® Fondue Party Book
Everything® Gluten-Free Cookbook
Everything® Glycemic Index Cookbook
Everything® Grilling Cookbook
Everything® Healthy Cooking for Parties Book, $15.95
Everything® Holiday Cookbook
Everything® Indian Cookbook
Everything® Lactose-Free Cookbook
Everything® Low-Cholesterol Cookbook

Everything® Low-Fat High-Flavor Cookbook, 2nd Ed., $15.95
Everything® Low-Salt Cookbook
Everything® Meals for a Month Cookbook
Everything® Meals on a Budget Cookbook
Everything® Mediterranean Cookbook
Everything® Mexican Cookbook
Everything® No Trans Fat Cookbook
Everything® One-Pot Cookbook, 2nd Ed., $15.95
Everything® Organic Cooking for Baby & Toddler Book, $15.95
Everything® Pizza Cookbook
Everything® Quick Meals Cookbook, 2nd Ed., $15.95
Everything® Slow Cooker Cookbook
Everything® Slow Cooking for a Crowd Cookbook
Everything® Soup Cookbook
Everything® Stir-Fry Cookbook
Everything® Sugar-Free Cookbook
Everything® Tapas and Small Plates Cookbook
Everything® Tex-Mex Cookbook
Everything® Thai Cookbook
Everything® Vegetarian Cookbook
Everything® Whole-Grain, High-Fiber Cookbook
Everything® Wild Game Cookbook
Everything® Wine Book, 2nd Ed.

GAMES

Everything® 15-Minute Sudoku Book, $9.95
Everything® 30-Minute Sudoku Book, $9.95
Everything® Bible Crosswords Book, $9.95
Everything® Blackjack Strategy Book
Everything® Brain Strain Book, $9.95
Everything® Bridge Book
Everything® Card Games Book
Everything® Card Tricks Book, $9.95
Everything® Casino Gambling Book, 2nd Ed.
Everything® Chess Basics Book
Everything® Christmas Crosswords Book, $9.95
Everything® Craps Strategy Book
Everything® Crossword and Puzzle Book
Everything® Crosswords and Puzzles for Quote Lovers Book, $9.95
Everything® Crossword Challenge Book
Everything® Crosswords for the Beach Book, $9.95
Everything® Cryptic Crosswords Book, $9.95
Everything® Cryptograms Book, $9.95
Everything® Easy Crosswords Book
Everything® Easy Kakuro Book, $9.95
Everything® Easy Large-Print Crosswords Book
Everything® Games Book, 2nd Ed.
Everything® Giant Book of Crosswords
Everything® Giant Sudoku Book, $9.95
Everything® Giant Word Search Book
Everything® Kakuro Challenge Book, $9.95
Everything® Large-Print Crossword Challenge Book
Everything® Large-Print Crosswords Book
Everything® Large-Print Travel Crosswords Book
Everything® Lateral Thinking Puzzles Book, $9.95
Everything® Literary Crosswords Book, $9.95
Everything® Mazes Book
Everything® Memory Booster Puzzles Book, $9.95

Everything® Movie Crosswords Book, $9.95
Everything® Music Crosswords Book, $9.95
Everything® Online Poker Book
Everything® Pencil Puzzles Book, $9.95
Everything® Poker Strategy Book
Everything® Pool & Billiards Book
Everything® Puzzles for Commuters Book, $9.95
Everything® Puzzles for Dog Lovers Book, $9.95
Everything® Sports Crosswords Book, $9.95
Everything® Test Your IQ Book, $9.95
Everything® Texas Hold 'Em Book, $9.95
Everything® Travel Crosswords Book, $9.95
Everything® Travel Mazes Book, $9.95
Everything® Travel Word Search Book, $9.95
Everything® TV Crosswords Book, $9.95
Everything® Word Games Challenge Book
Everything® Word Scramble Book
Everything® Word Search Book

HEALTH

Everything® Alzheimer's Book
Everything® Diabetes Book
Everything® First Aid Book, $9.95
Everything® Green Living Book
Everything® Health Guide to Addiction and Recovery
Everything® Health Guide to Adult Bipolar Disorder
Everything® Health Guide to Arthritis
Everything® Health Guide to Controlling Anxiety
Everything® Health Guide to Depression
Everything® Health Guide to Diabetes, 2nd Ed.
Everything® Health Guide to Fibromyalgia
Everything® Health Guide to Menopause, 2nd Ed.
Everything® Health Guide to Migraines
Everything® Health Guide to Multiple Sclerosis
Everything® Health Guide to OCD
Everything® Health Guide to PMS
Everything® Health Guide to Postpartum Care
Everything® Health Guide to Thyroid Disease
Everything® Hypnosis Book
Everything® Low Cholesterol Book
Everything® Menopause Book
Everything® Nutrition Book
Everything® Reflexology Book
Everything® Stress Management Book
Everything® Superfoods Book, $15.95

HISTORY

Everything® American Government Book
Everything® American History Book, 2nd Ed.
Everything® American Revolution Book, $15.95
Everything® Civil War Book
Everything® Freemasons Book
Everything® Irish History & Heritage Book
Everything® World War II Book, 2nd Ed.

HOBBIES

Everything® Candlemaking Book
Everything® Cartooning Book
Everything® Coin Collecting Book
Everything® Digital Photography Book, 2nd Ed.

Everything® Drawing Book
Everything® Family Tree Book, 2nd Ed.
Everything® Guide to Online Genealogy, $15.95
Everything® Knitting Book
Everything® Knots Book
Everything® Photography Book
Everything® Quilting Book
Everything® Sewing Book
Everything® Soapmaking Book, 2nd Ed.
Everything® Woodworking Book

HOME IMPROVEMENT

Everything® Feng Shui Book
Everything® Feng Shui Decluttering Book, $9.95
Everything® Fix-It Book
Everything® Green Living Book
Everything® Home Decorating Book
Everything® Home Storage Solutions Book
Everything® Homebuilding Book
Everything® Organize Your Home Book, 2nd Ed.

KIDS' BOOKS

All titles are $7.95
Everything® Fairy Tales Book, $14.95
Everything® Kids' Animal Puzzle & Activity Book
Everything® Kids' Astronomy Book
Everything® Kids' Baseball Book, 5th Ed.
Everything® Kids' Bible Trivia Book
Everything® Kids' Bugs Book
Everything® Kids' Cars and Trucks Puzzle and Activity Book
Everything® Kids' Christmas Puzzle & Activity Book
Everything® Kids' Connect the Dots
        Puzzle and Activity Book
Everything® Kids' Cookbook, 2nd Ed.
Everything® Kids' Crazy Puzzles Book
Everything® Kids' Dinosaurs Book
Everything® Kids' Dragons Puzzle and Activity Book
Everything® Kids' Environment Book $7.95
Everything® Kids' Fairies Puzzle and Activity Book
Everything® Kids' First Spanish Puzzle and Activity Book
Everything® Kids' Football Book
Everything® Kids' Geography Book
Everything® Kids' Gross Cookbook
Everything® Kids' Gross Hidden Pictures Book
Everything® Kids' Gross Jokes Book
Everything® Kids' Gross Mazes Book
Everything® Kids' Gross Puzzle & Activity Book
Everything® Kids' Halloween Puzzle & Activity Book
Everything® Kids' Hanukkah Puzzle and Activity Book
Everything® Kids' Hidden Pictures Book
Everything® Kids' Horses Book
Everything® Kids' Joke Book
Everything® Kids' Knock Knock Book
Everything® Kids' Learning French Book
Everything® Kids' Learning Spanish Book
Everything® Kids' Magical Science Experiments Book
Everything® Kids' Math Puzzles Book
Everything® Kids' Mazes Book
Everything® Kids' Money Book, 2nd Ed.
Everything® Kids' Mummies, Pharaoh's, and Pyramids
        Puzzle and Activity Book
Everything® Kids' Nature Book
Everything® Kids' Pirates Puzzle and Activity Book
Everything® Kids' Presidents Book
Everything® Kids' Princess Puzzle and Activity Book
Everything® Kids' Puzzle Book

Everything® Kids' Racecars Puzzle and Activity Book
Everything® Kids' Riddles & Brain Teasers Book
Everything® Kids' Science Experiments Book
Everything® Kids' Sharks Book
Everything® Kids' Soccer Book
Everything® Kids' Spelling Book
Everything® Kids' Spies Puzzle and Activity Book
Everything® Kids' States Book
Everything® Kids' Travel Activity Book
Everything® Kids' Word Search Puzzle and Activity Book

LANGUAGE

Everything® Conversational Japanese Book with CD, $19.95
Everything® French Grammar Book
Everything® French Phrase Book, $9.95
Everything® French Verb Book, $9.95
Everything® German Phrase Book, $9.95
Everything® German Practice Book with CD, $19.95
Everything® Inglés Book
Everything® Intermediate Spanish Book with CD, $19.95
Everything® Italian Phrase Book, $9.95
Everything® Italian Practice Book with CD, $19.95
Everything® Learning Brazilian Portuguese Book with CD, $19.95
Everything® Learning French Book with CD, 2nd Ed., $19.95
Everything® Learning German Book
Everything® Learning Italian Book
Everything® Learning Latin Book
Everything® Learning Russian Book with CD, $19.95
Everything® Learning Spanish Book
Everything® Learning Spanish Book with CD, 2nd Ed., $19.95
Everything® Russian Practice Book with CD, $19.95
Everything® Sign Language Book, $15.95
Everything® Spanish Grammar Book
Everything® Spanish Phrase Book, $9.95
Everything® Spanish Practice Book with CD, $19.95
Everything® Spanish Verb Book, $9.95
Everything® Speaking Mandarin Chinese Book with CD, $19.95

MUSIC

Everything® Bass Guitar Book with CD, $19.95
Everything® Drums Book with CD, $19.95
Everything® Guitar Book with CD, 2nd Ed., $19.95
Everything® Guitar Chords Book with CD, $19.95
Everything® Guitar Scales Book with CD, $19.95
Everything® Harmonica Book with CD, $15.95
Everything® Home Recording Book
Everything® Music Theory Book with CD, $19.95
Everything® Reading Music Book with CD, $19.95
Everything® Rock & Blues Guitar Book with CD, $19.95
Everything® Rock & Blues Piano Book with CD, $19.95
Everything® Rock Drums Book with CD, $19.95
Everything® Singing Book with CD, $19.95
Everything® Songwriting Book

NEW AGE

Everything® Astrology Book, 2nd Ed.
Everything® Birthday Personology Book
Everything® Celtic Wisdom Book, $15.95
Everything® Dreams Book, 2nd Ed.
Everything® Law of Attraction Book, $15.95
Everything® Love Signs Book, $9.95
Everything® Love Spells Book, $9.95
Everything® Palmistry Book
Everything® Psychic Book
Everything® Reiki Book

Everything® Sex Signs Book, $9.95
Everything® Spells & Charms Book, 2nd Ed.
Everything® Tarot Book, 2nd Ed.
Everything® Toltec Wisdom Book
Everything® Wicca & Witchcraft Book, 2nd Ed.

PARENTING

Everything® Baby Names Book, 2nd Ed.
Everything® Baby Shower Book, 2nd Ed.
Everything® Baby Sign Language Book with DVD
Everything® Baby's First Year Book
Everything® Birthing Book
Everything® Breastfeeding Book
Everything® Father-to-Be Book
Everything® Father's First Year Book
Everything® Get Ready for Baby Book, 2nd Ed.
Everything® Got Your Baby to Sleep Book, $9.95
Everything® Getting Pregnant Book
Everything® Guide to Pregnancy Over 35
Everything® Guide to Raising a One-Year-Old
Everything® Guide to Raising a Two-Year-Old
Everything® Guide to Raising Adolescent Boys
Everything® Guide to Raising Adolescent Girls
Everything® Mother's First Year Book
Everything® Parent's Guide to Childhood Illnesses
Everything® Parent's Guide to Children and Divorce
Everything® Parent's Guide to Children with ADD/ADHD
Everything® Parent's Guide to Children with Asperger's
        Syndrome
Everything® Parent's Guide to Children with Anxiety
Everything® Parent's Guide to Children with Asthma
Everything® Parent's Guide to Children with Autism
Everything® Parent's Guide to Children with Bipolar Disorder
Everything® Parent's Guide to Children with Depression
Everything® Parent's Guide to Children with Dyslexia
Everything® Parent's Guide to Children with Juvenile Diabetes
Everything® Parent's Guide to Children with OCD
Everything® Parent's Guide to Positive Discipline
Everything® Parent's Guide to Raising Boys
Everything® Parent's Guide to Raising Girls
Everything® Parent's Guide to Raising Siblings
Everything® Parent's Guide to Raising Your
        Adopted Child
Everything® Parent's Guide to Sensory Integration Disorder
Everything® Parent's Guide to Tantrums
Everything® Parent's Guide to the Strong-Willed Child
Everything® Parenting a Teenager Book
Everything® Potty Training Book, $9.95
Everything® Pregnancy Book, 3rd Ed.
Everything® Pregnancy Fitness Book
Everything® Pregnancy Nutrition Book
Everything® Pregnancy Organizer, 2nd Ed., $16.95
Everything® Toddler Activities Book
Everything® Toddler Book
Everything® Tween Book
Everything® Twins, Triplets, and More Book

PETS

Everything® Aquarium Book
Everything® Boxer Book
Everything® Cat Book, 2nd Ed.
Everything® Chihuahua Book
Everything® Cooking for Dogs Book
Everything® Dachshund Book
Everything® Dog Book, 2nd Ed.
Everything® Dog Grooming Book

Everything® Dog Obedience Book
Everything® Dog Owner's Organizer, $16.95
Everything® Dog Training and Tricks Book
Everything® German Shepherd Book
Everything® Golden Retriever Book
Everything® Horse Book, 2nd Ed., $15.95
Everything® Horse Care Book
Everything® Horseback Riding Book
Everything® Labrador Retriever Book
Everything® Poodle Book
Everything® Pug Book
Everything® Puppy Book
Everything® Small Dogs Book
Everything® Tropical Fish Book
Everything® Yorkshire Terrier Book

REFERENCE

Everything® American Presidents Book
Everything® Blogging Book
Everything® Build Your Vocabulary Book, $9.95
Everything® Car Care Book
Everything® Classical Mythology Book
Everything® Da Vinci Book
Everything® Einstein Book
Everything® Enneagram Book
Everything® Etiquette Book, 2nd Ed.
Everything® Family Christmas Book, $15.95
Everything® Guide to C. S. Lewis & Narnia
Everything® Guide to Divorce, 2nd Ed., $15.95
Everything® Guide to Edgar Allan Poe
Everything® Guide to Understanding Philosophy
Everything® Inventions and Patents Book
Everything® Jacqueline Kennedy Onassis Book
Everything® John F. Kennedy Book
Everything® Mafia Book
Everything® Martin Luther King Jr. Book
Everything® Pirates Book
Everything® Private Investigation Book
Everything® Psychology Book
Everything® Public Speaking Book, $9.95
Everything® Shakespeare Book, 2nd Ed.

RELIGION

Everything® Angels Book
Everything® Bible Book
Everything® Bible Study Book with CD, $19.95
Everything® Buddhism Book
Everything® Catholicism Book
Everything® Christianity Book
Everything® Gnostic Gospels Book
Everything® Hinduism Book, $15.95
Everything® History of the Bible Book
Everything® Jesus Book
Everything® Jewish History & Heritage Book
Everything® Judaism Book
Everything® Kabbalah Book
Everything® Koran Book
Everything® Mary Book
Everything® Mary Magdalene Book
Everything® Prayer Book

Everything® Saints Book, 2nd Ed.
Everything® Torah Book
Everything® Understanding Islam Book
Everything® Women of the Bible Book
Everything® World's Religions Book

SCHOOL & CAREERS

Everything® Career Tests Book
Everything® College Major Test Book
Everything® College Survival Book, 2nd Ed.
Everything® Cover Letter Book, 2nd Ed.
Everything® Filmmaking Book
Everything® Get-a-Job Book, 2nd Ed.
Everything® Guide to Being a Paralegal
Everything® Guide to Being a Personal Trainer
Everything® Guide to Being a Real Estate Agent
Everything® Guide to Being a Sales Rep
Everything® Guide to Being an Event Planner
Everything® Guide to Careers in Health Care
Everything® Guide to Careers in Law Enforcement
Everything® Guide to Government Jobs
Everything® Guide to Starting and Running a Catering
    Business
Everything® Guide to Starting and Running a Restaurant
**Everything® Guide to Starting and Running
    a Retail Store**
Everything® Job Interview Book, 2nd Ed.
Everything® New Nurse Book
Everything® New Teacher Book
Everything® Paying for College Book
Everything® Practice Interview Book
Everything® Resume Book, 3rd Ed.
Everything® Study Book

SELF-HELP

Everything® Body Language Book
Everything® Dating Book, 2nd Ed.
Everything® Great Sex Book
**Everything® Guide to Caring for Aging Parents,
    $15.95**
Everything® Self-Esteem Book
Everything® Self-Hypnosis Book, $9.95
Everything® Tantric Sex Book

SPORTS & FITNESS

Everything® Easy Fitness Book
Everything® Fishing Book
Everything® Guide to Weight Training, $15.95
Everything® Krav Maga for Fitness Book
Everything® Running Book, 2nd Ed.
Everything® Triathlon Training Book, $15.95

TRAVEL

Everything® Family Guide to Coastal Florida
Everything® Family Guide to Cruise Vacations
Everything® Family Guide to Hawaii
Everything® Family Guide to Las Vegas, 2nd Ed.
Everything® Family Guide to Mexico
Everything® Family Guide to New England, 2nd Ed.

Everything® Family Guide to New York City, 3rd Ed.
**Everything® Family Guide to Northern California
    and Lake Tahoe**
Everything® Family Guide to RV Travel & Campgrounds
Everything® Family Guide to the Caribbean
Everything® Family Guide to the Disneyland® Resort, California
    Adventure®, Universal Studios®, and the Anaheim
    Area, 2nd Ed.
Everything® Family Guide to the Walt Disney World Resort®,
    Universal Studios®, and Greater Orlando, 5th Ed.
Everything® Family Guide to Timeshares
Everything® Family Guide to Washington D.C., 2nd Ed.

WEDDINGS

Everything® Bachelorette Party Book, $9.95
Everything® Bridesmaid Book, $9.95
Everything® Destination Wedding Book
Everything® Father of the Bride Book, $9.95
Everything® Green Wedding Book, $15.95
Everything® Groom Book, $9.95
Everything® Jewish Wedding Book, 2nd Ed., $15.95
Everything® Mother of the Bride Book, $9.95
Everything® Outdoor Wedding Book
Everything® Wedding Book, 3rd Ed.
Everything® Wedding Checklist, $9.95
Everything® Wedding Etiquette Book, $9.95
Everything® Wedding Organizer, 2nd Ed., $16.95
Everything® Wedding Shower Book, $9.95
Everything® Wedding Vows Book, 3rd Ed., $9.95
Everything® Wedding Workout Book
Everything® Weddings on a Budget Book, 2nd Ed., $9.95

WRITING

Everything® Creative Writing Book
Everything® Get Published Book, 2nd Ed.
Everything® Grammar and Style Book, 2nd Ed.
Everything® Guide to Magazine Writing
Everything® Guide to Writing a Book Proposal
Everything® Guide to Writing a Novel
Everything® Guide to Writing Children's Books
Everything® Guide to Writing Copy
Everything® Guide to Writing Graphic Novels
Everything® Guide to Writing Research Papers
Everything® Guide to Writing a Romance Novel, $15.95
Everything® Improve Your Writing Book, 2nd Ed.
Everything® Writing Poetry Book